A Pilot's Guide to Washington

J. Gryphon Shafer

Steward House Publishers
Port Orchard, Washington, U.S.A.

Visit the Steward House website at www.stewardhouse.com

STEWARD HOUSE and the Steward House logo are registered trademarks of Steward House Publishers, LLC.

A Pilot's Guide to Washington

Chief Executive Officer, Steward House
Sharalyn Shafer (sharalyn@stewardhouse.com)

Editor-in-Chief, Steward House
J. Gryphon Shafer (gryphon@stewardhouse.com)

Manufactured in the United States of America.

The picture on the cover was taken by Gregg M. Erickson on an August afternoon and released under the Creative Commons license. It is a panorama from near the summit of Mount Ellinor in the Olympic Mountains of Washington State.

ISBN-13: 978-1-937097-11-0

Jim, Enjoy your many future flights to these wonderful airports, Yours Brainard

To my wife and children, who tolerate my obsession with aviation.
To my fellow aviators, who share my obsession.
To my Creator, who gave me my obsession.

Table of Contents

Chapter 0

Approach

When people learn I'm a pilot,[1] one of the first questions they ask is, "How long have you been a pilot?" The very next question is, "How long did it take you to become a pilot?" It's at this point I offer the cautionary tale of why it's a terrible idea to string out flight instruction over the expanse of more than a decade.[2] If the person hasn't lost interest by the time I'm done blabbing, they usually ask something like, "Where do you go?" or "What do you do?"

Many pilots talk about the $100 hamburger, something almost as famous as the FAA-certified 50-foot obstacle located at the end of nearly all hypothetical runways. These $100 hamburgers are the default excuses for private general aviation pilots to fly. Rent an airplane, fly for less than 2 hours, eat a hamburger, and fly home.

Many pilots will tell you that $100 hamburgers taste better than regular old hamburgers. They're wrong; it's instead just the twin psychological influences of cognitive dissonance and confirmation bias wreaking havoc on our bank accounts. Besides, given inflation and other market forces, a Cessna 172 now costs between $95 and $130 per Hobbs hour to rent, including fuel. When you factor in the

[1] People learn I'm a pilot often because I won't shut up about being a pilot.
[2] Don't do what I did. Commit to 3 flights per week minimum. Work with your CFI to setup a plan and schedule. You'll save a lot of money and enormous time.

money you pay the restaurant for the hamburger and something to drink, a $100 hamburger actually costs something like $250.

That being said, is the experience of flying to lunch for what amounts to a $250 hamburger and beverage worth it? Yes. Of course, yes. However, it can get old after a while; the same hamburger at the same restaurant, day after day.

Most pilots know a few restaurants located on nearby airport properties. There are even lists of these locations floating around in pilot communities.[3] But if we add to consideration the restaurants and entertainment activities available within walking distance of nearby airports, the depth of options expands dramatically.

Similarly, if we only ever fly to airports that we can reach in under an hour, we'll be cheating ourselves out of a majority of options. If we consider the possibility of staying overnight in a location, at a hotel or B&B within walking distance of the airport, we'll see our range of options expand exponentially in correlation to the range of flight.

The Point of this Book

Hanging out in pilots' lounges, both in the real world and the far more bizarre virtual world of online social networks, I've frequently overheard and participated in conversations about where to go, what to see, and what to do. This is especially prevalent in groups of pilots who only recently earned their wings. "I was thinking I'd fly south, maybe to X or Y or Z airport. But I'm not sure what I'd do when I get there. What's there to do?"

I wrote this book as a guidebook for private aviators in Washington State, or folks visiting the State. My hope is to provide you with

[3] One such list was the initial inspiration for this book.

useful hints and suggestions about places to go and things to do while there.

Washington State is among the most beautiful and diverse states in the Union. There are flat and dry desserts, stunning basalt formations, towering mountains, rolling grass hills, thick rain forests, island archipelagos, and lakes and rivers and straits and sounds. Well, one sound. And we have roughly a billion[4] airports to visit. It would be shame to be a pilot living in or visiting Washington State and not deeply partake of the richness of this opportunity.

Criteria for Inclusion

I didn't include every airport of the roughly one billion[5] airports in Washington State. Instead, airports will only get included if they are:

- Open to the public or have a widely published policy of openness to visiting pilots.
- Have some sort of minimum number of destinations worth visiting within walking distance after landing.

What does "minimum number" mean? Let's say at least one.

What does "walking distance" mean? Well, it's a relative value. I consider myself a fairly lazy person, so if I have to walk more than a few minutes from the airfield, I'd better be going to something worth it. Typically, I like walking less than 30 minutes, but I'll make exceptions and go maybe as much as double that if the destination is really worth it.

What does "worth visiting" mean? It's correlated with walking distance, but to be completely blunt, it's my own personal

[4] I'm exaggerating slightly.
[5] I'm exaggerating slightly again. You should probably get used to this. I do it a lot.

interpretation of what's interesting and worth the walk. There are several restaurants, for example, that are easily within walking distance of their nearby airports, but I did not include them because their quality was, at least in my opinion, overshadowed by other, better options.

I recognize my preferences are a single data point, and you're preferences will likely vary. That being said, I wrote the book, so I get to choose what to include and what to exclude.

There will inevitably come a time when you ask, "Why didn't he include X airport or Y business?" In such cases, just remind yourself that this book is really just a collection of my opinions. You're under no obligation to agree with them.[6]

Errors, Omissions, and Corrections

If you spot any errors or omissions, or if you'd like to offer some corrections to this book, please email me at g@shfr.us with your feedback.

Gryphon Ratings

Each airport I've included will come with a "Gryphon Rating," expressed by some number of these gryphon symbols:

These represent the rating I am personally giving to the destination. As the name implies, these ratings are entirely my opinion about the destination. The ratings range from 1 to 5, with 5 gryphons being the highest rating a destination can possibly achieve, the equivalent of a "must visit" location. Even airports with a rating as

[6] However, you'll be wrong if you don't agree. Just sayin'.

low as 2 should be considered as worthwhile destinations; it's just that they don't stack up against 5s.

It's a virtual certainty that you'll disagree with at least a few of these Gryphon Ratings, especially if I'm grading your home airport. Just remember that these are really just my opinion.

How does an airport get more gryphons? Well, it's a combination of a lot of factors. There are things that are beyond the airport and town's ability to change; for example, how beautiful the area surrounding the airport appears to me, the author, Gryphon. When flying into Friday Harbor or Electric City or Pullman, the landscape is particularly stunning, and that adds to my opinion of the place.

The number and diversity of restaurants, things to do, and places to stay overnight contributes significantly to the rating. And there are other things that are entirely within the control of the airport or town. For example, Electric City gets a big bump in rating because of their courtesy car. Tacoma gets a bump because of their restaurant on the field.

Restaurants on the Field

Speaking of restaurants on the field, any airport with a restaurant technically on the property or so close it's virtually on the property will be given this little symbol:

The associated entry for the restaurant will be marked with this little symbol to indicate it's on the airport property:

Any restaurant located on the airport property will be listed first in the set of restaurants listed.

Courtesy Cars

For airports with courtesy cars available, I'll include this cute little icon in the airport header section:

In all cases, don't completely trust the information I'm providing about courtesy cars. It's best to call ahead to inquire about availability instead of relying on the car to be where you expect it.

Day Trip Options

There's one last icon to talk about, which is the "day trip option" icon. It looks like this:

This is the most subjective of all the icons. If an airport destination gets this icon, it means I'd personally consider the airport to be worth visiting for just a day trip with my family. In other words, this destination has something for everyone in my family.

My family consists of me (also known as the pilot), my wife (also known as the responsible adult), my son of 14, and my daughter of 5. So for a destination to be interesting to all four of us, it has to have appeal to all of us.

Legal Disclaimer

Nothing in this book is intended to supersede any information published by any FAA-approved source. Where information of any kind presented herein differs from an FAA-approved source, consider the information from the FAA-approved source to be correct.

Chapter 1

San Juan Islands

The United States Geological Survey (USGS) defines the San Juan Islands as the archipelago north of the Strait of Juan de Fuca, west of Rosario Strait, east of Haro Strait, and south of Boundary Pass. Residents and visitors alike define it as paradise. I consider the landscape gorgeous, the mood mellow, and the weather almost always better than anywhere else west of the Cascades.

There are 172 named islands and reefs in San Juan County, but only 4 islands are reachable by ferry: San Juan, Orcas, Lopez, and Shaw. Although the ferry is usually on time and reliable, if visitors are traveling up from Seattle, it can be quite a time investment to come by car and ferry. Arriving by air is certainly the way to go. When I fly in, I often feel like I'm cheating my way into heaven.

We don't fly primarily because we want to get somewhere faster. Most of the time, it's best to not fly if you're on a tight schedule. That said, the San Juans just might violate that rule of thumb. And the payoff is tremendous. There's enough around the Islands to occupy you for weeks if not a lifetime, but by flying in, it's possible to experience bits and pieces of the Islands one afternoon at a time.

There are several of what one might call "climate zones" in Washington State, each with its own type of beauty. Looking at a map, it'd be easy to mistake the San Juan Islands as being just the northern part of the Puget Sound; however, there's something a bit different about them. I often fly from Bremerton (PWT) up to Friday Harbor (FHR), and something strange happens near the southern edge of the Strait of Juan de Fuca. It's like your passing through some sort of space warp. The weather changes. The winds change. And when you arrive over the Islands, even the landscape changes. What you see below you still has the Pacific Northwest evergreen trees, but the land itself looks somehow different.

The mood on the Islands is different. Friendly. Casual.

Keep in mind that a lot of the base materials that go into making things on the islands is shipped in, and prices reflect that fact. A sandwich on the islands is going to cost just a little bit more than on the mainland; however, it tastes better. Sometimes, a lot better.

Also keep in mind that if you visit during tourist season, you're going to have to share the islands with a lot of people, most of whom are not exactly as friendly and casual as the natives. Staff at retail shops and restaurants can sometimes feel overwhelmed by the onslaught. Be the nice aviator, not the rude tourist.

I've found the best times to visit are in the spring and fall. I've gone up as late as the end of October and found it an especially beautiful and almost magical place.

FHR – Friday Harbor Airport

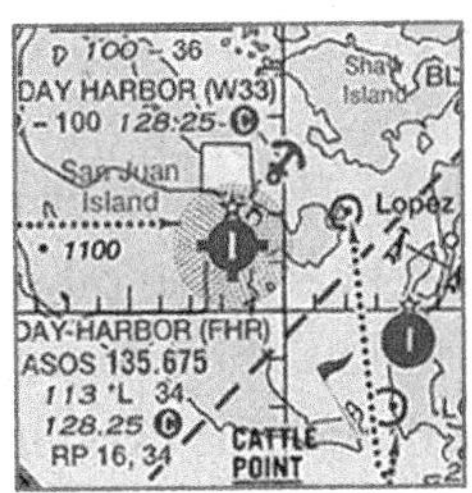

Location: 0 miles southwest of Friday Harbor
Coordinates: N48°31.32' / W123°1.46'
Altitude: 112 MSL
Fuel: 100LL (blue)
Transient Storage: Tiedowns (BYO Ropes)

Friday Harbor is the county seat for the San Juans and is the largest of its cities. The airport is on the southwest edge of town. The harbor and downtown area are a short walk down the hill from the airport.

This is one of my most favorite destinations for a variety of reasons. The airport is well-maintained, and the town is simultaneously charming and filled with a lot of things to do.

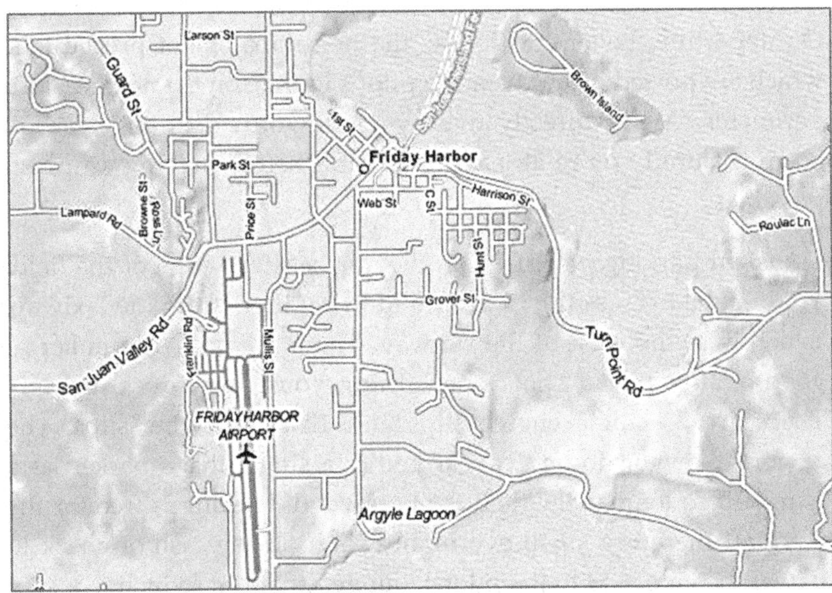

Airport Notes

The approach into FHR is easy and enjoyable. On clear days, which seems to be predominately the case in the San Juans, the airport is clearly visible from a great distance to the south. The southern approach inward is flat and mostly farm land. I've heard one pilot mention how he likes to start at Cattle Point and follow the eastern shoreline into a straight-in 34, though I've never flown this myself as it seems a bit too non-standard for me.

To the north is a bit of a hill that hugs the northern edge of the main section of Friday Harbor. Its peak is only about 450 MSL, but it looks taller to those of us with slow-climbing aircraft.

The runway slopes upward toward the north a bit, but I find it a bit difficult to see that from the air. I've never had a problem landing 34, but landing 16 I almost always float a few feet more than I intend despite repeatedly telling myself, "It slopes down. It slopes down."

On departure, be sure to follow the noise abatement procedures, which are posted in and near the pilot's lounge on the northeastern perimeter. Avoid directly overflying downtown Friday Harbor, and wait until you're at least 1,000 MSL before making a turn, if possible.

Transient parking is located on the northeastern edge of the field. You'll have to cross the 16 threshold to get there from the taxiway, which is to the west of the runway. There are quite a number of good-quality paved spots open. Bring your own ropes, though. There are 23 single engine slips and 10 twin-engine slips. The airport manager doesn't care if you're a single that's parked in a twin slip so long as the field isn't crowded. Parking is free for the day, but there is a small overnight charge. Bring cash or check to pay at the gate next to the pilot's lounge. If you're so inclined, sign the visitors' book in the pilot's lounge.

The fuel dock is located on the west side of the field near the north end, just north of the 16 threshold. If you're departing from transient parking, you'll need to taxi on the 1-way taxiway over the north end of the field, then turn south, and you'll be right at the fuel dock.

Transportation

I've always walked into town from the airport. It's maybe a 15 to 20-minute walk, and it's quite nice.[7] That said, you could call for a taxi with San Juan Taxi & Tours Service (360-378-3550) or Friday Harbor Taxi (360-298-4434), both of which are located downtown near the ferry dock.

You can rent a car from West Isle Rent a Car (360-378-2440), which is right on the airport, west side about midfield. There's also M & W Auto Sales & Rentals (360-378-2794), which is just off the north end of the field.

Depending on your needs, you could also try Susie's Moped Rentals (360-378-5244). You'll end up with a red scooter looking contraption, which is great for zipping around quickly from place to place on the island.

[7] If you're stopping by FHR for lunch, then it's best to walk because it'll make you feel better about consuming far too many ridiculously yummy calories.

Ernie's Café ✈

Café Food, Bulgogi, Popovers
West Side of Airport (Near Fuel Dock)
744 Airport Cir Dr, Friday Harbor, WA 98250
360-378-6605

Ernie's is right on the field on the northwest side. It's the building directly north of the fuel dock. Getting there from transient parking might be entertaining, but I suppose you could walk across the perimeter of the taxiway. Be mindful of aircraft.

The food is good. Many have commented positively about the bulgogi and popovers. They also make their own soups. They've got pretty good drip coffee.[8] I've heard the Korean tacos are great. The service is friendly and timely, and the prices are low. There's free wifi available.

One downside is that they're only open from 10am to 2pm weekdays.

Bakery San Juan

Bakery, Pizza, Sandwiches
0.5 miles or 9-minute walk
775 Mullis St, Friday Harbor, WA 98250
360-378-5810

This place is an absolute must-stop. Fortunately, it's located just outside the gate from the transient parking area, so you're likely walking right past it twice anyway. Their bread is crazy-good, and

[8] Any airport-based restaurant that doesn't have good drip coffee needs to have its owners taken out back and slapped several times with a wet trout.

their pizza is some of the best in this part of the state. As you'd expect from a bakery, they also offer cakes, pastry, and sandwiches.

They're open weekdays from 8am to 5pm in the winter and 6pm in the spring and summer. If you're going into town for lunch, consider picking up a loaf of bread from these guys on your way home.

Cask and Schooner

Seafood
1.0 miles or 19-minute walk
1 Front St, Friday Harbor, WA 98250
360-378-2922

This is a popular destination for a few pilot association lunch fly-ins. Show up there on Fridays in the summer around 1 PM or so, and you'll likely meet up with a few fellow pilots. The restaurant is located all the way downtown, just across the street from the marina.

The place is inspired by English seashore taverns. The decorations are fantastic. There's a gigantic model sailing ship just inside the door. The staff are always friendly, and the food is wonderful. Order the bacon-wrapped dates. You'll thank me.[9] There are about 3 places in western Washington where the fish and chips are excellent. This is 1 of those.

The prices are a bit high, but the food is great. The problem is that it seems like everyone else knows that the food is great. So sometimes, especially on busy weekends, you'll have to wait a considerable amount of time for your food.

[9] I know you're going to want to thank me because you're not a rude pilot.

San Juan Island Cheese

Cheese Shop, Sandwiches
0.9 miles or 16-minute walk
155 Nichols St, Friday Harbor, WA 98250
360-370-5115

This is a fantastic place to stop in if you like cheese or wine. Unfortunately, we pilots can't sample the wine if we're just making a day-trip to FHR, but the cheese alone is worth the stop in. As you're walking down Spring Street from the airport, veer off to your right onto Nichols Street, a few blocks up from the water.

These folks have wonderful hot and cold sandwiches and soups. The black forest ham grilled cheese is awesome. I've heard the smoked salmon chowder is great. If you're up for it, try the lavender lemon cheesecake.[10]

If you're making an overnight visit, consider picking up their "Romantic Picnic" package, which includes wine, cheeses, meats, breads, crackers, and other various yummy things. It's perfect for a picnic next to a beach or in a park somewhere.

Golden Triangle Thai Restaurant

Thai
1.0 miles or 19-minute walk
140 1st St, Friday Harbor, WA 98250
360-378-1917

If you're looking for a change from the typical island food fare, stop in to the Golden Triangle. The food isn't particularly fancy, but it's honest, authentic Thai food, and good. The portions are large. There are gluten-free options. This restaurant ranks up there with some of

[10] Yes, that's right: lavender lemon. I know it sounds weird, but trust me. It's good.

the better Thai places in major metropolitan cities, and yet it's tucked away in Friday Harbor. Outdoor seating is available.

Spring Street Deli

Deli Food
0.9 miles or 18-minute walk
135 Spring St, Friday Harbor, WA 98250
360-378-5959

If you like Reuben sandwiches, then you should stop in to the Spring Street Deli. It's right in the heart of downtown on Spring Street. The staff are friendly, and the food is fantastic. The portions are fairly large, so unless you're hungry, it may be wise to split an order with someone. These guys stack their sandwiches with a lot of meat, which is awesome.

Seating is somewhat limited. So it may make sense to get your sandwiches to go. Watch the ferry schedule, because a lot of folks getting off the ferry pop through the deli. You might have to stand in a line for a while, but such is the price you pay for greatness.

Things to Do

Island Wine Company

Wine Shop
1.0 miles or 19-minute walk
2 Cannery Landing, Friday Harbor, WA 98250
360-378-3229

As a pilot visiting a remote location for a day trip, stopping in at a wine shop is likely not such a great idea. This might be an exception. The Island Wine Company sells a variety of wines, but its chief export are wines from San Juan Cellars. The grapes come from

Eastern Washington and the wine is made by Rob Griffin, one of the most experienced and respected wine makers in the Northwest.

The company is owned by David Baughn and Kathryn Lawson Kerr who moved to the island in 1993. In addition to great wine, you can fine all sorts of related books, gadgets, and gizmos. Whatever you buy, David and Kathryn can if you like keep it for you in the back until your day is done. They'll of course ship anything you'd rather not take with you. And best of all, if you're a pilot and you buy at least 1 case of wine, David will drive you back up to the airport when you're ready to depart.[11]

Griffin Bay Bookstore

Bookstore, Coffee House
1.0 miles or 18-minute walk
155 Spring St, Friday Harbor, WA 98250
360-378-5511

There are several excellent bookstores in Friday Harbor, but this one seems to draw me in nearly every time I visit with my family.[12] The book selection is wide despite the bookstore not having a gigantic amount of space. There's usually something interesting for each person in our family, children included.

There's a small and charming coffee house in the back that serves wonderful coffee. I can't think of a more relaxing idea than buying a new book and thumbing through it whilst sipping a mocha. I've bumped into the occasional book club meeting in the back. The shop hosts wonderful events of local and off-island authors along with book signings. There's also free wifi.

[11] You get to walk downhill from the airport; then for the price of a case, David will drive you all the way back up. Since the airport slopes downward from the north, and the gate entrance is on the northern perimeter, you can accurately say you visited Friday Harbor and walked downhill both ways.

[12] This is despite the fact that its name is obviously misspelled.

A Place to Play

Arts & Entertainment
1.0 miles or 18-minute walk
55 Spring St, Friday Harbor, WA 98250
360-378-0378

If you fly with children, sometimes the little ones need a chance to play and let loose a bit. Fortunately, there's a place for that. They host a colorful indoor space that's filled with creative and imaginative play areas. It gives children a chance to build, create, socialize, and explore. More importantly, it gives parent pilots a chance to relax.

It's designed primarily for ages 1-10, but staff say children of all ages are welcome and enjoy the experience. All kids must be accompanied by an adult, except on scheduled "date nights" when childcare is provided. Light snacks, fresh baked cookies from The Bean, Keurig coffee, juices and a variety of beverages are available for purchase.

The place is immaculately clean and well-organized, impressive considering it's designed for children. The owner has gone to great lengths to make a fantastic place for play.

PedalAnywhere San Juan Islands

Bike Rentals
0.4 miles or 7-minute walk
845 Argyle Ave, Friday Harbor, WA 98250
360-797-5787

Technically, this is a 7-minute walk from the airport; however, the whole point of PedalAnywhere is that they'll deliver the bikes to you wherever you happen to be. Give them a call to reserve whatever you need: bikes, helmets, bike racks, carrying equipment, or other accessories.

The bikes are of high quality and are fairly new. They're well-maintained and properly serviced. You won't be getting a beat-up bike.

Rates are low, but you get a better per-day rate if you rent for longer durations. If you're planning just a few hours on the island, it's probably not worth it; but if you're staying for a few days and want to pedal around, these guys are great.[13]

Boat Charters and Tours

There are numerous boat charter and water tours and sports operations, most located near the marina area. What follows is a partial list of the highest-rated companies:

Springtide Paddlesports

Paddleboard Rentals
180 East St, Friday Harbor, WA 98250
360-298-5317

Outdoor Odysseys

Tours, Boating, Rafting/Kayaking
0.3 miles or 5-minute walk
86 Cedar St, Friday Harbor, WA 98250
800-647-4621

Discovery Sea Kayaks

Rafting/Kayaking, Bike Rentals, Tours
0.9 miles or 17-minute walk
260 Spring St, Ste 1, Friday Harbor, WA 98250
360-378-2559

San Juan Kayak Expeditions

Boating, Rafting/Kayaking
0.9 miles or 17-minute walk
275 A St, Friday Harbor, WA 98250

[13] One of the best reason to rent a bike is that you can pretend the peddling will help shed some of the calories consumed at the island's numerous fine restaurants.

360-378-4436

San Juan Classic Day Sailing

Boating
1.0 miles or 19-minute walk
1 Spring St, Friday Harbor, WA 98250
360-378-6700

Naknek Charters & Diving

Diving
1.0 miles or 19-minute walk
2 Spring St, Friday Harbor, WA 98250
360-378-9297

Western Prince Whale Watching Tours

Boat Charters, Tours
1.0 miles or 19-minute walk
1 Spring St, Friday Harbor, WA 98250
360-378-5315

Schooners North

Boating
1.0 miles or 19-minute walk
1 Front st, Friday Harbor, WA 98250
360-378-2224

Friday Harbor Cruises

Tours
1.0 miles or 19-minute walk
San Juan Island, WA
360-317-4321

All Aboard Sailing

Tours, Boat Charters, Boating
1.1 miles or 20-minute walk
Spring St Landing, 204 Front St, Friday Harbor, WA 98250
360-298-1918

The Whale Museum

Museums
1.0 miles or 19-minute walk
62 First St N, Friday Harbor, WA 98250
360-378-4710

Up on 1st off Spring is the Whale Museum. There's a self-guided tour available, so you can look through at your own pace. The museum is dedicated to the different species of whales that abound the waters of the San Juans. The exhibit is housed on two floors with most displays on the second floor. There's also a gift shop that offers what you might expect in the way of souvenirs like postcards, magnets, keychains, jewelry, and clothing.

Overnight Lodging

Wharfside Bed & Breakfast

Hotels, Bed & Breakfast
0.9 miles or 17-minute walk
Friday Harbor Marina Slip K, Friday Harbor, WA 98250
360-378-5661

This is a charming B&B that's built on a boat moored in the marina. Being that it's a boat, you're not exactly going to have a lot of space to sprawl, but the space you do get is wonderful. The breakfast bit of the B&B is served up on deck, weather permitting. The owners are extremely friendly, and the food is great.

The Kirk House

Bed & Breakfast
0.9 miles or 16-minute walk
595 Park St, Friday Harbor, WA 98250
360-378-3757

The Kirk House is near the high school, on Park Street, which you can get to via Blair off Spring. While close to the airport and downtown, it feels just a bit removed from the touristy feel of Friday Harbor. The owners Doug and Roxie have taken great care to build a wonderful experience for you. The house is meticulously arranged, and the breakfasts are fantastic. Staff leaves fresh coffee in a basket outside your door at 7 AM. You can order picnic lunches if you'd like to take some food with you for the day.

Bird Rock Hotel

Hotels
1.0 miles or 18-minute walk
35 1st St, Friday Harbor, WA 98250
360-378-5848

The Bird Rock is right in the heart of downtown on 1st street. The rooms vary in size and shape. Some are small, but all are quite nice. Breakfast is included with your stay. Some rooms don't have their own bathrooms, so you'll need to play to share, but this isn't a problem. The hotel offers free bicycles for use around town. There's a nice patio or deck area where you can sit and enjoy being in the center of everything Friday Harbor. There's free wifi. The major problem with this hotel is that it'll make you want to extend your stay.

Argyle House Bed & Breakfast

Hotels, Bed & Breakfast
0.6 miles or 11-minute walk
685 Argyle Ave, Friday Harbor, WA 98250
360-378-4084

The Argyle House is somewhat closer to the airport, about half-way between the airport and the core of downtown. It's run by a husband and wife who take great care as to the quality of the lodging. There's gorgeous landscaping, free wifi, and a good selection of books. The breakfasts are fantastic as are the cookies in your room each day. A downside is that things are a bit cramped and tiny. Rooms feel tight. You're also clustered in tight to other houses in the neighborhood.

W33 – Friday Harbor Seaplane Base

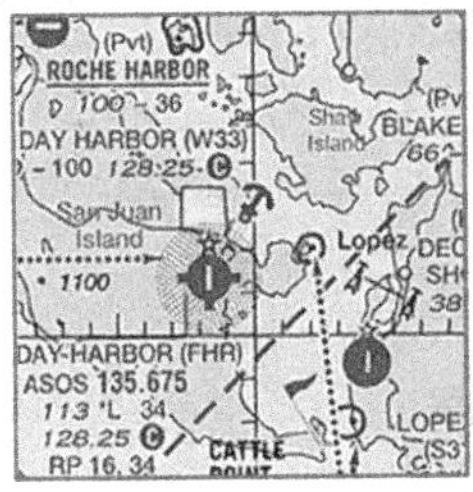

Location: 0 miles northeast of Friday Harbor
Coordinates: N48°32.24' / W123°0.58'
Altitude: 0 MSL
Fuel: None
Transient Storage: None

Another way to get into Friday Harbor is by seaplane. There's far less of a walk to get into town, since town is literally right off the dock. The problem is that lengthy seaplane parking is difficult to come by. Check with the Port of Friday Harbor at 360-378-2688 for arrangements.

Airport Notes

All takeoffs and landings should be performed north of Browns Island, the large island right in the middle of the harbor. Watch out for ferries coming or going over the north side of Browns Island. Check for the boat traffic in the area before setting up for an approach, especially in the warmer months.

There's no ramp to use, but there are docking locations. On the southeastern edge of the breakwater dock is an extension dock suitable for a brief tie-up. Ensure you leave enough room for other seaplanes. This is a very popular destination.

Whatever you do, call ahead to make arrangements and get the latest on how to be a good seaplane visitor.

Destination Notes

See the entry for FHR - Friday Harbor Airport on page 13.

WA09 – Roche Harbor Airport

Location: 1 mile northeast of Roche Harbor
Coordinates: N48°36.74' / W123°8.31'
Altitude: 100 MSL
Fuel: None
Transient Storage: None

Roche Harbor is a sheltered harbor on the northwest side of San Juan Island. The landscape here is particularly exquisite with lots of small inlets, bays, islands, and elevations. The harbor itself provides one of the better protected anchorages in the islands. The Roche Harbor marina is a designated port of entry for pleasure boats and is one of the best marinas in the Western United States.

Visiting the town of Roche Harbor itself is almost like walking into a postcard. It's immaculate, perfect.

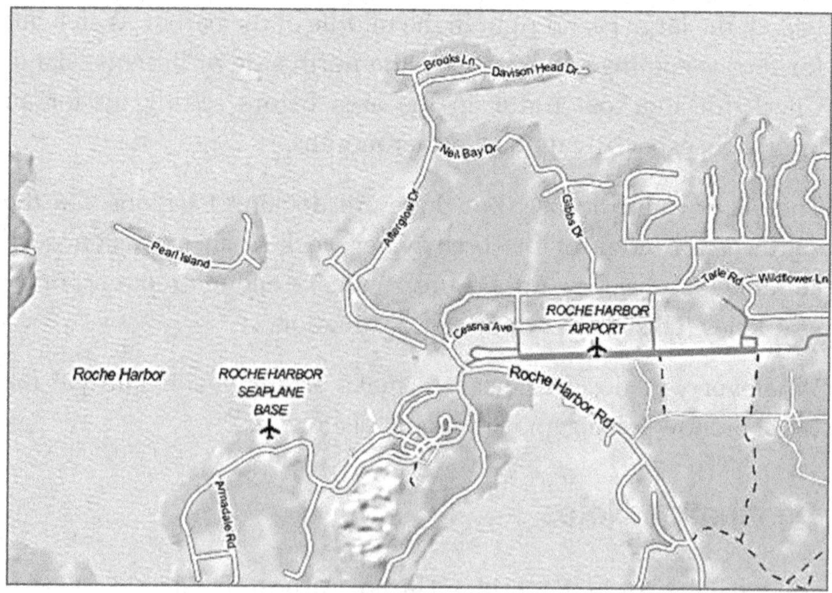

Airport Notes

The area around the airport is quite pretty, but don't let that distract you as you're on approach. There's some mild elevation to the south a bit, but it's all over a nautical mile or more away, so nothing to be worried about.

There's a windsock about 500′ east of the 07 threshold, but don't take what it's indicating too seriously if you hear others in the pattern. The runway slopes downward as it runs west to the water, so a lot of folks like to land 07 even with a light tailwind.

There's a small taxi-turnaround area on the east end and a tight but usable turnaround area on the west end. Otherwise, plan on taxiing on the runway.

Parking is up on a field on the northwest end of the runway. Immediately west of the 07 threshold is a taxiway that leads you up slightly, then turn left onto the open field. It's grass, and it slopes south toward the runway. Use chocks. A lot. Really. More than one airplane has experience an unintentional visit to the ditch between the parking area and the runway due to insufficient chocking. Note also that after long periods of considerable rain, the parking area can become something less resembling a field of grass and something more closely resembling a swamp.

The airport is private. Any visit, however brief, requires a fee be paid on the board that's on the west edge of the airport property. Bring cash or check. If you forget, pick up an envelope and mail in payment when you get back home. It's on the honor system, so please be honorable.

To get into the main part of town, cross the street to the west of the airport, then follow the trail that runs briefly south then turns west into a thick bit of trees. It's a short walk of about 0.2 miles.

Lime Kiln Café

American (Traditional), Breakfast & Brunch, Pizza
0.3 miles or 5-minute walk
248 Rueben Memorial Dr, Roche Harbor, WA 98250
800-451-8910

If you're stopping in at Roche Harbor for lunch,[14] make the Lime Kiln Café your first stop. As you exit the Reuben Memorial road that extends from the airport to the center of town, you'll pass by the Roche Harbor gardens and resort. Walk out on the main pier, and just before you get to an open green grass space, you'll find the café.

The place runs like a typical café with large seat area. You get in line just as you come in the door, order what you like at the counter, and then seat yourself. Just about everything is fantastic. If you're lucky enough to spot any donuts, buy one.[15] You'll thank me.[16] I've heard whispers the pancakes are even better than the donuts, but I consider that akin to blasphemy.

All the food is crazy-good. There's a "five-way burger" that comes with bacon, cheddar, ham, guacamole, and a fried egg. Yes, really. I also recommend the fish and chips.

The café is only open for breakfast and lunch, so keep that in mind when you're planning. If you're staying overnight, there are other places you should visit, but make this place one of your morning or

[14] When I write, "lunch," I of course include in that group the traditional American fried dough confectionery feast of donut. The donut's history is disputed. One theory states they were invented in North America by Dutch settlers. Given the historical obsession the Dutch have with coffee, I subscribe to this theory.

[15] If you're married, buy two. There are some things a spouse considers unforgivable. Failing to purchase a second donut is among these.

[16] One way to thank me is to submit a positive review of this book with an online book retailer.

mid-day stops. If you're doing a lunch-only visit to Roche, this is your go-to location.

McMillin's Dining Room

American, Seafood
0.3 miles or 5-minute walk
248 Reuben Memorial Dr, Roche Harbor, WA 98250
360-378-5757

If you're staying overnight, or if you're stopping in to Roche for dinner in the mid-summer months, then McMillin's is a fancy treat. As you're walking into town from the airport, you'll walk right past them. They're up the trail from the park area, a few paces downward from the Our Lady of Good Voyage Chapel. The place sits just at the edge of the water and has stunning views of the marina and landscape beyond. If you have a postcard of Roche Harbor, there's a high probability McMillin's will be in the picture.

While the Lime Kiln Café is open for breakfast and lunch only, McMillin's is open typically for dinner only. I've noticed their operating times fluctuate based on the season, so check in with them for their schedule and to place a reservation.

There's general seating on the lower level, a deck with umbrellas overlooking the marina and harbor, and a bar with seating upstairs.

The service is first-class, as is the food. Some call this the best restaurant on the whole of San Juan Island. They offer a killer prime rib, prawn stuffed Dungeness crab risotto, salmon ratatouille, and so much more.

Remember that during the height of the tourist season, these guys are going to get slammed. So make reservations, show up on time, and be nice to the staff. They'll treat you right and give you a fantastic experience.

Madrona Bar & Grill

American (Traditional)
0.4 miles or 6-minute walk
248 Rueben Memorial Dr, Roche Harbor, WA 98250
800-451-8910

The Madrona is down slightly from McMillin's in physical location. Still a fantastic place, but a bit less fancy. Think of Madrona as the casual alternative to McMillin's. They too have deck seating.

The food options are more bar-and-grill-ish in nature, to which the name properly alludes. Crab mac and cheese, salmon Caesar "salad,"[17] prime rib dip with blue cheese, and so on. All the food is excellent, and the service is top level.

Madrona's open for lunch and dinner, but call ahead if you're making this a day-trip. They can sometimes get quite busy during the height of the tourist season, so plan accordingly.

Things to Do

San Juan Islands Sculpture Park

Art Galleries
0.6 miles or 11-minute walk
9083 Roche Harbor Rd, Friday Harbor, WA 98250
360-370-0035

The sculpture park is impressive, large, and well organized. It's located near the airport, just on the other side of Roche Harbor Road from the airport. There's a small cost (donation) to get in. If you're at all interested in art or sculpture in particular, it's worth a stop.

[17] I don't understand this thing called "salad." I hear it mentioned in several places, so I'm passing along this information to you. But I've never tried "salad." It seems strange. Certainly, it's scary. I wouldn't try it.

We have two children, and for them, it was almost like visiting a large park that had many lovely and interesting[18] pieces of art to enjoy.

McMillin Mausoleum

Park
0.7 miles or 12-minute walk
Afterglow Dr, Roche Harbor, Friday Harbor, WA 98250

The McMillin Mausoleum is a stunning place to visit, located on the top of the small elevation to the north of the harbor. From the west end of the airport, head north along Afterglow Drive. Follow that street northwestward, and then follow the signs up the hill to the mausoleum.

The mausoleum itself is beautiful with some hidden and not-so-hidden meaning in its design and construction.

Village Artist Booths

Shopping
0.3 miles or 5-minute walk
248 Rueben Memorial Dr, Roche Harbor, WA 98250

From late June through early September, local artisans showcase their work along a stretch of ground that's just west, or inland, of the main resort dock.

[18] And some weird.

Bocce

Games
0.3 miles or 5-minute walk
248 Rueben Memorial Dr, Roche Harbor, WA 98250

Something fun for a small group might be playing a few games of bocce on the twin lanes that are just west of the Village Artist Booths area.

Bocce is a ball sport that's sort of like bowling with tiny balls and no pins or like curling without ice.[19] You can play a game between two players or two teams of two, three, or four. Pick a side at random to throw a smaller ball, the jack, from one end of the court into a zone 16′ in length, ending 8.2′ from the far end of the court. If the first team misses twice, the other team is awarded the opportunity to place the jack anywhere they choose within the prescribed zone.

The side that first attempted to place the jack is given the opportunity to bowl first. Once the first bowl has taken place, the other side has the opportunity to bowl. From then on, the side which does not have the ball closest to the jack has a chance to bowl, up until one side or the other has used their four balls. At that point, the other side bowls its remaining balls. The team with the closest ball to the jack is the only team that can score points in any frame. The scoring team receives one point for each of their balls that is closer to the jack than the closest ball of the other team. The length of a game varies from 7 to 13 points.

Players are permitted to throw the ball in the air using an underarm action. This is generally used to knock either the jack or another ball away to attain a more favorable position. Tactics can get quite

[19] Fair warning. If you see either of my children playing, ensure you have proper ear protection prior to approaching the area. They get excited when they play bocce.

complex when players have sufficient control over the ball to throw or roll it accurately.

Just Walk Around

Roche Harbor offers an extensive trail network directly on the property and on connected National Monument lands, tying together dozens of miles of outdoor footpaths. Many miles of paths start from the resort core and fan out into the forests and farmland near Roche Harbor. These trails are typically on Roche Harbor-owned property. They give you the chance to walk through woods, pastures, lagoons, quarries, and marshes. Bring your camera.

Overnight Lodging

Roche Harbor Resort

Resorts
0.4 miles or 6-minute walk
248 Reuben Memorial Dr, Roche Harbor, WA 98250
360-378-2155

If you're planning an overnight or multi-night stay at Roche Harbor, the obvious choice for lodging is the Roche Harbor Resort. There are many accommodations options including waterfront condos and historic hotels. There's a "Harbor View" and "Lagoon View" condos. There's also the McMillin Suites, four deluxe suites in an historic home perched on a bluff overlooking the marina.

There's also the Hotel de Haro with its historical hotel rooms and old charm. Many of the rooms feature original furniture from the hotel in 1886. Note that only 4 of the 20 hotel rooms have private toilets or showers in the room. Access to four shared bathrooms are down the hallway.

The newest addition to the deluxe offerings is the Quarryman Hall, which rests majestically in the center of the village next to the Hotel de Haro. This boutique-inspired hotel features contemporary amenities without losing the ambience of the turn of the century.

In addition, there are 3 and 4-bedroom village homes for larger parties.

Most popular are the historic cottages. Each one has two bedrooms and a fully equipped kitchen, making them the perfect place for a family or two couples to relax in comfort. The five front-row cottages have full views of the harbor and sunsets, and feature a gas fireplace to warm the great room. If the weather's nice, all cottages have picnic tables and fire pits with wood.

W39 – Roche Harbor Seaplane Base

Location: 0 miles southwest of Roche Harbor
Coordinates: N48°36.49' / W123°9.58'
Altitude: 0 MSL
Fuel: None
Transient Storage: None

Another way to get into Roche Harbor is by seaplane. A fair bit of commercial traffic comes and goes, but private flights are allowed so long as they don't interfere with commercial activities. The Roche Harbor dock is owned by Roche Harbor Marina. Give them a call at 360-317-6171 and/or 360-378-3500 to arrange your arrival and docking options.

Airport Notes

When arriving, take a careful scan of the both the harbor and the land-based airport. Traffic often departs the land-based airport to the west, low and slow. Keep a careful eye out for water craft of all types and sizes.

Avoid takeoffs between Pearl Island and Roche. All takeoffs outside Pearl must taxi to a point midway between the northeast corner of Pearl Island an Barren Island.

Destination Notes

See the entry for WA09 - Roche Harbor Airport on page 28.

7WA5 – Stuart Island Airpark

Location: 2 miles southeast of Stuart Island
Coordinates: N48°40.37' / W123°10.54'
Altitude: 10 MSL
Fuel: None
Transient Storage: Hangars

There's not much to do on Stuart Island, but maybe that's the whole point. The 2.8 square mile island is north of San Juan and west of Waldron. It is home to two communities: a state park and the Stuart Island Airpark.

The island is not served by ferry. There are almost no commercial services, so you'll need to plan accordingly. Also, most everything including the airpark are private. So don't plan on a trip here without getting someone to bless it first. More on that in a bit.

Airport Notes

The approach into the airport overflies some of the most charming and interesting shoreline I've ever seen. Don't let that distract you. The airpark is grass turf, and it's only 2,000 feet long. There are beaches on either end of the strip's run. The runway is kept in reasonable condition, but it may be wise to treat it as soft field to protect your gear.

The airport is private, and you must obtain permission before visiting. The runway is often not safe to land on. When you solicit permission, you'll be given a surface report and, if it's not deemed safe, you'll be denied permission to land. It's critical to follow this procedure every time you want to visit.

Washington Pilots' Association Cabin

"Rustic" Cabin
0 miles or 1-minute walk
360-825-6777

For us pilots, this island has a special draw, but it's only available to pilots who are members of the Washington Pilots' Association (WPA).[20] There's a cabin next to the airpark formerly owned by a pilot who gave it to WPA for WPA pilots to use.

Folks like to call the cabin "rustic," which it is in every sense of the word. You'll need to bring in whatever you need for your stay.

You must get permission before landing. Call Tom Jensen at 360-825-6777 or 253-350-7442 to check on availability and reserve your stay. Remember, this only applies to WPA members.

[20] If you're a pilot living in Washington State and you're not a member of WPA already, stop reading right now and sign up at wpaflys.org. Go ahead. I'll wait.

S31 – Lopez Island Airport

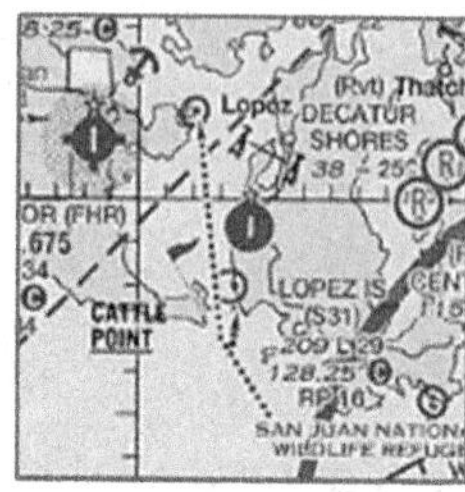

Location: 3 miles south of Lopez
Coordinates: N48°29.03' / W122°56.26'
Altitude: 209 MSL
Fuel: None
Transient Storage: Tiedowns

Lopez is the third largest island in the San Juans, but it's quite a different sort of experience visiting here as compared to Friday Harbor or Eastsound. Lopez is a quiet place, as delightful as the islands but with a different, more muted feel.

As peaceful as the island is, it's equally if not even more friendly. People wave at you all over the place.

Lopez is not a great place for a day-trip necessarily, unless you want to go golfing. Rather, Lopez is great as an overnight option.

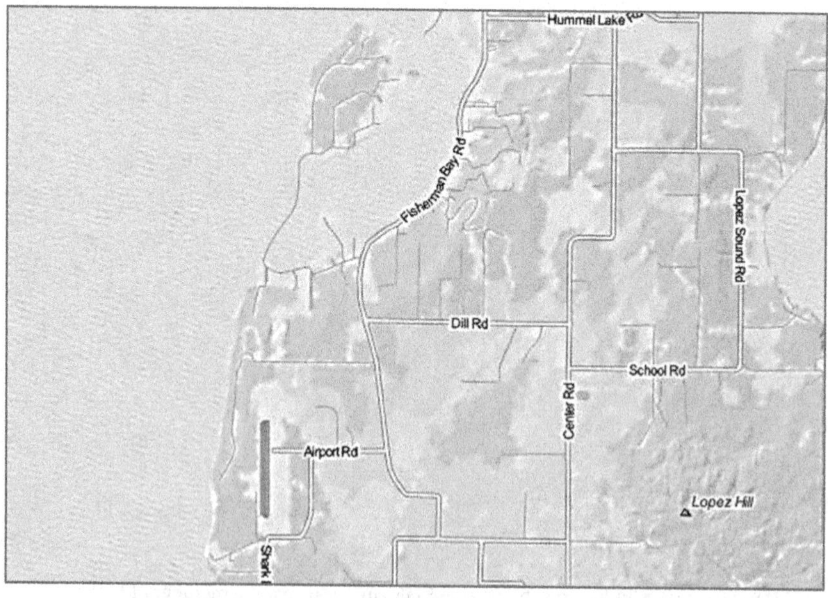

Airport Notes

The airport is well maintained and easy to work with. Traffic should stay always towards the water, the west of the airport, for noise abatement. The runway slopes downward as it runs to the south.

There are 60′ trees near both ends of the runway, but given the nearly 3000′ of runway and additional space beyond before the trees, they aren't an issue. There's plenty of parking in the northeast parking lot, plainly visible. There's no fuel, though.

Transportation

As far as I know, there aren't a lot of good transportation options on Lopez. However, most of the time that's not terribly important. Most overnight accommodations include shuttles you can use to pick you up from the airport.

Things to Do

Lopez Island Golf Club

Golf
0.2 miles or 3-minute walk
589 Airport Rd, Lopez Island, WA 98261
360-468-2679

There's really nothing to do within a short walk of the airport apart from a round of golf. The Lopez Island Golf Club is right next to the airport, convenient for pilots. The club offers a small 9-hole course that varies to 18 with tee and pin placements.

The Garden Cottages

Guest Houses
1.6 miles or 31-minute walk
7 Hanson Ln, Lopez Island, WA 98261
360-468-2259

If you follow Airport Road (northeast side of the airport) east then turn north on Fisherman Bay Road, you'll eventually end up at the Garden Cottages. It's a bit of a walk if you're carrying overnight bags, but it's a lovely walk. You'll likely notice at least a couple cars drive by on Fisherman Bay Road with drivers who'll wave at you. Unlike other lodging options, I don't believe the Garden Cottages offers shuttle service to the airport.

The cottages are in a great location in the bay, near shops and a grocery store. There's also beach access. However, when you're in the cottages area, you'll get a feeling of separation from the outside world. It's very peaceful.

The idea with the cottages is that you bring in your own food and treat the place like a vacation home. There's a kitchen with kitchen ware, microwave, oven stove, and refrigerator.

Edenwild Inn

Hotels, Bed & Breakfast
3.0 miles or 57-minute walk
132 Lopez Rd, Lopez Island, WA 98261
360-468-3238

The Edenwild Inn is near the north end of Fisherman Bay. It's a large house that's been converted into a fine-looking hotel. There are 9 guest rooms in all. All the rooms have either water or garden views. For visiting pilots, the inn does offer a shuttle service.

Many of the rooms have brick fireplaces. There's free wifi, private gardens to enjoy, and bicycle rentals.

This is probably one of the ideal locations for pilots to stay overnight. There's also a restaurant on the premises.

Lopez Lodge

Hotels
2.9 miles or 56-minute walk
37 Weeks Point Way, Lopez Island, WA 98261
360-468-2071

Lopez Lodge is at the north end of Fisherman Bay, right at the entrance to the bay. The rooms are cozy but nice. The staff are extremely attentive to your needs.

There's wifi in each room along with full kitchen, dining, and living areas.

Food Options

There aren't any food options within a reasonable walk from the airport. However, if you stay overnight near the north end of the bay, you have a few great options to try.

Vita's Wildly Delicious

Cafés
77 Village Rd, Lopez Island, WA 98261
360-468-4268

The food here is even more awesome than its wonderful location. It's tucked away in a garden. It's something like a high-end deli, a bit on the expensive end of the spectrum, but worth it. The food is grown in their own greenhouse or by local farmers on the island.

When you arrive, you're walking into the kitchen area, so you get to see all the ingredients laid out before you.

Many speak highly of their shrimp cakes, meatloaf, macaroni and cheese, and stuffed peppers. There's extraordinary attention to detail with flavors and combinations.

This is a mid-day sort of restaurant, closing at 5pm except on Fridays when they stay open until 8pm. They're closed on Sundays. Give them a call to find out specific closing times if you're expecting to be arriving toward the later part of the day.

The Bay Café

Seafood, American
9 Old Post Rd, Lopez Island, WA 98261
360-468-3700

The Bay Café is located just outside the mouth of the bay right on the water with extraordinary views westward. The food is top-quality on all counts. Everything on the menu is great. If when you're there for dinner weather permits, sit on the deck and enjoy the sunset while the staff treat you like royalty.

Especially highly rated dishes include the crab cakes, anything with clams including the chowder, and scallops.

Haven

American (Traditional)
210 Lopez Rd, Lopez Island, WA 98261
360-468-3272

This is a more casual food experience than the Bay Café, but worth a stop. Folks rave about the fish tacos, pork sliders, and something they call the "hot Mexican mess". The crab cakes are good as well.

ORS – Orcas Island Airport

Location: 1 mile north of Eastsound
Coordinates: N48°42.50' / W122°54.63'
Altitude: 34 MSL
Fuel: 100LL
Transient Storage: Tiedowns

Orcas Island is quickly becoming one of my favorite places to visit. It's a big island, the largest of the San Juan Islands at 57 square miles; but more than that, it's spread out in such a way that it almost acts like multiple separate islands all merged together.

There's Westsound and Deer Harbor to the southwest, Moran State Park and Doe Bay to the southeast, and Eastsound (the city) at the north end of Eastsound (the sound), which cuts the island nearly in two. Eastsound (the city) seems like a natural place for the largest town on the island because it sits on a bridge between the west and east arms of the island in a low and mostly flat stretch.

The natural beauty of Orcas cannot be overstated. As magnificent as it is from the ground, it's even more breathtaking from the air. Mount Constitution and Mount Pickett in Moran State park rise up tall, the former of which is the tallest point in all of the San Juans at 2,400′.[21]

At Eastsound (the city) itself, down just off the edge of the water, sits a small island turned bird sanctuary. At low tide, one can walk along an exposed land bridge out to the island.[22]

[21] 2,770′ if you count the buildings and antennas, which you should.

[22] If you do, please read the sign as you step on to the island and follow all its instructions. Keep a careful look out for nests tucked into the rocks and avoid them.

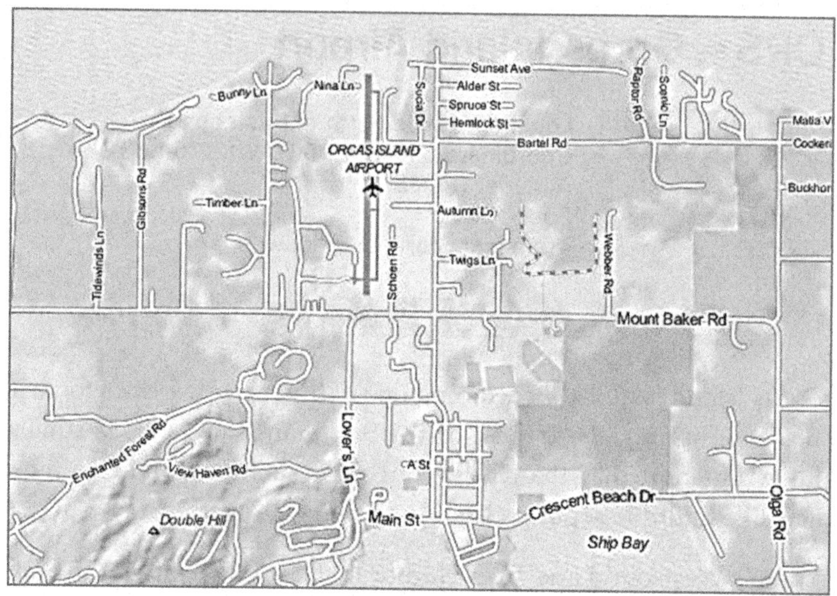

Airport Notes

The approach into Eastsound (the airport) is easy but fraught with peril due to the extent of the visual distractions you'll encounter along the way. Stay focused. Traffic is always to the east of the field because there's a pretty nice rise in terrain immediately to the west of the field.

If you're trying for a straight in approach from the south, you'll come right over the top of Mount Woolard. Alternatively, some hot shot pilots like to follow Eastsound (the sound) at a lower altitude then swing onto a straight-in 34 near Osprey Hill.

The runway slopes down as it runs north, so if you're approaching from the south, keep your speed and altitude in check so you can make the first turnoff and impress your friends. There are some trees to the south of the field just off to the east of the centerline that may alarm you if you're coming in low off the water, but they're nothing to worry too much about.

Parking and the small passenger terminal are toward the southeast end of the field. The fuel dock is on the north side of the ramp here. There's parking both north and south of the passenger terminal and hangars in the middle of the ramp area.

If it's your first time to Eastsound, stop by the passenger terminal area to pick up a tourist map of the area. Regardless of where you park, if you're going to stay overnight, there's a small landing fee payable with envelopes and box that's on the ramp side door to the passenger terminal area.

You can exit the airport either through the passenger terminal, nearby gates, or from the very south of the field through a walking gate. If you park in the south parking area and call a taxi, there's a parking lot and small gate just to your north.

Transportation

A courtesy car is reportedly available. It's a 1970s Mercedes 240D. Call Tony Simpson at 360-376-5285 to inquire. Alternatively, you can call for a taxi. I've used and like Orcas Island Taxi Service, at 360-376-8294. You can also try New Orcas Taxi Tours at 360-298-1639.

That said, unless you're heading away from town or are carrying in a lot of luggage and your hotel doesn't offer a shuttle, you've really got to try the nature trail that runs conveniently from the southern end of the airport all the way into town. To pick up the trailhead, exit the south of the airport by the road, cross the street, and immediately ahead just to the right side of the road is the trail.

The Madrona Bar & Grill

American (Traditional)
1.0 miles or 19-minute walk
310 Main St, Eastsound, WA 98245
360-376-7171

After you've enjoyed your stroll into town via the nature trail, make your way to the water and to the very center of town, the intersection of Main and North Beach. There you'll find a small plaza, and if you follow the pier out, you'll end up at the Madrona Bar and Grill, which overlooks Eastsound (the sound).

Many have taken up the task of ranking the best places in Washington for pilots to get fish and chips. Many claim it's at PWT. Others say FHR. All, however, recognize that Madrona needs to be on the list if not at the top of it.

One problem with Madrona is they seem to always be busy around lunch time, even in the off-season. There's good reason for that, though. Beyond the fish and chips, they've got great oysters, burgers, chowder, ravioli, and more.

Enzo's Italian Café

Cafés, Gelato, Breakfast & Brunch
0.8 miles or 15-minute walk
365 N Beach Rd, Eastsound, WA 98245
360-376-3732

Another great location is Enzo's Café. It's not open for dinner, but it's a great place for breakfast or lunch. It's located in the group of buildings on the northwest corner of Beach and A Street. As you're coming off the nature trail, just keep heading east past the Post Office, and you'll pass right by it.

These guys have great coffee and sandwiches. There's free wifi, so you can pick up your food and sit down with your laptop or tablet and get some work done. Great paninis and pizza. The crepes and gelato are available during the main tourist season. There are gluten-free fresh-baked cookies.

Half the enjoyment of this place is the grounds. You'll be surrounded by landscaped gardens.

New Leaf Café

American (New)
0.9 miles or 18-minute walk
171 Main St, Eastsound, WA 98245
360-376-2200

This café is part of the Outlook Inn.[23] It's worth a stop even if you're not staying the night at the Inn. Try the crab cakes, sockeye salmon pasta, or smoked salmon eggs benedict. The apple upside-down cake is great, if you like apples.[24]

The view is amazing, looking across the street out onto the Eastsound (the sound). The atmosphere is wonderful as well. There's free wifi, although I doubt you'll use it.[25]

[23] See my comments about the inn in the overnight lodging section. You'll thank me. Or at least, you should if you're a courteous pilot, which I'm sure you are.
[24] I don't.
[25] You'll be too busy eating the yumminess.

Mijitas

Mexican
0.8 miles or 16-minute walk
310 A St, Eastsound, WA 98245
360-376-6722

I don't know about you, but when I think Pacific Northwest islands near the Canadian border, I think Mexican food.[26] Mijitas doesn't disappoint. These guys blend local food stuffs with a Mexican slant, and the results are wonderful. They incorporate a lot of seafood into their dishes. As an example, take the kale enchiladas. Try the quinoa cakes stuffed with goat cheese with sweet potatoes mashed with chills. There's also prawn tacos and Dungeness crab enchiladas.

Brown Bear Baking

Coffee & Tea, Breakfast & Brunch
1.0 miles or 18-minute walk
29 N Beach Rd, Eastsound, WA 98245
360-855-7456

This breakfast and brunch spot is along Beach Road about half way to the water from the end of the nature trail on A Street. They serve bakery type food. Think chocolate muffins, almond croissants, and bread pudding. The tea selection is good, but the coffee is hit or miss.

[26] Actually, no, I don't. But I've noticed in my travels a strange correlation of good Mexican food at locations near the Canadian border.

Just Walk Around

One of the best things to do in Eastsound (the city) is to just walk around. There are so many wonderful and gorgeous things to see. To the west of Madrona along Main Street by the water is the Emmanuel Episcopal Church. On its grounds is a picturesque labyrinth open to the public to traverse.

To the west of the church is a pathway, trail, and steps to get down to the beach. At low tide, you can and should walk out to the small island that sits about 500′ offshore. Read the signs and keep a close watch for bird nests. Avoid disturbing any of the birds or their nests.

The Eastsound Village Green Country Park is a nice place, weather permitting, to sit down for a picnic.

A-1 Wildlife Cycles

Bikes, Bike Rentals, Bike Repair/Maintenance
0.8 miles or 15-minute walk
350 Northbeach Rd, Ste 1048, Eastsound, WA 98245
360-376-4708

A great way to get around this part of Orcas Island is on a rented bicycle, and the best place to rent a bicycle is at A-1. These guys rent quality mountain and performance road bicycles. They're also quite good at repairs and maintenance, so they keep their rental bicycles in good condition.

These guys can also recommend various routes to take around the island, depending on your capabilities and interests.

A-1 is located just east of the intersection of A Street and North Beach Road.

Emerald Isle Sailing Charters

Boating, Tours
0.3 miles or 6-minute walk
Eastsound, WA 98245
360-376-3472

If you have some time you can invest, try a sailing charter from Emerald Isle. They run one of the largest and nicest boats on the island. They offer scheduled tours, day charters, and multi-day cruises.

Consider splurging on a multi-day trip with them, because you'll enjoy your cabin stay with multiple bedrooms, full kitchen, and gigantic deck. The captain is a naturalist and possesses extensive knowledge of the area, its history, the native tribes, and more.

Overnight Lodging

Outlook Inn on Orcas Island

Hotels, Restaurants
0.9 miles or 18-minute walk
171 Main St, Eastsound, WA 98245
360-376-2200

There are several good options for overnight lodging in Eastsound (the city); however, few offer quite what the Outlook Inn can and does. The Outlook is on Main Street just a tiny bit west of the beach access location. You'll get an amazing view of Eastsound (the sound) and be right in the heart of everything.

The rooms aren't cramped and are setup with care to reflect an Orcas Island feel. As much as possible, the rooms are furnished and stocked with items from the island.

There are some low-cost rooms where the prices are extremely reasonable, almost unbelievably so.

Kangaroo House B & B

Hotels, Bed & Breakfast
0.2 miles or 4-minute walk
1459 N Beach Rd, Eastsound, WA 98245
360-376-2175

If you're like me[27] and feel the need to sleep closer to your airplane, Kangaroo House is a good option. It's up north on North Beach Road, not far from the northern shoreline. The B & B is established in a magnificent historic house, a 1907 Craftsman, on lovely grounds. There's an incredible garden toward the front of the house, and the grounds are surrounded by large, old trees. The breakfast in the morning is a top-quality, 3-course meal made with fresh ingredients mostly grown in the B & B's own gardens.

Golden Tree Inn & Hostel

Hotels
0.3 miles or 5-minute walk
1159 N Beach Rd, Eastsound, WA 98245
360-317-8693

If you'd like to stay near your airplane and simultaneously congregate with other visitors to the island, Golden Tree is a good option. It's located on North Beach Road just around the corner from the airport. It's also quite inexpensive compared to other options on the island. They offer both private and communal rooms, all with shared baths and a fully-equipped kitchen. During the regular season, they offer a campfire at night. You can relax and play a game of pool or soak in the hot tub.

[27] If you're like me, I'm very sorry.

W49 – Rosario Seaplane Base

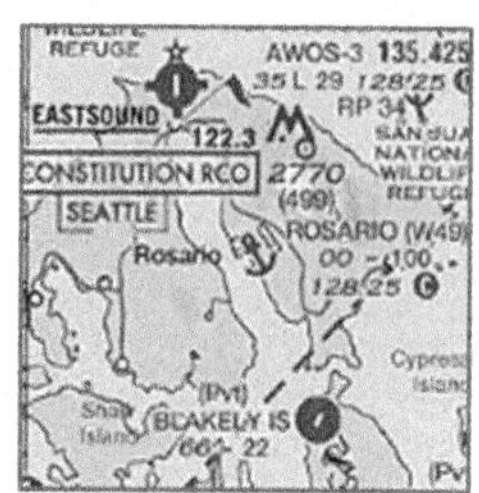

Location: 0 miles south of Rosario
Coordinates: N48°38.74' / W122°52.08'
Altitude: 0 MSL
Fuel: None
Transient Storage: None

A special treat that's a short taxi ride away from Eastsound (the city) is Rosario Resort, located a bit more than halfway down Eastsound (the sound). If you lack the ability to land on water more than once, just park at Eastsound (the airport) and call up Orcas Island Taxi Service at 360-376-8294. If, however, you have the ability to safely depart after a water landing, there's a seaplane base just for you.

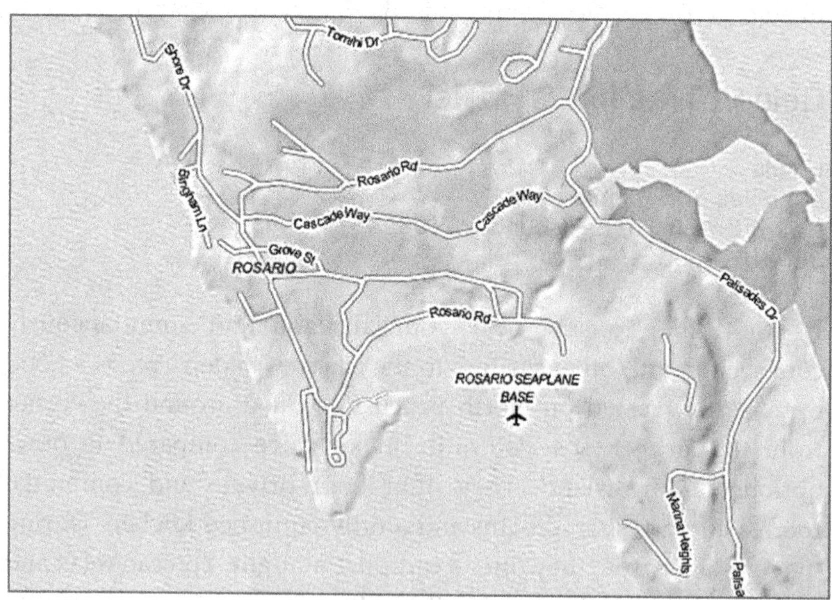

Airport Notes

Given the height of Mount Constitution and the fact that Eastsound (the sound) has a channeling effect, keep a sharp eye out for strange things going on with the wind as you're coming in. There's a very sharp hill coming up off the shore along the east, and there's a medium-grade hill rising up from the beach as you move north.

It may be best to circle over the point to the west of the resort to get a read on the winds, water, and boat traffic. As you're coming down, watch for the buoys area that extends from the eastern shoreline out about a third to halfway into the resort cove. Generally speaking, the cove is sheltered from the winds to some degree, but keep a sharp eye on the water because the winds do some strange things on the water that's often not obvious.

The seaplane dock is the first dock you'll see as you head in toward the marina. There's plenty of space there for a small number of float planes to tie up temporarily. That said, you shouldn't plan on tying up there for any duration more than a few minutes.

Call the harbormaster at 360-376-2222. He's extremely accommodating and will figure out a good spot for you. For hull planes, if you're only stopping in for food, you could try the beach to the east of the marina. Either way, check with the harbormaster.

Transportation

The resort itself has a courtesy shuttle that can get you around the resort property. If you need or want to go anywhere beyond, you'll need to make other arrangements.

The Mansion Restaurant

American (New)
0.3 miles or 4-minute walk
1400 Rosario Rd, Eastsound, WA 98245
360-376-2152

I've been particularly blessed to enjoy the best cuisine on the planet. It takes a lot to impress me. The restaurant at the Mansion in Rosario Resort impressed me with its dinner service. The food was on par with the finest restaurants and private clubs I've ever had the privilege to patronize. The service is spectacular.

My only complaint is that breakfast, while being very good, is something of a letdown when compared to dinner.

As you walk from the main doorway of the Mansion to the entrance to the restaurant, you'll pass through the lounge, which is a good place to relax in front of the fireplace.

Cascade Grill

American (New)
0.1 miles or 2-minute walk
1400 Rosario Resort, Eastsound, WA 98245
360-376-2222

Open during the main tourist season, the Cascade Grill is a more informal food option to the Mansion. The food is still great, but it has more of a beach grill vibe to it, as you'd expect. The fish and chips are great. The oysters and other seafood are top quality.

The presentation of the dishes is basically non-existent, but the taste more than makes up for this. If you want presentation, go to the

Mansion. If you want a casual yummy lunch, the Grill should be your choice.

Things to Do

Moran Mansion Museum

0.3 miles or 4-minute walk
1400 Rosario Rd, Eastsound, WA 98245
360-376-2222

When time permits, it's well worth it to visit the Mansion's upstairs areas. The Museum is a tribute to the man that built Rosario as his home: shipbuilder and former Seattle mayor Robert Moran. The Museum features original photographs taken from the early 1900s, period furnishings, and models of the ships built by the Moran Brothers Company in Seattle.

Organ Concert and Rosario History Narrative

0.3 miles or 4-minute walk
1400 Rosario Rd, Eastsound, WA 98245
360-376-2222

Christopher Peacock, accomplished musician, author and Rosario historian, offers a presentation of music and photography that walks guests through the history of the Moran family and the Rosario estate. Highlights of the presentation include the historic Moran Photograph Collection, Phantom of the Opera music played on the Mansion's 1,972 pipe Aeolian organ with silent film, stories of the Mansion's most colorful residents, and Christopher's original piano compositions played on the 1900 Steinway Grand Piano.

These events are on only on Saturday afternoons; however, they're complimentary and open to the public.

Rosario Resort and Spa

Hotels, Resorts
0.3 miles or 4-minute walk
1400 Rosario Rd, Eastsound, WA 98245
360-376-2222

If you're going to bother getting to Rosario Resort and you need to stay overnight, the default choice is staying at the Resort. The property covers the whole of the shoreline of the bay. The Mansion is towards the western point, but most of the overnight lodgings are to the east as the elevation starts to rise. This is not a problem, though, since the Resort makes available a shuttle to get you from one place to another.

The actual rooms themselves are a bit tight and outdated. That said, there's little reason to hunker down in your room.

The staff are all, every one of them, extraordinarily professional, helpful, and friendly. They each and all genuinely want to serve you and ensure you have a wonderful time.

Chapter 2

Olympic Peninsula

The Olympic Peninsula is about 3,600 square miles of mostly wilderness bracketed by the Pacific, Strait of Juan de Fuca, and Hood Canal. It has the unique qualification of being the last unexplored area of the lower 48 of the United States. It remained unmapped until just prior to 1900 when it was first surveyed for its topography and timber resources.

Even today, it remains quite empty compared to most places in Washington State. Flying over lands west of the slopes of Olympic National Park, I feel like I'm flying over an ocean of trees.[28]

The westernmost parts of the continental United States are Cape Flattery and Cape Alava, both breathtakingly stunning landscapes we pilots can view from above 2,000 AGL. Cape Flattery has the distinction of being the oldest permanently named feature in Washington State, having been named by James Cook in 1778.

Clallam County runs along the north rim of the Olympic Peninsula and includes most of the airports in the area. Just to the south is Jefferson County, which is split in half by the towering Olympic Mountains in all their glory.

The weather in these areas can be entertaining. Along the western side of the Olympics, raw ocean weather rolls in and can slam up

[28] If I fly a bit more to the west, I feel like I'm flying over an ocean of ocean.

against the rising western slopes to form all sorts of visual degradations. The mountains themselves are frequently obscured behind billowing cloud forms. Ceilings to the west can plummet rapidly, depending on what systems are flowing in from the Pacific.

Along the northern rim, in central Clallam County, the weather is often surprisingly good by comparison. It resembles in some ways the weather in the San Juans. When I fly up to Friday Harbor (FHR) from Bremerton (PWT), I often encounter a shift from an overcast cloud layer to scattered or few clouds right about the time I overfly Jefferson County Airport (0S9).

If you can fit your bicycle into your airplane,[29] this area has some wonderful cycling options.

[29] Don't try hooking up a bicycle rack to the empennage. This is a bad idea.

0S9 – Jefferson County Intl Airport

Location: 6 miles southwest of Port Townsend
Coordinates: N48°3.23' / W122°48.64'
Altitude: 110 MSL
Fuel: 100LL
Transient Storage: Hangars, Tiedowns

 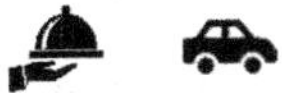

There are multiple reasons to visit "JeffCo" or Jefferson County International Airport, sometimes called Port Townsend. However, the greatest of these reasons is pie. Very good pie. Pie so good it doesn't last long. Pie that seems to make all the problems of the world fade away. Pie so good it'll actually distract you from the gorgeous view from the airport looking south toward the Olympics. Pie as spiritual experience.[30] But we'll get to that later.

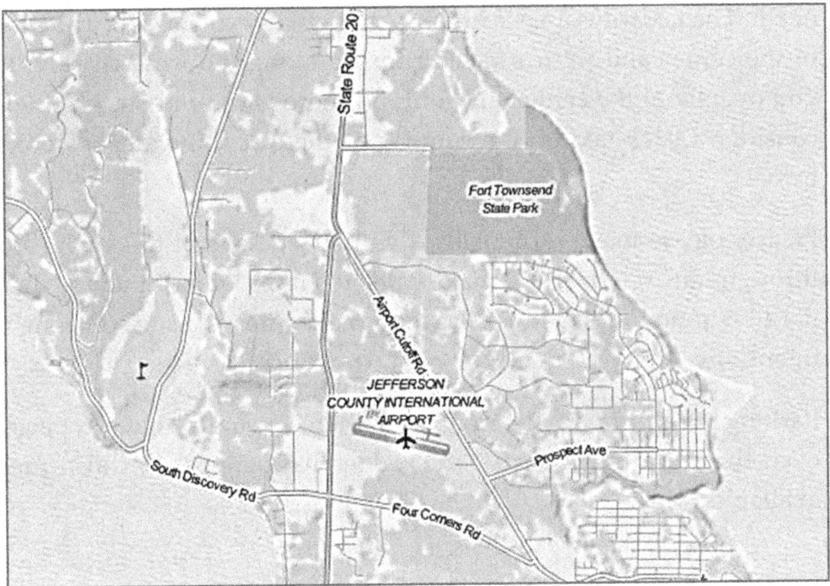

[30] I might be overselling this pie ever so slightly, but probably not.

Airport Notes

JeffCo sits in the middle of the Port Townsend peninsula, tucked in just east of a cove in Discovery Bay to the west. When approaching, avoid the airspace to the east below 2,900′ MSL so the Navy doesn't get too annoyed with you. If you keep to the western shoreline of the bay to the east, you should avoid the Navy's ire.

Winds are almost always out of the west, but check weather and traffic before committing to 27. Traffic pattern is always to the south of the field.

One of the neat things about JeffCo is there are well-traffic-ed roads just beyond the thresholds of both 27 and 09, so you'll often get opportunities to scare drivers.[31]

Once on the ground, use the runway exit in the center of the field to go straight up the slight incline to the ramp that's quite a distance north. The taxiways area is organized such that you exit the runway in the center and return to the runway along the western side. If you overshoot the center turn off and there isn't someone on final, consider a back-taxi on the runway to the exit if the airport looks busy.

Please, please make radio calls. I've noticed several folks who fly through JeffCo who don't make calls. It's not required they do, but it's a bit annoying when you have to make guesses as to someone's intentions.

Parking is up north on the ramp, and there's usually enough spaces even during a lunch rush, which does happen. There's also fuel available.

[31] These roads are also great for scaring first-time passengers. Not that I'm recommending doing so. Fly a reasonable glide slope.

Transportation

There is a report of a courtesy car available. Give "Tailspin Tommy's" a call at 360-385-1308 to inquire.

Food Options

Spruce Goose ✈

American (Traditional)
0.1 miles or 1-minute walk
310 Airport Rd, Port Townsend, WA 98368
360-385-3185

Pie. The Spruce Goose has some yummy diner food and a wonderful view from its deck seating that looks out over the center of the field and includes the northeast Olympics beyond. The interior is extremely pilot-friendly, including old sectionals as table decorations. Airplanes hang from the ceiling, and the wall posters might make you smile.

Pie. The fish and chips are good, but I'm a big fan of their Ruben and their shrimp sandwich. The Monte Cristo is also pretty good.

Now a brief note about the pie: order some.

When you first arrive, take a look at the chalkboard behind the register. It'll list out the pies *currently* available. That word "currently" is important. The list changes. A lot. When the waitress first greets you, ask her to set aside some pie. If you don't, there's a good chance your preferred flavor won't exist by the time you get done with lunch.

I have three complains about the Spruce Goose. First, they run out of pie far too frequently. Second, they aren't open past 4pm. Third, it should be called the Hercules so the ghost of Howard Hughes doesn't get upset. Pie.

San Juan Taqueria

Mexican
0.6 miles or 12-minute walk
23 Kala Square, Port Townsend, WA 98368
360-344-2891

The San Juan Taqueria[32] is a good restaurant and really does deserve your patronage, but it has one big problem: It's not the Spruce Goose. To get to the Taqueria, you need to walk past the Spruce Goose,[33] then walk down Highway 19 until you get to Kala Square.

The Taqueria serves fairly authentic Mexican food. The tostada with pork carnitas is wonderful. The carne asada is heavenly.

Things to Do

Port Townsend Aero Museum

0.1 miles or 1-minute walk
105 Airport Rd, Port Townsend, WA 98368
360-379-5244

The Aero Museum on the field is a great place to visit. Airplane models hang from the ceiling, and restored aircraft are placed around the floor. Unlike many other museums where planes go to die, several of the planes here are flight ready and are used in active flight training operations.

[32] Not located on San Juan Island.

[33] If you have the will power to land at JeffCo and walk past the Spruce Goose, you have my respect and admiration.

W28 – Sequim Valley Airport

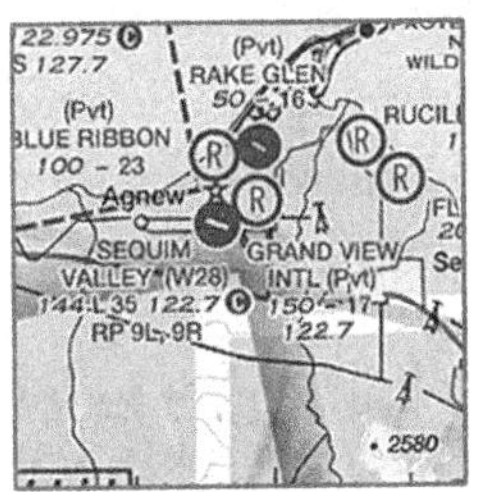

Location: 4 miles northwest of Sequim
Coordinates: N48°5.84' / W123°11.25'
Altitude: 152 MSL
Fuel: 100LL
Transient Storage: Tiedowns

Sequim is both a town and a mini region of Clallam County. The town itself is just to the west of Discovery Bay a bit, but the mini region stretches wide from the banks of Sequim Bay west about half-way to Port Angeles, and from the Strait of Juan de Fuca south to the northern rim of the Olympics. Sequim is unusually nice with pleasant weather as a norm.

A river runs through it, the Dungeness River, which runs from deep within the Olympic National Park out into Dungeness Bay.

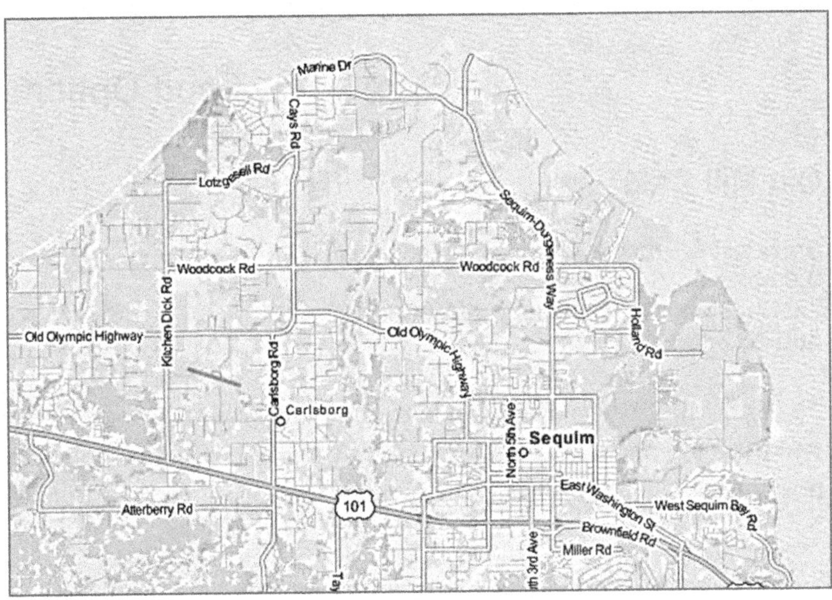

Airport Notes

The airport is a fair bit west of the center of Sequim. There are quite a few smaller, private fields in the area, so be sure you're picking out the right place. Winds tend to favor 27, but get current weather before committing. Traffic is always to the south of the field.

As you're coming in on final on 27, there's a rectangle of trees that has its southwestern point terminate looks and feels pretty much right where you want to be. In reality, there's sufficient clearance where it shouldn't be a problem, but it's close enough that on my first arrival, I did a pair of side slips to give myself extra spacing.

There is a small landing fee, payable at a board in roughly the middle of the northern perimeter of the ramp. There's also a pilot's lounge to the west of that board.

If you're going to stay for a while, park in the grass that's between the paved ramp and the runway, but keep to the north side of that grass area.

Food Options

Old Mill Café

Breakfast & Brunch, American (Traditional)
0.8 miles or 16-minute walk
721 Carlsborg Rd, Carlsborg, WA 98324
360-582-1583

The Old Mill Café is a not-too-bad of a walk from the airport, but you have to go in a rather out-of-your-way route to get there. Head north up to Old Olympic Highway, then south on Carlsborg Road.[34]

[34] You can probably get there a bit faster by walking across the runway, trespassing through some guy's farm land, then follow a small access road out to Carlsborg Road. For the record, I'm not recommending you do this.

The place itself has something of a rustic and interesting feel to it. The coffee is good, the food is good, and the atmosphere is good. The seafood benedict is yummy.

You should be prepared for a bit of a wait for your food, but when it arrives, you'll be happy.

Gabby's Java

Restaurants
0.9 miles or 17-minute walk
471 Business Park Loop, Sequim, WA 98382
360-683-8839

Just a skip away from the Café is Gabby's Java. They have a good hot sandwich selection and deserts. The bread pudding is a wise choice. The cinnamon rolls will add your waistline, but they're yummy enough you may not care.

CLM – William Fairchild Intl Airport

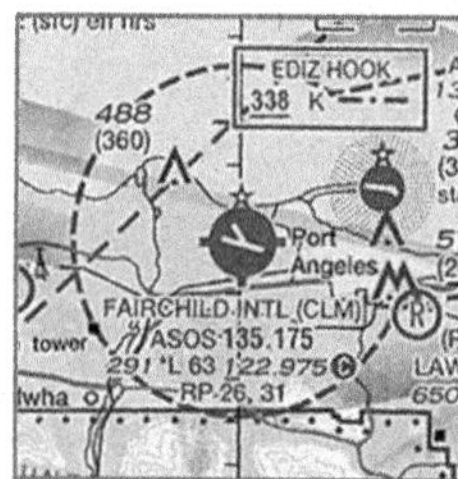

Location: 3 miles northwest of Port Angeles
Coordinates: N48°7.21' / W123°29.98'
Altitude: 291 MSL
Fuel: 100LL
Transient Storage: Tiedowns

Fairchild is a good place to stop off to get fuel, but there isn't much really to do near the airport. You'll have to get into Port Angeles itself.

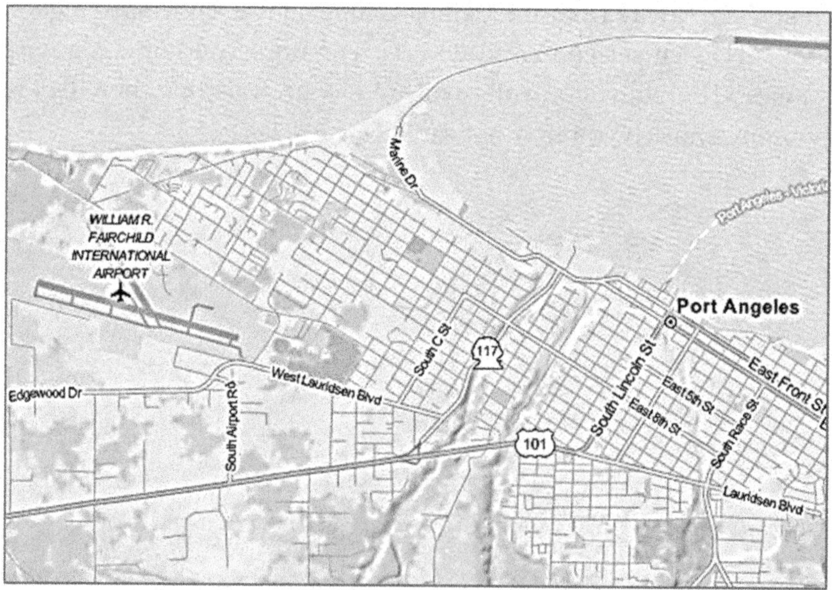

Airport Notes

This is a well-maintained and large airport with easy access. Pattern is always to the north.

Parking is available just to the east of the main terminal building. Fuel and other parking is to the west.

Transportation

Courtesy cars are available: a Windstar and an actual operating Astrovan. Call Rite Brothers Aviation at 360-452-6226 for information and/or reservations.

Things to Do

Harbinger Winery

Wineries
1.2 miles or 24-minute walk
2358 Highway 101 W, Port Angeles, WA 98363
360-452-4262

While there are several things to do in Port Angles proper (away from the airport), there's really only the winery within walking distance of the field. From the main terminal area, make your way south along South Airport Road, then walk west on Highway 101.

Of course, if you're only doing a walking visit from the airport, visiting a wine tasting room will be of questionable wisdom unless your intention is to buy without tasting.

11S – Sekiu Airport

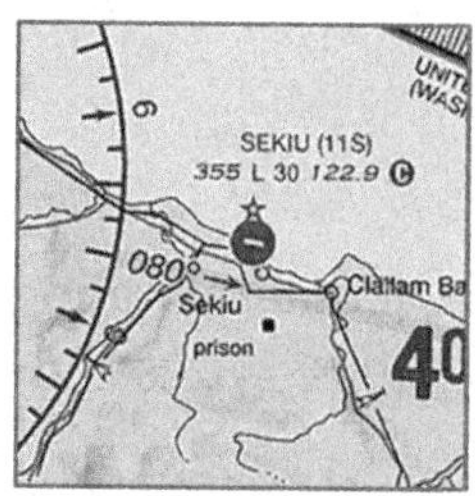

Location: 0 miles northwest of Sekiu
Coordinates: N48°15.97' / W124°18.84'
Altitude: 355 MSL
Fuel: None
Transient Storage: Tiedowns

Sekiu is a town and airport living on the edge, so to speak. The small, unincorporated community is nestled to the western shores of Clallam Bay along the north rim of the Olympic Peninsula. Just to the north of the town at the northwestern corner of the bay is a nearly 500′ hill that shields the town. The airport itself is up on a rise west of the town, the runway itself sitting at 355′ MSL.

The feeling you get is one of remoteness and quiet. There is a year-round population here, but the town is mostly known as a summer destination for fishing and birdwatching.

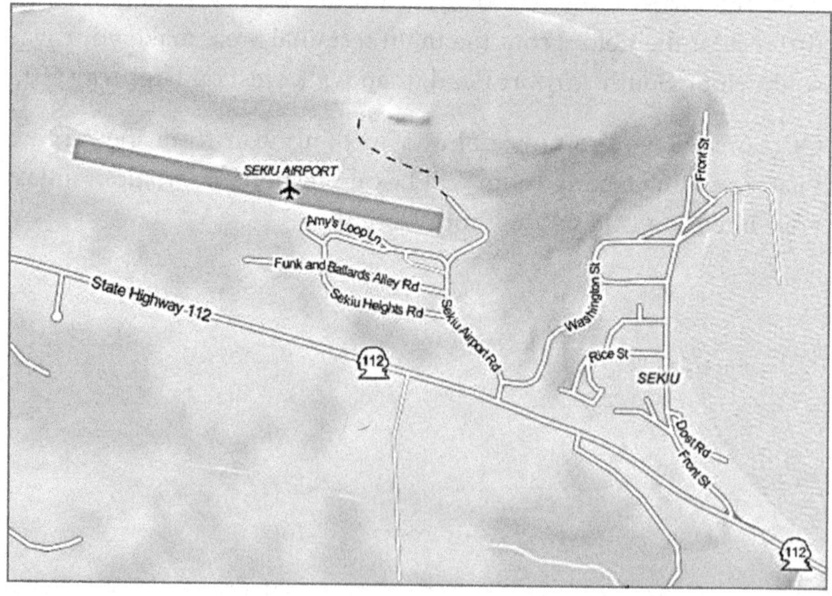

Airport Notes

This airport is entertaining to get into when there's wind. There's a non-trivial rise in terrain to the north, which in most places would result in right pattern for 8, but not here.

Winds tend to favor 26, but watch out for turbulence on the east end of the approach over the water due to the rising terrain lifting off the water and the Gibraltar-inspired 500′ hill just off to the right.

If winds are from the north, plan on a few go arounds and exercise caution. The hills to the north aren't what you might call uniform, so the wind does things you wouldn't normally expect. Also, the landscape sets up a pretty good situation of a strong downdraft that presents itself just as you're approaching the 26 threshold.

And of course, just to make it all even more fun: deer.

Food Options

By the Bay Café

American (Traditional)
0.6 miles or 11-minute walk
343 Front St, Sekiu, WA 98326
360-963-2998

Dining options up in this neck of the woods are scarce, but the Café is a solid choice. They're open for breakfast, lunch, and dinner. They offer fairly standard style picks like a meatloaf sandwich, ham breakfast sandwich, burgers, fries, and other choices that seem perfect for filling up after a cold day of hard fishing.

It's a small operation, sometimes with only a single person running the whole thing: taking orders, cooking, and cleaning.

A great plus is you get an abundant view of the bay from the café.

Things to Do

There's little to do here from the perspective of businesses to visit, but there's plenty of scenery to enjoy. There are all sorts of hiking trails to the north of the airport. Head westward along some and you'll end up at the ridgetop, and the trail there follows the ridge west and slightly downward to the north with stunning views northward of the Strait and Canada.

Overnight Lodging

Van Riper's Resort

Hotels
0.6 miles or 12-minute walk
280 Front St, Sekiu, WA 98381
360-963-2334

Van Riper's is a combination RV park and motel located right on the water. The walk from the airport is short, only about 12 minutes, but you do have to contend with the hill down from the airport to the water.

The actual hotel itself consists of a number of small apartments of various sizes. There are rooms as small as a 1 bedroom and as large as a 3 bedroom. All rooms include a refrigerator, kitchen, microwave, and stove. During fishing seasons, they have a 2-night minimum stay on weekends and a 3-night minimum stay on holiday weekends, so call ahead.

If you're a fan of fishing, these guys can set you up with poles and nets, tackle, bait, and fishing licenses.

Straitside Resort

Hotels
0.6 miles or 12-minute walk
241 Front St, Sekiu, WA 98381
360-963-2100

On the opposite side of the street from Van's is Straitside. They offer apartment-style accommodations, which include a refrigerator, kitchen, and small stove. Some rooms include electric fireplaces. There's a fire pit in front with a slight view of the bay for those evenings where such activities are warranted.

S18 – Forks Airport

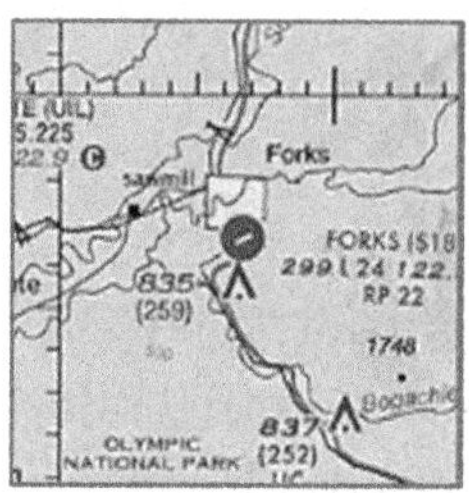

Location: 1 mile southwest of Forks
Coordinates: N47°56.26' / W124°23.76'
Altitude: 299 MSL
Fuel: None
Transient Storage: Tiedowns

I found Forks more scenic and delightful than I assumed I would. Forks is a town of somewhere over 3,500 people set into the western foothills of the Olympics. It's named after the forks in the nearby Quillayute, Bogachiel, Calawah, and Sol Duc rivers. The town historically was a timber economy, but more recently it has been growing from tourism.

Forks has an oceanic climate. Not a single month of the year goes by without it receiving at least 1.6 inches of rain. The average monthly temperature is never higher than 72 degrees.

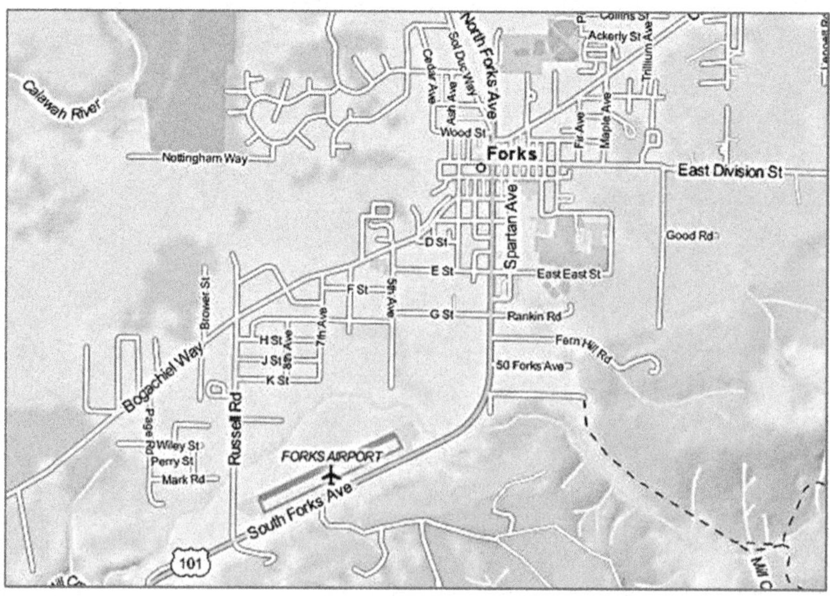

Airport Notes

The Forks airport is to the southwest of the town tucked up next to the edge of a hill rising up to the south. Traffic pattern is always to the north of the field to avoid this rise.

There's no fuel here. The nearest is at Port Angeles, so plan accordingly. Parking is in the middle of the south side of the field.

Food Options

Blakeslee's Bar & Grill

Bars, American (Traditional)
0.3 miles or 5-minute walk
1222 S Forks Ave, Forks, WA 98331
360-374-5003

Just off the field, walking northeast along Highway 101 past the Forks Chamber of Commerce office, you'll encounter Blakeslee's. It's so close you can smell it when you're holding short of runway 22.

It has great bar and grill food: burgers, steaks, sandwiches, wraps, and something locals call "salad" that you can get with shrimp, normal chicken, or oriental chicken. There's also clam strips, fish and chips, and a gigantic seafood plate.[35]

[35] If you're departing after your meal, it's a wise idea to calculate weight and balance factoring in the residual effects of the seafood plate.

Pacific Pizza

Pizza
0.6 miles or 10-minute walk
870 S Forks Ave, Forks, WA 98331
360-374-2626

Just up the road a bit more from the BBG is Pacific Pizza. They're located just as 101 turns true north, next to Forks Outfitters.

The place is a pretty typical late 80s style pizza place where you order up at the counter, and they serve you at your table. The pizza is great, the garlic bread is good. They also offer pasta dishes like Portobello mushroom ravioli with pesto.

Things to Do

Native to Twilight

Art Galleries
1.0 miles or 18-minute walk
10 Forks Ave, Forks, WA 98331
360-374-2111

Continue to walk north past the High School, you'll encounter Native to Twilight. If you're a fan of the Twilight book and movie franchise, you'll probably enjoy a stop here. It's a shop filled with all things Twilight. There are souvenirs, clothing, and knick knacks. You can have your picture taken whilst standing between life-sized cardboard cutouts of the actors from the movie series.

Sunset Lanes

Bowling
0.8 miles or 16-minute walk
261 E E St, Forks, WA 98331
360-374-5323

I know, I know; why would you fly to Forks to simply go bowling. Well, when in Forks, do as the Forkians do. Sunset isn't particularly big; it only has about 10 lanes, but it's pretty classic. The ball return is above ground, which is pretty interesting. At $3.50 per person per game and $2 shoe rental, it's not bad on the wallet either.

Forks Timber Museum

Museums
1.0 miles or 19-minute walk
1421 S Forks Ave, Forks, WA 98331
360-374-9663

For a brief stop off before you depart from the airport, you could consider the Forks Timber Museum. It's fairly small, and it contains details of the logging history for the area. There are exhibits of tools, chainsaws, axes, and other equipment. There are also many old photographs of timber history.

Wood Street Guest House

Guest Houses
1.1 miles or 20-minute walk
60 Wood Ave, Forks, WA 98331
360-640-4469

Wood Street is a bit of a walk for lodging, being at a bit over a mile away. That could get annoying if you're pulling luggage. However, it's one of the cutest places to stay in Forks.

The Guest House itself is rustic, cute, cozy, and yet spacious. There's a gas fireplace, kitchen, microwave, refrigerator, and dining room. There are even books in your room to read. There's a private entrance within a small fenced yard.

Misty Valley Inn Bed & Breakfast

Hotels, Bed & Breakfast
2.1 miles or 41-minute walk
194894 Highway 101, Forks, WA 98331
360-374-9389

At over 2 miles from the airport, it's not exactly ideal from a location perspective. However, the Misty Valley will make you glad you picked it once you're there. Depending on your arrival and departure times, you may be able to get a ride to or from the airport.

From the deck, you'll get a handsome territorial view of the Olympic foothills. Each morning, you'll receive a tray at your door with your preferred morning beverages. Breakfast is served downstairs at a communal table. The food is almost unreal in its quality and is meticulously prepared. It's all served on fine dishware, which adds to the experience.

UIL – Quillayute Airport

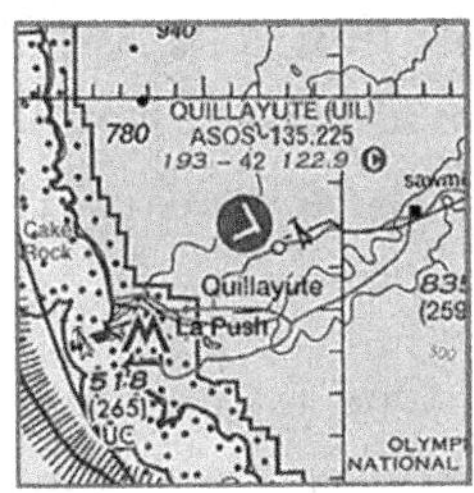

Location: 0 miles southwest of Quillayute
Coordinates: N47°56.19' / W124°33.76'
Altitude: 193 MSL
Fuel: None
Transient Storage: Tiedowns

Quillayute Airport feels like the airport time forgot. It's a rather large airport in the middle of nowhere. It was originally a Naval Auxiliary Air Station, but it was deeded to the City of Forks by the Washington State Department of Transportation in 1999.

You might consider a visit to Quillayute if you'd like to go hiking down to the ocean or go bicycle riding around the area. The emptiness you'll experience at the field is almost Zen-like in a way.

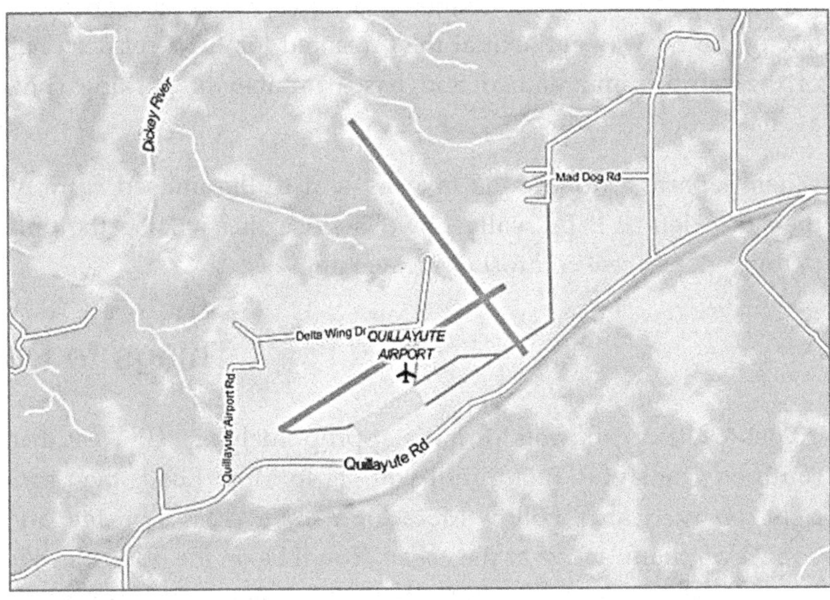

Airport Notes

From the air, there's not much remarkable about this field. On a clear day, it's visible from great distances. As you approach, you'll notice there are two runways, but only the east-west runway is open. Winds tend to favor 22, of course.

Be sure to note the displaced threshold on 22. One thing you'll notice quite quickly is how most of the airport's concrete square block surface is separated by grass, in some places quite tall grass. The main runway and some of taxiway sections are maintained to allow for landing. However, if you don't pay attention to the displaced threshold and land short on 22, I can't promise your airplane will remain particularly happy with you.

Even the maintained runway sections aren't exactly the smoothest surface.

If you want to stay on maintained areas, proceed all the way to the end of the runway and exit at the threshold for 4. The eastern half of the ramp is maintained and has a number of parking spots available.

When departing, follow the taxiway east to the unused runway, then turn left. It'll be really obvious since this will be the only pathway you'll feel comfortable traversing.

Things to Do

To get to the ocean, walk or more appropriately bicycle west then south on Quillayute Road until you get to Mora Road, then turn right (or westward). Follow Mora for a ways, cross a bridge, and you'll eventually arrive at the ocean. You'll be on the opposite side of James Island and La Push. If you'd like to get to La Push, you'll need to backtrack east on Mora until you get to La Push Road.

Quillayute River Resort

Hotels, Resorts
1.7 miles or 32-minute walk
473 Mora Rd, Forks, WA 98331
360-374-7447

On you way out to La Push, you'll pass by two locations worthy of overnight stay consideration. Both are quite close to the Mora Road Bridge. First, on the near side of the bridge, is Quillayute River Resort.

The suites are connected in series in a long building, which is great because each suite has its own direct entrance onto the shared yard space and river view and access. The whole place is quite picturesque and romantic.

Three Rivers Resort

Cabins, Campgrounds
2.0 miles or 39-minute walk
7764 LaPush Rd, Forks, WA 98331
360-374-5300

Just a bit beyond the Mora Road Bridge is the Three Rivers Resort. It's predominately an RV park and campground, but there are cabins available for rent. Each cabin comes with a living room, bathroom, and 2 bedrooms. It's cozy and tight, but it's simple and completely works.

On site is a small restaurant as well. The food is reasonable, with options like burgers, pizza, and fish and chips. The milkshakes are rather amazing and will make you miss Luna's down at Hoquiam.

Chapter 3

Southern Pacific Coast

The southern half of the Pacific coast of Washington offers a variety of places to visit, and unlike the northern half does not have the waters adjacent to its coastline prohibited to us below 2,000′. The zone extends from the southern edge of the Olympic MOA and Copalis State Airport (S16) down to Ilwaco (7W1) at the mouth of the Columbia River.

Two great land features let in the ocean seas deep inland: Grays Harbor and Willapa Bay. Grays Harbor to the north of the zone is an estuarine bay about 17 miles long and 12 miles wide. The Chehalis River flows into its eastern end at the city of Aberdeen. The somewhat smaller city of Hoquiam is immediately to its northwest, along the shoreline of the bay. Grays Harbor is home to Ocean Shores, Westport, and Hoquiam airports.

To the south is Willapa Bay at a size of over 260 square miles, which unlike Grays Harbor actually has about half of its water empty out at low tide. The bay is an estuary formed when the Long Beach Peninsula, a long sand spit from the Columbia River to the south, partially enclosed the estuaries of several smaller rivers. The area is well-known for its extensive biodiversity. The whole of Long Island to the west side of the Bay is set aside as a wildlife refuge.

HQM – Bowerman Airport

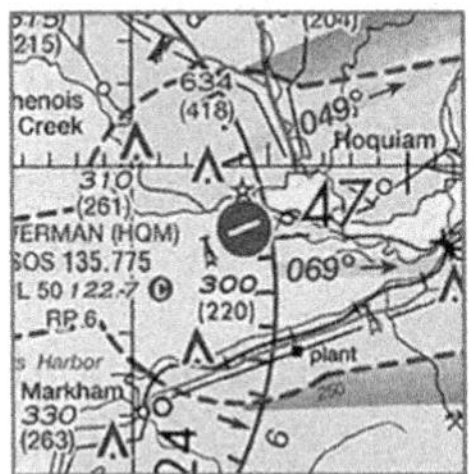

Location: 2 miles west of Hoquiam
Coordinates: N46°58.27' / W123°56.19'
Altitude: 17 MSL
Fuel: 100LL, Jet-A
Transient Storage: Tiedowns

The largest airport in the zone is Bowerman at Hoquiam. This used to be one of my favorite places to visit until Luna's on the field relocated.[36] It's still a hoot of an airport to visit, surrounded on 3-and-a-half sides by water. If you enjoy nature walks and picnics, this can be a nice destination still.

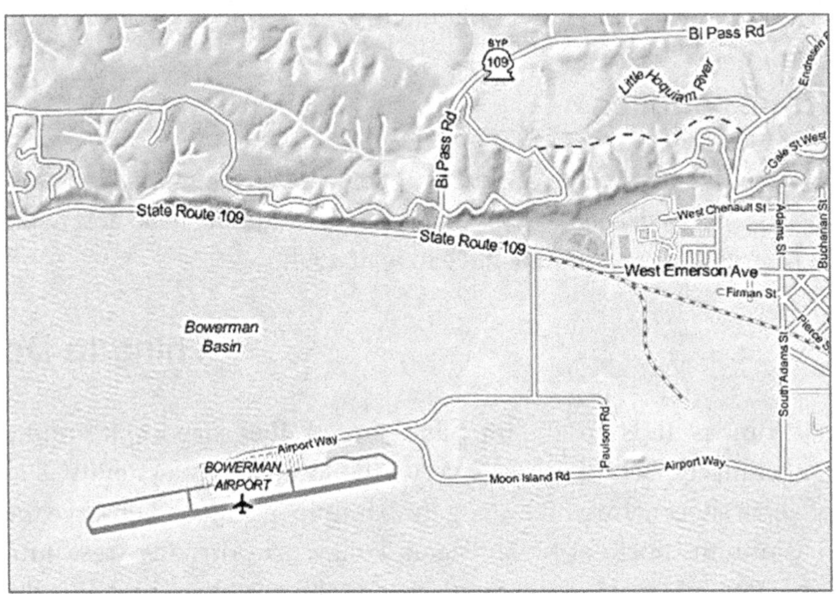

[36] Luna's had pretty typical diner food. The fries were good. But the milk shakes were phenomenal and alone were worth a trip. You could get a $100 hamburger, but the $100 shake was even better. Now, I say "was" because Luna's relocated away from the field. It still exists, I hear. But because it's too far from the field, it's unfortunately dead to me. Much sadness is the result.

Airport Notes

Traffic patterns are always to the south of the field over the bay. Winds typically favor 24. In such cases, if you're flying straight in, I've noticed some turbulence just before you cross the Hoquiam River.

The airport is built on top of Moon Island, which isn't an island anymore.[37] Be here warned about the extremely not-scared-of-you deer nearby and often on the field. I once taxied out to 6, and there was a cluster of about 4 or 5 of these guys just past the hold short line. As I approached, they looked more annoyed than afraid.

Parking and fuel is to the northeast of the field. 100LL is available on demand. For Jet A, call 360-593-0949.

The old Luna's building is still there.[38]

Transportation

Your best bet for car transport to get off Moon Island are the people at Tri City Taxi, 360-532-7777. Probably best to call ahead and make a reservation, or you may have to wait a while.

Thing to Do

As fun as it is to fly into and out of this airport, it's quite anticlimactic because there's very little to do. One possibility is to go on a short nature hike along the Sandpiper Trail and observe the basin to the north of Moon Island. Follow Airport Way west until you get to its very western end, then in the northwest corner is the trailhead. There are several picture-taking spots along the way.

[37] But it's such a catch name, so I guess that's why they kept it.
[38] Flowers can be placed on steps to the entrance on the west side of the building.

W04 – Ocean Shores Municipal Airport

Location: 2 miles northeast of Ocean Shores
Coordinates: N46°59.95' / W124°8.54'
Altitude: 15 MSL
Fuel: None
Transient Storage: Tiedowns

If you're shooting an IFR ILS 24 into HQM and you mistakenly tune in HQM (117.7) instead of I-HQM (108.7), all is not lost (except maybe your checkride and/or pride). Just make a hard right and (weather permitting) make for Ocean Shores.

Ocean Shores is a 6,000-ish population city along the northern arm of land that encloses Grays Harbor. It's a popular recreation and retirement destination sporting golf courses, a casino, and several hotels. And of course, a huge sand beach.

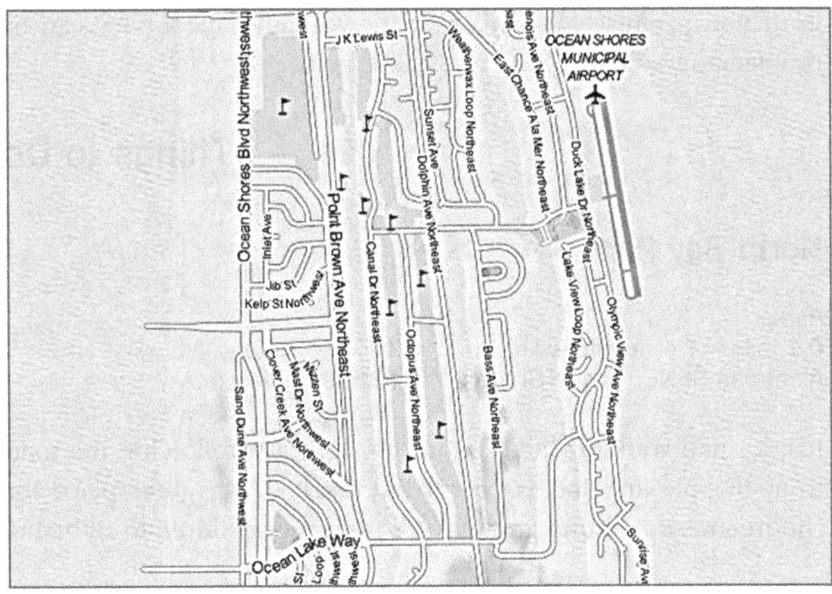

Airport Notes

The airport is located toward the north edge of the boundary of the city, but that boundary is not particularly well-defined visually from the air. Look about two-thirds of the way up the inside coastline for a bit of land without houses that sticks out ever so slightly.

You'll land and depart over a shallow marsh and the water; no need to worry about obstructions. Traffic pattern is always to the east over the water.

There's plenty of parking in the ramp at the center-west of the field, but there's no fuel available.

Transportation

Getting off the field will require a bit of ingenuity. Most of the larger hotels have shuttles, and the casino will send someone to pick you up if you promise to gamble a little. Getting taxi service can be problematic, so plan ahead and call ahead.

Things to Do

North Bay Park

Parks
0.2 miles or 4-minute walk
Albatross St NE, Ocean Shores, WA 98569

Just a small walk off the field to the west, just following the road from the parking lot, is North Bay Park. It's a great place for children to run around and play, or for us not-children to sit by the dock of the bay[39] while we waste time. There's a soccer field, baseball diamond, tennis court, basketball court, swing set, a pair of docks, and a lot of open space. Bring a Frisbee.

Ocean Shores Municipal Golf Course

Golf
0.7 miles or 14-minute walk
500 Canal Dr NE, Ocean Shores, WA 98569
360-289-3357

If you're into golf and you don't mind carrying your clubs on a 14-minute walk, the Ocean Shores Municipal Golf Course might be worth a visit. From the field, pass by the North Bay Park along Albatross Street, cross a bridge, and keep going until you reach Canal Drive.

The municipal golf course is a nice although as you might expect sandy golf course. It's well maintained, and when winds pick up, it adds a bit of an extra challenge from your average course. The front is more of a traditional course whereas the back sports more of a links style.

Overnight Lodging

Several options exist for overnight lodging, all within what some would call walking distance of the airport. If you figure out transportation, there are even more beyond what would be considered a sane walking distance.[40] That said, the closest is still nearly a mile away. If you've got an overnight backpack, great; but if you're sporting a suitcase or two, these "casual walks" will be

[39] It's not really a bay, but the locals named it, so that's what I'm calling it. It's actually one of several small lakes. When in Rome, or Ocean Shores, right?
[40] I realize this range will vary by person, but I'm not super into long walks on or near the beach, so my range is going to be on the smaller end of the spectrum.

draining. Call ahead to your hotel of choice to see if they can offer transportation options.

Windjammer Condominiums

Hotels
0.9 miles or 17-minute walk
605 Point Brown Ave NW, Ocean Shores, WA 98569
360-289-3388

The Windjammer is the closest option to the airport, and it'll provide you reasonable accommodations, but it's certainly not the top-rated place in the city. The condo-style rooms are a bit larger than you'd expect from a typical hotel stay, but they're a bit dated. The location is nice being that it's not far from the airport or golf course, and it's a nice mid-point to other locations including the beach.

Oasis Motel

Hotels
1.2 miles or 23-minute walk
686 Ocean Shores Blvd NW, Ocean Shores, WA 98569
360-289-2350

A bit more of a walk but perhaps worth it is the Oasis Motel. It's located just across the street from the beach, about half-a-block from a major walkway entrance area to the beach. Look for a pyramid or teepee sort of looking building. The room rates are inexpensive, and you aren't cramped into a tiny space. There's free wifi.

The Grey Gull

Hotels
1.2 miles or 23-minute walk
651 Ocean Shores Blvd Nw, Ocean Shores, WA 98569
800-562-9712

A bit south from the Oasis Motel, but on the beach-side of the road, is the Grey Gull. This is a huge place, a tad more expensive than other options but well worth it. During the summer months, the place can get full fast, so book ahead if possible.

The Grey Gull sports an outdoor pool and hot tub. The walls are thin and noise travels between floors, but you're right next to the beach, so you shouldn't spend much time in your room anyway. There's free wifi, but it's marginal quality. The decks from the upstairs rooms are phenomenal and offer unparalleled views of the ocean.

Morning Glory Hotel, Resort & Suites

Hotels, Guest Houses, Bed & Breakfast
1.3 miles or 24-minute walk
685 Ocean Shores Blvd NW, Ocean Shores, WA 98569
360-289-4900

This is a much more classic hotel-looking hotel. It's in an ideal location, right on the main road with direct beach access. They provide a laundry room, pool, and hot tub. There is also a work out room with treadmill, elliptical, and stationary bikes.

There's no kitchen, but you do get a mini fridge and microwave. There's a breakfast bar offered in the morning, which is reasonable.

14S – Westport Airport

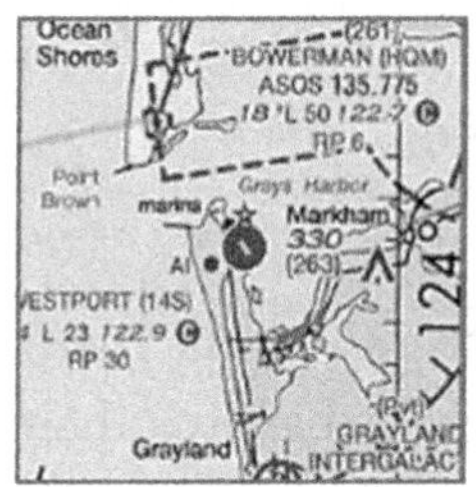

Location: 1 mile north of Westport
Coordinates: N46°53.82' / W124°6.04'
Altitude: 14 MSL
Fuel: None
Transient Storage: Tiedowns

Just south of the gap to the ocean from Grays Harbor is the always fun town of Westport, home of the Westport Airport and other attractions. During the summer months, this place gets rather busy with its fishing expedition rentals, huge retail boardwalk by the marina, state park, and beaches. Even in the winter[41] months, this place has a certain charm worth a visit.[42]

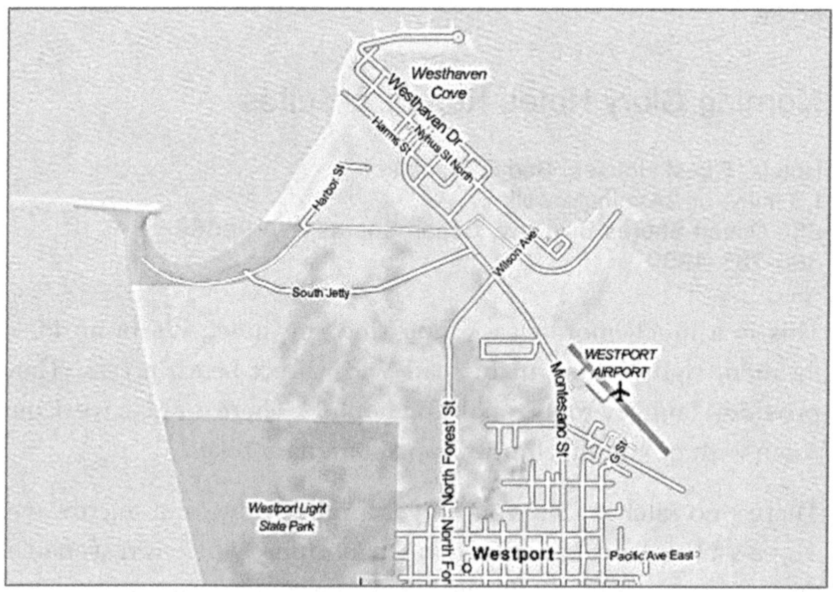

[41] To be completely honest, they don't really have winter here, nor really the usual 4 seasons. Instead, they have summer, late summer, wet, and damp.
[42] I prefer the off-season because, while there are still tourists, their numbers are dramatically reduced.

Airport Notes

On a VFR day, this airport is impossible to miss unless hidden by the curvature of the Earth. Coming in from the east, you'll probably be over Grays Harbor at some point, so just look to the left side of the opening to the ocean. The runway is to the left of the marina. It's bracketed by a line of buildings and a road on one side and a large marsh on the other.

Traffic pattern is always over the marsh/water side. Off the southeast end is marsh followed by water. But off the northwest end is a go-cart track, and just to the north of that is a non-trivial sized building. Try to avoid overflying the building. If you don't feel comfortable turning crosswind before then, just fly straight over the go-carts, then turn crosswind just beyond the building. You'll fly over a parking lot, but then be pretty much over water.

Be considerate with noise abatement best practices, especially in the summer.

There's no fuel here, but there's a healthy number of good parking spaces.

Transportation

The main retail boardwalk area, marina, state park, and beaches are all within walking distance. However, if you need a vehicle to get out a bit further, give Beach Taxi a call at 360-581-9270. There's only a single guy running the business, so sometimes you might have to wait a few minutes, but he's extremely nice.

Original House of Pizza ✈

Pizza
0.3 miles or 5-minute walk
1200 N Montesano St, Westport, WA 98595
360-268-0901

While not technically "on the field," the Original House of Pizza is so close to the ramp's gate that I'm going to call it "practically" on the field. This Original House offers wings, fries, something called "salad," breadsticks, fried fish, and sub sandwiches. Oh, and pizza.

All the food is great, particularly the pizza. The service is also extremely good, very friendly, and as fast as humanly possible. That said, you may want to try this place in the off-season or at not-exactly-dinner time times during the summer because everybody else seems to realize how good it is. Still, even at its most busy, the staff goes to great lengths to accommodate the crowds.

Tinderbox Coffee Roasters

Cafés, Coffee & Tea
0.5 miles or 9-minute walk
101 N Montesano St, Westport, WA 98595
360-612-0555

Tinderox is south of the airport right on Montesano Street, which is the main road that goes past the airport. This place is the classic sit-and-relax coffee house with various areas of old and new styles. I particularly like the very soft sofa, weathered wood table, and bookshelves area, but there are also more modern tables and chairs for small meetings.

As the name of the business implies, they roast their own beans, and they put equally substantial care into the crafting of their coffee as they do the roasting.

There's free wifi. There's also outdoor seating during the dry months. If you like loose leaf tea, these guys have over 30 to choose from.

Westhaven Drive Retail Boardwalk

Various Restaurants
1.0 miles or 20-minute walk
Westhaven Dr, Westport, WA 98595

There are quite a few restaurant options on what I'm calling the "retail boardwalk" section of town, which is just across from the marina on Westhaven Drive. From the airport, head northwest on Montesano Street until you reach Patterson, then turn right until you reach the water. Here are a selection of the better options:

Aloha Alabama

Barbeque
1.0 miles or 19-minute walk
2309 Westhaven Dr, Westport, WA 98595
360-268-7299

Bennett's Fish Shack

Fish & Chips, Seafood Markets
1.2 miles or 22-minute walk
2581 Westhaven Dr, Westport, WA 98595
360-268-7380

Blue Buoy Restaurant

Seafood, Breakfast & Brunch
1.0 miles or 19-minute walk
2323 Westhaven Dr, Westport, WA 98595
360-268-7065

Odysseus

Greek
1.0 miles or 18-minute walk
1155 W Ocean Ave, Westport, WA 98595

If you're a fan of good Greek food,[43] then look to Odysseus. It's a bit of a walk to get to from the airport, but if you hit it as part of a circuit through the state park or along with a visit to the beach, then it's right on your way. Head south along Montesano Street, then turn right (or west) on West Ocean Avenue.

Things to Do

Westport Light State Park

Parks
0.9 miles or 18-minute walk
Ocean Ave, Westport, WA 98595

The Westport Light State Park is the 212-acre block of land west of Forrest Street from the marina all the way down to Ocean Avenue. From the air, its dimensions are obvious. Park activities include hiking, fishing, beachcombing, and birdwatching. There's a nice 1.3-mile concrete walkway to enjoy.

The park is adjacent to the historic Grays Harbor Light, the tallest lighthouse in Washington. There are regular tours of the lighthouse, conducted by the Westport-South Beach Historical Society.

[43] I realize "good Greek food" is a bit redundant. I could have just written "Greek food." Sorry.

Westport Maritime Museum

Museums
0.9 miles or 16-minute walk
2201 Westhaven Dr, Westport, WA 98595
360-268-0078

The Westport Maritime Museum is on Westhaven Drive toward the southeast end of the strip. It's the gorgeous 3-story beach-island-style white building with black trim sporting a crow's nest at the top.

There's a $5 fee to get in, and the docents are quite friendly and knowledgeable. There are several small exhibits and paintings. There's also a "discover room" for children.

Westport Aquarium

Amusement Parks, Aquariums
1.0 miles or 19-minute walk
321 E Harbor St, Westport, WA 98595
360-268-0471

The Aquarium is in an unassuming and easily overlookable building on Harbor Avenue, just off Westhaven Drive. The inside is impressive in that it's actually more depressing than the outside.[44] The sea creatures seem like zombies in a bad horror movie from the mid-1970s.

[44] You'll understand why such a feat is impressive when you see the outside.

Westport Bayside Bed and Breakfast

Bed & Breakfast
1.4 miles or 27-minute walk
1112 S Montesano St, Westport, WA 98595
360-268-1403

Stay here. Stay here. Stay here. I will grant you that the idea of walking with luggage for nearly half an hour is probably not on your short list of things to do on your visit to Westport, but having actually done the trek,[45] I can say unequivocally it's worth it. That said, call ahead to the B&B, and one of the owners will gladly pick you up from the airport.

Bayside is what all B&Bs should aspire to be. In nearly every respect. Really. Richard and Tracy ensure everything is, quite literally, perfect. Every room is setup beautifully, the views from nearly every window are great, and there are lots of quite spaces in the shared areas downstairs to curl up with a book.[46] Outside, there's a large yard with a trail that leads down through a thicket of trees and out onto a boardwalk over the marsh. And they offer you fresh, home-baked cookies upon your arrival.

Now, yes, all of this is wonderful, but I'm a big fan of B&Bs that don't skimp on that second B: Breakfast. Here, they don't skimp. They set the standard.[47] The food is so good it cannot adequately be described using mere words. As Jodie Foster said, they should have sent a poet. They are great with accommodating special diets.

[45] Both directions.
[46] There are also several spaces to spread out your aviation charts while sipping some exceptionally good drip coffee.
[47] Well, at least the standard that would be set if you were to appointment me King of B&B Standards.

Breakers Boutique Inn

Hotels
0.2 miles or 3-minute walk
971 N Montesano St, Westport, WA 98595
360-268-0848

If for some reason you really want to sleep as close to your airplane as possible, the Breakers Boutique Inn is a great option. The Inn is just across the street and south half a block from the airport. Look for the go-cart track in front.

The rooms are spacious and clean, and the upstairs rooms have nice balconies with views. The owners really care about ensuring your stay is enjoyable.

If you're staying with children, the Inn is probably a very wise choice for several reasons. The go-cart rides are fun, but just behind the Inn is a park with lots of options for children to enjoy including baseball, climbing gym thing, tennis, and trails to explore.

Glenacres Historic Inn

Hotels
0.7 miles or 12-minute walk
222 N Montesano St, Westport, WA 98595
360-268-0958

Glenacres is just south down Montesano from the airport. The main building is an historical large house converted into a hotel set on spacious grounds. There are also three cottages available for rent. One of these is a 2-story house with separate bedrooms, full kitchen, and downstairs bathroom.

S16 – Copalis State Airport

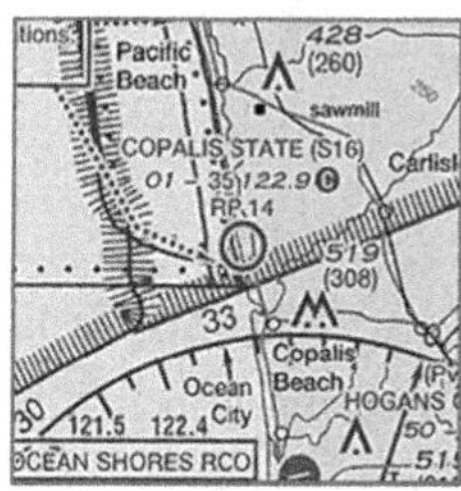

Location: 2 miles northwest of Copalis
Coordinates: N47°8.68' / W124°11.34'
Altitude: 1 MSL
Fuel: None
Transient Storage: None

Copalis State Airport is a state-owned airport open to the public, but its key unique quality is that it's the only official airport located on a beach in Washington State. It's located on the beach front immediately north of the mouth of the Copalis River.

Technically, the airport covers 16 acres of beach at 1 foot MSL. However, keep in mind that you shouldn't stay here long since you'll need to time the tides appropriately. Come in near low tide and be prepared to leave before it crawls back up. That said, it does make for an adventurous and entertaining destination.

Airport Notes

The first challenge with Copalis is finding the airport. Look for the mouth of the Copalis River. The landing area's southern end is close to the river. The runway is designated 14 and 32, with a right pattern in 14 to keep traffic over the ocean and away from the homes just up off the shore.

Most residents are aircraft friendly, but there are those that aren't.[48] Do whatever you can to keep noise levels low. You'll need to plan on at least one low-altitude fly-over to inspect the landing zone prior to landing.[49] Try to do this at a low RPM and over the water to keep the noise down. If you're flying in with multiple planes, you may want to consider having only one go low for the visual pass, then land, and then report by radio the conditions to the others so they can make straight in.

Expect a lot of foot and car traffic on the beach from Labor Day until April 15 and during open razor clam digging season.

The Washington State Department of Transportation (WSDOT) placed orange reflective markers near the north and south ends of the authorized landing area. There's also a windsock roughly midfield up toward the embankment from the shore.

As you're coming in for landing, which ideally should be just before low tide, you should see three different types of sand: dry, damp, and soggy. The dry stuff is up from the shore and should be avoided. The soggy stuff is right next to the water and might do alright if you're airplane isn't too heavy. As Goldilocks learned, the

[48] There have been reports that at least one resident has focally confronted pilots who legally and responsibly landed at Copalis. If that happens to you, just remain professional and polite.

[49] There have been reports that anti-aircraft obstacles have in the past been purposely planted within the landing zone by those wishing to keep aircraft away. Take all necessary precautions for a safe landing.

best stuff is in the middle: the damp sand. It's quite hard, enough that I can't leave a footprint in it, which is saying something.

After landing, park along the high-tide mark, but before the sand gets so soft that you'll have to dig out your airplane.

Remember that there's no fuel, tie-downs, FBO, or pilots' lounge. There's a sign-in area near the windsock about midfield, but otherwise, you're on your own.

Some sections of the beach are closed to vehicle access from April 15 through Labor Day, so you'll need to get permission for limited vehicle access within these dates. Contact Ocean City State Park at 360-289-3553 and WSDOT Aviation Division at 360-651-6300 for approval.

Things to Do

Basically, you can do beach things on the beach. WSDOT suggests clam digging, surfing, fishing, or beach combing.[50] Oddly enough, WSDOT has not publicly endorsed long walks on the beach, but they do not openly oppose them either.

Overnight Lodging

As tempting as an overnight beach camping stay might sound, WSDOT prohibits it due to risk from tidal activity. There are a few overnight lodging options, one right near the mouth of the river, but since you can't leave your plane overnight on the beach, there's no point.

[50] The phrase "beach combing" reminds me of Spaceballs.

7W1 – Port of Ilwaco Airport

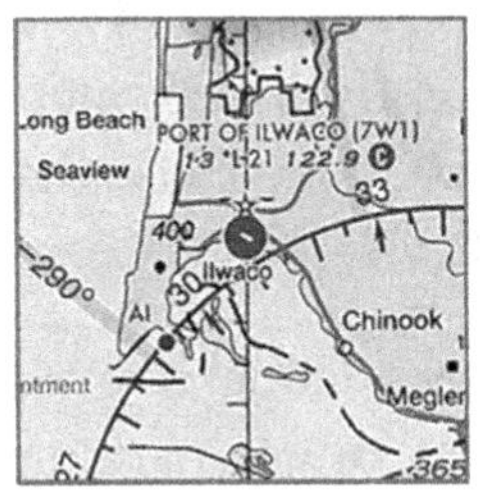

Location: 2 miles east of Ilwaco
Coordinates: N46°18.89' / W124°0.23'
Altitude: 13 MSL
Fuel: None
Transient Storage: Tiedowns

If you're looking to fly to the edge[51] and unplug for a while, Ilwaco may be a good option. It's located on the northwestern side of Baker Bay just inside the mouth of the Columbia River on the Long Beach peninsula. The southwestern corner of Washington is within walking distance of the town.

The area gets warm and dry summers with monthly average temperatures never climbing above 72.

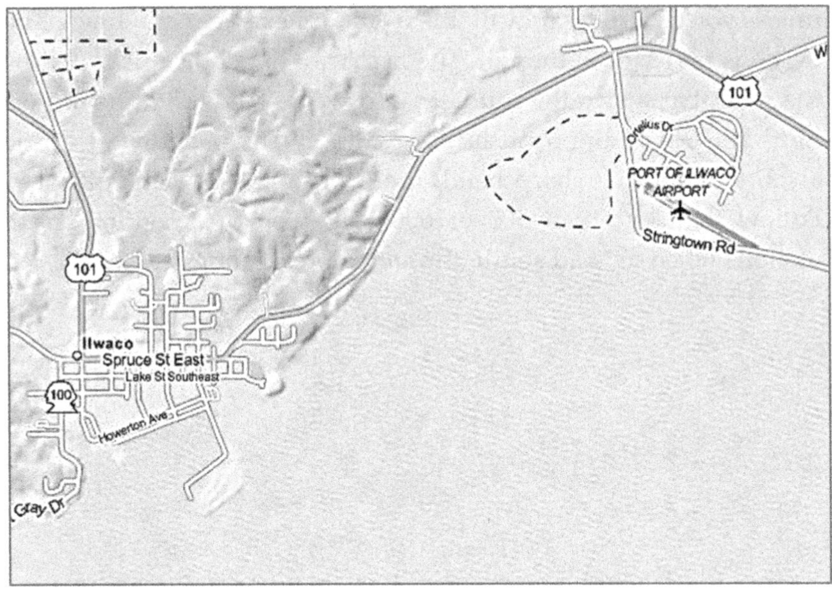

[51] By that I mean of course the edge of Washington State. Ilwaco is just inside the mouth of the Columbia, so pretty close to the southeast edge.

Airport Notes

The airport is east of the town by a couple miles, basically at the midpoint of the northern rim of Baker Bay, just up from the water. Watch out for trees on either end of the runway, but otherwise the airport is easy to access.

The northern side of the runway is rimmed with residential homes. Park along the southern side, toward the west end, or in a parking area about midfield toward the road. There are gates to both areas that connect up with the road that runs past.

The locals are friendly, but don't go traipsing through their yards uninvited.

Things to Do

There's not much to do here apart from walking out to the beach unless you're willing to walk the over 2 miles to get into town. The beach is pretty nice, though. The best way to get there is to follow the road that wraps the southern and western edges of the airport until you get to the bend in the road, which is southwest of the airport. From that sharp bend, there's a trail that leads off west. Follow that for about 500 or 600 feet, then turn south. It'll be obvious when to head south, through a break in the trees.

Ilwaco / Long Beach KOA

RV Parks, Campgrounds
0.4 miles or 7-minute walk
1509 State Route 101, Ilwaco, WA 98624
800-562-3258

If you follow the road on the west side of the airport north, cross the Wallacut River, then turn right or east on 101, you'll find yourself at the Ilwaco / Long Beach KOA (Kampgrounds of America). The camp is a great place to stay with a family. There are large campsites, private fire pits, tables, and large grass areas to play around in. There's a playground for children and a game room for the whole family.

There's a KOA store stocked with what you might not be able to fly in with, including firewood, beach toys, games, and coffee. There's also wifi near the office in case you have difficulty unplugging from civilization. There's a laundry room available.

2S9 – Willapa Harbor Airport

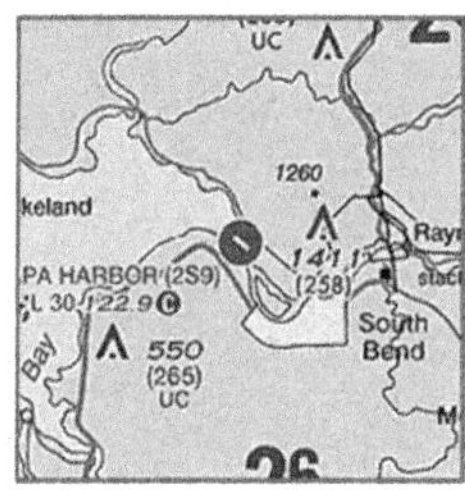

Location: 2 miles northwest of South Bend
Coordinates: N46°41.86' / W123°49.40'
Altitude: 13 MSL
Fuel: None
Transient Storage: Tiedowns

Willapa is less of a town than is it a zone. The government calls it a "census-designated place" or CDP. As of the 2010 census, there were 210 people living in the area. Although South Bend is just across the river and a bit south from the airport, you have to go all the way east to Raymond before you can find a bridge to get you across the river.

That said, Willapa might be a good location for overnight camping near your airplane. You'll just need to pack in whatever you need.

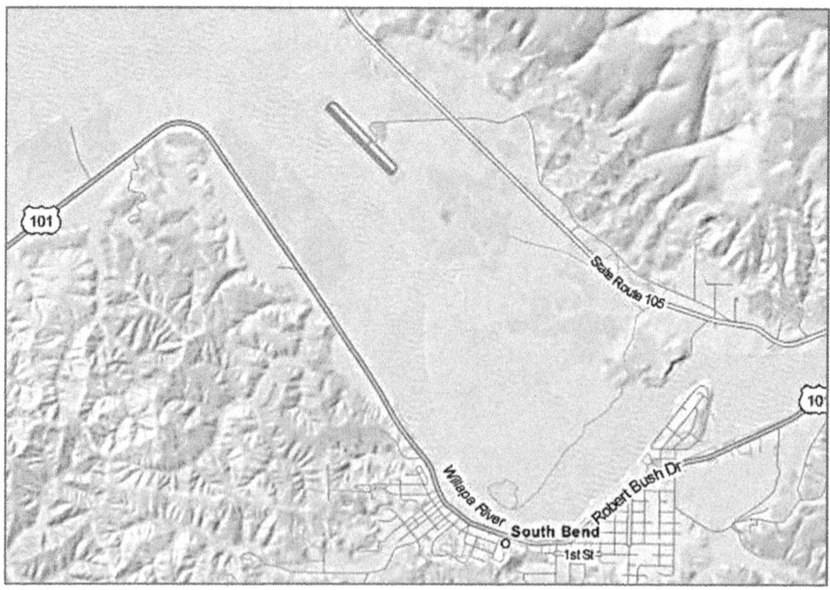

Airport Notes

The airport itself is in pretty good condition considering the feeling of isolation you get when you're there. There are trees on either end, but they aren't really in the way, and there are no serious obstacles to worry about. The wind can do some weird things if it's coming from the north down from the slopes.

Parking is to the north of midfield with spots for 8 tie-downs, but there's more space in the grace.

Transportation

If you need to get into either South Bend or Raymond, your best bet is to call Al O'Neal at 360-875-6192.

Things to Do

If you can bring along an off-road bicycle, you might enjoy riding it off the run way south toward the river. There's an initially paved, then dirt roadway that leads south from the runway. It connects with a dirt roadway that rims the southern and western sides of the airport along the river.

4W8 – Elma Municipal Airport

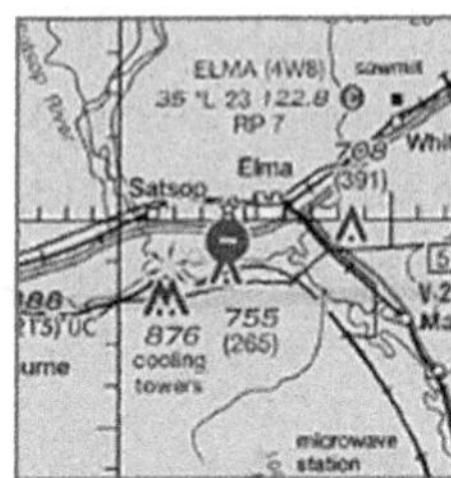

Location: 1 mile southwest of Elma
Coordinates: N46°59.43' / W123°25.78'
Altitude: 35 MSL
Fuel: None
Transient Storage: Tiedowns

Elma lies within the Chehalis River Valley and is self-described as the "gateway to Grays Harbor." The airport is small but cute, but the big problem is that it's located on the wrong side of the Olympic Highway, away from town.

There once was a restaurant on the field, and the building looks inviting to a would-be restaurant entrepreneur; but alas, you can't order a burger.

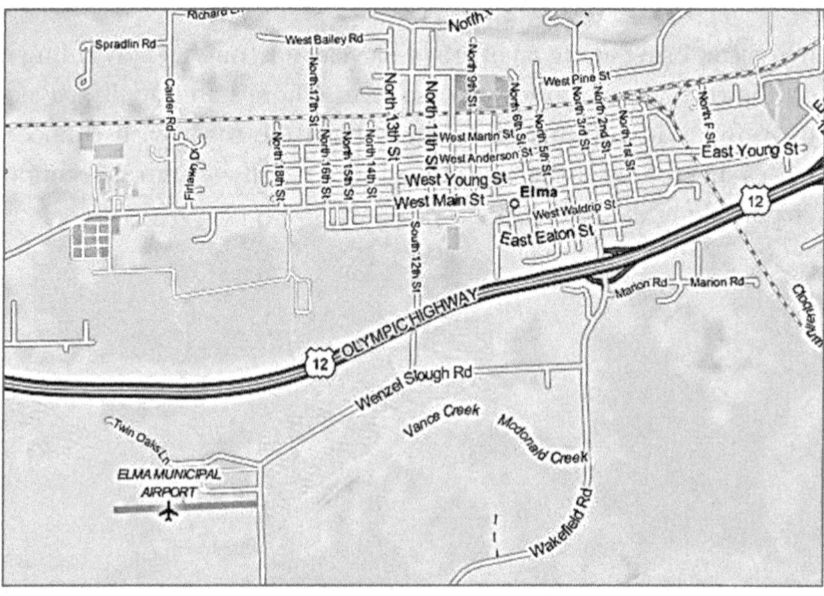

Airport Notes

The airport is tucked between two sets of lakes southwest of town. The runway is small, 2280 by 30. Traffic patterns is always to the south of the runway. Both ends have trees you'll need to clear, but the 07 end is particularly entertaining in this regard. The trees surround the end and almost hide it completely. They're chopped down and cleared directly in front of 07's threshold, but it's still a tight fit down the stretch.

Park in the grass that's just in front of the old restaurant building. There are several good spots there.

There's ample space around the airport for camping, but check with Jeff Wysong at 360-482-2292 before setting up tents.

Chapter 4

Seattle Terminal Area West

If airplanes are like blood cells, the heart of Washington State aviation would be the Seattle terminal area. It just so happens that a majority of Washington flights happen therein, and it naturally contains a high concentration of airports. It's a bit unfair to lump airports in the Seattle TAC together, since they often have quite different personalities. So I'm going to somewhat arbitrarily divide up the airports into those mostly west of the Puget Sound versus those mostly east.

While the western zone lacks the population density of the eastern side of the Puget Sound, it never-the-less sports several high-density areas including Bremerton, Tacoma, and Olympia. Simultaneously, there are great tracks of land[52] with tall tress masking most of the human presence. There are small airports with tight approaches and almost no traffic like Port Orchard (4WA9) all the way up to relatively larger airports, some towered, some not, with moderate traffic.

The weather in this zone can be simultaneously diverse with a complex set of microclimates. Although close to each other, it's not uncommon for Shelton (SHN), Bremerton (PWT), and Tacoma (TIW) to all report remarkably different weather.

[52] Great tracks of land, some of which include swamps. Also curtains.

OLM – Olympia Regional Airport

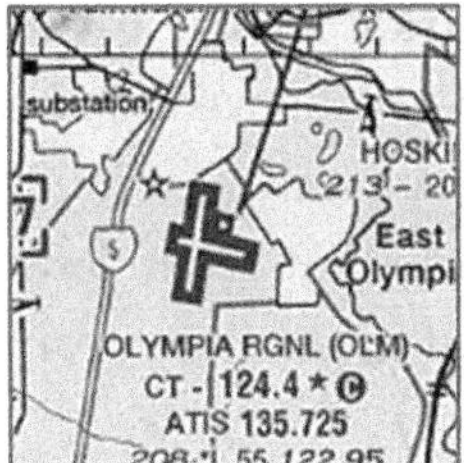

Location: 4 miles south of Olympia
Coordinates: N46°58.16' / W122°54.15'
Altitude: 207 MSL
Fuel: 100LL (blue), Jet-A
Transient Storage: Hangars, Tiedowns

The Olympia airport is a nice-size and well-maintained, towered airport with a pair of lengthy runways and a flight museum. The unfortunate bit about the airport is its location: 4 miles south of Olympia, which is a bit too far to walk.[53] Fortunately, there are mitigating circumstances: There are several things to do within a short walk of the airport, and there's also a courtesy car available to get into town.

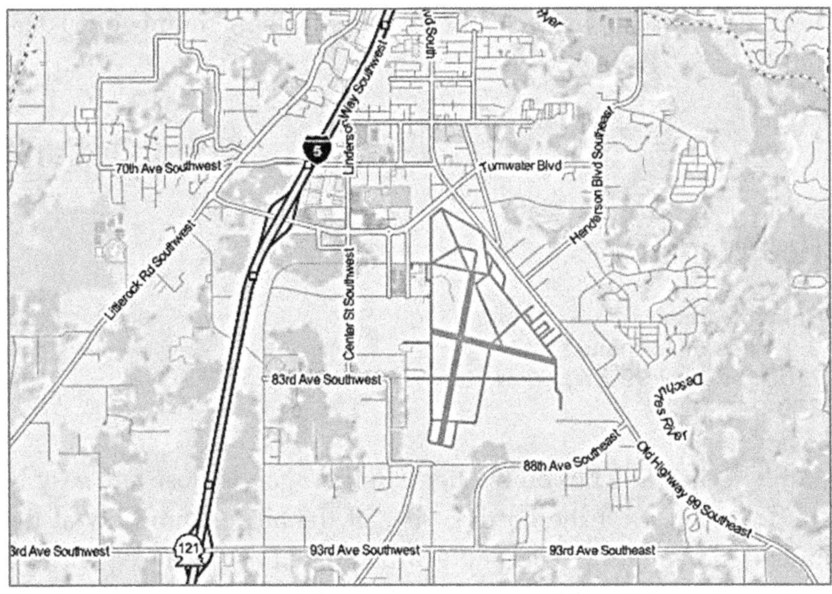

[53] This is in my own personal definition of "too far to walk" as it pertains to walking from an airport to something to do near the airport after having landed there. Yes, it's subjective; but I'm writing this book, so I get to make the rules.

Airport Notes

The approach to the airport is easy and unremarkable. The tower controllers are always nice and helpful.[54] Traffic is to the west of the north-south runway and south of the east-west runway. You'll likely get cleared for the north-south runway. Note that if you land 35, the rise of the terrain will block the other end of the runway from view.[55]

Parking is on the northeast side of the field, just off the delta taxiway.

Transportation

A courtesy car is reportedly available. Contact JAS Air at 360-754-4043 for more information. Alternatively, there are several local taxi companies, and Uber has good coverage of the area. Capital West is based out of Olympia. Contact them at Phone number 360-923-5818.

Food Options

Red Wagon

Burgers, Cheesesteaks, Soup
0.9 miles or 18-minute walk
7205 Old Hwy 99 SW, Tumwater, WA 98501
360-943-6234

While technically not on the field, Red Wagon is close and easy to get to. It's just off the north corner of the airport property at the intersection of Tumwater Boulevard and Old Highway 99. This is a

[54] Although, I sometimes wonder if I'm waking them up on slow weekday mornings.
[55] At least, it does in my airplane, which puts my eyes mere inches above the pavement.

classic burgers, fries, and onion rings sort of place. They also offer Philly Cheesesteaks.[56] They claim they've got the best burgers in town, and they might be right. The burgers are bigger than your mouth[57] and flame broiled to perfection. The onion rings are yummy. They also offer something called "salad."

The location has indoor and outdoor seating. You order at the counter, then eat wherever you'd like. During lunch rushes, the food can take a while to get made. So if time is a consideration, you can call-in your order for pick-up. These guys are a lunch and dinner place, open until 9 PM weekdays and 8 PM Saturdays. They're closed on Sundays.

Koibito Japanese Restaurant

Japanese
0.9 miles or 18-minute walk
7205 Old Hwy 99 SE, Tumwater, WA 98501
360-570-0450

If you're into sushi,[58] this is the place to try. They have some of the best sushi in the south Sound area. If you don't like sushi, try the teriyaki salmon, then seek counseling to overcome your sushi issues. There's also several Korean options on the menu.

Koibito has a very relaxed atmosphere, the complete opposite of formal. It's usually crowded during lunch, especially on weekends.

---

[56] On a business trip to Philly several years back, I ordered one of these famous cheesesteaks. I was unimpressed. Granted, it wasn't from Geno's or Pat's or Jim's, so that could have made all the difference in the world. I've had better Philly Cheesesteaks outside of Philly. That said, I did pick up some local lingo. You order your cheesesteak by saying "one whiz with," which means one sandwich with cheese-whiz as your cheese of choice and with onions. Ordering "one whiz without" is socially acceptable. Although you can vary the cheese type, I've heard that you should get your first with "whiz" for the authentic experience.

[57] Unless you have an unusually large mouth.

[58] And really, who except close-minded people aren't?

Enjoy Teriyaki & Wok

Japanese, Chinese
1.0 miles or 19-minute walk
125 Tumwater Blvd SE, Olympia, WA 98501
360-943-1421

If you're more into a pure teriyaki place, walk west on Tumwater Boulevard from the Old Highway 99 intersection until you reach Enjoy. They offer great Mongolian beef, chicken teriyaki, egg rolls, and the usual assortment of teriyaki and wok foods. There are good combination and lunch specials.

All Fed Up

Sandwiches, Food Trucks
1.5 miles or 28-minute walk
6450 Capital Blvd SE, Tumwater, WA 98501
360-464-5757

Keep walking north on Old Highway 99 and you'll get to All Fed Up. Think sandwiches, breakfast burritos, "salads," and soups. By all accounts, the food is all around great. There have been reports of unusual or unpredictable hours of operation, though. These guys are a breakfast and lunch place, closing daily at 3 PM, and theoretically opening at 7:30 AM. In practice, however, it may be mid to late morning before they open.

Things to Do

Olympic Flight Museum

Museums
0.5 miles or 9-minute walk
7637 Old Hwy 99 SW, Tumwater, WA 98501
360-705-3925

If you're stopping by the Olympia airport during the museum's open hours, you sort of owe it to aviation to visit. It's a fairly small museum as far as aviation museums go, but worth your patronage. They have several restored airplanes and helicopters. They have an airworthy Kaman HH-43B Huskie helicopter, a P-51D, and a FG-1 Corsair. The museum also sponsors or offers flights in vintage aircraft to help raise money for restoration efforts.

Overnight Lodging

Comfort Inn Conference Center

Hotels
1.3 miles or 24-minute walk
1620 74th Ave SW, Tumwater, WA 98501
360-352-0691

The Comfort Inn is a fairly typical hotel of its type located west of the field off Tumwater Boulevard. There's free wifi, good clean rooms, and usual offerings from a Comfort Inn. There's a pool and hot tub.

Best Western Tumwater Inn

Hotels
2.2 miles or 42-minute walk
5188 Capitol Blvd SE, Tumwater, WA 98501
360-956-1235

This is a bit of a hike northward toward the city; however, you can comfort yourself knowing that once you check-in, you'll be about half-way into town already. Just follow Old Highway 99 north. It'll change into Capitol Boulevard, and then you'll end up at the Best Western.[59]

This is a typical Best Western with all the usual amenities and comforts. Free wifi, although the speed and quality is hit-or-miss sometimes. Breakfast buffet. There's a small gym with an elliptical, treadmill, and weights.

[59] Ever notice how Best Westerns are everywhere? They're all the same. Good quality, clean rooms, and friendly staff. They pretty much all have gyms of some kind, good wifi, and an included breakfast.

SHN – Sanderson Field Airport

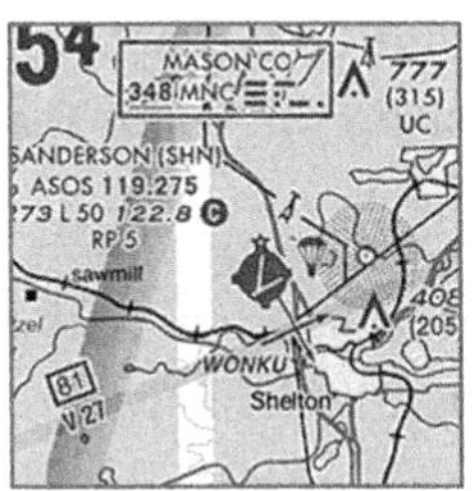

Location: 3 miles northwest of Shelton
Coordinates: N47°14.01' / W123°8.85'
Altitude: 272 MSL
Fuel: 100LL (blue), Jet-A
Transient Storage: Tiedowns

Sanderson is a large and friendly looking field northwest of Shelton. The field is on a plain that rises up a few miles inland from the water. While Shelton itself is a lovely place to visit, sporting several fine coffee shops and other welcoming businesses, Sanderson is unfortunately too far of a walk from downtown to make non-automobile-assisted visit practical. That said, if you bring along a bicycle and don't mind climbing back up 101 or the Olympic Highway to the field, it may be worth a stopover.

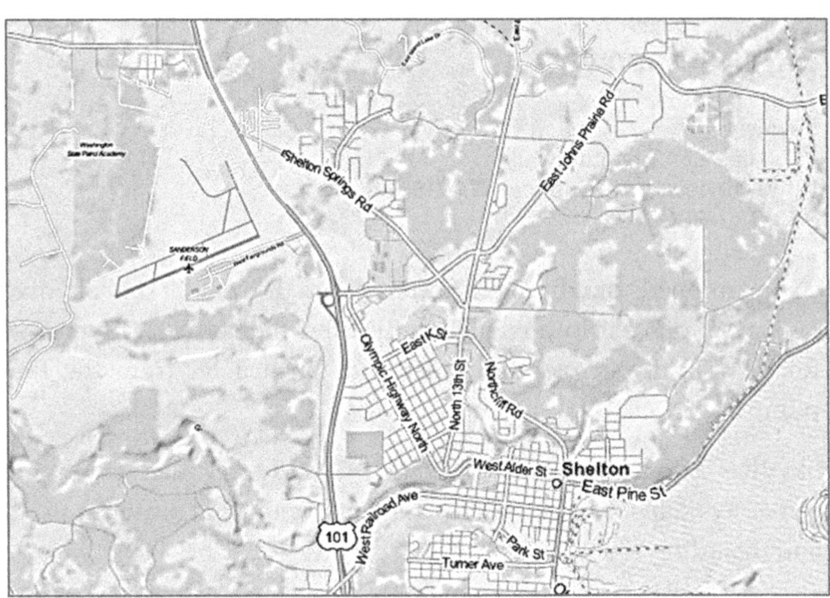

Airport Notes

The airport sports a 5005′ runway in good condition. The fuel pumps are up past the hangars on the northeast perimeter of the field.

Note that traffic should remain to the south of the field when in the pattern. One big reason for this is parachute operations. If you're planning to even transition the airspace, check NOTAMs and lurk on CTAF.

Transportation

There's no courtesy car here, but if you need to get into town, you can try Mason County Taxi (based in Shelton) at 360-426-8294.

Things to Do

Skydive Kapowsin

Skydiving
0.7 miles or 12-minute walk
141 W Airview Way, Shelton, WA 98584
360-432-8000

As mentioned, skydiving is offered on the field. The Skydive Kapowsin office is located just on the other side of West Enterprise Road, basically across the street and north a bit from the fuel pumps.

Skydive Kapowsin boast of being the only certified skydiving center available 7-days a week. They offer jumps at altitudes up to and including 13,000′.

Super 8 Motel

Hotels
1.0 miles or 19-minute walk
2943 Northview Circle, Shelton, WA 98584
800-536-9326

The closest overnight lodging option, and really the only one within walking distance to the airport, is the Super 8 about a mile south of the field. From the field, head out to 101, then follow that south until you get to Wallace. Go east a small bit on Wallace until you reach Olympic Highway, then south. The hotel is behind the Jack in the Box on Olympic.

TIW – Tacoma Narrows Airport

Location: 4 miles west of Tacoma
Coordinates: N47°16.08' / W122°34.69'
Altitude: 294 MSL
Fuel: 100LL (blue), Jet-A
Transient Storage: Hangars,Tiedowns

Tacoma Narrows Airport sits on the Gig Harbor side of Tacoma Narrows bridge, right on the southern edge of a cliff that drops dramatically to the water. It's in an ideal location if you're visiting friends or family from either Gig Harbor or Tacoma who are willing to pick you up from the airport.[60] If you're not so lucky, there's a lot less to do within walking distance of the airport. Still, there are several reasons to make this a destination.

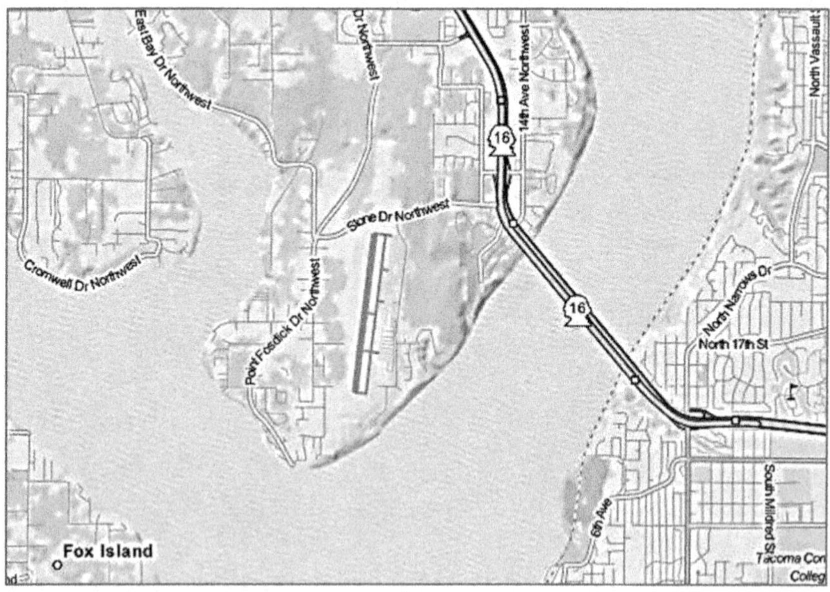

[60] If they aren't willing, maybe bribe them with a scenic flight. The area around Tacoma Narrows is quite pretty.

Airport Notes

The tower here is always friendly and professional. The controllers don't speak a mile-a-minute. If you want to try different approaches, touch-and-goes, or even have the tower flash its light cannon at you, I've found these folks are always accommodating.

Note that traffic pattern is to the east of the field, which is over the hangars and tower.[61]

Transportation

There's no courtesy car, but Uber covers the area well. So I'd use that as your go-to option for getting into either Gig Harbor or Tacoma.

Food Options

The Hub ✈

American (Traditional), Pizza
0.3 miles or 5-minute walk
1208 26th Ave NW, Gig Harbor, WA 98335
253-853-1585

This is a fairly new and upscale restaurant, which tends to get really busy Friday evenings and weekends, but for good reason. The food is quite nice.

After landing, tower will typically ask you where you'd like to go before having you monitor ground. Just say the restaurant, and you'll get directed to park right in front. It's directly to the south of the tower, in a building that's attached to the tower building. There's enough parking for 6 or 8 airplanes, but if it's full, you can

[61] That feels backwards to me, but I suspect it's because the folks in the houses to the west of the field requested it.

park in the spaces immediately to the south if you're there just for a meal.

The Hub is offers a variety of pizza options. One of my favorite dishes is their blackened chicken mac and cheese. Oy, it's good.

One possible thing to keep in mind is that I've experienced inconsistent wait times. Sometimes I can get in and out for lunch in under an hour, but other times it takes far more time. The degree to which the restaurant is busy at the time doesn't seem to correlate.

Fredda & Lori's Deli

Delis, Sandwiches
1.2 miles or 22-minute walk
2601 Jahn Ave NW, Ste A-9, Gig Harbor, WA 98335
253-858-7212

If for whatever reason you want to visit a deli instead of eat at the Hub, try Fredda & Lori's. From 26th Ave NW (the street just on the eastern edge of the airport property), turn east or right on Stone Drive, then north on Jahn Avenue.

Things to Do

Narrows Park

Beaches
0.7 miles or 13-minute walk
1502 Lucille Pkwy NW, Gig Harbor, WA 98335

The Narrows public park is right on the water, a short but somewhat steep walk down the hill from the airport. From the airport, walk south on 26th Avenue until you reach Defenders Northwest. Roughly in the middle of the northern parameter of their parking lot is a trailhead, somewhat difficult to find. You can follow that down the hill all the way to the water.

From the water, you're treated to a great view of the bridge and waterway. There's one small Gazebo, a couple of free telescopes, and beach access.

Things Not to Do

Don't fly under the Tacoma Narrows Bridge. I realize the bridge is tall and there's plenty of space to fly under. Believe me, I completely understand the temptation. It's like every time you fly past it, there's some strange siren song pulling you in. Resist the temptation.

Don't fly between the upper supports of Tacoma Narrows Bridge. I realize the upper supports look like goal posts and that by flying through them you'll be in effect kicking a field goal with your airplane. Believe me, I completely understand the temptation.

Don't fly a loop around the Tacoma Narrows Bridge. I realize if someone were recording it from a nearby observation point, the video would go viral in seconds because of how epic it would be. Believe me, I completely understand the temptation.

Don't think of an elephant.

PWT – Bremerton National Airport

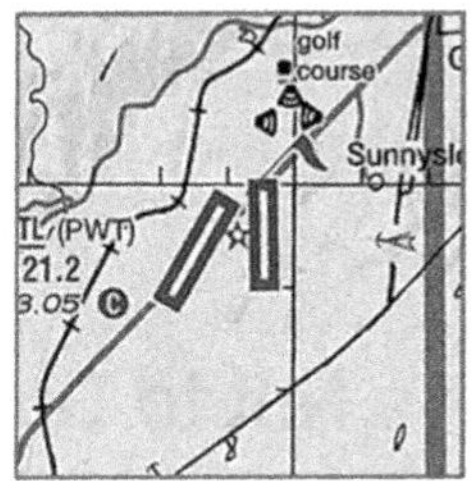

Location: 7 miles southwest of Bremerton
Coordinates: N47°29.42' / W122°45.89'
Altitude: 443 MSL
Fuel: 100LL (blue), Jet-A
Transient Storage: Tiedowns

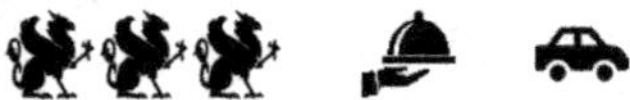

Bremerton feels quite similar to Sanderson in that it's up on a plain that rises from the water, this time from the inlet by Gorst. It's a large field, very well maintained. There's fuel and an FBO, but unlike Sanderson, there's an excellent restaurant on the field and a courtesy car. Similar to Sanderson, though: there's little to do (other than the restaurant) within walking distance.

That said, with the courtesy car or a rental the FBO can set you up with, the cities of Bremerton and Port Orchard are close by.

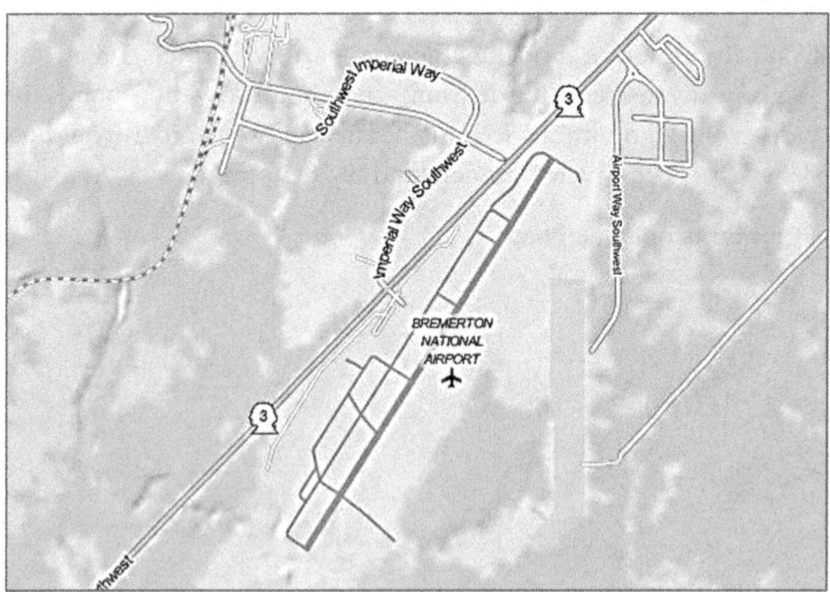

Airport Notes

Traffic pattern is always to the southeast of the field. Note that while it looks like there are two runways, only the 2/20 runway is available. The other has been converted into a racetrack.

On nice, sunny days, especially on the weekends, this airport can get fairly busy. Be sure you make good radio calls, and keep an eye out for traffic. There are usually a fair number of visitors, plus helicopter and military traffic. Be courteous and communicative.

Transportation

There's a courtesy car available from Avian Flight Center. Call ahead of time to 360-674-2111 to reserve it. Alternatively, the FBO can set you up with a rental. Uber does cover the area, but drivers are limited, so you may have to wait a while.

Food Options

Airport Diner ✈

Seafood, American (Traditional), Breakfast & Brunch
0.7 miles or 14-minute walk
8830 State Hwy 3 SW, Port Orchard, WA 98367
360-674-3720

Chances are if you're a visitor to the Bremerton airport, you're coming for a meal at the Airport Diner, and for good reason. The food is typical diner fare, and yummy. There's ample airplane parking within a few feet of the restaurant. Use the gate that's immediately to the south of the restaurant, and you can ascend either stairs or a ramp to the side entrance. Seat yourself, and your waitress will be over to you shortly.

The interior is decorated with many airplane models. There's free wifi.

The fish and chips are good here as is the clam chowder. There are burgers, sandwiches, and a few entrée type dishes as well. On Sundays there's an all-you-can-eat buffet that's quite popular. If you intend on visiting on a Sunday before the late afternoon, expect the place to be packed.

My only complaint is the speed. Even when not busy, it can sometimes take quite some time to get your food. It's always worth the wait, though.

Casey's Bar and Grille

Bars, American (New)
0.5 miles or 9-minute walk
24090 NE Hwy 3, Belfair, WA 98528
360-275-6929

Across the street and north a bit from the Airport Diner is Casey's. This is a small but enjoyable bar and grill that offers great burgers and free wifi. There's darts, pool, weekly poker, and occasionally live music.

4WA9 – Port Orchard Airport

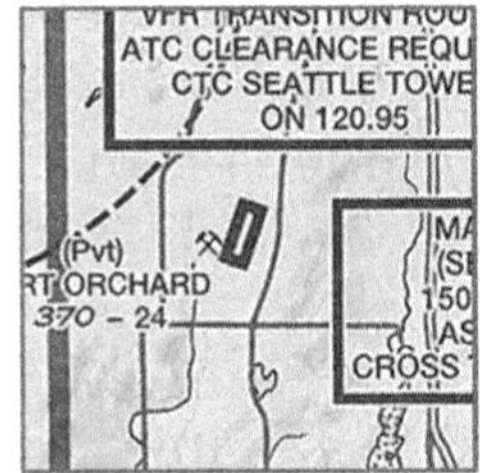

Location: 7 miles southwest of Port Orchard
Coordinates: N47°25.94' / W122°40.07'
Altitude: 370 MSL
Fuel: None
Transient Storage: None

Port Orchard is both a small city and a large, unincorporated region of Kitsap County. Nestled roughly in the middle of this unincorporated region, close to Bremerton Airport, and surrounded by tall trees, is Port Orchard Airport. It's technically a private airport; however, I have it on good authority that visitors are welcome, especially if they partake of the pizza from the restaurant on the field.

Apart from the pizza, there's really not much to do here.

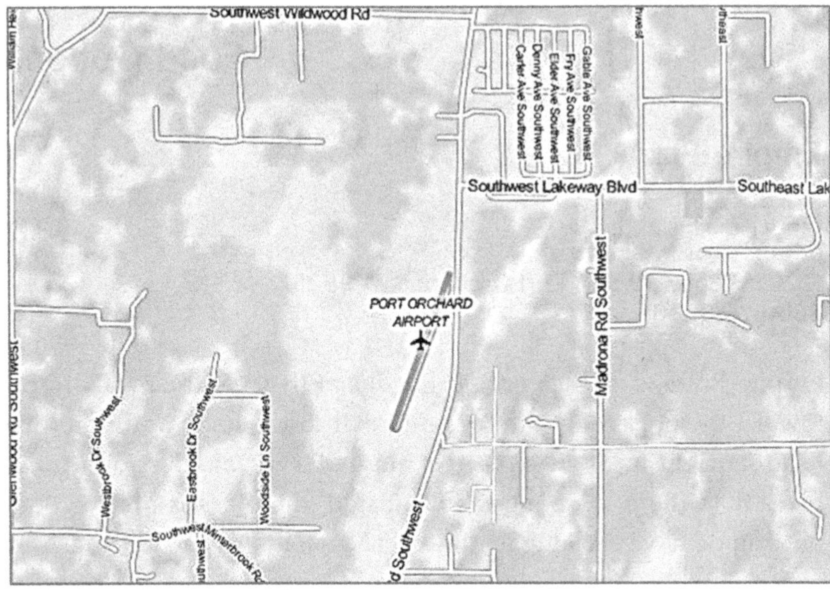

Airport Notes

Port Orchard Airport is fairly easy to spot given that it's next to a large strip-mining operation that shows up as a large, light-colored area immediately to the west of the field. The field itself borders along Sidney Road.

The runway hugs the northern edge of the property, making approaches from the north entertaining. Just north of the runway is Sidney Road and then a cluster of tall, intimidating trees. Approaching from the south is another story. The 2,460′ runway ends with over 1,500′ of flat, undeveloped grass beyond before you have to worry about trees. As such, it may be wise to favor a south takeoff, winds permitting of course.

Toward the north end are hangars and other buildings. From the 18 threshold, the first taxiway exit to the northwest will take you to a large segment of grass in front of a row of hangars. You can park there while you eat your pizza.

Food Options

Empire Pizza ✈

Pizza
0.5 miles or 9-minute walk
12292 Sidney Rd SW, Port Orchard, WA 98367
360-874-8336

Empire Pizza is on the very north edge of the field. Just walk north toward the only road entrance and exit to the field, and you'll be heading right for it. The place is more of a bar and less of a pizza place than the name suggests. That said, the pizza is pretty good, but you do have to navigate the "local customs" when placing your order.

83Q – Poulsbo Seaplane Base

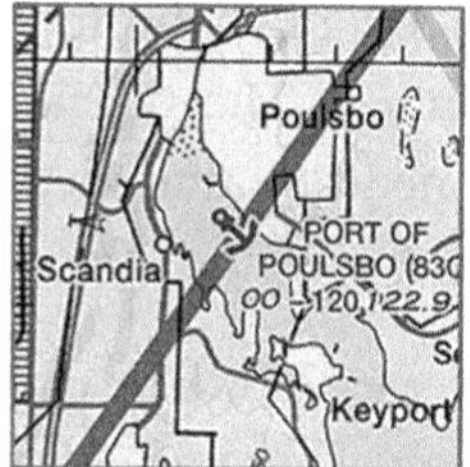

Location: 0 miles north of Poulsbo
Coordinates: N47°43.26' / W122°38.52'
Altitude: 0 MSL
Fuel: None
Transient Storage: Day-Only Dock

There are several gems in Kitsap County worthy of a day-trip, but only Poulsbo has a seaplane base right in the heart of one. Poulsbo is on the northeastern side of Liberty Bay and is the fourth largest city in Kitsap County. The city is well-branded a Scandinavian village in honor of the early immigrants to the area in the 1880s. In fact, well into the 20th century many Poulsbo residents kept Norwegian as their first language.

Nowadays, the city has a vibrant downtown area that attracts tourists from far and wide.

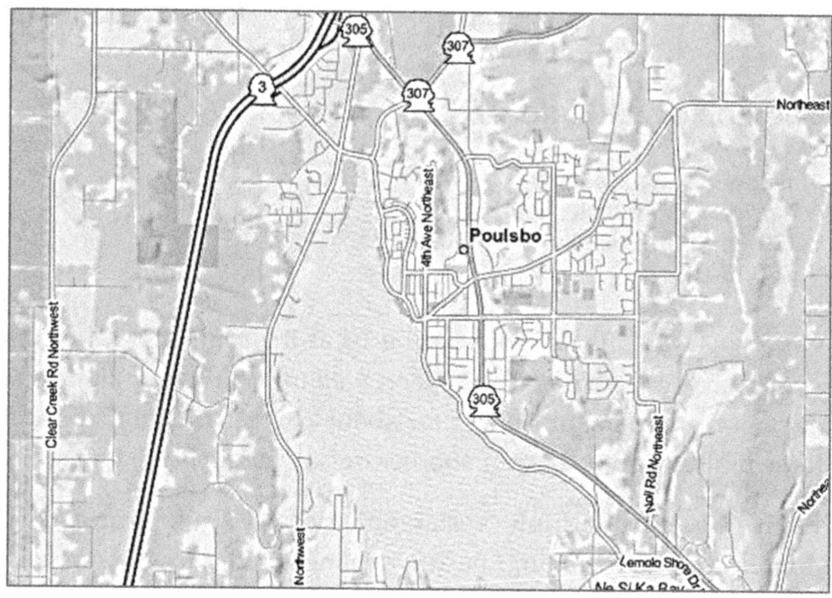

Airport Notes

Liberty Bay is large, but it's also often populated by a fair number of boats at anchor. Plot your approach accordingly. The official seaplane base waterway is 13/31, but you may need to alter that. Use caution for moving and unmoving objects on the water.

At low tide, the mud flats will get exposed all the way out to nearly the marina that's the closest in to heart of the bay. There are also mud flats to the southwestern edge of the bay. It may be wise to prefer setting down near but a safe distance away from the middle of the three marinas.

Once on the water, displacement taxi up to the northernmost marina. There's a seaplane dock on the very north part of the marina along the shore.

Be mindful of the posts that stick up from the dock. They like to eat airplane wings.

Food Options

The Loft at Latitude 47.7

American (New), Seafood
0.9 miles or 16-minute walk
18779 Front St, Poulsbo, WA 98370
360-626-0224

Once you walk off the dock, you'll be at the southern end of the Liberty Bay Waterfront Park. Keep walking southwest along the edge of the parking area there for about 200 feet and you'll be at a large building at the base of another dock. Therein is the Loft.

From the outside, this restaurant doesn't look particularly impressive or welcoming, but that changes radically the moment you walk in the doors. The place is huge, with two stories and a deck. It's open for lunch and dinner, offers free wifi, and on nice days offers one of the best view of Liberty Bay in town.

The style of the place is a little scattered, but good all around. There's burgers and seafood, high quality cuisine and feel-good food.

Tizley's Europub

German, Pubs, Scandinavian
0.9 miles or 17-minute walk
18928 Front St NE, Poulsbo, WA 98370
360-394-0080

From the marina, walk northeast across the parking lot and through a small pedestrian open area between buildings, then cross Front Street, and you'll find Tizley's. The restaurant is upstairs, and so it may be slightly tricky to locate. Head into a small alley, then look for the stairs and signs.

Tizley's almost feels like it belongs in Leavenworth instead of Poulsbo, but it's certainly an enjoyable experience regardless. Schnitzel, meatballs, mash potatoes, and other yummy Germanic dishes grace the menu. There's a bar and several small rooms suitable for small groups. There's a small terrace area with outdoor seating that overlooks the main Poulsbo strip.

Poulsbohemian Coffeehouse

Coffee & Tea, Cafés
1.0 miles or 20-minute walk
19003 Front St NE, Poulsbo, WA 98370
360-779-9199

If you just want to grab some coffee and sit for a long time enjoying a great view of the Bay, your best bet is the Poulsbohemian Coffeehouse. It's located up the street from the marina. From the marina, head up to Front Street, then turn left and walk up the hill. The coffeehouse is on the left side of the street overlooking the Bay.

This place has just about everything you could want in a good coffeehouse: the coffee is good, the pastries are excellent, and there's ample space to find a table and relax. There's free wifi.

Paella Bar

Tapas Bars, Spanish
1.0 miles or 19-minute walk
19006 Front St, Poulsbo, WA 98370
360-930-8446

Just a bit down the street from the Poulsbohemian is a great tapas bar called Paella. It opens at 1pm and stays open through dinner service. They offer an extensive list of tapas selections. The food and service are excellent.

Given that it's tapas, remember the portions are not large; you'll need to order several things to share. And a full meal can get expensive. That said, if tapas is your thing, it's worth a visit. Unfortunately, a lot of other people believe this too, which makes the place crowded often. You can try calling ahead for reservations, but be sure you're making reservations at Paella when you call since it shares a line with another restaurant.

Liberty Bay Waterfront Park

Parks
0.1 miles or 2-minute walk
18809 Anderson Pkwy
Poulsbo, WA 98370

Being that you'll be docking up at the marina right next to Liberty Bay Park, you might as well take a stroll through and enjoy it. This 1.5 acre park was first opened in 1976, but improvements made in 2007 updated this gem into something even more special. There's a pavilion toward the northern half of the park available for private rentals. My children especially enjoy climbing on the giant rock that's not far from the entry ramp to the marina.

Sluys' Poulsbo Bakery

Bakeries
1.0 miles or 18-minute walk
18924 Front St NE, Poulsbo, WA 98370
360-779-2798

On the far side of Front Street almost mid-point along this Poulsbo strip is the famous Poulsbo Bakery. They're most famous for their bread and donuts. This is a place you'll enjoy visiting if you have fully embraced the philosophy that a life well lived is a life filled with good bread.[62] The marquee reads, "Give us this day our daily bread," and the Poulsbo Bakery delivers on this promise.

[62] If you haven't yet embraced this philosophy, I invite you to consider that you cannot "break bread" without bread. Bread pudding is, unquestionably, the best kind of pudding. And nothing on this planet rivals the heavenly scent of freshly brewed coffee except for perhaps freshly baked bread.

Man shall not live on bread alone, and so the Bakery also offers pastries, cupcakes, gingerbread, cookies, doughnuts, cakes, scones, and more.

If you decide to visit the Bakery, be sure to recalculate your weight and balance before takeoff.

Poulsbo Marine Science Center

Aquariums, Museums
0.8 miles or 15-minute walk
18743 Front St NE, Poulsbo, WA 98370
360-598-4460

The Poulsbo Marine Science Center is located just to the southeast of the The Loft along the shoreline. From The Loft, just continue across a small parking lot, and the large building in front of you is the Center.

The Center is an aquarium with a science and education bent that's great for children and families. They offer among other things a tidepool touch tank allows folks to interact with most of the animals found around Puget Sound. Everything in the tanks is hands on and child-friendly.

The exhibits are fairly limited, but the price is right: free, although a donation will help keep this place going.

2S1 – Vashon Municipal Airport

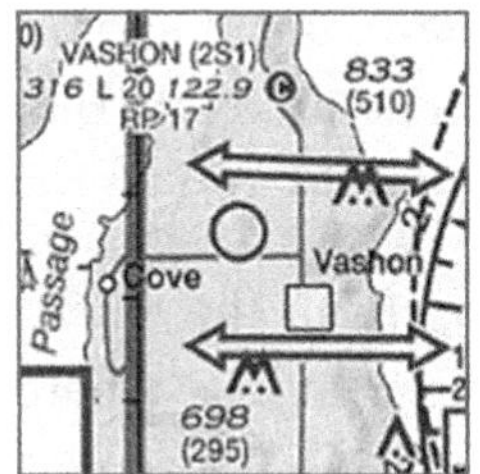

Location: 1 mile northwest of Vashon
Coordinates: N47°27.52' / W122°28.45'
Altitude: 316 MSL
Fuel: None
Transient Storage: Tiedowns

Vashon Island or Vashon-Maury Island is the largest island in Puget Sound south of Admiralty Inlet. Boasting a population of over 10,000, this community prides itself in being self-described as weird. Although connected to the outside world by two ferry docks at the northern and southern ends, the island maintains a distinctive isolated and rural character.

Flying to Vashon can be a treat due in no small part to its airport sporting the longest grass runway in the state.

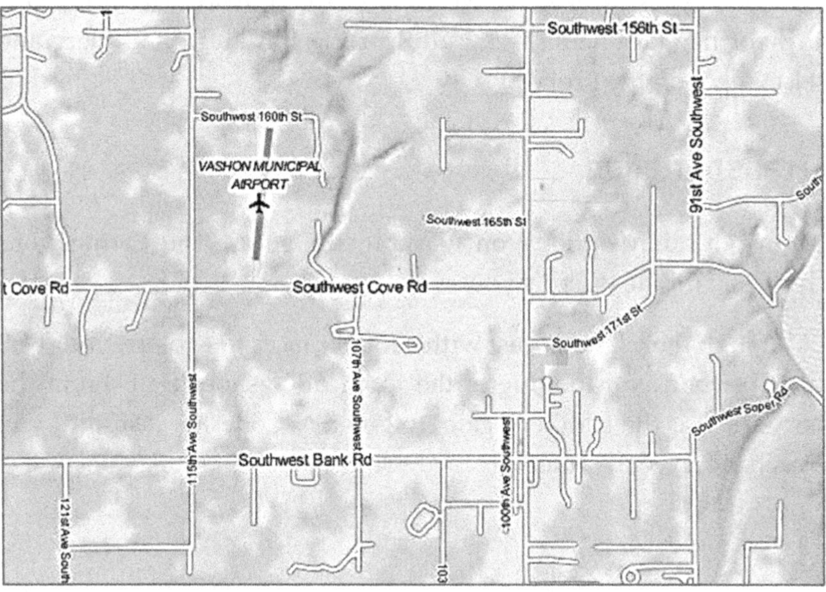

Airport Notes

The airport is the largest grass runway in the state, but it should still be approached with caution and attention to detail. Note that traffic patterns should always be to the west of the field.

The island itself is a relatively flat plateau rising from the water, which gives the island the opportunity to provide ravines where you least expect them. Such is the case as you approach the airport from the north. Be watchful for a thick line of trees directly to your left as you land. You'll cross over a small and rarely trafficked road just before touchdown.

From the south, note the threshold of the runway is 460 feet or so north of a well-trafficked road. As you line up on final from the south, the local pilots speak of using a pair of trees just below your glide path as height reference points. They call these the "Vashon VASI."

Transient parking is on the west side of the runway just south of the row of hangars here. Be mindful of the hill and ditch there and elsewhere on the property.

Transportation

Transportation options on Vashon are sparse, but bring your bicycle, and the island's yours.

Although the island is vast with a lot of places to explore, your best bet for food and lodging is the town of Vashon itself. From the airport, exit the southern gate, follow SW Code Rd east until you reach 99th Ave SW, then proceed south.

Rock Island Pub & Pizza

Pizza, Pubs
0.9 miles or 17-minute walk
17322 Vashon Hwy SW, Vashon, WA 98070
206-463-6814

If you're on Vashon and you want great pizza, Rock Island is here to serve you. The place reminds me of the family pizza restaurants from the 80s where you order at the counter, find a table, and they bring out the food to you. There's even a small game room and a small bar. The pizza itself is thick crust with ample toppings.[63]

If you're flying in to Vashon with a decent sized group, Rock Island won't disappoint.

May Kitchen & Bar

Thai, Cambodian, Wine Bars
1.0 miles or 20-minute walk
17614 Vashon Hwy SW, Vashon, WA 98070
206-408-7196

Near the corner of Vashon Highway (99th) and Bank Road in the heart of Vashon township is the May Kitchen and Bar. These guys are a dinner-only, Wednesday through Sunday operation offering Thai and Cambodian dishes.

While the outside isn't all that impressive, the interior décor is breathtaking and includes wood carvings, candles, and little touches of Thai on every wall. There are lots of nooks and crannies

[63] When it comes to pizza toppings, if you can see through the toppings near the center to a spot where there's just cheese, then there's not enough toppings. Cheese is like glue. Its purpose is to hold toppings on the pizza. While cheese is yummy, toppings plus cheese is more yummy. Therefore, any pizza where you can see cheese is insufficiently awesome. Rock Island does not serve insufficiently awesome pizza.

to offer a great secluded even romantic atmosphere. The food menu is extensive and well-received.

Snapdragon

Vegetarian, Bakeries, Pizza
1.1 miles or 21-minute walk
17817 Vashon Hwy SW, Vashon, WA 98070
206-463-1310

Down the street and across from May's is Snapdragon, a vegan bakery and pizza shop. It's open most every day except Mondays and Tuesdays.

The Snapdragon offers such yumminess as a breakfast tostada, stuffed sopes, ricotta pancakes, veggie bean burger, ricotta and broccoli fritters, Turkish pizza, and a whole assortment of different "salads."

Zamorana

Mexican
1.1 miles or 21-minute walk
17722 Vashon Hwy SW, Vashon, WA 98070
206-356-5684

If you're looking for authentic Mexican food, Zamorana should be your destination. The owner greets you at the door, and the atmosphere is warm, friendly, and welcoming if perhaps a bit tight on busy days. The restaurant offers outdoor seating, weather permitting.

The tacos are particularly worth your consideration. Their salsa is of high quality and sufficiently spicy.[64] Try the pork nachos, and ask for roasted jalapeños or the jalapeño salsa.

Things to Do

Vashon Maury Island Heritage Association

Museums
0.9 miles or 18-minute walk
10105 SW Bank Rd, Vashon, WA 98070
206-463-7808

Just to the west of the central intersection in town along Bank Road is the Island Heritage museum.

The building was originally built as a Lutheran Church in 1907. Later, it was the Vashon Allied Arts and the Vashon Children's Centre. The Museum houses permanent exhibits and periodic special exhibits. There's also a History Resource Room and an extensive archive of island photographs.

The Museum is open Wednesday through Sunday from 1pm to 4pm, and admission is by donation.

[64] "Spicy" is such a relative term. My son used to think if food had any flavor at all, if it didn't taste like cardboard, it was "too spicy." I have family who think that if after the meal their insides aren't screaming to dive into a vat of sour cream, it was "not spicy enough." So when I say "sufficiently spicy," I mean the spice was sufficient that you notice, you enjoy it, and you don't have to intersperse every bit with three gulps of water.

Lodges on Vashon

Vacation Rentals
0.8 miles or 15-minute walk
17205 Vashon Hwy SW, Vashon, WA 98070
206-693-3750

Roughly across the street from the Ober Park District, just a bit north from the center of town, are the Lodges on Vashon. The lodges are vacation rental mini-homes. They're constructed in something of an ultra-modern style and yet are impressively comfortable and enjoyable.

Each contemporary lodge features keyless entry, a king-size bed, gas fireplace, flat-panel TV, and high-speed internet. Everything from soaps to coffee are sourced from artisans on the Island.

Chapter 5
Seattle Terminal Area Northeast

Although the western half of the Seattle terminal area couldn't be properly described as terrifically sparse as compared to the state average, it might certainly seem so when compared to the eastern half of the terminal area. More people live here than any other place in the state, and as you might expect, there are more and bigger airports here than elsewhere.

The northeast section of the Seattle terminal area is as urban as urban gets. Multiple large cities and several smaller cities link up together to form a sprawling metropolis. Everett in the north links up with Seattle in the center, Lake Washington, Lake Union, and all the smaller sub-communities in the area. There are multiple flights in the air all day and night, so if you're from a less dense area, keep your eyes peeled for traffic.

As urban as the Seattle to Everett corridor is, things change rapidly as you head eastward just out of the corridor, roughly toward the northeast edge of the Class Bravo airspace. The population density thins out, and the terrain returns to something that looks a lot closer to the west side of the terminal area.

Consequently, there are both multiple high-density urban airports and more remote, isolated airports all within this beautiful area of the state.

PAE – Snohomish Airport (Paine Field)

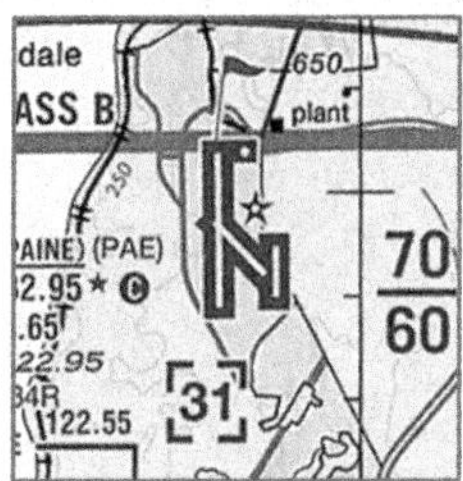

Location: 6 miles southwest of Everett
Coordinates: N47°54.42' / W122°16.89'
Altitude: 607 MSL
Fuel: 100LL (blue), Jet-A
Transient Storage: Hangars, Tiedowns

The Snohomish airport (otherwise known as Paine Field) is home to one of Boeing's important plant facilities and prides itself on friendly but strict tower communications. Much like Boeing field in the south, the majority of traffic here consists of small GA aircraft interspersed with periods of large traffic.

The area is especially urban, and it's fairly removed from downtown Everett some 6 miles away. While not necessarily the best pick for a relaxing overnight stay, the area has a lot to offer for visiting pilots and aviation enthusiasts.

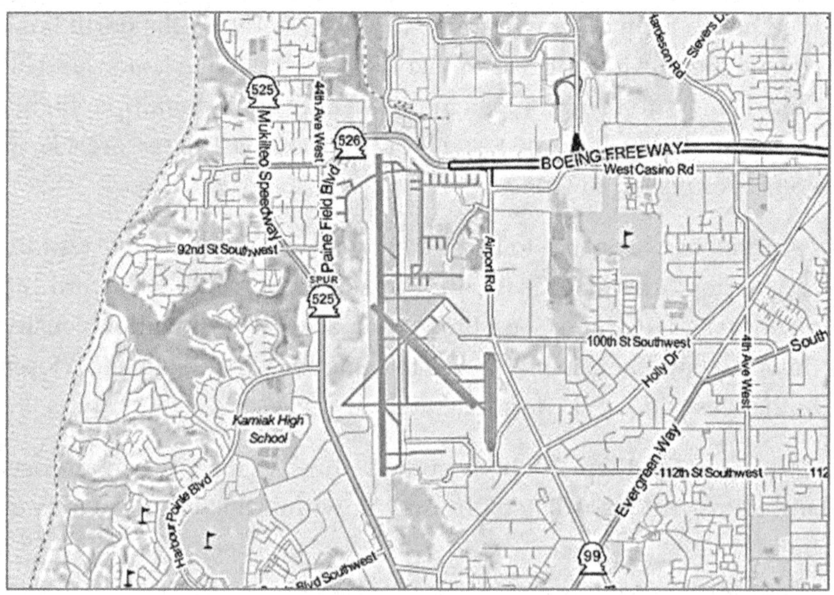

Airport Notes

Other than maybe SeaTac, there's hardly another airport in all the state that's as easily identifiable at a distance as Paine. It's a well-developed and significant airport property that sits on top of a plateau, half surrounded by water, and rimmed with various greenbelts and other non-airport-looking structures. So it stands out.

On the easternmost runway, if you're landing toward the south, you'll be flying almost right over a major roadway on your way in.

You'll probably want to park on the central ramp, northwest slightly from the 34R/16L midpoint.

Transportation

There's a courtesy car available from the folks at Castle and Cook Aviation. Give them a call at 425-355-6600 to check on availability.

Alternatively, Uber has very good coverage and availability here. And of course the FBO can set you up with a rental.

Food Options

Café Soleil

Japanese, Sushi Bars, Asian Fusion
0.6 miles or 10-minute walk
9999 Harbour Pl, Ste 105, Mukilteo, WA 98275
425-493-1847

Café Soleil is a family-owned restaurant offering "Euro-Japanese" cuisine located just to the west of the airport. They're typically a lunch and dinner place, but they're closed on Mondays and open only at 5pm on Sundays.

The restaurant offers what they call a tapas menu that includes a wide range of selections including Japanese Kurobuta pork sausage,[65] shrimp dumplings, fried oysters, various tempura dishes, and garlic organic tofu steak.[66] There's a small sushi menu and an entrée menu including various salmon, udon, and tempura dishes.

Seating can be a bit limited during busy times.

Grouchy Chef

French
1.0 miles or 18-minute walk
4433 Russell Rd, Ste 113, Mukilteo, WA 98275
425-493-9754

The Grouchy Chef is off the Mukilteo Speedway on the southwest side of the airport. If you liked, feared, or respected the Soup Nazi from Seinfeld, this place might be right for you. This restaurant is perfectly named. The head chef is quite grouchy, but the food is insanely good and shockingly reasonable on price. If you follow the rules, you'll get 5-star crazy-good food for less money than you'd pay anywhere in this hemisphere.[67]

Chef Masumoto wants you to follow the rules. He intentionally keeps his operation small, working multiple jobs at the restaurant, so you pay only for the food.[68] He also demands a certain level of respect from the customer. One sign lists things he considers a dishonor of his restaurant. It lists, among other things: flip flops, jeans, and "man with shorts." Don't put your elbows on the table.

[65] Yummy.
[66] No comment.
[67] I'm not exaggerating.
[68] You're not allowed to tip, but you can make a donation to cancer research.

Don't eat too fast. When ordering, say the full name of the dish you're ordering. Don't shorten the name.

When you arrive, you'll be given a list of the rules, so as long as you read that and do your best to follow them, you'll be fine.[69]

Dining is by reservation only. Cash only. And you pay up front. The experience is, well, an experience.

Sakuma Japanese Restaurant

Japanese
0.8 miles or 14-minute walk
10924 Mukilteo Speedway, Mukilteo, WA 98275
425-347-3063

Sakuma is located southwest of the airport off 525. They offer an extensive Japanese menu, and it's all of very good quality. The sushi is great, fresh and well-balanced. Bento boxes are a common sight.

The interior is spacious and clean. There's a sushi bar and general seating.

Gyro Stop

Mediterranean
1.1 miles or 20-minute walk
11811 Mukilteo Speedway, Ste 110, Mukilteo, WA 98275
425-374-8137

Gyro Stop offers you an opportunity to eat traditional Mediterranean in a fast food environment. Hand-made hummus, fresh made-to-order falafel, and gyros that will impress. They even offer a beef and lamb gyro "salad" dish.

[69] You're a pilot, after all. Following a lot of seemingly arbitrary rules shouldn't be that difficult or unusual for you.

Flying Heritage Collection ✈

Museums
0.5 miles or 10-minute walk
Paine Field, 3407 109th St SW, Everett, WA 98204
877-342-3404

The Flying Heritage museum is located in the central-southern area of Paine Field, roughly between the southern ends of the two north-south runways. The museum exhibits an almost overwhelming number of aircraft from the 1930s and 1940s, with the bulk being warbirds from World War 2. Paul Allen began acquiring and preserving these iconic airplanes starting in 1998. The aircraft are all well-maintained, and many are still flight-ready.

Historic Flight Foundation ✈

Museums
0.6 miles or 11-minute walk
10719 Bernie Webber Dr, Mukilteo, WA 98275
425-348-3200

The Historic Flight Foundation is out toward the west side of the airport property. This museum offers a collection of what the curators call the "most important aircraft produced between 1927 and 1957." Every aircraft is fully restored and flight ready.

The museum was established in 2003 as the "John T. Sessions Historic Aircraft Foundation" with the intention to collect, restore, and share significant aircraft from the period between the solo Atlantic crossing of Charles Lindbergh and the first test flight of the Boeing 707.

Museum of Flight Restoration Facility ✈

Museums
0.4 miles or 7-minute walk
2909 100th St SW, Everett, WA 98204
425-745-5150

The Flight Restoration Facility is located a bit north of the 16L threshold. This is the restoration facility for aircraft that end up at the Museum of Flight. While this place may not necessarily be as fancy and presentable as the other flight museums around, here you'll be able to chat far more informally with mechanics working on restoration efforts.[70]

Overnight Lodging

Staybridge Suites Seattle North-Everett

Hotels, Venues & Event Spaces
0.7 miles or 12-minute walk
9600 Harbour Pl, Mukilteo, WA 98275
425-493-9500

The Staybridge Suites are located west of the airport about midfield, on the west side of the Speedway.

This place is rather amazing for a hotel. The staff remember you by name and treat you like royalty. After check-in, you're invited to a complimentary dinner and drinks. The pool and hot tub are open 24-hours a day. There's an on-site free laundry facility and a large, well-equipped workout room.

There's free popcorn in the room along with the usual big-screen TV and excellent wifi.

[70] Make friends here, because every so often, they sell off parts of airplanes. Years ago, my wife bought me a couple rows of 1st class airplane seats from the Vancouver Canucks jet, which even now still grace our basement recreation room.

S43 – Harvey Field Airport

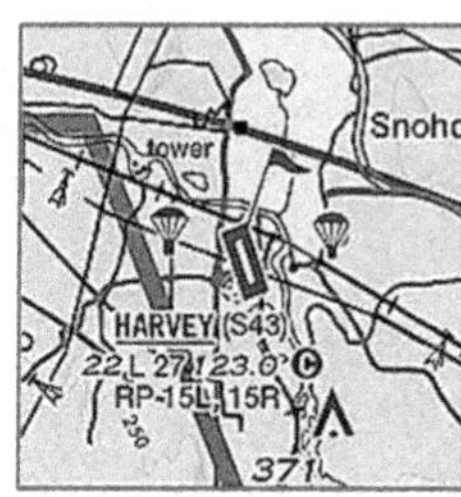

Location: 1 mile southwest of Snohomish
Coordinates: N47°54.29' / W122°6.16'
Altitude: 22 MSL
Fuel: 100LL (blue), Jet-A
Transient Storage: Hangars, Tiedowns

Harvey Field is just about as perfect a small-town airport experience as you can get. The airport itself has one 2,750-foot asphalt runway and another 2,660-foot turf runway.

The airport was established in 1944 by Noble and Eldon Harvey and Wesley Loback on the Harvey family's property. In 1947, the family added a restaurant, administration building, and a maintenance shop. Harvey Field provides flight training in both airplanes and helicopters, and there's a parachute school and operation on the field.

Airport Notes

If it's your first time to the airport, you can locate it by looking for the turn or hook in the Snohomish river. The airport property is tucked up into that bend. Traffic pattern is always to the west, over a farm and field.

Noise abatement procedures are in place. Do what you can to keep the prop noise down when you're north of the river. When landing from the north, keep an eye out for power lines near the river. They're well-marked with orange balls.

On nice days and even some not-so-nice ones, be mindful of parachute operations. The drop zone is just to the east of the runways toward the north end.

Transient parking is in the grass along the north-south taxiway.

Transportation

There's no courtesy car here, but Uber is a good bet since there's good coverage and availability in the area.

If you're just going into town for a while, which is an excellent reason to visit this destination, just walk north off the property and cross the bridge. It's not a far walk. Bring your camera.

Buzz Inn Steakhouse ✈

Steakhouses, American (Traditional)
0.2 miles or 4-minute walk
9900 Airport Way, Snohomish, WA 98296
360-568-3970

The Buzz Inn Steakhouse is right on the field toward the northeast end. If you're heading into town, you'll pass right by it. As you'd expect from a steakhouse, its top offerings include steak: rib, New York, T-bone, porterhouse, and more. The restaurant also offers chicken and seafood dinners and baskets, burgers, and sandwiches. They also offer all-day breakfast and good drip coffee.

Roger's Riverview Bistro

American (New)
0.6 miles or 10-minute walk
1011 1st St, Snohomish, WA 98290
360-563-2800

This amazing bistro is across the Snohomish River from the airport, just down on 1st Street a ways. The food is locally sourced, and the quality is extremely high. They offer dishes like pork Milanese, seared steak, roasted salmon, chicken cordon blue, and more.

There's deck seating that overlooks the river, perfect for warm, summer evenings.

The Hungry Pelican

Diners, Gluten-Free
0.6 miles or 10-minute walk
113 Ave C, Snohomish, WA 98290
360-243-3278

Just up from 1st Street on Avenue C is the Hungry Pelican. It's a cute café offering a wide range of great good, much of it gluten-free.[71] They offer a wide range of sandwich and soup options. The decor is comfortable, warm, and homey with mismatched furniture.

Andy's Fish House

American (New), Seafood
0.5 miles or 9-minute walk
1229 1st St, Snohomish, WA 98290
360-862-0782

At the corner of Airport Way and 1st, just after you cross the bridge, is Andy's Fish House. There seems to always be a happy crowd here. Patrons attest Andy's offers the best seafood in the area. Many locals recommend Andy's on a regular basis.

If you're in a rush, you might want to skip Andy's since some have reported the wait times can be considerable, especially when they get busy.

[71] While my family is gluten-free, I love gluten. I'm pretty sure "gluten" is Swedish for "yummy," so I enjoy loading up on it.

Thai Naan

Thai
0.6 miles or 11-minute walk
1020 1st St, Ste 106, Snohomish, WA 98290
360-863-6426

Thai Nann is another of the restaurants along 1st Street, offering wonderful Thai food, but despite its name, not offering naan. The menu is filled with a wide range of curry options along with the usual suspects of Thai food like: pad thai, orange chicken, lemongrass chicken, spring rolls, chicken satay, and more.

Things to Do

Skydive Snohomish ✈

Skydiving
0.2 miles or 4-minute walk
Harvey Airfield, 9906 Airport Way, Snohomish, WA 98296
360-568-7703

Right on the field toward the northern end is Skydive Snohomish, a family-owned and operated, full-service skydiving operation. They specialize in the first-skydive experience. They offer jumps from 13,500 for both first-time jumpers and more experienced solo jumpers. During the busy season, wait times for your flight up can be significant, so bring a book.

Snohomish River Front Trail

Hiking
0.4 miles or 7-minute walk
Snohomish, WA 98291

Starting from the intersection of Airport Way and 1st, near Andy's Fish House, is the Snohomish River Front Trail. It runs from there down to the river and along the river to Cady Park and Maple Avenue, some 6 blocks away. It's not a particularly long walk, but the area is beautiful. Due to the steep northern slope of the river, the trail area is quiet and feels secluded from the commercial district.

Everything Tea

Tea
0.6 miles or 11-minute walk
1015 1st St, Snohomish, WA 98290
360-568-2267

If you're a fan of tea, you owe it to yourself to visit Everything Tea. The place is wall-to-wall tea and tea-making supplies. They have an enormous wall filled with sorts of loose leaf teas including: herbal, black, green, and pu-ehrs.

Snohomish Bakery

Bakery
0.7 miles or 12-minute walk
101 Union Ave, Snohomish, WA 98290
360-568-1682

No visit to Snohomish or any small town community like it is complete without a visit to the local bakery. The Snohomish Bakery sports the usual fare: donuts, pastries, bread, and good coffee.

Thomas Family Farm

Arts & Entertainment, Pumpkin Patches, Paintball
0.6 miles or 11-minute walk
9010 Marsh Rd, Snohomish, WA 98296
360-568-6945

On the opposite side of the field from the bridge to town is the Thomas Family Farm. These guys offer all sorts of family activities depending on the time of year. Day activities include: mining, a corn maze, pumpkin patch, monster truck ride, and kid's painball. Nighttime activities include: a haunted house, flashlight maze, beer garden, and fire pits. They also offer "zombie paintball," a delightful apocalyptic battle with the undead.

Overnight Lodging

Country Man Bed & Breakfast

Hotels, Bed & Breakfast
0.7 miles or 13-minute walk
119 Cedar Ave, Snohomish, WA 98290
360-568-9622

This BnB is just a bit off the main commercial district. Head east on 1st until you get to the Snohomish Bakery. Then turn slightly southeast, then left on Cedar. The house itself is an old, tall, regal-looking Queen Ann Victorian house set on beautiful grounds. These guys also offer a shuttle, so you don't necessarily have to hike in with your bags from the airport.

Pillows & Platters

Hotels, Bed & Breakfast
0.9 miles or 17-minute walk
502 Avenue C, Snohomish, WA 98290
360-862-8944

A bit further up Airport Road after crossing the bridge from the airport is the Pillows and Platters BnB. This cut late-Victorian home sits on a quiet corner in a residential neighborhood. It's rimmed with a white picket fence.

It's a bit of a hike from the airport by comparison to the Country Man, and there's no shuttle. However, it's a fine establishment if closer alternatives are unavailable.

W16 – First Air Field Airport

Location: 2 miles northwest of Monroe
Coordinates: N47°52.28' / W121°59.71'
Altitude: 50 MSL
Fuel: None
Transient Storage: Tiedowns

Monroe hosts a population of around 20,000 on the shores of the Skykomish River. Settled in the 1800s as stop along the Great Northern Railway, the town has grown over the years whilst maintaining its connection to its history.

Monroe hosts the Evergreen State Fair annually, which runs for 12 days up to and through Labor Day. The Fair is the largest county fair in the Pacific Northwest. The Evergreen State Fairgrounds features permanent facilities used year-round for horse shows, trade shows, swap meets, and auto races.

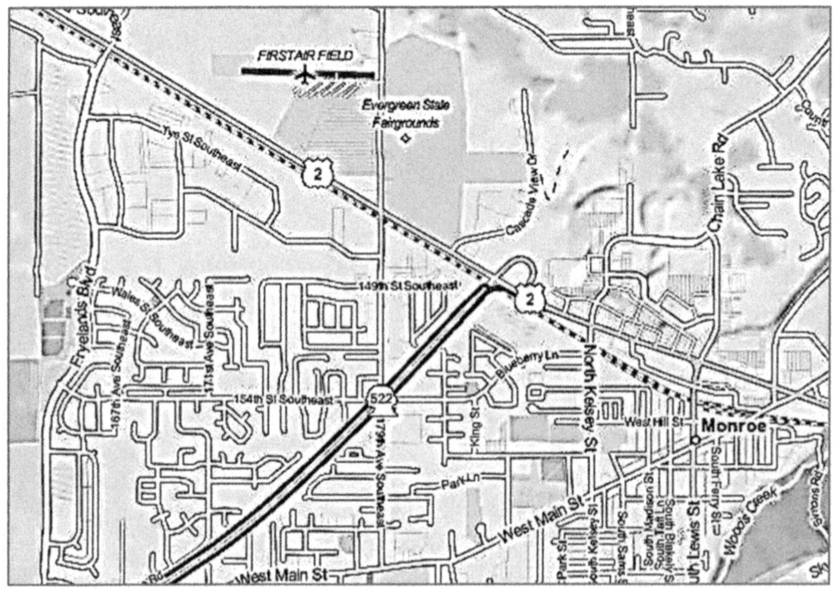

Airport Notes

Monroe is fairly flat, although there's a short ridge of trees north and east of the runway, but it's not a factor. The airport is to the northwest of the fairgrounds, which are to the northwest of town. Traffic pattern is always to the south.

The runway is on the shorter side, close to 2,087'. The bigger concern is the width. The payment is 34', but the spacing around that is tight with transient parking just inches to the south.

Transient parking is in the grass to the southern edge of the runway across from the hangars. The tiedowns don't have ropes, so remember to bring your own.

Food Options

Asian Spice

Chinese, Thai, Asian Fusion
0.8 miles or 14-minute walk
14655 Fryelands Blvd SE, Monroe, WA 98272
360-805-9292

Head south from the airport, cross Stevens Pass Highway, and then proceed west until you're right by Lake Tye, and you'll find Asian Spice. This is a Chinese and Thai restaurant in the style of a Teriyaki fast food place. The prices are reasonable, and the menu is fairly extensive.

Entrées include the Mongolian Beef, Chicken Japchae, and the Funny Spicy Chicken.[72]

[72] Don't ask me why it's funny. I don't know.

El Lago Mexican Restaurant & Bar

Mexican, Bars
0.7 miles or 13-minute walk
14090- Fryelands Blvd, Monroe, WA 98272
360-794-4272

North of Asian Spice along Fryelands Blvd and right next to Lake Tye resides El Lago. Open for lunch and dinner, this place offers the typical Mexican menu, but the quality is a noticeable notch above the average. The restaurant prides itself on its authentic, traditional Mexican recipes. The portions are huge, but that doesn't dilute the flavor.

There's a deck seating area with umbrella-covered tables that overlooks the lake and lands beyond.

Things to Do

Evergreen State Fair

Local Flavor, Festivals
0.6 miles or 10-minute walk
Monroe Fairgrounds, 14405 179th Ave SE, Monroe, WA 98272
360-805-6700

The Evergreen State Fair itself runs for 12 days up to and through Labor Day. That'd certainly be the best time to fly in to Monroe, although parking your airplane might be slightly more challenging. That said, the fairgrounds offer near year-round event hosting. There are events perhaps half the days each week, sometimes more. Check out their website at evergreenfair.org for details.

Evergreen Speedway

Race Tracks
0.6 miles or 10-minute walk
14405 179th Ave SE, Monroe, WA 98272
360-805-6100

The Evergreen Speedway is an auto racetrack draws crowds for events year round. The facility can accommodate up to 7,500 spectators in the covered grandstand and an additional 7,500 in the uncovered modular grandstands.

The track is the only sanctioned NASCAR track in Washington State. It hosts Formula D the third weekend in July every year. Along with NASCAR, the multi-purpose track can be configured to road courses with sanctioned SCCA, USAC, ASA, and NSRA events.

Overnight Lodging

Guest House Inn & Suites

Hotels
1.2 miles or 22-minute walk
19103 State Rt 2, Monroe, WA 98272
360-863-1900

The Guest House Inn and Suites is a fair walk from the airport, down Stevens Pass Highway from the Fairgrounds. Once there, you'll be greeted with hotel's amenities including: pool, exercise room, and wifi. Morning breakfast includes cinnabons, muffins, bagels, make your own waffles, and yogurt.

S86 – Sky Harbor Airport

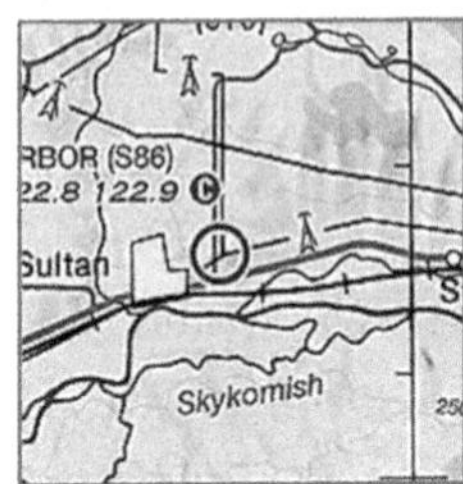

Location: 1 mile east of Sultan
Coordinates: N47°52.24' / W121°47.54'
Altitude: 282 MSL
Fuel: None
Transient Storage: None

Located where the Sultan River flows into the Skykomish, Sultan is a small town of about 5,000. Sultan was originally settled around 1880 but not officially incorporated until 1905.

Normally, there's very little to do near the grass airport, but there are a few places to eat. In July each year, the town puts on a 3-day street fair called the "Sultan Shindig." In includes carnival rides, street vendors, and logging games.

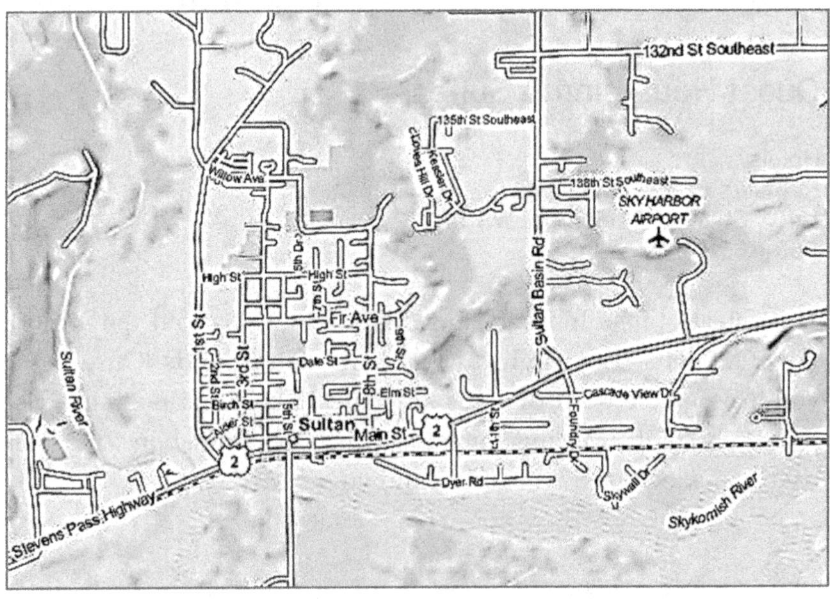

Airport Notes

The airport is a bit tricky to spot being that it's a grass runway surrounded by trees mixed in with a bunch of areas filled with trees and grasslands. Look north of the main highway, just east of a large church and its open grounds. The runway sits between two small, winding residential developments.

If winds allow, land to the west and depart to the east so that you'll avoid the tall trees to the west of the airport. The turf can get very soft in winter and spring. It's probably a good idea to call ahead for information prior to use.

You can park in a clearing on the northeast end of the runway or to the southwest end just to the west of the old hangars.

There are a few different but hidden ways to exit the airport property, but the easiest is probably a tight dirt road that passes by the house that's to the south of the field about midfield. Follow that road south, and you'll exit onto the highway.

Food Options

Vick's Burger Shack

Burgers
0.9 miles or 17-minute walk
930 Stevens Ave Hwy 2, Sultan, WA 98294
360-863-6796

After exiting onto the highway, walk west three-quarters of a mile, and you'll encounter Vick's Burger Shack. Vick's is a classic burger place offering the usual burger menu options, some with bacon and/or cheese. If you want to go crazy, there's the Double Bacon Cheeseburger.

In addition, Vick's offers some great root beer floats, shakes, and ice cream sundaes.

Bubba's Roadhouse

Bars, American (Traditional)
0.9 miles or 17-minute walk
924 Stevens Ave, Sultan, WA 98294
360-793-3950

Quite close to Vick's is Bubba's Roadhouse.[73] Here you can experience great food, good beer and wine, live music, and even dancing, if you're so inclined.[74] The food is inspired by typical burger or roadhouse food, but then kicked up a notch to the extraordinary. Bubba's offers a "WTF," which is a sandwich with every meat imaginable, but don't order it unless you're extremely hungry or want to feed a table of twelve.[75]

The interior is clean and inviting, with natural wood walls, a fireplace, and a stage for live music.

---

[73] I suppose it's just me, but when I see a name like "Bubba's Roadhouse," I can't help but take a look. Everything you assume about a place based on a name like that turns out to be true in this case. It's pretty awesome.
[74] No, I don't dance. Not when people can see. Please don't ask me. Under article 3 of the Geneva Convention, it's considered a war crime.
[75] Or both.

Dutch Cup Motel

Hotels
0.9 miles or 17-minute walk
819 Main St, Sultan, WA 98294
800-844-0488

If after your meal at Bubba's or Vick's you can't fit in your airplane, just wander north a block or two until you reach the Dutch Cup Motel. It's nothing fancy, but you'll get a clean and somewhat dated motel room for not too much dough.

BFI – King County Airport (Boeing Field)

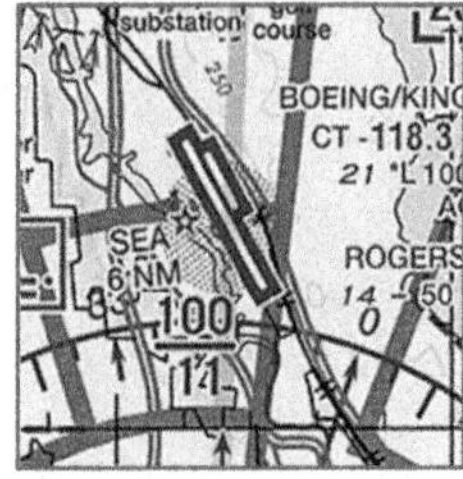

Location: 4 miles south of Seattle
Coordinates: N47°31.80' / W122°18.12'
Altitude: 21 MSL
Fuel: 100LL (blue), Jet-A
Transient Storage: Hangars, Tiedowns

Located just 4 miles south of downtown Seattle, Boeing Field (King County International Airport) is about the most urban airport Washington State has to offer. It's also tucked into airspace that's about as tight as tight can be, with SeaTac's Class Bravo to the southwest and over the top and Renton's Class Delta tucked up to the southeast.

Being so close to Seattle means that a short taxi or Uber ride gets you into the heart of the largest city in the state, to enjoy all the amenities, recreational and otherwise, the city has to offer.

Airport Notes

The biggest consideration when flying to Boeing Field is the airspace. SeaTac's Class Bravo overshadows Boeing Field, so your approaches and departures need to be tight. Note especially that at from about midfield to the south, the Class Bravo airspace extends down to 1,100′. When Boeing Tower instructs you to stay below 1,000′, they're not kidding.

Check the usual resources for updated information about VFR approaches and departures. If you have questions, call the tower.

Care should be taken not to drift into the approach/departure way for the other runway.[76]

There are numerous GA businesses around the field. If you've never been before, call up your intended destination and get a briefing of the field and what to expect.

Transportation

There are multiple courtesy car options available. There's Aeroflight at 206-762-6476, Landmark at 206-763-0350, and Clay Lacy at 206-762-6000. In addition, Uber has excellent coverage here, and the FBOs can certainly hook you up with a local taxi or rental car.

A lot of restaurant options in the area require a walk over the 16th Ave Bridge on the west side of the field. The actual distance isn't all that far, but depending on where you park, the path you have to take might get a bit awkward. Depending on your preferences, it

[76] Otherwise, big airplanes with large wakes. Very bad.

may be worth it to order up an Uber to get you where you want to go. That said, if you're going to go Uber, you should consider going into downtown Seattle, which has a list of restaurants so large it would fill its own book.

Food Options

Cavu Café ✈

Sandwiches, Cafés
0.5 miles or 9-minute walk
7277 Perimeter Rd S, Georgetown, Seattle, WA 98108
206-762-1243

Cavu Café is on the field in the main terminal building on the east side. It offers a variety of snack items and coffee. You can pick up cookies or sandwiches here.

Via Vadi Caffe

Cafés
0.6 miles or 12-minute walk
8600 14th Ave S, South Park, Seattle, WA 98108
206-762-7519

The Via Vadi is across the 16th Ave Bridge near the intersection with Cloverdale. It's a nice little café tucked behind a pizza shop. It's cozy and friendly. The coffee is typically well made. Cappuccinos actually look and taste like cappuccinos ought.

There's free wifi, and while the place is small, seating is usually not a problem.

Napoli Pizzeria

Pizza, Italian
0.6 miles or 12-minute walk
8600 14th Ave S, South Park, Seattle, WA 98108
206-768-9615

Next to Via Vadi is Napoli Pizzeria. In a lot of ways, this is close to the ideal simple pizza joint. The menu is simple, so you're not overwhelmed with difficult decisions. The pizza is well-made, loaded with toppings, and perfectly cooked.

After a day at the Flight Museum, this place can make for a perfect dinner spot.

Loretta's Northwesterner

Bars, American (New), Burgers
0.7 miles or 13-minute walk
8617 14th Ave S, South Park, Seattle, WA 98108
206-327-9649

This 21-and-over burgers bar offers some good grub at reasonable prices. It's something of a nice hole-in-the-wall spot with a simple menu. The food isn't superb, but it's reasonable. The atmosphere is eclectic. There's an old RV parked inside the restaurant.

Phorale

Vietnamese, Asian Fusion, Tex-Mex
0.8 miles or 14-minute walk
8909 14th Ave S, South Park, Seattle, WA 98108
206-519-0810

Phorale is in the same neighborhood as Napoli and Loretta's. They offer a Vietnamese-Mexican fusion menu, which sounds insane at first, but it actually works. Another odd quirk about this place is that it's located inside a mini-mart. Not joking.

That said, the food is surprisingly interesting and good. I know of no other place on earth where you can order pho with "Al Pastor" egg rolls and Korean spicy pork.

Mexican Restaurants

There are a handful of typical Mexican style restaurants in the area. Here are few of the better options.

Muy Macho Taqueria

Mexican
0.7 miles or 12-minute walk
8515 14th Ave S, South Park, Seattle, WA 98108
206-763-3484

Mi Fondita del Itsmo

Mexican
0.7 miles or 12-minute walk
8525 14th Ave S, South Park, Seattle, WA 98108
206-747-3681

Jalisco Restaurant

Mexican
0.7 miles or 12-minute walk
8517 14th Ave S, South Park, Seattle, WA 98108
206-767-1943

Sabor A Mi

Mexican
0.7 miles or 13-minute walk
8709 14th Ave S, South Park, Seattle, WA 98108
206-764-9379

The Museum of Flight ✈

Museums
0.8 miles or 15-minute walk
9404 East Marginal Way S, Seattle, WA 98108
206-764-5720

As an aviator visiting Boeing Field looking for something to do, the obvious choice is the Museum of Flight. This museum has one of the best aviation and space collections in the United States. It boasts such greats as the Concorde, Dreamliner, 747, SR-71, and old Air Force One, and much more.

When arriving by air, you'll need to call ahead to reserve a parking spot and arrange entrance from the ramp. The day before you arrive, call Museum Security at 206-764-5710 to set things up.

When you arrive, tell the tower and/or ground controller your intentions, and they'll route you to an area of aircraft parking that's just to the northeast side of the museum area. There are 6 transient parking spaces inside a blue box outline.

Charles Smith Wines Jet City

Wine Tasting Room
1.3 miles or 25-minute walk
1136 S Albro Pl, Georgetown, Seattle, WA 98108
206-745-7456

Up past the northern end of the field is the Charles Smith Wines tasting room and winery. It also hosts the largest urban on the west coast. The facility features two tasting room: the main floor is designed with a rustic Northwest feel, and the larger upstairs space exudes an early 60's vibe, with nod to the aviation industry.

Flip Flip, Ding Ding

Arcades, Bars
1.5 miles or 28-minute walk
6012 12th Ave S, Georgetown, Seattle, WA 98108
206-508-0296

Flip Flip, Ding Ding is a pinball arcade center with a vast array of pinball games located a couple blocks off the north end of the Boeing Field airport property.

Overnight Lodging

Georgetown Inn

Hotels
1.5 miles or 29-minute walk
6100 Corson Ave S, Georgetown, Seattle, WA 98108
206-762-2233

The Georgetown Inn is located a few blocks off the north end of the airport. It's a small but clean and minimalist hotel. There's a basic continental breakfast provided, and the hotel has reasonable wifi and friendly staff.

This would be a good place to stay if you're planning on flying in to catch a game at CenturyLink or Safeco. You can catch either the 106 or 124 bus lines just a few blocks from the hotel at Doris and Airport Way, and either will take you to within 2 blocks of the sports stadiums.

RNT – Renton Municipal Airport

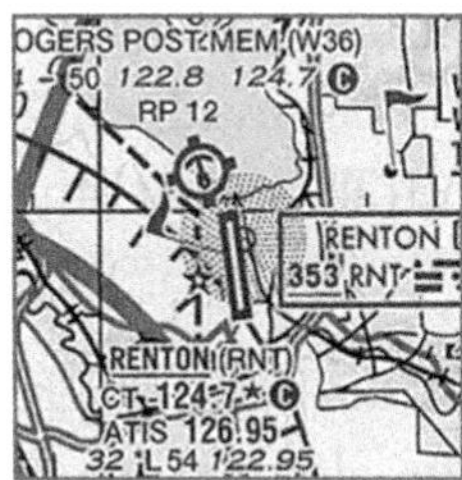

Location: 0 miles northwest of Renton
Coordinates: N47°29.59' / W122°12.94'
Altitude: 32 MSL
Fuel: 100LL (blue), Jet A-1+
Transient Storage: Tiedowns

Straddling the southeast shore of Lake Washington at the mouth of the Cedar River resides Renton the city, and plopped directly in its heart is Renton the airport. The airport is perhaps best known for being the final assembly point for the Boeing 737 family of commercial airplanes.

Despite Seattle and Bellevue being only minutes away,[77] Renton itself is no small city, being the 8th largest in the state. Certainly there's a strong urban feel to the area, especially near the airport.

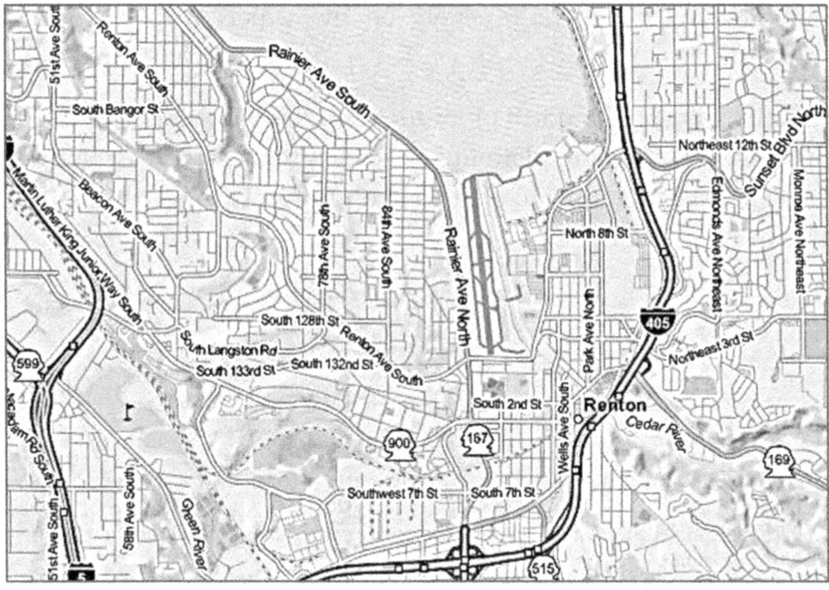

[77] Depending on traffic.

Airport Notes

Tower controllers across the state come in all varieties. Some are sociable, others more robotic, but all are professional. And while many if not most are friendly, it seems[78] the controllers at Renton are the friendliest of the bunch.[79]

Traffic patterns are typically on the east side of the field. There aren't any real obstacles to concern yourself with, although there are a few perceived obstacles that add to the excitement of the flight. Coming in on 16, you'll be over the water until a bit over 300′ before touchdown.[80] Coming in on 34, you'll cross over a busy urban road and a jet blast wall before touchdown. There's a displaced threshold of 500′ from the blast wall, but it still might catch the eye if you're below glide slope.

There's a seaplane base to the north end along the water that sports a dock and ramp. Renton tower controls the base as well as the airport and class D airspace. Be friendly back at them by announcing when you're safely on the water as they typically request.

The FBO is slightly north of midfield on the west side. Operations are busy, so if you're planning on staying for lunch or longer, call the FBO ahead of time to give them opportunity to plan.

[78] As in, "it seems to me," which really is what matters since I'm the author of this book and all.
[79] They're still as professional as any other tower controllers, so don't think they're lax or anything.
[80] This can be a weird experience. For anyone who's not a seaplane pilot, the reasons are obvious. And for those of us who are, it's a weird experience but for entirely different reasons.

Lake Thai Cuisine

Thai
0.6 miles or 10-minute walk
11425 Rainier Ave S, Seattle, WA 98178
206-420-1180

Almost directly west of the seaplane base along Rainier Avenue is Lake Thai Cuisine. This place offers some spectacular Thai food despite its strange exterior. The Pad See Ew is excellent as is the Phad Thai.

El Kiosko

Mexican
0.9 miles or 16-minute walk
526 S 2nd St, Renton, WA 98057
425-271-2341

Walk south along Rainier Avenue, cross over Airport Way, then turn left or east on 2nd Street, and you'll pass by the Performing Arts Center on you way to El Kiosko on the corner. It's a very small, yellow building with red trim. It's essentially what happens to a really great taco truck when it grows up and turns into a permanent restaurant.

When you walk in, you'll see a very small counter from which to order and a full wall behind it with pictures of all the yummy you can order. The number of choices is almost overwhelming.

Big Island Poke

Hawaiian, Seafood, Live/Raw Food
0.8 miles or 15-minute walk
235 Rainier Ave S, Renton, WA 98057

If you're on your way to El Kiosko and get tired or change your mind and want Hawaiian food, Big Island Poke is at the corner of Rainier and 2nd. The restaurant has a modern yet simplistic feel to it. You can customize your order to however you like. Start with your base, like rice, arugula, or tortilla chips, then add protein, toppings, and sauces.

Melrose Grill

Steakhouses
1.1 miles or 21-minute walk
819 Houser Way S, Renton, WA 98057
425-254-0759

Beyond El Kiosko and a bit of a walk is Melrose Grill, but worth every step to get there. This small white building with rail tracks along the road by it may not seem like much from the outside, but you'll be glad you set foot inside after your order arrives.

New York strip, filet mignon, porterhouse, and more grace the menu. The Grill also offers salmon filet, pork medallions, and a Bavarian sausage plate among other things. The atmosphere is fairly relaxed given the classy food. The staff are friendly and accommodating.

Jimmy Mac's Roadhouse

American (Traditional)
1.4 miles or 26-minute walk
225 SW 7th St, Renton, WA 98057
425-227-6881

A fair walk south from the airport along Rainier Avenue, just off on 7th street, sits Jimmy Mac's Roadhouse. This is the place where you throw peanut shells on the floor.[81] It's a self-proclaimed "Texas-style" family restaurant with an extremely casual style. While you wait for your food, you can eat the free peanuts, tossing the shells on the flood.

They offer Dungeness crab cakes, crawfish chowder, BBQ baby back pork ribs, fresh grilled salmon, shrimp, burgers, grilled chicken entrées, and smoked pork, among other things.

Things to Do

Liberty Park and Cedar River Park

Parks
1.0 miles or 18-minute walk
1101 Bronson Way N, Renton, WA 98057

Follow 2nd Street east, and it'll turn north 45° and into Bronson Way. Follow that across the Cedar River and you'll encounter Liberty Park. Here you'll find the Renton Public Library, baseball, tennis, and basketball courts, a skate park, and a slide/playground area.

The Renton Public Library straddles the Cedar River. It was recently remodeled and looks quite nice on the inside. That said, it's fairly loud; it's more of a community center now than a quiet place to read. Still, if you bring noise-canceling headphones, you can find

[81] Yes, really.

a spot by the windows to read that overlooks the river that flows under you.

Cross under 405 and you'll find Cedar River Park, which is home to the Renton Community Center and the Carco Theater.

Cedar River Trail Park

Parks, Trails
0.2 miles or 3-minute walk
1060 N Nishiwaki Ln, Renton, WA 98057

The Cedar River Trail and Park runs along the Cedar River from just south of its mouth, next to the 16 threshold, southward past Liberty Park and Cedar River Park. The trail extends all the way into Maple Valley. The loop from the stadium parking lot to the water and back takes about 40 minutes. Along the way, there are plenty of picnic spots and benches.

Cascade Canoe & Kayak Centers

Boating, Rafting/Kayaking
0.5 miles or 9-minute walk
1060 Nishiwaki Ln, Renton, WA 98057
425-430-0111

Situated just past the very northern end of the Cedar River on the southern shores of Lake Washington is the Cascade Canoe and Kayak Center. As you might expect, here you can rent a canoe or kayak and explore the lake or river. You can also sign up for guided tours by kayak.

Luther's Table

Coffee & Tea, Venues & Event Spaces
0.9 miles or 16-minute walk
419 S 2nd St, Ste 1, Renton, WA 98057
425-970-3157

Across the street from the Performing Arts Center is Luther's Table, a coffee house with a lot of activities available. After picking up a good cup of coffee, you can enjoy locally-based live music, art shows, lectures, and movies.

Overnight Lodging

Larkspur Landing Renton

Hotels
2.0 miles or 38-minute walk
1701 E Valley Rd, Renton, WA 98057
425-235-1212

There are closer overnight lodging accommodations to the hotel than Larkspur, which sits just south of the 405 intersection with 167; however, none of the closer options I'm willing to recommend. Larkspur Landing is a good quality lodging location that's easily approachable for pilots because they offer free shuttle service to the airport.[82]

Rooms are nice, clean, and large enough to fit a small family. There's a dishwasher, microwave, stove, and dishes. Breakfast is provided and there is a good selection of breakfasts such as: cereals, yogurt, pastries, eggs, cheeses, and a toaster. The wifi service is good.

[82] Be sure to specify which airport. If you don't, they'll assume you mean SeaTac.

Hampton Inn Seattle-Southcenter

Hotels
2.5 miles or 47-minute walk
7200 S 156th St, Tukwila, WA 98188
425-228-5800

Another hotel, a bit further away but equally as good, is the Hampton Inn. It's actually over in Tukwila, but it offers a shuttle to and from the airport as well.[83] One nice feature about the Hampton Inn is it's within walking distance of Southcenter mall area, so you'll have half-a-billion food and entertainment options available to you.

The floors aren't carpeted, which gives the place almost a Malaysian feel to it. The wifi service is good. The breakfast area is large, unlike many hotels where you feel squeezed into a small space with many other guests for breakfast.

[83] And again, remember to specify which airport to the hotel when you request the shuttle.

Chapter 6

Seattle Terminal Area Southeast

The southeast section of the Seattle terminal area has a mixture of dense urban and scenic rural zones. At the upper end of density is the Seattle-Tacoma (SEA) International Airport, the largest and busiest airport in the Pacific Northwest, set in a sprawling urban metropolis between the cities of Seattle and Tacoma. At the other end of the spectrum might be Swanson (2W3) out by Eatonville or Crest (S36), a wooded residential community airport.

As with the northeast terminal area, the southeast is dominated by the SeaTac Class Bravo, but due to the twin military airports being offset to the west, there's a wide area to the south that's easy to navigate around and through.

Flying over this area, you'll enjoy some beautiful scenery, especially out by Enumclaw and all along the lower step edge of the Cascade Mountains. On good days, Rainier will loom large to your southeast. Lake Tapps sits south of Auburn and east of Puyallup and is usually filled with a few boaters on nice days.

The land in this area starts to look a lot the same from the air, the father out you get from the urban centers. The first time I flew over this area, I nearly got lost. It's not as easy to pick out landmarks as it is in the other spots in the terminal area. Turn off your GPS and have a little fun with pilotage and dead reckoning.

SEA – Seattle-Tacoma Intl Airport

Location: 10 miles south of Seattle
Coordinates: N47°26.99' / W122°18.71'
Altitude: 432 MSL
Fuel: 100LL (blue), Jet-A, Jet A-1
Transient Storage: Tiedowns

The mothership of all airports in the Pacific Northwest is unquestionably SeaTac. It sports the largest airspace, most traffic, and greatest cumulative wake turbulence of any airport in the state. Its easternmost runway is 11,901′ long.[84] It has a T taxiway that gets mistaken for a runway. It has a Z taxiway.[85] Unless you *really* want some sort of gold star in your logbook for later bragging, avoid.

[84] This means I can land to a full stop and take off about 8 times without having to turn. Of course, doing so would likely annoy tower controllers a lot and result in a very large bill in the mail, since I suspect the Port of Seattle would charge me a landing fee for each of those 8 landings.

[85] Because I guess it's fun to use all the letters in airport diagrams…

Airport Notes

This airport is usually busy. Very busy. If you arrive and expect a prompt landing when there's a stack of heavies on approach, you'll be disappointed.[86] But there are breaks in the traffic. If you can time your arrival for one of those breaks, or you're willing to sit in a hold for a while, the tower is happy to fit you in.[87]

The actual approach is extremely easy. Just follow the tower's instructions. They'll usually give you a squawk code quickly then have you hold somewhere like over Vashon Island or Westpoint until they can fit you in. Their biggest concern it seems is your time on the runway. They don't want to be in a situation where they have to force one of the heavies into a go-around.

If you've not been to SeaTac before, it may be wise to consider doing a VFR transition to get comfortable with the tower and airspace before attempting a landing. There are two VFR transition routes; one will be active depending on traffic flow. See the terminal area chart for details.

There are landing fees at SeaTac. The Port of Seattle will bill you based on whatever the current policy is at the time. It's typically not a crazy amount.[88] There's been chatter about how if you're cleared for the option as opposed to a touch-and-go, you won't be charged since the fee is only for wheels down rather than airspace transition. However, there's also other chatter that says this loophole no longer exists.

[86] I once thought it'd be a good idea to fly GA to SeaTac to catch a commercial flight to the east coast. We arrived right about when there was a parking lot all the way up to Class A. When we called tower and requested landing, there was a pause, and then the controller said, "Uh... Hold south of Three Tree. Be advised, expected wait of 45 minutes." I'm not joking.

[87] Honest. They don't mind working with GA flights at all.

[88] This is not gospel. Check with the Port of Seattle if you want to know the correct current fee.

If you do land and plan on taxiing somewhere, have the airport diagram in front of you and review it in detail before your flight. The tower and ground controllers are nice and accommodating, but SeaTac is a tight operation. You don't want to be the pilot that hiccups the efficiency.

After landing, taxi to ASIG General Aviation Services. They're on the southern end of the field close to where taxiway T terminates. They can set you up with fuel, parking, and other typical FBO services. If you give them prior notice, they can drive you over to the main terminal building in their passenger van.

Transportation

ASIG does have courtesy car available. Call them at 206-433-5481 to confirm availability. The FBO can also secure you a rental, and Uber coverage in the SeaTac area is excellent.

Food Options

The BBQ Schacht

Barbeque, Caterers
1.4 miles or 26-minute walk
19231 Des Moines Memorial Dr, SeaTac, WA 98148
206-878-8931

From the FBO, follow Des Moines Memorial Drive west and south past 188th and 192nd, and you'll end up at The BBQ Schacht.

If you're into "award winning BBQ and tasty down-home grub," The BBQ Schacht is for you. They're a lunch and late-lunch sort of place, open from 11am through 5pm Tuesday through Friday. As you'd expect from a BBQ catering place, the meats are phenomenal.

Don't arrive hungry; arrive starving. The portions are galactic. The "Schacht Attack" consists of three choices of meat, two sides, two piece of corn bread, and a soda for $25.

Aunt Becky's Deli

Delis
1.3 miles or 25-minute walk
19110 Des Moines Memorial Dr, SeaTac, WA 98148
206-246-1115

If you're not ready yet for a third heart attack, just up the street from BBQ is Aunt Becky's Deli. They're open Monday through Friday from 6:30am to 4pm, and they offer good wifi.

The sandwiches are great, both in taste and size. The full sandwiches come with a cup of soup. They offer various daily specials. Such might include things like Mongolian beef, beef and chicken fried rice, and baked potatoes.

It's a small community restaurant, and many folks have set this as their regular lunch spot. So don't be too surprised if it gets busy.

Overnight Lodging

There are between 17.4 and 18.2 billion overnight lodging options in and around SeaTac.[89] Most of these are either mediocre, poor, or downright scary. Here are a few of the better options that are within walking distance.

Cedarbrook Lodge

Hotels
1.4 miles or 27-minute walk
18525 36th Ave S, SeaTac, WA 98188
206-901-9268

[89] I'm exaggerating only slightly.

Hampton Inn & Suites

Hotels
1.3 miles or 25-minute walk
18850 28th Ave S, SeaTac, WA 98188
206-244-5044

Sleep Inn Sea Tac Airport

Hotels
2.3 miles or 44-minute walk
20406 International Blvd, SeaTac, WA 98198
206-878-3600

Crowne Plaza Seattle Airport

Hotels, Venues & Event Spaces
0.8 miles or 15-minute walk
17338 International Blvd, Seattle, WA 98188
206-248-1000

Seattle Airport Marriott

Hotels
1.1 miles or 20-minute walk
3201 South 176th Street, Seattle, WA 98188
206-241-2000

La Quinta Inn & Suites

Hotels
1.2 miles or 23-minute walk
2824 South 188th St, Seattle, WA 98188
206-241-5211

S50 – Auburn Municipal Airport

Location: 2 miles north of Auburn
Coordinates: N47°19.66' / W122°13.60'
Altitude: 63 MSL
Fuel: 100LL (blue)
Transient Storage: Hangars, Tiedowns

Auburn is a city and Seattle suburb that's predominately in King County but also spans into Pierce County and is home to some 70,000 residents. Auburn is bordered by the cities of Federal Way, Pacific, and Algona to the west, Sumner to the south, Kent to the north, and unincorporated King County to the east.

The Muckleshoot Indian Reservation is in or near the southern city limits. The one-mile oval track of Emerald Downs, a thoroughbred racetrack, is located to the east of the airport and west of highway 167.

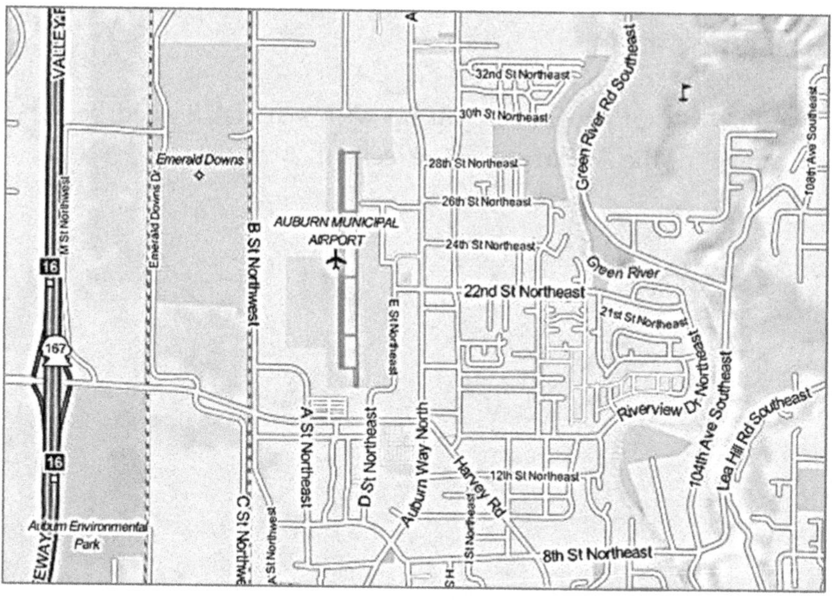

Airport Notes

Be mindful of the Class Bravo overhead as you're approaching. Its floor is at 3,000′ over the airport, but about 6,000′ to the west it drops down to 1,800′.

The airport itself sits in the middle of a north-south valley that runs from Renton/Tukwila in the north down past Sumner and into Orting in the south. The airport is about 2 miles north of the downtown Auburn area. It's easy to spot. Just look for Emerald Downs, then look just east of that.

Traffic pattern is always to the west of the field. Avoid what are called "extremely noise-sensitive residential areas" east of the field.

The FBO is just south of midfield to the east. Transient parking is yellow box between the FBO and runway, but if those spots aren't available, the FBO can put you almost anywhere else. Speaking of which, those folks are some of the friendliest aviation peoples around.

Transportation

The FBO can of course set you up with a rental if need be. Uber coverage for the Auburn area is excellent.

Belen Pupuseria

Salvadoran
0.3 miles or 6-minute walk
1833 Auburn Way N, Auburn, WA 98002
253-887-5608

This one's not so obvious how to get to. From the FBO, walk out to E Street, then head south about half-way to the end of the airport property. You'll encounter the back side of a long and non-descript 1-story building at 1833 Auburn Way. It's right across from the last couple of hangars and before you get to the back parking lot for The Truck Shop. Follow the alley on the north side of the non-descript building and walk around until you reach the east side. About mid-point on the east side is Belen Pupuseria.

If you've never had traditional Salvadoran food, you ought to give this place a try. A pupusa is a traditional Salvadoran dish made of a thick, handmade corn tortilla that's usually filled with a blend of cheese, pork, and refried beans. Belen offers this excellent traditional dish at low prices.

In addition to the papusas, Belen also offers tacos, soups, burritos, quesadillas, carne asada, fajitas, taquitos, and similar.

Pho Dinh

Vietnamese
0.4 miles or 8-minute walk
2822 Auburn Way N, Auburn, WA 98002
253-804-8688

Turn north instead of south on E Street, and you'll reach Pho Dihn. It's near but not quite at the northern end of the airport property. This is a pretty typical pho restaurant with several other

Vietnamese dishes available. Beyond the usual wonderful selection of pho, they also offer Com Dia (rice plates), Banh Mi (sandwiches), and Bun (bowls filled with all sorts of yummy meat and vegetables).

Jack's Tavern

Burgers, Music Venues, Bars
0.2 miles or 4-minute walk
2425 Auburn Way N, Auburn, WA 98002
253-833-0840

To find Jack's, head north on E Street, past where the road bends, and stop at the alley on the north side of Fritz Towing. From there, walk east, and Jack's will be on your left.

There are many reasons to love Jack's, not the least of which is the model yellow Canadian Beaver on floats hanging from the ceiling. Jack's is a typical tavern business with pool, pull tabs, a large bar, and good grub. The double bacon cheeseburger will increase your risk for a heart attack, but you should order it anyway.[90]

Taqueria El Rinconsito

Mexican
0.3 miles or 4-minute walk
2101 Auburn Way N, Auburn, WA 98002
253-939-6627

If you're looking for some excellent authentic Mexican food, look to Taqueria El Rinconsito, just south of midfield and 22nd on Auburn Way. These guys offer the usual stuff like tacos, burritos, enchiladas, and so on, but everything is made from top-quality ingredients and in a way that sets it apart from the typical Mexican restaurant. The food and restaurant are fairly authentic, so don't

[90] As pilots, we don't fly because we want a life of perfect safety. We take calculated risks all the time. Ergo, I suspect most pilots will enjoy ordering the double bacon cheeseburger. Like flying, it's worth the added risks.

expect an Americanized Mexican place. It's essentially "Mexican fast food."

Things to Do

Brannan Park

Parks
0.6 miles or 11-minute walk
1055 28th St Ne, Auburn, WA 98002

Brannan Park is to the east of the field a few blocks. Head north on Auburn Way until you reach 28th, which is not quite as far north as the northern end of the airport property. Then walk east, and you'll run right into the park, which sits along the Green River.

Here you'll find several baseball fields, a skate park, basketball and soccer, a playground for younger children, and a magnificent paved trail that follows along the Green River. The trail is fairly long, but probably too short for a bicycle ride if you're accustomed to long rides.

At the southern end of the trail is Dykstra Park, a smaller park area, and a walking bridge across the river. Crossing the river and walking north, you'll reach Isaac Evans Park, which is next to the Auburn Golf Course.

Emerald Downs

Horse Racing, Stadiums & Arenas
0.5 miles or 9-minute walk
2300 Emerald Downs Dr, Auburn, WA 98001
253-288-7711

Just to the west of the airport, across B Street and the railroad tracks, sits Emerald Downs, is a thoroughbred racetrack. The track hosts live racing events Fridays, Saturdays, and Sundays from April through September. It also offers simulcast race events every day from April through December.

Avoid concessions when here since the wait times can be extraordinary.

Overnight Lodging

Guesthouse Inn

Guest Houses
0.5 miles or 10-minute walk
9 14th St NW, Auburn, WA 98001
253-735-9600

Just at the southern end of the field and a bit to the west near B Street is the Guesthouse Inn. It's not an especially fancy hotel, but it'll do. The amenities are a bit limited, and the place has some repair needs. However, it's a not-too-bad place that's close to your airplane.

La Quinta Inn & Suites Auburn

Hotels
1.7 miles or 33-minute walk
225 6th Street South East, Auburn, WA 98002
253-804-9999

If you're willing to walk a fair bit south past highway 18, or better yet, use Uber or a taxi to get there, you'll find La Quinta a nice place to stay. Everything is clean and updated nicely. There's the standard spread of hotel breakfast offerings.

The wifi works but isn't particularly fast. There are fresh cookies in the afternoon.

S44 – Spanaway Airport

Location: 1 mile south of Spanaway
Coordinates: N47°5.21' / W122°25.88'
Altitude: 385 MSL
Fuel: 100LL (blue)
Transient Storage: Tiedowns

Spanaway is an unincorporated area near Tacoma. It resides along the eastern side of the Fort Lewis Military Reservation and McChord Air Force Base.

The town was established in 1890 when the Lake Park Land, Railway and Improvement Company purchased all the nearby land east of Spanaway Lake with the intent of turning the area into a recreation destination. When Mount Rainier National Park was established in 1899, tourists took the train to its terminus in Lake Park and from there made the 2-day journey to Mount Rainier.

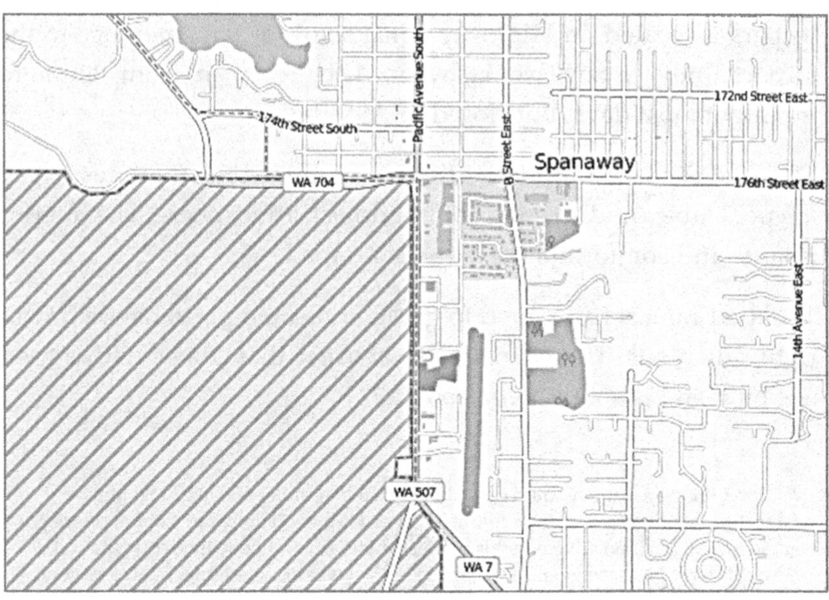

Airport Notes

Note the terminal area chart carefully when planning a trip to or from Spanaway. The class D airspace of Joint-Base Lewis-McChord overhangs the airport at 1,000 MSL, or roughly 615 AGL.[91]

Traffic pattern is always to the east of the field. There's a 215′ displaced threshold on 16.

The runway is narrow, only 20′ across, but long at over 2700′. Parking and fuel are available about midfield on the west side.

Food Options

Jeepers Bar and Grill

American (Traditional)
0.2 miles or 3-minute walk
18823 Pacific Ave S, Spanaway, WA 98387
253-271-0236

Jeepers is located on Highway 7 just south of the enterence to the airport, only a few blocks walk. They're open from 11am to midnight most days, but closed on Mondays.

The food is good, and there's live entertainment on Sundays. There are pool tables and an enjoyable, laid-back atmosphere. The interior is large and comfortable, not at all cramped.

The food ranges from good to great, and some portions are downright ridiculous. There's one cheeseburger that comes with a fried egg on it and is about half-a-foot tall.[92]

[91] I don't know about you, but I don't like cruising at under 600′ AGL. So maybe talking to the friendly tower people at McChord is a good idea. But I'm not offering any practical aviation advice in this matter what-so-ever. Just telling you what I'd do.

[92] You'd think I was exaggerating, but I'm not. I never exaggerating. Ever. I've gone my entire life without even once exaggerating.

Samurai's Japanese Steakhouse

Japanese, Steakhouses
0.4 miles or 7-minute walk
19321 Mountain Hwy E, Spanaway, WA 98387
253-846-5557

Almost right off the southern end of Spanaway Airport is Samurai's Japanese Steakhouse. This is your typical Japanese steakhouse where the chefs cook the food right in front of you while they put on a little show. All the usual Japanese steakhouse dishes are available. There's also "Samurai's Choice" dishes including "Shogun," a lobster, scallops, and shrimp dish.

As with any Japanese steakhouse, arrive hungry. The portion sizes will require you recalculate your weight and balance for the flight home.

Umai Bento

Japanese, Sushi Bars
0.9 miles or 17-minute walk
17306 Pacific Ave S, Spanaway, WA 98387
253-537-3222

If you're looking for a more sushi-Japanese experience, then Umai Bento is a good choice. They're a bit of a walk, but not that far. Head north from the airport along Highway 7, then cross 176th. Umai is a couple blocks north.

The sushi menu is extensive, and all the sushi is well-made and well-styled. They also offer 17 dishes made on a wok including Mongolian chicken and beef, orange chicken, broccoli beef, and so on. They also offer donburi and a huge assortment of bento box options.

Hidalgo Mexican Restaurant

Mexican
0.6 miles or 11-minute walk
17807 Pacific Ave S, Spanaway, WA 98387
253-847-5455

Hidalgo's is located north from the airport right on Highway 7, before you reach 176th. It's a cozy and clean family restaurant.

The food is quite authentic, not Americanized. The "Hidalgo Plate" is a plate of steak, bacon wrapped prawns, and chicken breast with rice and beans.

PLU – Pierce County Airport, Thun Field

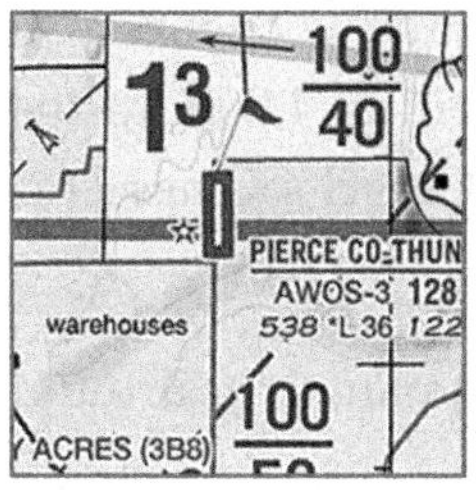

Location: 5 miles south of Puyallup
Coordinates: N47°6.24' / W122°17.23'
Altitude: 537 MSL
Fuel: 100LL (blue)
Transient Storage: Tiedowns

Just at the southern edge of the Puyallup density area resists the Piece County Airport, also known as Thun Field.

Puyallup itself is home to about 40,000 people. It's named after the Puyallup Tribe, a name that means "generous people." The city is home to the Washington State Fair, the state's primary fair. The town was established in 1877 by Ezra Meeker who later became its mayor.

The fairgrounds and city are about 5 or 6 miles to the north, but there's still a fair bit to do around the airport itself.

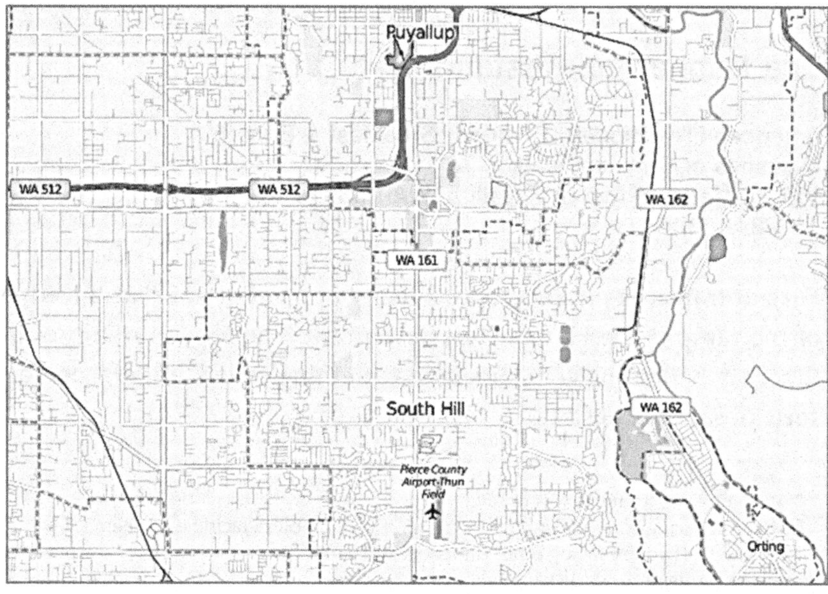

Airport Notes

As you approach PLU, keep an eye on your altitude to ensure you don't stray into the Class B that overlaps it at either 4,000' to the north or 5,000' to the south. Note also that McChord's Class D is only about 3nm to the west.

The airspace by the airport itself is very easy to maneuver around in and presents no obvious obstacles.[93]

Fuel and transient parking are on midfield to the west.

Transportation

There are possibly 2 courtesy cars available. The first is from Safety in Motion Flight Center. Give them a call at 253-840-5758 to inquire about availability. The second option is from Spencer Aircraft at 253-848-9349.

Food Options

The Hangar Inn Restaurant ✈

American (Traditional), Seafood, Breakfast & Brunch
0.3 miles or 6-minute walk
16919A Meridian Ave E, Puyallup, WA 98375
253-848-7516

Park at transient parking, and directly in front of you[94] at the edge of the ramp is the Hangar Inn Restaurant. The food is in a typical diner style: hamburgers, omelets, something called "salad," and all sorts of sandwiches.

93 Well, obvious to me, that is to say.

94 If you're facing west, it'll be right in front of you. If you're facing east, then it'll be behind you. If you're facing other directions, turn until you're facing either west or east, then consult the earlier instructions.

There's a descent sized deck facing the airport so you can keep a close eye on your beloved airplane while you eat. No wifi, though.

Nearby Chain Restaurants

There are a handful of chain restaurants nearby, some very close to the airport. Here's a non-comprehensive list:

Red Robin Gourmet Burgers

American (Traditional), Burgers
0.3 miles or 6-minute walk
16904 Meridian East, Ste 105, Puyallup, WA 98375
253-845-5127

Applebee's

American (Traditional), Bars, Steakhouses
0.3 miles or 6-minute walk
16518 Meridian E, Puyallup, WA 98374
253-770-7300

Quiznos

Sandwiches, Fast Food
0.7 miles or 13-minute walk
17526 Meridian E, Ste C101, Puyallup, WA 98375
253-445-6747

Subway

Fast Food, Sandwiches
0.5 miles or 9-minute walk
16116 Meridian Ave E, Puyallup, WA 98375
253-848-9211

Taco Bell

Fast Food, Mexican, Chicken Wings
0.4 miles or 8-minute walk
17514 Meridian East, Puyallup, WA 98375
253-840-9030

Happy Bento

Sushi Bars, Japanese
0.5 miles or 8-minute walk
9909 168th St E, Ste 103, Puyallup, WA 98375
253-445-7909

From midfield, head west a couple blocks and you'll find Happy Bento. This is a fairly old-school and dated Japanese restaurant with excellent sushi and bento options. They have very friendly and professional staff. The food, especially the sushi, is prepared fast.

Modoo Teriyaki

Chinese
0.7 miles or 13-minute walk
17530 Meridian E, Ste 101, Puyallup, WA 98375
253-445-7033

Toward the southern end of the field and off to the west near Fred Meyer is Modoo Teriyaki. While this place is predominately a teriyaki place and calls itself Chinese, there's really a wide variety of offerings. Don't be surprised to see Thai, Japanese, and Vietnamese influences on the menu.

Jersey Mike's Subs

Sandwiches, Fast Food, Delis
0.8 miles or 14-minute walk
10306 156th Street East, Puyallup, WA 98374
253-268-3617

Up just past the north end of the field next to Target and LA Fitness is Jersey Mike's Subs. This place is about as good as it gets for subs and wraps. The restaurant is clean, open, and inviting. They offer cold and hot subs; things like the "Big Kahuna Cheese Steak, grilled pastrami Reuben, and the "Super Sub."

These guys literally slice the meat you order at the time of your order. The price is slightly higher than a run-of-the-mill sub place, but the quality is substantially higher and well worth it.

Qdoba Mexican Grill

Mexican
0.8 miles or 14-minute walk
Sunrise Village Shopping Center, 10306 156th St E, Ste 108, Puyallup, WA 98374
253-770-4802

Also located in the Sunrise Village near Jersey Mike's is the Qdoba Mexican Grill. These folks offer up familiar Mexican dishes but with distinctive flavors and an authentic feel. Tacos, burrito bowls, 3-cheese nachos, tortilla soup, quesadillas, and similar dishes grace the menu.

2W3 – Swanson Airport

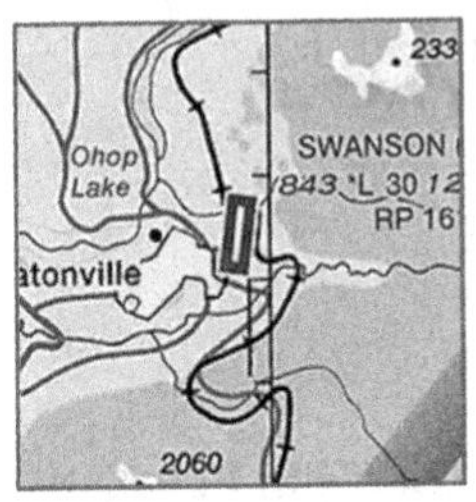

Location: 1 mile northeast of Eatonville
Coordinates: N46°52.30' / W122°15.43'
Altitude: 843 MSL
Fuel: None
Transient Storage: Tiedowns

Eatonville is a town in Pierce County tucked up next to the western edge of the Cascade foothills. It hosts a population of a little under 3,000.

In 1889, Indian Henry, a member of the Nisqually tribe, was one of those who guided the town's founder, Thomas Van Eaton to the present site of Eatonville. It's said that upon arrival, Henry declared, "This good place. Not much snow."

In the 1970s, the Northwest Trek wildlife park was opened. It remains one of the more popular tourist attractions in the area.

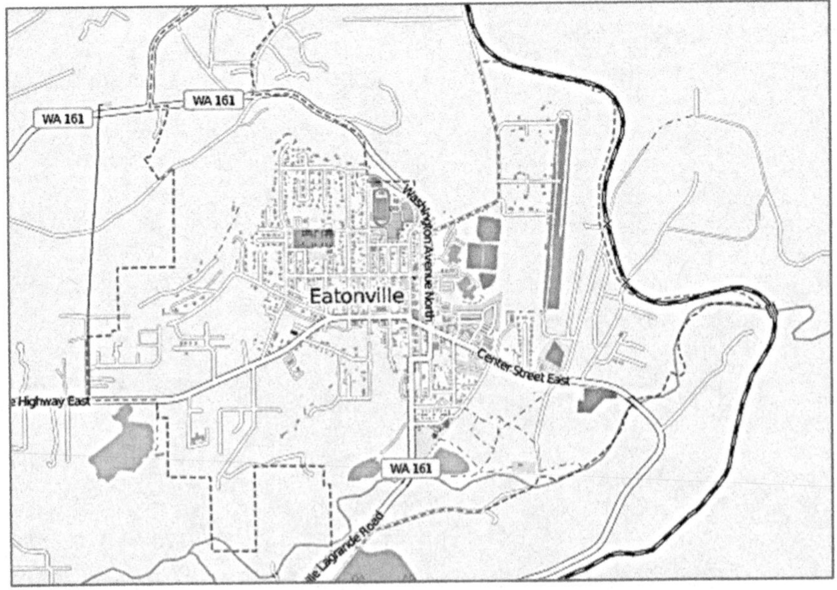

Airport Notes

Note the rising terrain mostly to the east but also north and a bit off to the south. This shouldn't be a concern, though, since the traffic pattern is always to the west of the field. There's good clearance from trees and other obstructions on either end of the runway.

There are buildings close to the runway, especially on the eastern side about midfield.

Food Options

The Pour House

Burgers, American (Traditional)
0.5 miles or 9-minute walk
119 Mashell Ave S, Eatonville, WA 98328
360-832-4782

From the south end of the field, hike down the hill via Weyerhaeuser Road south then Center Street west until you reach Mashell, in the heart of town. There you'll find the Pour House.

This is a solid hamburger bar. The hamburgers can be ordered with buffalo, elk, or venison meat, provided what you want is in season. They also offer pizza. Their fries are fresh cut, well-seasoned, and a bit on the greasy side.[95]

[95] I say this only to warn you about your need to use a napkin, not to dissuade you from ordering them.

Bertoglio's Pizza

Pizza
0.5 miles or 8-minute walk
102 Weyerhaeuser Rd N, Eatonville, WA 98328
360-832-6006

From the south end of the field, hike down Weyerhaeuser Road a bit until you reach Center Street. As you do, you'll pass a baseball field, and just at the end, a very tiny pizza joint tucked into a little green building with a red door. That's Bertoglio's Pizza.

These guys offer some good pizza options. The space is small but clean and well kept. The pizza comes with a thick cut and made with fresh quality toppings. The sizes are larger than average.

Bruno's Family Restaurant & Bar

American (Traditional), Bars
0.5 miles or 9-minute walk
204 Ctr St E, Eatonville, WA 98328
360-832-7866

Down toward the center of town along Center Street, right next to the Mill Village Motel, is Bruno's. This is a full-range American-style family restaurant offering burgers, sandwiches, steaks, seafood, and chicken dinners. There are such things as elk burgers. In fact, you can "Bruno size" your burger into a double, or add buffalo, elk, or wild boar.[96]

The interior sports a great vaulted wood ceiling with ceiling fans, and there's plenty of space for a small crowd.

[96] I'm seriously not joking. I would never joke about wild boar.

Eatonville Mill Village Motel

Hotels
0.5 miles or 9-minute walk
210 Center St E, Eatonville, WA 98328
360-832-3200

After eating wild boar[97] at Bruno's, you can roll yourself conveniently to your room had you booked yourself into Eatonville Mill Village Motel. It's a clean and comfortable, which is saying it's rather special compared with most small-town motels. The complimentary breakfast includes self-made waffles, cereal, eggs, sausage, and sausage gravy with a variety of juices, teas, and coffee.

[97] And really, if you're going to eat at Bruno's, why not order wild boar? How often in life do you get to eat wild boar? This is not to say that something that's rare in life is necessarily a good thing because it's rare. Rather, I'm saying wild boar is simultaneously a yummy meal and a great brag at dinner parties. Being able to brag about having eaten wild boar seems to me to be worth the effort to find and eat wild boar. Imagine being invited over to a summer backyard dinner party, and the hosts serve ribs. You can say with complete honesty and total truthfulness, "These ribs are great, but it's difficult to compare them with the wild boar I ate this one time at Bruno's." Your friends will marvel at your total truthfulness. Your neighbors will respect your complete honesty. Both your friends and your neighbors will be secretly envious of your wild boar eating experience. Perhaps one of them will take you aside and confess his or her envious feelings, which would make that one of them a rare person amongst your friends and neighbors. This is not to say that the rare person amongst your friends and neighbors is necessarily a better person because he or she is rare. Rather, I'm saying: It's wild boar!

Chapter 7

Southern I-5 and Nearby Cascades

Interstate 5 or I-5 south of Olympia forms something of a corridor through southern western Washington on its way south to Portland. It links up several large and small cities along its way including Centralia, Chehalis, Toledo, Kelso, and Vancouver. The region is mostly flat and open around Centralia and southward for maybe 20nm.

The Cowlitz River, starting up in Riffle Lake south of Morton, initially progresses westward, but once it meets up with the I-5 valley around Vader[98] and Toledo, it turns south. The river and interstate highway follow each other through the valley all the way south to Kelso and the Columbia.

While the I-5 corridor itself is mostly flat, the natural topography of the land around this area seems especially designed to capture nasty weather and hold on to it for a while. When a low pressure area moves inward from the Pacific, gentile southwest winds can often push onshore moisture flow up into and through the Columbia area or across the land toward the north. With the rising Cascade foothills to the east, the clouds can get boxed in between

[98] This is the one and only obligatory reference I'll include in this book to Darth Vader, the namesake of Vader, Washington. I include this footnote for historical reasons, but out of respect for the countless who suffered as a direct result of the Darth Vader administration, I will not mention his name again.

the Morton valley, Toledo, and Vader[99] areas. I've heard many a weather briefer refer to this as the "Toledo gap" where conditions may hold IMC for a bit longer than everywhere else.

The southern Cascades in Washington stick out a bit to the west here, the most notable peak perhaps being Mount Saint Helens at 8,365'.[100] Mount Adams just a bit beyond towers at over 12-thousand feet.

A brief note about mountain flying, given that the last two airports in this section are tucked up into the western slopes of the Cascades: We aviators do not choose to fly because it's perfectly safe. We take calculated risks every time we get into the cockpit.

Mountains can take a soft and consistent breeze and turn it into a rollercoaster of turbulence.[101] They take lazy clouds and turn them into storms. They take happy little trees and throw them thousands of feet into the air, sometimes holding them right in front of you. In short, they're evil; and they're magnificent.

There are old pilots, and there are bold pilots, but there are no old, bold pilots. The old pilot has become old because he or she has sought official weather briefings, crafted flight plans, determined alternate routes and landing options, and followed checklists.[102] Mountain flying with its high peaks of vast nothing is, yes, more risky than flying over flat lands littered with airports. But in much the same was as flying is better than driving, so is mountain flying better than flat-land flying. Know your route, know your risks, know your craft, and know yourself.

[99] Turns out, I can't help myself. Look, look! It's a town with the same name as Darth Vader!

[100] That is to say, this is the height as I observe it while writing this book. Your results may vary. Because, you know, volcano.

[101] As William Shakespeare famously wrote, "There are more wind currents in heaven than on earth, Horacio."

[102] It also helps if you do all the other things your CFIs told you to do.

CLS – Chehalis-Centralia Airport

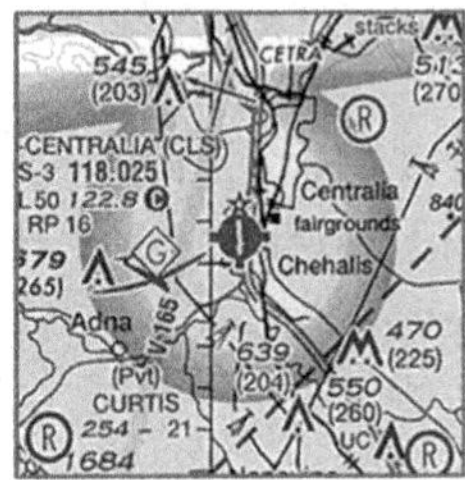

Location: 1 mile west of Chehalis
Coordinates: N46°40.62' / W122°58.96'
Altitude: 177 MSL
Fuel: 100LL (blue), Jet-A
Transient Storage: Tiedowns

The Chehalis-Centralia Airport sits between the twin cities of Chehalis and Centralia.[103] Centralia to the north is home to some 17,000 people, and Chehalis to the south supports about 8,000. Both were incorporated in the 1880s and have an interesting history behind them.

Chehalis was once known as "The Maple-Leaf City" due to the shape of the convergence of the Chehalis River, tributaries, and railroads.

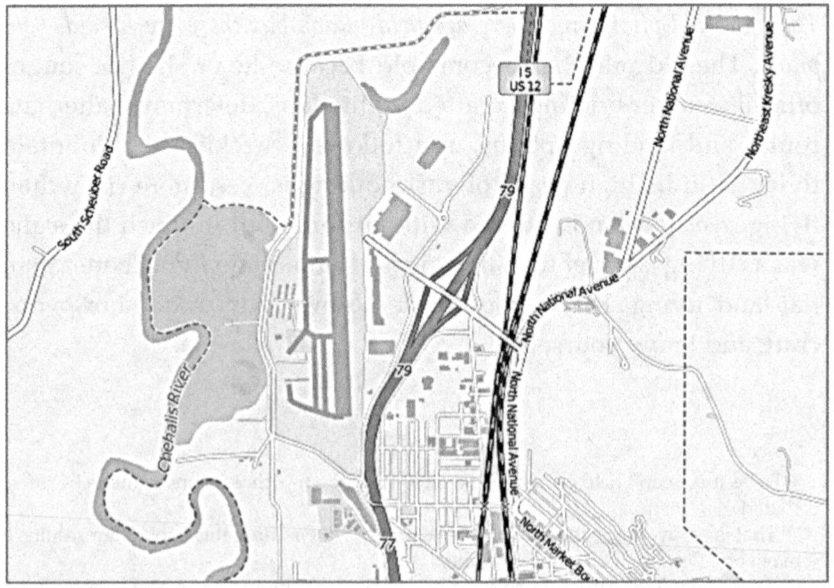

103 Please tell me you weren't surprised by this fact.

Airport Notes

The airport itself sits in a flat, open area with no obstructions and plenty of space. Traffic pattern is always to the west. Just remember to overfly the golf course, where you might get hit with golf balls, instead of over the shopping mall, where you might annoy customers.

Transient parking and fuel is available on the west side toward the south.

Just west of the fuel island is a small pathway that if followed will take you up and over a larger trail running north-south and then to the road that runs between the golf course and the airport. This makes visiting the golf course quite easy.

There's a similar mini-bridge and pathway on the east side leading toward the mall, but it's probably better if you use the courtesy car if you're going that direction.

Transportation

There is a courtesy car available. Call 360-748-1230 to inquire about availability. The FBO can also set you up with a rental car if you're going to be staying a while.

Riverside Golf Club Bistro and Bar

Golf, American (New), Bars
0.3 miles or 6-minute walk
1451 NW Airport Rd, Chehalis, WA 98532
360-748-8182

As mentioned above, getting to the Golf Club Bistro is fairly easy. Just follow the pathway west of the fuel island, cross the road, and you're there.

The food is fairly good, mostly consisting of burgers, sandwiches, "salads," and wraps for lunch. Dinner entrees include ribeye steak, bourbon glazed chicken, and blackened salmon.

There's good wifi and outdoor seating. Prices are slightly high, but it's a golf club bistro, after all.

Mackinaw's Restaurant

American (New)
1.0 miles or 18-minute walk
545 N Market Blvd, Chehalis, WA 98532
360-740-8000

Most everything other than the Golf Club requires a bit of a walk around the southern perimeter of the airport and into the main commercial district. The first among these further away options is Mackinaw's. Follow the airport road until you cross under I-5 and it turns into NW West Street.[104] Follow that a few blocks and you'll end up at Mackinaw's.

[104] Yes, that's "North West West Street." I'm not making that up.

The food and ambiance here are wonderful. Brick walls and lots of seating available. The menu changes daily.

Market Street Pub & Grill

Pubs, American (Traditional), Cocktail Bars
1.0 miles or 19-minute walk
523 N Market Blvd, Chehalis, WA 98532
360-748-6777

Close by to Mackinaw's is the Market Street Pub and Grill. This is a more casual place with burgers, sandwiches, and fish. There's good wifi. There's tiny bit of outdoor seating, but it's not exactly worth the effort. The staff are all quite friendly. The tater tots are great.

The Shire Bar & Bistro

Beer, Wine & Spirits, American (Traditional), Seafood
1.0 miles or 20-minute walk
465 NW Chehalis Ave, Chehalis, WA 98532
360-748-3720

The Shire is half-a-block south of the Market Street Pub. The inside will take you back in time. It's classy yet comfortable and casual. The food is excellent. This place can prepare a killer breaded catfish along with "shire cake" (a fried potato pancake, more or less). Smoked pheasant, crab stuffed halibut, and a wide variety of other perfectly designed plates await you at The Shire.

Things to Do

Lewis County Historical Museum

Museums
0.9 miles or 18-minute walk
599 NW Front Way, Chehalis, WA 98532
360-748-0831

After you finish a meal at any of the restaurants listed above (except for the bistro at the golf course), you'll be nearly next door to the Lewis County Historical Museum.

The Museum is right next to the railroad tracks. It's located in the historic 1912 Northern Pacific Railway depot. The museum offers interesting displays depicting the early settlements and pioneer life in Lewis County.

The Museum is also the starting point for the Historic Chehalis Downtown Walking Tour.

Overnight Lodging

Holiday Inn Express & Suites

Venues & Event Spaces, Hotels
1.1 miles or 20-minute walk
730 NW Liberty Plz, Chehalis, WA 98532
360-740-1800

From the airport, follow the airport road southeast onto NW West Street, then make your way south past NW St Helens Avenue and cross Prindle Street. There you'll find the Holiday Inn.

This is a pretty typical high-quality Holiday Inn. The rooms are nice, the staff are friendly and professional, and the wifi works reasonably well.

TDO – Ed Carlson Memorial Field

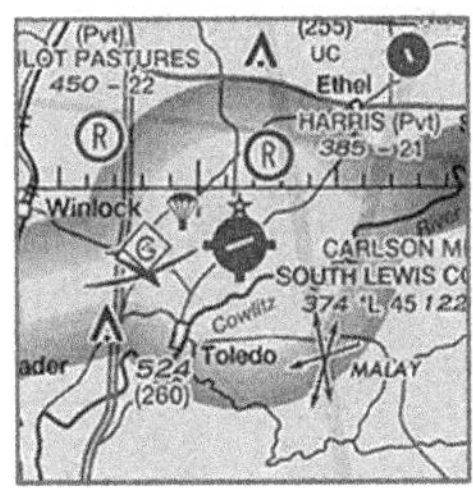

Location: 3 miles north of Toledo
Coordinates: N46°28.63' / W122°48.39'
Altitude: 374 MSL
Fuel: 100LL (blue)
Transient Storage: Tiedowns

Toledo is a very small town, supporting only about 725 people. There are a handful of things to do there, but the town is 3 miles from the airport, so it's a bit far for a short walk.

The airport itself sports a surprisingly large and well-crafted runway, despite its proximity to almost nothing.[105] It's got a few names including: Ed Carlson Memorial Field, South Lewis County Airport, and Toledo Airport.

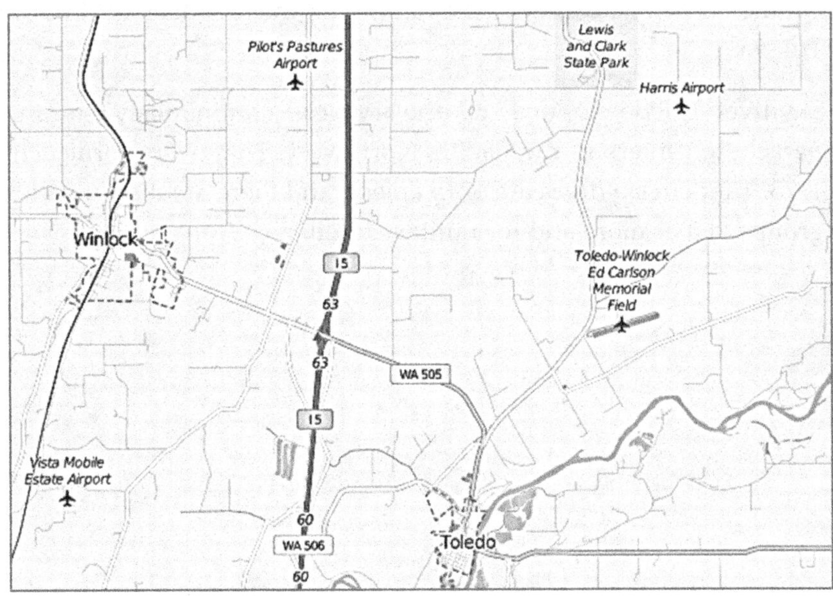

105 That is to say, nothing of commercial visiting interests. The homes off Skyhawk Drive are quite nice, and I'd consider myself blessed to own a property there.

Airport Notes

There are no obstacles of note near the airport, and the runway is extraordinarily easy to spot.

Fuel and transient parking are toward the western end. If you're going to stay for a bit, park in the grass that's just off the ramp toward the runway. There are several tie-down spots.

Things to Do

Skydive Toledo ✈

Skydiving
0.3 miles or 6-minute walk
5239 Jackson Hwy, Toledo, WA 98591
360-864-2230

On the northwest corner of the ramp with the fuel dock is Skydive Toledo.

Skydive Toledo is one of the longest continuously-running parachute centers in the Pacific Northwest. They were formed in 1973. Tandem skydives are $215 apiece, and there are discounts for groups of 5 or more and for military families.

KLS – Southwest WA Regional Airport

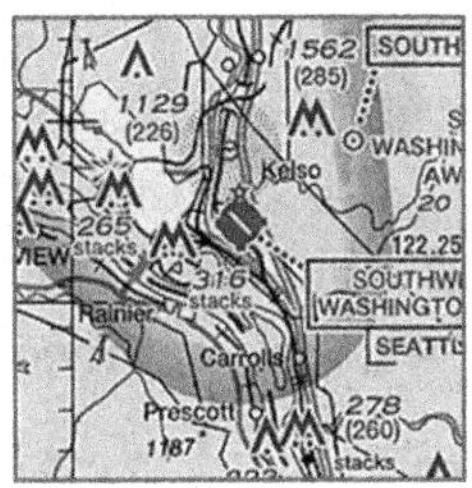

Location: 2 miles southeast of Kelso
Coordinates: N46°7.08' / W122°53.90'
Altitude: 20 MSL
Fuel: 100LL (blue), Jet-A
Transient Storage: Tiedowns

Kelso has a long and storied history. It was founded by a Scottish surveyor in 1847, and it was later incorporated in 1889. In its early days, Kelso obtained the nickname "Little Chicago" as it became famous for its large number of taverns and brothels that catered to local loggers. The FBI finally forced the mayor to shut them down in the 1950s with the last closing in the mid-1960s.

The economy continues to be based largely on wood products. Sitting on the junction of the Cowlitz and Columbia rivers, Kelso is an obvious keystone for visual aviators.

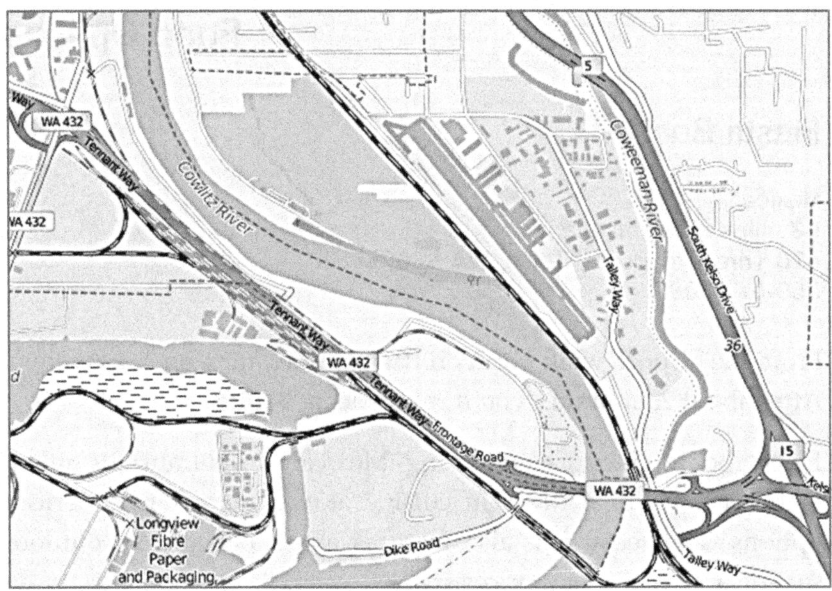

Airport Notes

The airport is easy to spot being just 1.8nm northeast of the Columbia and Cowlitz river junction. The airport is situated on the eastern shore of the Cowlitz, between the river and I-5. Although there is a mild rise in terrain toward the east and some hills to the southeast, there are not real obstructions or terrain to be concerned about when maneuvering.

Traffic pattern is always to the west of the field, over the river.

Transient parking is midfield to the east. The fuel dock is in front of the FBO, wedged between it and the primary taxiway.

Transportation

If you need to get around town, the FBO can set you up with a rental. Alternatively, call Owl Taxi at 360-577-6777 or Uptown Taxi at 360-577-8294.

Food Options

Fiesta Bonita

Mexican
1.3 miles or 25-minute walk
420 Three Rivers Dr, Kelso, WA 98626
360-577-9087

From the airport, walk north on Parrott Way, then on 13th Avenue. After about 25 minutes, you'll reach Fiesta Bonita.

Fiesta Bonita is a casual-dining Mexican restaurant. Its menu features traditional Mexican cuisine as well as a few American options. The restaurant also features a full bar and an outdoor seating area. The menu prices are at an average price point between

$11 and $30. Fiesta Bonita offers a take-out menu but not delivery services. They also have available space for large group dining as well as offering pre-booked reservations.

Fiesta Bonita is a family-friendly dining environment set in a traditional Mexican/Aztec style building.

Izzy's

Buffets, Pizza, Salad
1.5 miles or 29-minute walk
1001 Grade St, Kelso, WA 98626
360-578-1626

In the same area as Fiesta Bonita, just past the Three Rivers Mall, is Izzy's.

They serve some of the best food in town and their staff is very well trained to make sure you enjoy your meal. They will go out of their way to make sure it is an enjoyable time for you, and there are many cool people to hang out here so you will enjoy your stay.

Things to Do

Gearhart Gardens Off-Leash Dog Park

Dog Parks
0.7 miles or 13-minute walk
200 Freedom Rd, Longview, WA 98632

Gearhart Gardens Off-Leash Dog Park is a 3-acre fenced dog park that is quaintly located on the river. As the name indicates, dogs are able to get exercise on a large grassy area without being leashed. The park includes small pools and water hoses for the dogs to cool off on a hot summer day. Included within the park is a separate park specifically for small dogs and shaded benches for dog owners to relax on while their dogs exercise. The operating hours are sunrise to sunset, although the park may occasionally be closed for rain or maintenance.

Overnight Lodging

Comfort Inn Kelso - Longview

Hotels
1.4 miles or 26-minute walk
440 Three Rivers Dr., Kelso, WA 98626
360-425-4600

The Comfort Inn is located between the Three Rivers Mall and the Cowlitz River. They are competitive in their prices for comparable locations and offers a two story building full of comfortable and clean rooms. It's a good location that's accessible at night to the late night traveler who didn't make reservations ahead of time.

This is a smoke-free environment, which makes it great for families with children. This hotel offers a continental breakfast like no other and at no additional cost. The breakfast included eggs, waffles, sausage, hard boiled eggs, and more. The staff is friendly, and there is a 24-hour pool with hot tub.

Guesthouse Inn & Suites

Hotels
1.6 miles or 30-minute walk
501 Three Rivers Dr, Kelso, WA 98626
360-414-5953

The Guesthouse Inn & Suites is located northeast of the Three Rivers Mall. The staff are helpful, and the rooms and common areas are spacious and accommodating. The place is clean and inviting. The service is good.

Super 8 Kelso Longview Area

Hotels
1.6 miles or 31-minute walk
250 Kelso Dr., Kelso, WA 98626
800-536-9326

The Super 8 motel in Kelso is located just off I-5. The motel offers rooms with one queen bed, two queen beds, or a king bed. Room rates include good wifi. Complimentary continental breakfast includes cereal, bagels, yogurt, boiled eggs, and fresh fruit. The motel has an indoor pool and Jacuzzi. The motel is pet-friendly.

W27 – Woodland State Airport

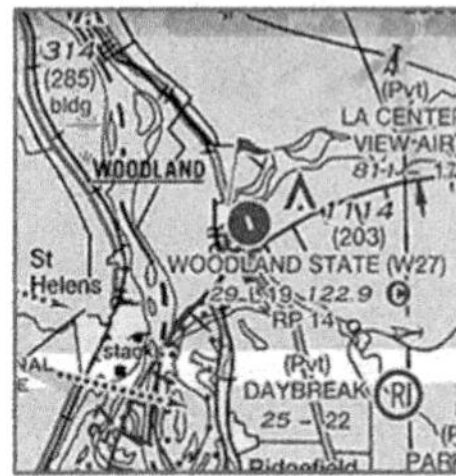

Location: 1 mile southeast of Woodland
Coordinates: N45°53.93' / W122°44.24'
Altitude: 29 MSL
Fuel: None
Transient Storage: Tiedowns

Woodland, Washington is a small town of about 6,000 situated along I-5 where the Lewis River turns south to parallel the freeway for a bit before joining up with the Columbia. The town was incorporated in 1906, but settlement dates back to the 1850s.

Woodland hosts "Planter's Day," which was first held in 1922 and is the longest continuously running civic celebration and community festival in the State of Washington.

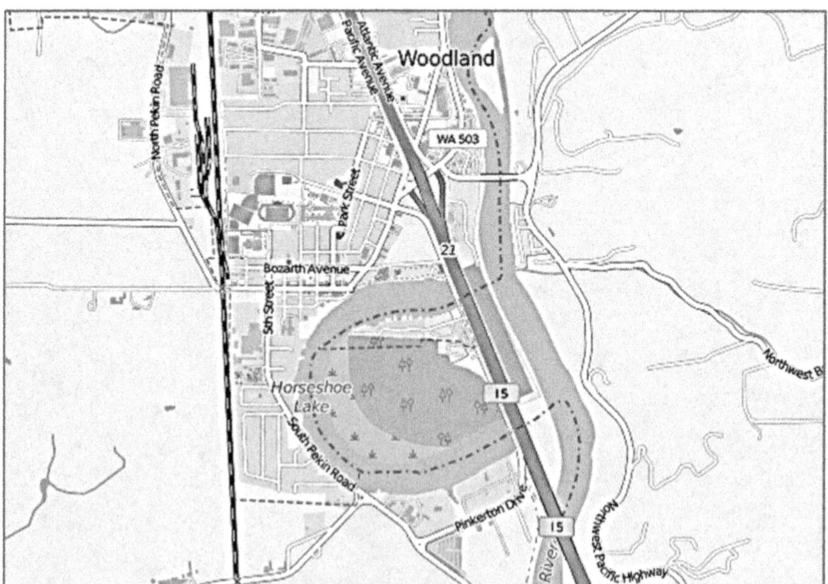

Airport Notes

This airport is a bit scary to use, so proceed with care and caution, but it's also is a thrill. At less than 2,000′, the runway doesn't offer much forgiveness for excess speed on landing or an imperfect takeoff.

As you approach, look for Horseshoe Lake, a horseshoe-looking half-circle lake that's immediately west of I-5 and Lewis River. The airport is immediately to the east of I-5, wedged between it and the Lewis River.

Traffic pattern is always to the west of the field, essentially over I-5 or perhaps slightly beyond. If landing to the north, note the hill and cliff on final that's right next to the bridge along I-5.

The runway sits on what feels like sunken land compared to its surroundings. I-5 borders the west, which is raised up. To the north is a similar rise in the land. To the south is a turn in the river, and the whole eastern side of the airport is lined with tall trees.

Transient parking is on the north end of the field near the west side.

Food Options

Old Town Grill

Diners, Breakfast & Brunch, Bars
0.5 miles or 10-minute walk
128 Davidson Ave, Woodland, WA 98674
360-225-5649

From the field, walk north to Lewis River Road, then cross under I-5. Continue on Goerig Street for a bit, and you'll find the Old Town Grill off Davidson.

This grill is a home-style cooking location with a huge variety of food including hamburgers, prime rib, "salads," chicken, and more. They also have a large bar in the back with lots of sports on TV. All of the food is based on homemade recipes from the owners and their families and friends. This place also has a horseradish sauce usable in almost any type of food and enjoyed. It's quite popular.

Los Pepe's

Mexican
0.5 miles or 8-minute walk
611 Goerig St, Woodland, WA 98674
360-225-7753

Nearby The Old Town Grill is Los Pepe's, a family-owned Mexican restaurant. People describe them as being authentic and friendly. Their quick service is also another highlight of this place. Their seafood enchilada is considered one of the best around. Customers love coming in for the chips and salsa, and the large drinks they offer is a plus. They are respected by customers for providing great service and remembering repeat customers. This is a friendly and welcoming restaurant for anyone who wants to enjoy a real taste of Mexico.

America's Family Diner

American (Traditional), Breakfast & Brunch, Caterers
0.9 miles or 17-minute walk
1447 N Goerig St, Woodland, WA 98674
360-225-3962

If you're looking for a long walk along the Lewis River, then America's Family Diner might be the right pick. From the airport, walk north, then follow Lewis River Road north until you reach the diner.

The diner is mostly known for their breakfast offerings. Many people say this business's egg dishes are quite excellent. All dishes have fresh ingredients, and seasonings are such that they bring out the flavors of the food. The service is outstanding, friendly, welcoming, and professional. The portion sizes are very generous. They also have discounts for military.

China Garden Restaurant

Chinese
0.6 miles or 11-minute walk
265 Millard Ave, Woodland, WA 98674
360-225-1818

China Garden Restaurant is a relatively unknown gem. It's located a few streets away from the heart of town and has a local, hole-in-the-wall charm. They always have plenty of choices. There's something for everyone, and the portions are generous, which makes this place such a good value. During the daytime, the lunch specials make that value even better. Dine in and takeout are both quick and easy. Service is good and the owner is friendly. China Garden Restaurant isn't fancy, but it's full of character and has a loyal following.

Burgerville

Burgers, Fast Food
0.6 miles or 12-minute walk
1120 Lewis River Rd, Woodland, WA 98674
360-225-7965

Burgerville is located on Lewis River Road, north of the airport.

Sometimes you just can't beat a good burger. You can go to the nicest five star restaurant in the world and still be in the mood to have a burger. Reportedly, the best burger in town is at Burgerville. It may not have the ambience of that five-star restaurant, but it is a relaxing place to enjoy your burger. They also have some of the best fries you will ever eat.

Casa Tapatia

Mexican
0.6 miles or 12-minute walk
1175 Lewis River Rd, Woodland, WA 98674
360-225-3104

This restaurant is a Mexican restaurant where they cook home-made meals for the public at reasonable prices. This place is mostly known for their "worldwide famous" fajitas which are seasoned to perfection and handled delicately. This place also has a dance floor.[106] The staff is also very nice. Their bean-dip is also "famously known" to be boarding on perfection.

Things to Do

Lucky 21 Casino

Casinos
0.6 miles or 12-minute walk
1020 Atlantic Ave, Woodland, WA 98674
360-841-8567

After having taken on some risk and gambled with your life to fly into Woodland Airport, it may be fitting to consider taking on more risk and gambling some of your hard-earned money at the Lucky 21 Casino, located off the north end of the runway on the other side of 503.

Lucky 21 Casino is a full service casino and a great restaurant that has everything from American to Chinese and authentic

[106] No, I can't dance. I can't sing. Please don't ask me. Only thing about me is the way I walk.

Vietnamese. The games are fun and the dealers are friendly in this cozy casino. In the lounge, you can enjoy drinks and food specials almost every night of the week. It is a non-smoking facility so playing your hand and enjoying your complimentary hot pot can be done without the cloud of smoke typical in many casinos. Enjoy monthly tournaments, daily lunch specials, and even shuffle board games. They also have a full size pool table in the restaurant area.

Overnight Lodging

Lewis River Inn

Hotels
0.6 miles or 11-minute walk
1100 Lewis River Road, Woodland, WA 98674
360-225-6257

The Lewis River Inn is a family owned motel featuring both regular and riverfront rooms. It's located north of the airport along Lewis River Road.

All riverfront rooms have private balconies with chairs that overlook either the garden or river and king size beds. Regular guest rooms include a queen size bed, reclining chair, good wifi, hair dryer, microwave, coffee maker, and refrigerator. Certain rooms are pet friendly and can be rented for an additional fee. All guests have access to the included continental breakfast in the lobby.

Best Western Woodland Inn

Hotels
0.8 miles or 16-minute walk
1380 Atlantic Ave, Woodland, WA 98674

The Woodland Washington Best Western[107] is a clean and comfortable hotel. The rooms are spacious and the staff is friendly and helpful. The rooms are well kept and quiet, perfect for a peaceful stay. The breakfast is also really good. This Best Western also has a pool and Jacuzzi. This hotel is a great value for all that you get.

Lewis River Bed & Breakfast

Hotels, Bed & Breakfast
2.3 miles or 44-minute walk
2339 Lewis River Rd, Woodland, WA 98674
360-225-8630

Lewis River Bed and Breakfast is a quaint five bedroom bed and breakfast adjacent to the river. The property features five rooms with numerous amenities including high speed internet, TV, private bathrooms (some of which include jetted tubs), and exterior decks.

Hairdryers and robes are provided for no additional cost. A home-style breakfast, snacks, and beverages are served to all guests. Meals can be enjoyed in either a common room or a 60 foot deck that overlooks the river. Wine tours can also be arranged upon request.

---

[107] YABW: Yet Another Best Western.

VUO – Pearson Field Airport

Location: 2 miles southwest of Vancouver
Coordinates: N45°37.23' / W122°39.39'
Altitude: 28 MSL
Fuel: 100LL (blue)
Transient Storage: Tiedowns

Pearson Field is the oldest continuously operating airfield in the Pacific Northwest and one of the two oldest continuously operating airfields in the United States, receiving recognition in 2012 as an American Institute of Aeronautics and Astronautics historic aerospace site.

It's also the only airport in the United States that operates totally within the boundaries of a national historic reserve. It resides within the Fort Vancouver site, originally an important 19th century fur trading outpost established in 1824.

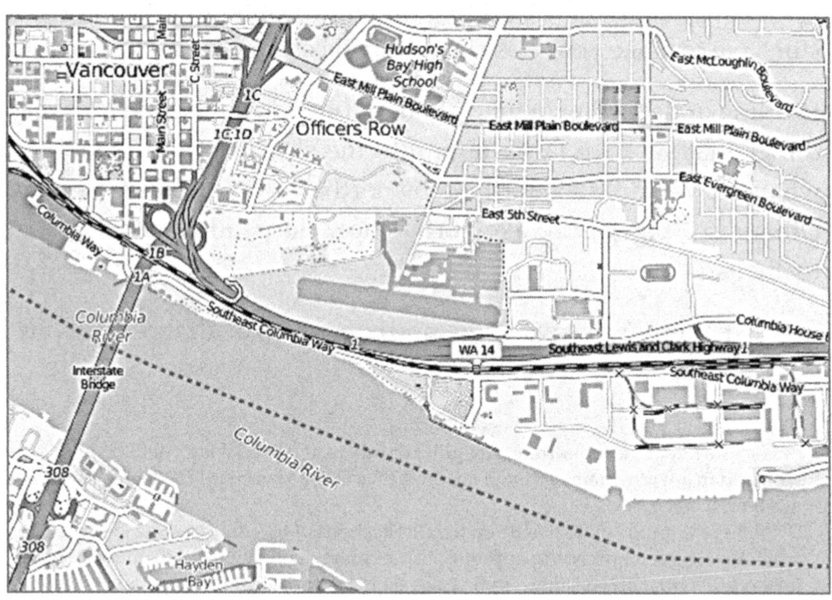

Airport Notes

The first and perhaps most important think to consider when flying in or out of Pearson is its proximity to Portland International. The eastern end of Pearson's runway is less than 2nm from the western end of PDX's 13R/31L. PDX's class C airspace covers over Pearson like a warm blanket.[108] The class C over Pearson descends all the way down to 1,100′ MSL.

The other thing to consider is that the airspace directly over Pearson is class D, but Pearson has no tower.[109]

The PDX Approach controllers are friendly, helpful, and professional. So typically, if flying VFR, it's easiest to get clearance into PDX's class C and ask for a transition. Just be prepared to juggle a few things quickly. Cockpit resource management, and all that jazz.

If you're going to be grumpy and not want to talk to Approach, you could fly in low over Vancouver Lake. Stay well below 1,800′ MSL. Then drop below 1,100′ before you enter Pearson's class D. You'll still have to make your class D radio call before you enter it, though.

Landing or departing in this way does put you quite close to several things that stick up fairly high into the sky. Don't hit them. And whatever you do, stay north of the northern shore of the Columbia. Otherwise, big jets. Wake turbulence. Suspended privileges. A really bad day.

Traffic pattern is always to the north, because of all those reasons I just discussed.

108 For some, that's a comforting thought. For others, it's like saying you'll be wrapped in a warm blanket as you lay on the San Diego beach in 104-degree sunny weather. It can get hot.

109 I'll leave it up to you to decide on the implications of this, since for me to say anything official might not be appropriate. Let's just say that when I fly into any non-towered airport, I always make radio calls. At Pearson, I consider these radio communications mandatory.

Note the rather significant displaced threshold on 26. Despite the fact that you need to stay low, don't stray too low and hit the building just past the end of the runway to the east.

Transient parking is inside a yellow box east of the FBO and fuel dock. The fuel dock is on the southwest side of the FBO.

Transportation

Uber and Lyft coverage here is quite good. You usually won't have to wait much more than a couple minutes for your ride. Alternatively, the FBO can set you up with a rental.

Food Options

Beaches Restaurant & Bar

Seafood
0.4 miles or 8-minute walk
1919 SE Columbia River Dr, Vancouver, WA 98661
360-699-1592

Beaches is fairly close to the airport, but it takes a bit of wandering to walk there. You have to exit off the airport property to the north, then follow East 5th Street until you get to Grand. Head south, then west, and follow the road until you get to the river.

There are quite a number of great restaurants around Vancouver, and Beaches is definitely in the top tier. They have a lengthy drink selection and a big menu with a large variety of different foods to choose from. They take great pride in making sure that the meals they serve are high-quality.

McMenamin's on the Columbia

American (Traditional), Pubs, Breweries
0.4 miles or 7-minute walk
1801 SE Columbia River Dr., Vancouver, WA 98661
360-699-1521

In the same area as Beaches is McMenamin's. It serves American and pub fare such as sandwiches and burgers, and it's is classified as a mid-price restaurant with meal prices ranging from $11 to $30. It serves lunch, dinner, and dessert, operating from 11am every day to late in the evening. There is a happy hour and the restaurant also offers outdoor seating. While the restaurant does not offer delivery, it does offer takeout. It is a casual atmosphere that also caters to children, and there's also a full bar.

Mama's Kitchen

American (Traditional), Comfort Food
0.8 miles or 15-minute walk
611 Main St, Vancouver, WA 98660
360-597-3260

After departing the airport property, turn west along East 5th Street, then turn north on Fort Vancouver Way. You'll be able to cross under I-5 using Evergreen, then make your way south to Main Street. There, you'll find Mama's Kitchen.

Mama's Kitchen is a Southern style restaurant located right in the center of downtown. The ambiance makes it feel just like walking into a home in New Orleans. The owner treats you like family making it feel more like it really is your Mama's Kitchen. The restaurant is open 7 days a week from 9 am to 9 pm. It serves breakfast, lunch, and dinner. Breakfast is available all day. There is mention of catering on the website, but call ahead to confirm. Entrees range from a grilled cheese sandwich, to fried catfish and chicken. If you really want to dive deep into the South, you can try the frog legs.

Willem's On Main

French, Italian, Breakfast & Brunch
0.9 miles or 17-minute walk
907 Main St, Vancouver, WA 98660
360-258-0989

Just north up on Main from Mama's is Willem's. Willem's On Main is a neighborhood restaurant in the heart of historic downtown Vancouver. Here you can enjoy homemade meals that will amaze.

Service and cleanliness of the restaurant is good as well is the friendly and knowledgeable service given. The Chef is a native from the Netherlands and brought his European influence to Portland's Pearl District in 1998 and then established a restaurant that is extremely successful.

Lapellah Restaurant & Bar

American (Traditional)
0.6 miles or 12-minute walk
Grand Central Station, 2520 Columbia House Blvd, Ste 108, Vancouver, WA 98661
360-828-7911

Lapellah Restaurant & Bar is a moderately expensive restaurant, locally-owned, and advertises its sustainable approach to cooking. Ingredients are sourced from local farms in the area. The restaurant is open for brunch, lunch, and dinner. It also has a happy hour.

The business advertises its artisanal cocktails and wood-fired food. Along with this, they offer the "Chief's Counter" for parties of four or less. This allows patrons to watch the chefs prepare their meals. The "Chef's Counter" has to be reserved ahead of time. There is also a communal table that can seat up to twenty. Lapellah also offers outside eating.

Things to Do

Pearson Air Museum

Museums
0.2 miles or 4-minute walk
1115 E 5th St, Vancouver, WA 98661
360-816-6232

As you leave the airport property, you'll walk past the Pearson Air Museum, located on the west side of the road. It's in a set of buildings with painted yellow and black checker roofs.

Admission is free, and the museum is in great shape with a lot to offer packed into a tiny space. Everything is well documented. There are great interactive displays for children from toy planes to play on to landing a wooden plane on an aircraft carrier. The old hangar that houses the collection is itself interesting.

On the way down to the smaller hangar, non-pilots should stop by the flight center and take a seat at the flight simulators and try flying a Cessna 172 or a Boeing 747.

North Bank Artists Gallery

Art Galleries, Community Service/Non-Profit
0.9 miles or 17-minute walk
1005 Main St, Vancouver, WA 98660
360-693-1840

The North Bank Artists Gallery is a non-profit gallery that features mostly contemporary artists. The gallery is open Wednesday through Saturday from 11:00am until 4:30pm. They are closed Sunday, Monday, and Tuesday. Visitors are welcome to walk around and view the art in the gallery, and if they choose, they may buy a piece to take home. Being in the heart of the Art's District, this is a great place to visit on First Friday's Art Walk.

Magenta Theater Company

Performing Arts
1.0 miles or 19-minute walk
1108 Main St, Vancouver, WA 98660
360-635-4358

The Magenta Theater Company is an all-volunteer run community theater. The theater includes a multitude of events ranging from storytelling events to improvisation shows interspersed between their larger scale productions. Tickets are available at the box office and can be purchased online. They also offer season tickets at a few levels for discounted prices.

The theater also prides itself on offering acting classes for all ages and takes a real stand in supporting their community. The theater holds open auditions for their productions and a schedule for those auditions can be found on their website. They accept donations and volunteers for all areas of the theater experience.

Source Climbing Center

Climbing
1.0 miles or 19-minute walk
1118 Main St, Vancouver, WA 98660
360-694-9096

Source Climbing Center is a great way to stretch your legs between flights. You will have a great time learning how to climb and mastering your new craft.

Clark County Historical Museum

Museums
1.1 miles or 21-minute walk
1511 Main St, Vancouver, WA 98660
360-993-5679

The Clark County Historical Museum is dedicated to cataloging, preserving and displaying the cultural history of the Pacific Northwest. The museum has existed in one form or another for nearly 100 years, making it a piece of living history as well as a place to display history.

The museum contains a wide array of exhibits, including artifacts dating back to the 13th century. Numerous events are hosted at the museum, with workshops and walking tours being the most common.

The museum is open from Tuesday through Saturday, 11am to 4pm. Admission is $4 for adults, $3 for seniors and students, $2 for children, and $10 for families. Guided group tours are also available for groups of 5 or more.

Waterfront Renaissance Trail

Parks
0.3 miles or 5-minute walk
115 Columbia Way, Vancouver, WA 98661
360-487-8311

The Waterfront Renaissance Trail is a walking path along the beautiful Columbia River. It is a 5 mile trail connecting two parks. This trail is perfect for walking, jogging, biking, or rollerblading. While you walk the trail, you can stop at any number of shops, restaurants, and bars that run parallel to the trail. The trail includes a beautiful view of two bridges that go over the water. The trail also has beautiful vegetation along the way.

Comfort Inn & Suites

Hotels
0.9 miles or 16-minute walk
401 E 13th Street, Vancouver, WA 98660
360-696-0411

Comfort Inn & Suites in located near I-5. It's a pet-friendly hotel with good-quality wifi, as well as a hot breakfast and free coffee service. Check-in starts at 3pm; check-out is at noon, giving guests plenty of time to get some rest in the available queen and king sized beds. There's a seasonal pool and exercise room for added convenience.

Hilton Vancouver

Hotels
0.9 miles or 17-minute walk
301 W 6th St, Vancouver, WA 98660
360-993-4500

The Hilton is a seven story building modeled after the convention center of the city. It's in a great location overlooking the Colombia River. The staff here are friendly and welcoming. The hotel offers amenities such as wifi and free underground parking as well as an indoor pool and a large fitness center.

Breakfast is served to order rather than a choosing from a buffet. The rooms are a great size and they are clean and updated.

39P – Strom Field Airport

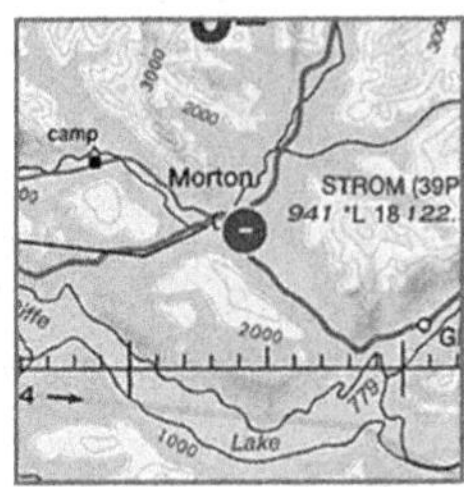

Location: 0 miles southeast of Morton
Coordinates: N46°33.02' / W122°16.00'
Altitude: 941 MSL
Fuel: None
Transient Storage: Tiedowns

Morton is a small town, home to about 1,200 people, located north of Riffe Lake at the intersection of highways 12, 508, and 7. From an aviation perspective, it sits at the entrance to a long channel through the Cascades that progresses along highway 12 through Packwood.

Morton was first settled in 1871 and was incorporated in 1913. Historic sources of revenue included logging, harvesting of cascara bark, and mining for mercury ore in local mines.

Morton has played host to the The Loggers Jubilee annually since the 1930s.

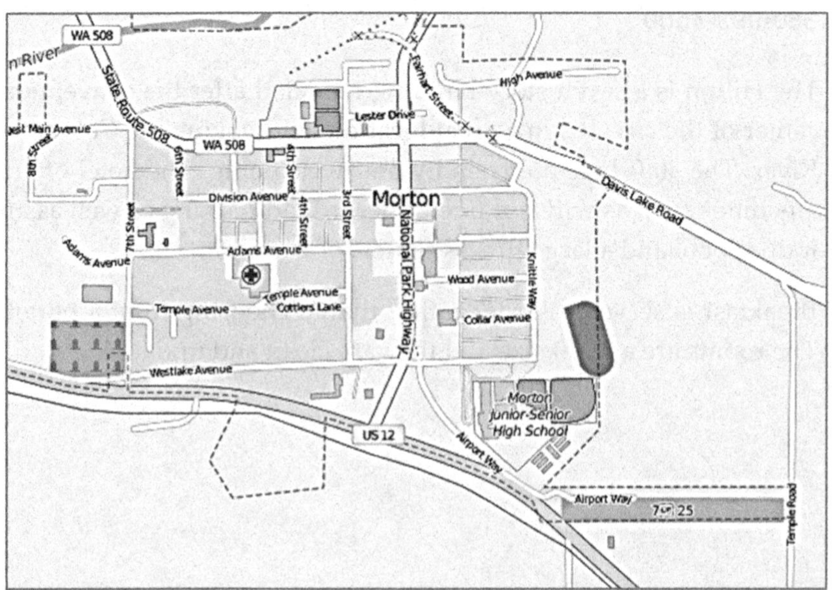

Airport Notes

Morton sits basically in the center of 4 valleys, or rather 2 valleys that intersect. The airport is on the southeast of town, and it's tucked up near one of the edges of one of the valleys. As such, there are quite a few things to consider when approaching. First and most obvious is the very tall ridge that runs from south of the airfield in a northwesterly direction. At its top is Cottlers Rock at over 2,700' MSL. That's about an 1,800-foot jump up from the airport elevation, and the ridge begins its rise about a thousand feet from the runway.

Given the high hills to the north and west of Morton, you'll likely encounter a strong wind flowing southwest down the valley. Expect a crosswind every time, most likely a right crosswind when you come around for 25.

Technically, if you're departing on 25, you should make a left turn for a standard pattern.[110] There are displaced thresholds at both ends of the runway due to the roads just beyond.

Transient parking can be found just to the west end of the row of hangars near the west end of the runway, north side.

Food Options

Spiffy Dine In Drive In

American (New), Burgers, Sandwiches
0.4 miles or 7-minute walk
104 W Lake, Morton, WA 98356
360-496-5472

From the airport, just follow Airport Drive in a semi-circle arc for less than half a mile, and you'll end up at this joint.

[110] Personally, I'd likely not fly this if the crosswinds were strong. I'd try for a right pattern if there weren't other airplanes in the area.

The Spiffy Dine In Drive In is a 1950s-inspired boutique diner offering walk-up, drive-in, and traditional dining services, both indoor and outdoor. The diner specializes in the All-American experience, serving burgers, a variety of sandwiches, milkshakes, ice cream, as well as a fresh "salad" bar and food buffet.

Spiffy's caters to patrons of all ages and any occasion. All food is homemade and cooked to order, served in generous portions. The delicious food coupled with great value and quality staff, makes the experience at this diner one to remember.

Cody Café

Diners
0.7 miles or 13-minute walk
216 Main Ave, Morton, WA 98356
360-496-5787

Cody Café is conveniently located on Main Avenue in the heart of downtown Morton. Look no further because this classic American diner has it all. Serving a full breakfast menu and plenty of delicious lunch options, everyone's tastes are sure to be satisfied. Bring the whole family, because the kids will love the home-style cooking. Order the enormous pancakes and French toast and relax at the counter or at a table or booth setting.

Things to Do

Roxy Theater

Cinema, Performing Arts
0.7 miles or 13-minute walk
233 W Main St, Morton, WA 98356
360-496-0541

The Roxy is a theater with an old time feel and low prices. The theater is only opened during the weekend, and it only shows on a single screen. Concessions prices are cheap. The outside of the movie theater has an old time look to it. There are wooden chairs with cushions inside; very old school.

Overnight Lodging

Seasons Motel

Hotels
0.5 miles or 10-minute walk
200 Westlake Ave, Morton, WA 98356
360-496-6835

The Seasons Motel is to the west of highway 7 off Westlake, not far beyond where Airport Way meets Westlake.

The staff is quite friendly and helpful. This hotel is nice, and it's accommodating to people with pets. Despite allowing pets, the place is very clean and comfortable. It's nothing special, but it'll do if you're overnighting in Morton. It's not particularly expensive either. The hotel offers good wifi. They serve breakfast in the morning, and coffee makers are in the rooms.

55S – Packwood Airport

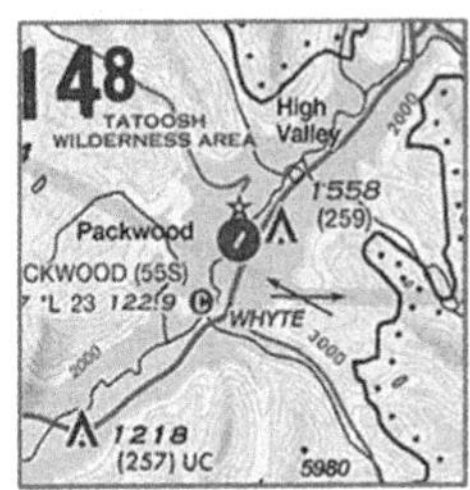

Location: 0 miles west of Packwood
Coordinates: N46°36.25' / W121°40.67'
Altitude: 1057 MSL
Fuel: None
Transient Storage: Tiedowns

Packwood is tucked up close to the end of a channel valley that cuts through the western side of the Cascades south of Rainier. It's located at the intersection of US Highway 12 and Gifford Pinchot National Forest Road 52. A small town of only about 1,400 people, Packwood is surrounded by natural beauty.

Packwood's remote location and small town charm appeal to the visitor who's looking for a wonderful place to relax and refresh. Scenic beauty and recreational opportunities include hiking, fishing, bird and wildlife watching, skiing, and camping.

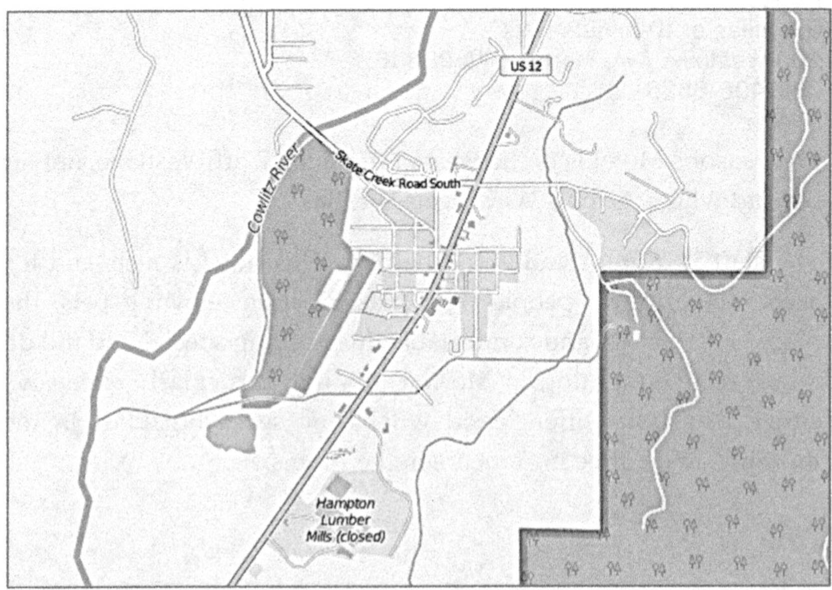

Airport Notes

Although there are tall mountains all around you, they're sufficiently far from the airport as to be of little concern. Winds at altitude are squirrely, but down toward the ground they get more predictable.

The runway itself is not exactly in the best of condition, but it's perfectly usable. If you're landing 19, note the road that at one point is only 140 feet from the end of the runway. Maybe come in a bit steeper than usual, and keep an eye out for cars. Landing on runway 1, it's not quite as bad. The road down there is a dirt road about 220 feet from the runway, but it's seldom used.

The ground on either side of the runway can be quite soft, so use the runway to back-taxi. Transient parking is on the north end toward the east side.

Most everything in town is right on highway 12, a short 950 feet from where you park your airplane.

Food Options

Cliff Droppers

Burgers, Hot Dogs, Sandwiches
0.2 miles or 4-minute walk
12968 US Hwy 12, Packwood, WA 98361
360-494-2055

Cliff Droppers offers American style fare specializing in the ever classic staples burgers and hot dogs. For cravings of a full Americana experience, Cliff Droppers offers locally loved hand mixed milk shakes.

The atmosphere is family friendly but also versatile, serving beer and wine for the adults. The restaurant is a frequent stop for hikers, visitors, and locals alike. Although most notorious for their burgers, the menu is also able to cater to people with vegetarian interests. The establishment is also known for using fresh ingredients and serving above average portions. The inside of the building promotes a casual eating environment, and ski related pictures adorn the walls along with other local scenic images. A more eclectic and unusual item on the menu is the Huckleberry Shake.

Cruisers Pizza

Pizza
0.4 miles or 8-minute walk
13028 Us Hwy 12, Packwood, WA 98361
360-494-5400

A great lunch and dinner spot for the pizza fans. This small mom and pop restaurant has a homely feel to it. The food in this place is great for us over-indulgers. They offer pizza that is thick, cheesy, and so heavy it's hard to lift. The size of the slices are gigantic. They also offer omelets, particularly a western omelet that fills over half the plate and still comes with hash browns.

This is a family friendly location with great parking and accessible for the disabled. The casual setting does offer beer and wine, but nothing else alcoholic.

Blue Spruce Saloon

American (Traditional)
0.4 miles or 7-minute walk
13019 US Hwy 12, Packwood, WA 98361
360-494-5605

The Blue Spruce Saloon is a traditional American restaurant and bar. It's a family friendly location during the day but turns into a drinker's bar as the night progresses. The menu is typical American bar fare. The burgers and wings are some of the locals' favorites. The beer selection is superb and drink prices are quite reasonable.

Dooby's Restaurant

Restaurants
0.3 miles or 6-minute walk
12970 US Hwy 12, Packwood, WA 98361
360-494-8100

Dooby's Restaurant offers home-style cooking in a home-like atmosphere. The rates are reasonable and the portions are large. The restaurant is family owned and operated, obvious by the quality of the food. The porch is the first thing one might notice with its rocking chairs and house cat. The menu options include old favorites and some with creative takes. They offer many dessert choices including homemade hot cocoa. The restaurant can accommodate groups and is child friendly.

Overnight Lodging

Hotel Packwood

Hotels
0.3 miles or 6-minute walk
104 Main St, Packwood, WA 98361
360-494-5431

Similar to a boarding house, this nice hotel has been around since 1912. With an antique personality and a homey feel, the customer service is exceptional from owner Marilyn. The hotel accommodates most everyone with extra features such as wifi, coffee pot, and refrigerator in the room. Rooms are inexpensive, in the range of $45, especially considering Hotel Packwood is in high demand. Some guests have reported elk coming to graze nearby.

Cowlitz River Lodge

Hotels
0.6 miles or 11-minute walk
13069 Us Hwy 12, Packwood, WA 98361
360-494-4444

This is a privately run hotel that offers comfortable and clean rooms and is unique due in large part to the elk that graze on the grass around the hotel. The elk are accustomed to humans being around and pleasant to watch. This hotel also is pet friendly, offers a continental breakfast, and offers good wifi access to guests. The doors to the rooms open to the outside of the building which is especially enjoyable for the guests on the top floor because they are able to see quite a distance. There is a lot of open space surrounding the hotel which may be enjoyed by the guests and the hotel is within walking distance to restaurants. The staff is very friendly and accommodating.

Mt View Lodge

Hotels
1.1 miles or 20-minute walk
13163 Hwy 12, Packwood, WA 98361
360-494-5555

The Mountain View Lodge is a quiet hotel in a wooded setting. The lodge has 23 rooms, which include cabins, kitchen rooms, fireplace rooms, single rooms and double rooms. Adjoining rooms are available for groups. Rooms can be rented nightly or weekly. Lodge amenities include a covered hot tub, a gazebo, a maintained lawn area with picnic tables, breakfast area in the lobby, in room televisions, and good wifi. Certain rooms have kitchens, dining rooms, and bunk beds. Staff will assist with finding outdoor activities, and the lodge itself features scenic views of a nearby mountain. All rooms are non-smoking and no pets are allowed.

Crest Trail Lodge

Hotels
1.1 miles or 21-minute walk
12729 US Highway 12, Packwood, WA 98361
360-494-4140

Crest Trail Lodge is a conveniently located hotel with clean, ample sized rooms and good quality furnishings. The staff is friendly and very accommodating, ensuring that you have whatever you need to make your stay enjoyable. It has reasonable wifi available. The views are nice, and occasionally you'll see the local wildlife wandering through the trees. If you like to travel with your dog, this hotel is pet friendly. A full breakfast is included and you can also opt to have two glasses of wine in the evening.

Chapter 8

Northern I-5, Whidbey, and Loop

The northern I-5 zone, essentially the combined areas of Sedro-Woolley, Arlington, and Whatcom valleys are in every way as beautiful as the lands to the south, but they seem to carry with them a little more "edge" or *je ne sais quoi,* making them unique to fly through and around.

Tucked up tightly to the northern border with Canada are the communities of Lynden, Custer, Birch Bay, Blaine, and Everson, all in the shadow of Bellingham to their south. In the next valley below resides Mt Vernon, La Conner, Burlington, and Conway.

To their west is Whidbey Island, the largest of the islands of Island County, and the largest and longest island in Washington State. It is ranked as the fourth longest and fourth largest island in the contiguous United States.

To the east are the rolling foothills of the Cascades, sticking out into Skagit and northern Snohomish zones. A curious geographical anomaly is a favorite of some aviators. Due to glacier and other river erosion effects, a wide valley loop has formed that links Sedro-Woolley to Concrete to its east, then Darrington to its south, then Arlington to its west. The whole loop is about 90nm, and it takes the aviator through some beautiful countryside surrounded by tall hills thick with trees. Some call it the "Darrington Loop" or the "Cascade Loop" or the "Skagit Loop."

38W – Lynden Airport, Jansen Field

Location: 1 mile north of Lynden
Coordinates: N48°57.35' / W122°27.49'
Altitude: 106 MSL
Fuel: 100LL (blue)
Transient Storage: Tiedowns

Lynden is the second largest city in Whatcom County after Bellingham. It's tucked up near the northern border with Canada and is surrounded by seemingly countless acres of beautiful (and very flat) farm lands.

The town lies in a broad valley along the winding path of the Nooksack River. The surrounding area is filled with dairy, raspberry, strawberry, and blueberry farms. If you're flying below 1,500′ MSL on a summer day, you can smell the dairy farms.[111]

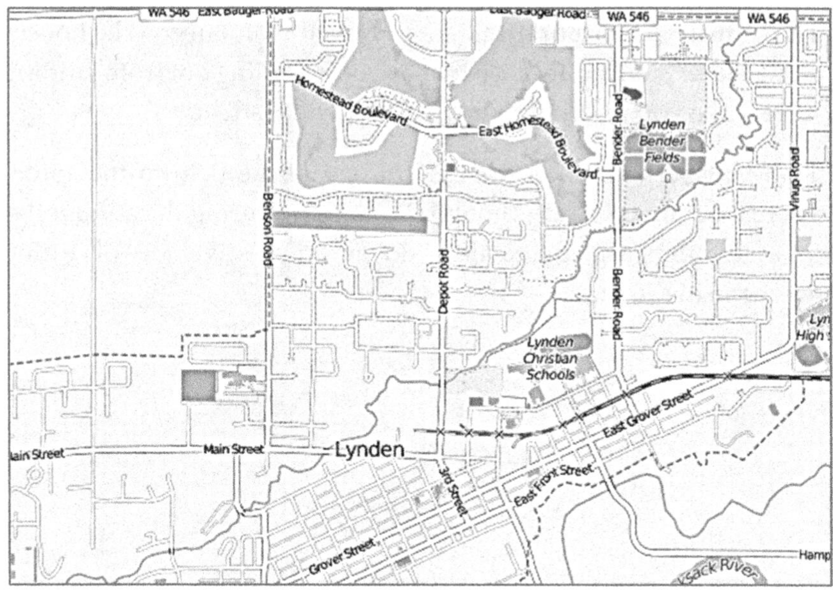

[111] This is one reason why I never fly below 1,500′ MSL in this area except to land.

Airport Notes

Spotting the town of Lynden is fairly easy since it's really the only such city-looking area in the whole valley (apart from Bellingham to the south). Spotting the airport is a bit more tricky as it's tightly packed into a small space between two rows of tall homes. Once you spot the city center, look for large, bright roof tops of the warehouses and schools. From there, look north about 0.5nm and slightly west.

It may be wise to plan on overflying the airport 1,000 feet above pattern altitude to get a good look before joining the pattern.

Both directions of the runway have displaced thresholds, the eastern end being rather significant. The reason are the roads at each end, but there's an extra bonus for folks landing 25. There are some lovely and very tall trees about 500 feet from the airport to the east. Depending on your glideslope preference, those tree tops can be entertaining.

The runway and airport itself are very well-maintained. The houses along either side are so close that as you're rolling out from landing it feels like you're driving down a residential street.

Transient parking is on the eastern end of the field to the south. There's not much space, though. Park tight. During the annual fly-in at Lynden, the marshalers do an impressive job of fitting everyone in safely.

Steakhouse 9 Bistro & Lounge

American (New), Steakhouses, Venues & Event Spaces
0.6 miles or 11-minute walk
115 E Homestead Blvd, Ste A, Lynden, WA 98264
360-778-2849

From the airport, exit east onto Depot Road, then walk north half a mile. There, you'll find the Steakhouse.

Serving as part of the Homestead Golf Course, the Steakhouse 9 Bistro & Lounge offers quality service and catering, amazing food and a breathtaking view of the Canadian Cascades and Mt. Baker, all in a picturesque, modernized yet classy and upscale environment. The restaurant offers wifi and is both biker and kid friendly.

Lynden Dutch Bakery

Bakeries, American (Traditional), Delis
0.9 miles or 18-minute walk
421 Front St, Lynden, WA 98264
360-815-4468

The Bakery, is in the heart of downtown Lynden. It seems far, but that's only because the town is small. It's a short walk, heading south on Depot Road, then on 3rd or 4th until you reach Front Street.

The Lynden Dutch Bakery is a quaint bakery, and as the name suggests, it serves traditional Dutch baked goods. Scones, cookies, doughnuts, breads, dutch muffins, and cinnamon rolls are a few of the bakery items on the menu. Breakfast items such as egg croissants are also available.

The Bakery also serves deli items like Reubens and sliders. Split pea with ham soup, beef & bean chili, and a daily special soup are served daily as well. Much of their food is also locally sourced. The Bakery has outdoor and indoor seating, which is perfect for any type of weather.

Chandara House

Thai, Asian Fusion
1.0 miles or 18-minute walk
655 Front St, Ste 10, Lynden, WA 98264
360-393-3068

Chandara House is a Thai Fusion restaurant and the only Thai food available in Lyndale. It is located in the old Dutch Mall. The setting is very natural with water running throughout the building via a waterfall and a koi pond. The food is authentic and the service is polite. Chandara House has a full beverage lineup, including beer and wine. They offer take out as well. They accept credit cards, and they're children and group friendly.

Jofish Seafood & Grill

Seafood
0.9 miles or 17-minute walk
312 Front St, Lynden, WA 98264
360-922-0187

Jofish Seafood & Grill offers a wide variety of seafood dishes featuring salmon, halibut, shrimp, oysters, scallops, clams, and calamari. For patrons who are not of the seafood persuasion, they offer a selection of hamburgers and chicken sandwiches. The restaurant is open Monday through Saturday, and they are closed on Sunday. They offer indoor and outdoor dining in a relaxed, casual atmosphere.

Dutch Mothers Family Restaurant

American (Traditional), Breakfast & Brunch, Sandwiches
0.9 miles or 18-minute walk
405 Front St, Lynden, WA 98264
360-354-2174

Dutch Mothers Family Restaurant offers homemade style cuisine. The Dutch style of the cuisine is old-fashioned and will remind you of the good old times when everything was genuine and yummy. The pannekoken is a special Dutch dish served here. Meats, soups like split-pea soups, and pies, are amazing in this one of a kind restaurant. It provides a unique experience of traditional Dutch cuisine. All the entrees are served in huge portions so that you can be completely satisfied.

Syros Greek & Italian Restaurant

Italian, Greek
0.9 miles or 18-minute walk
311 Front St, Lynden, WA 98264
360-354-6586

Syros is a good choice for a casual meal. It caters to the whole family. The restaurant would also be good for groups of people. It has a full bar and the ambiance is quiet. The prices seem quite reasonable for a substantial amount of food. The pizza is quite popular, and they offer "salads" filled with feta cheese.

The Firehall Café

Music Venues, Coffee & Tea
0.9 miles or 17-minute walk
321 Front St, Lynden, WA 98264
360-354-3600

Located inside Lynden's Jayden Art Centre, the Firehall Café provides amazing food and drinks in a creative environment and offers diners stimuli for various senses simultaneously. The way food is offered here reflects its creative surroundings as diners are able to select meals by picking a recipe cup full of fresh ingredients and deciding how the meal should be prepared. Gluten-free and vegetarian options also mean there is something here for everyone.

The free live music twice a week as well as other artistic activity going on within the café itself means there is never a dull moment and diners can watch their meals being prepared on the spot while being serenaded. The deck also offers stunning views of Mount Baker and a lovely garden.

Lynden Pioneer Museum

Museums
0.9 miles or 18-minute walk
217 Front St, Lynden, WA 98264
360-354-3675

Lynden Pioneer Museum covers a half city block in Lynden. The property contains many historical artifacts dating back to the founders of the city and includes informational displays of the area's natural, agricultural, and military history. Displays are laid out in a clear, concise manner, and the staff is helpful in pointing out the highlights of the exhibits.

The museum charges reasonable rates compared to others of the same nature, and they even include a discount for students. The museums old time feel is not to be overlooked, as it will take you back to a simpler time in life.

Lynden Skateway

Skating Rinks
1.0 miles or 19-minute walk
421 Judson St, Lynden, WA 98264
360-354-3851

Lynden Skateway was established in 1976. There are skating hours open to everyone on Wednesdays, Fridays, Saturdays, and Sundays. You can purchase and rent skates at the facility. The shop also cleans and repairs skates. They can accommodate private parties, roller derby, and even hockey. They offer skating lessons for beginners and the atmosphere is great for birthday parties. Their "Learn to Skate" classes are all ages and happen almost every Saturday. They offer adult skating classes during the afternoons and at night and the schedule for these classes can be found on their website. The prices for lessons and open skate start at $4.50 for children and are reasonably priced for adults as well.

Overnight Lodging

The Inn At Lynden

Hotels
0.9 miles or 17-minute walk
100 5th St, Lynden, WA 98264
360-746-8597

The Inn at Lynden is located inside the The Waples Mercantile Building and is therefore one of very few hotels in Washington State that resides in a structure listed on the National Registry of Historic Places.

Each of the 35 rooms offers stylish and serene comfort housed in a genuinely historical setting that highlights elements of the building's rich history. Choose from one of 19 Town Rooms, 9 Loft Rooms, or 6 Skywell Suites. Or splurge on the deluxe Celebration Suite. You will find each room presents a distinctive personality that provides for a unique guest experience.

The inn also allows guests to borrow their bicycles to get around town.

BLI – Bellingham International Airport

Location: 3 miles northwest of Bellingham
Coordinates: N48°47.56' / W122°32.25'
Altitude: 170 MSL
Fuel: 100LL (blue), Jet-A
Transient Storage: Tiedowns

Bellingham is the largest city in and the county seat of Whatcom County, supporting about 86,000 residents. It's also the 6th-largest metropolitan area after Seattle-Tacoma, Spokane, Vancouver, the Tri-Cities, and Yakima.

Bellingham's climate is generally mild and typical of the Puget Sound region. Western Whatcom County has a marine oceanic climate strongly influenced by the Cascades and Olympics. The Cascades to the east retain the temperate marine influence, while the Olympics provide a rain-shadow effect.

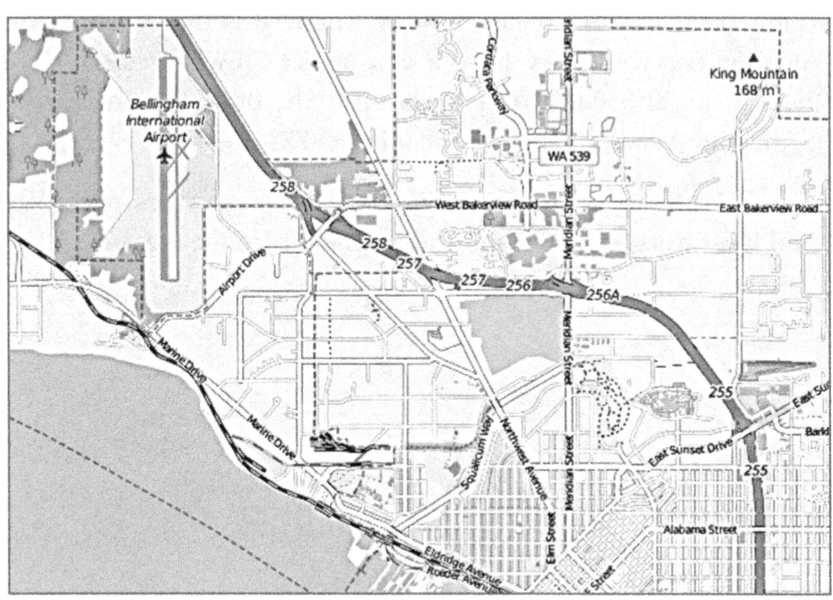

Airport Notes

The airport, situated off to the west of town, offers regularly scheduled commuter flights to and from Seattle and Friday Harbor and regularly scheduled jet service to major cities in California, Nevada, and Arizona. In 2010, Alaska Airlines began regularly scheduled direct flights to Hawaii. As such, the airport is busier than the typical airport in Washington.

The airport is a class D and is always attended. Traffic pattern is always to the west of the field.

Transient parking is northwest of the rows of hangars to the east of the field, directly south of the main commercial ramp area by the terminal buildings. The best spots to park in are those that are the most northeasterly of the set. They're directly northwest of the Heritage Flight Museum.

Transportation

There are two courtesy car options. The first is from Bellingham Aviation Services. They have a van and a Crown Victoria. Give them a call at 360-676-7624 to inquire. The other option is from Command Aviation. Their number is 360-773-3174.

The FBO can set you up with a rental car for longer stays, of course. And Uber has good coverage and availability in the area.

Food Options

Mykonos Greek Restaurant

Greek, Mediterranean
0.7 miles or 14-minute walk
1650 W Bakerview Rd, Bellingham, WA 98226
360-715-3071

Mykonos Greek Restaurant is a gem in the community. The fun Greek themed decor and the knowledgeable and friendly wait staff provide a welcoming atmosphere in which to enjoy your meal. They serve only the best, freshly made authentic Greek foods. Some of the local favorites are the lamb, Greek "salad," moussaka, and deliciously crispy fries. It's the perfect place for a romantic date or special dinner. You'll feel like you've been transported to the Mediterranean.

Overnight Lodging

Shamrock Motel

Hotels
0.7 miles or 14-minute walk
4133 W Maplewood Ave, Bellingham, WA 98226
360-676-1050

The Shamrock Motel is a reasonable, economical motel. They offer reasonable wifi. You can call from the airport for a free ride to the motel and return trip back if needed. Single rooms and double rooms with queen sized beds that are clean.

Hampton Inn

Hotels
0.8 miles or 15-minute walk
3985 Bennett Dr, Bellingham, WA 98225
360-676-7700

Your stay at the Hampton Inn includes wifi and a hot breakfast with coffee or tea service in the common areas. There are conference and meeting rooms for any business needs. To relax, you can enjoy the outdoor pool and sleeping on a double or queen sized bed. Rooms are either smoking or non-smoking. Management is friendly and helpful. The Hampton Inn also offers a fitness room and a laundry facility. Free shuttle service is also provided.

La Quinta Inn & Suites Bellingham

Hotels
1.3 miles or 25-minute walk
1063 W. Bakerview Rd., Bellingham, WA 98226
360-738-7088

La Quinta Inn & Suites offers first-class style accommodations with coach value in mind. From in-suite desks and wifi to full-length breakfast bars to indoor pool and gym to professional round-the-clock service, La Quinta Bellingham meets professional and family expectations over and beyond for a moderate rate. Dogs are accepted.

Spring Hill Suites Bellingham

Hotels
1.4 miles or 27-minute walk
4040 Northwest Avenue, Bellingham, WA 98226
360-714-9600

Spring Hill Suites is part of the Marriott chain of hotels and was built in 2013. Amenities include a hot breakfast, wifi, and a flat screen TV in each suite. Rooms are designed to accommodate both the leisure and business traveler and are equipped with a mini-refrigerator, microwave, and coffee maker. There is a pool, fitness center, and restaurant on-site. Shuttle service is available to and from the airport. Room rates are moderate and accessible rooms are available. Dogs are under 40 pounds are welcome.

Towne Place Suites Bellingham

Hotels
1.4 miles or 27-minute walk
4050 Northwest Avenue, Bellingham, WA 98226
360-714-9700

This pet friendly property offers shuttle service to and from the airport. The room rate includes wifi and breakfast. The hotel also offers onsite laundry, a fitness center, pool, and hot tub. Locally, there are plenty of recreational opportunities including bike trails, river rafting, hiking, and kayaking. Local restaurants deliver to the property with just a phone call. Alternatively, you can cook your own meals in your fully outfitted kitchen. Rooms go from a studio up through 1 and 2 bedroom apartments.

74S – Anacortes Airport

Location: 2 miles west of Anacortes
Coordinates: N48°29.91' / W122°39.75'
Altitude: 241 MSL
Fuel: 100 (green), Jet-A
Transient Storage: Tiedowns

Anacortes is sometimes referred to as the gateway to the San Juans[112] due to its heavily-used ferry docks. The city's name is a consolidation of the name "Anna Curtis," who was the wife of early Fidalgo Island settler Amos Bowman. The city boasts a population of about 16,000.

Anacortes is on Fidalgo Island. It is surrounded by the north Puget Sound and San Juan Islands on three sides, and by the Swinomish Channel and the flats of Skagit Valley to the east.

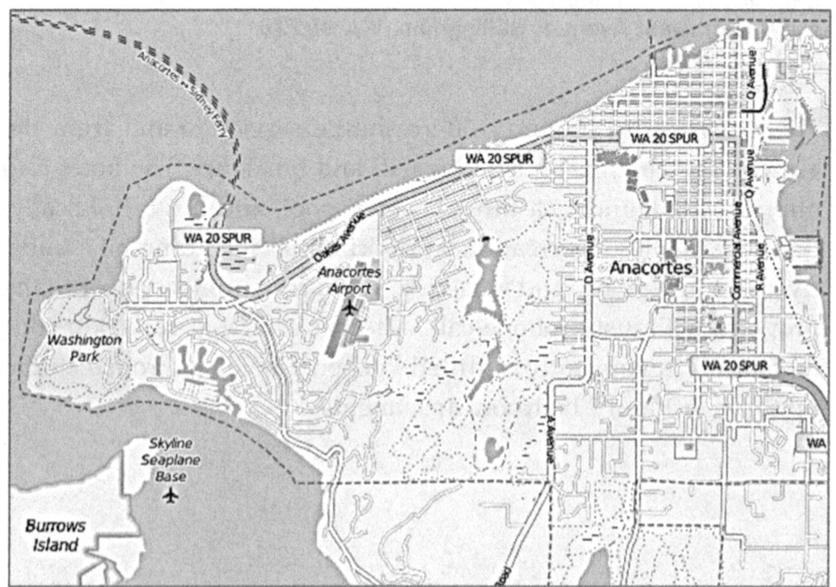

[112] Usually by people who don't have airplanes.

Airport Notes

The airport is easily visible west of the main part of town, northeast of Flounder Bay marina and southeast of the ferry dock. It sits under the northern edge of the class C airspace of Whidbey Island NAS, so keep that in mind when you make your approach.

Traffic pattern is always to the west of the field. There's rising terrain to the east.

There's quite a lot of well-marked transient parking on the east side of the runway. The fuel dock is well-positioned right in the middle of the ramp.

Food Options

Anacortes Ship Harbor Inn

Cafés, Beer, Wine & Spirits
0.6 miles or 11-minute walk
5316 Ferry Terminal Rd, Anacortes, WA 98221

The Anacortes Ship Harbor Inn is a quaint tranquil hotel for a relaxing moment away from the hustle of city life but close enough to have access to all the city has to offer. From the airport, you'll need to exit along Airport Road, then Anacopper Road until you reach Oakes. From there, just walk west until you reach the ferry terminal building.

The views from the cottages include the Puget Sound and the San Juan ferry. The staff is not only attentive but willing to serve their guests above and beyond. The menu offers a variety of options and is served within minutes.

Cheesecake Café

Bakeries, Sandwiches
0.9 miles or 17-minute walk
2100 Ferry Terminal Rd, Anacortes, WA 98221
360-588-0234

The Cheesecake Café is conveniently located in the on Ferry Road right before you the ferry. Known especially for their mini frosted cookies and other sweet and sugary treats it makes for a convenient stop for snacks or hotdogs, sandwiches, or "salads." The service is fast and friendly. They also serve espresso-based drinks.

Things to Do

Anacortes Kayak Tours

Rafting/Kayaking, Tours
1.1 miles or 20-minute walk
2201 Skyline Way, Ste 203, Anacortes, WA 98221
360-588-1117

If you are going to be taking a trip to Anacortes and want to do some kayaking, then this is the best place for you. They have been giving tours in this area for many years and know the land like the back of their hand. If you want a good guide to show you around the area and teach you wilderness survival, then this is a great company.

Blackfish Tours by Outer Island Expeditions

Tours, Fishing, Boat Charters
1.1 miles or 20-minute walk
2201 Skyline Way, Anacortes, WA 98221
360-376-3711

Blackfish Tours by Outer Island Expeditions provides tours and fishing and boat charters in the area. Daily whale watching tours are offered from May to October. Orcas, humpbacks, porpoises, and other wildlife can be viewed on the tours. Fishing and private charters are available year round. Fishing includes crab, lingcod, kelp greenling, halibut, and more. Blackfish Tours also offers an alternative to the Ferry with a water taxi available to tour the San Jan Islands at a leisurely pace.[113]

Overnight Lodging

Anacortes Ship Harbor Inn

Hotels
0.6 miles or 11-minute walk
5316 Ferry Terminal Rd, Anacortes, WA 98221
360-293-5177

Anacortes Ship Harbor Inn is both a restaurant and hotel. (See above.) A variety of top-rated rooms, cabins, and apartments are available, all including wifi, gym access, on-site laundry, and outdoor BBQs, as well as accepting dogs. Whilst being close to the city, the Hotel is set away from the commotion on 6 acres of peaceful woodland. All rooms have a beautiful view of the Wetlands and the San Juan islands.

[113] Why any pilot would want to do that instead of fly there is beyond my comprehension, but if this sort of thing floats your boat, then they have boats that float.

The Heron House Guest Suites

Bed & Breakfast
1.1 miles or 22-minute walk
11110 Marine Drive, Anacortes, WA 98221
360-293-4477

The Heron House Guest Suites is a bed and breakfast with beautiful views of the water and occasional views of the namesake herons that inhabit the area. The rooms themselves are good sized and well apportioned, with some of the rooms having decks overlooking the cove where you'll be able to hear the waves crashing against the cliff. The breakfast provided is of exceptional quality and the hosts are warm, welcoming, and inviting. They're very focused on ensuring your stay is even better than you expected and have been recognized for their exceptional customer service.

The Troll House

Guest Houses
1.3 miles or 24-minute walk
3895 Sea Breeze Lane, Anacortes, WA 98221
360-293-5750

The Troll House guest cottage offers accommodation for two adults with flexible reservation arrangements. The cottage boasts of its own private deck with a hot tub, an indoors wood stove, a kitchenette with barbeque and much more. Everything needed to enjoy some quiet time away is available, and guests will be able to prepare their own meals or stroll into town for a bite to eat. How little or how much interaction with the town or with the amazing surroundings nature has so graciously provided is entirely up to the visitors.

BVS – Skagit Regional Airport

Location: 3 miles west of Burlington
Coordinates: N48°28.23' / W122°25.30'
Altitude: 145 MSL
Fuel: 100LL (blue), Jet-A
Transient Storage: Tiedowns

The Skagit Regional Airport supports the communities of Burlington and Mount Vernon. Mount Vernon itself is a city first settled in 1870 and incorporated in 1889. It's home to about 32,000 residents. It hosts the annual Tulip Festival.[114] Each year, millions of tulips are grown in the Skagit Valley. The climate of Skagit County is similar to that of Northern France.

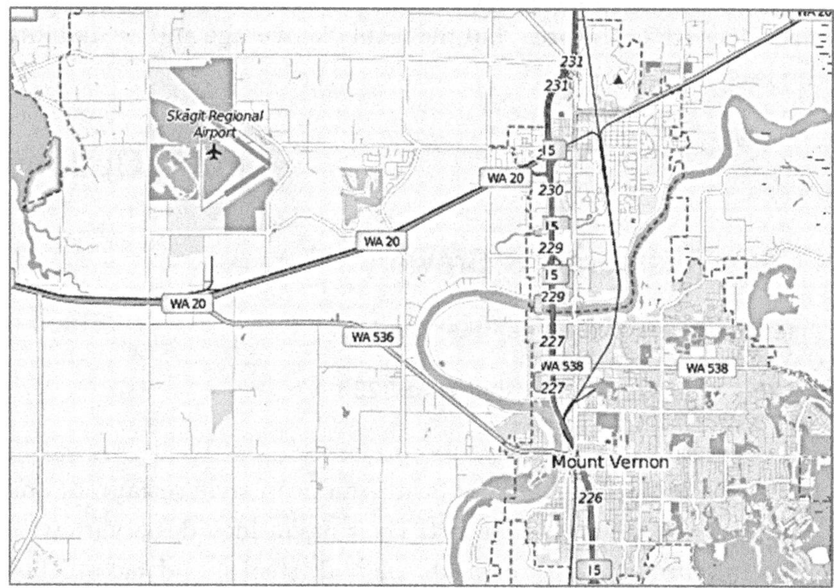

114 The Tulip Festival is great. If you enjoy sitting in your car for long periods of time while it inches along a clogged freeway, then the Tulip Festival is perfect for you. If instead, you enjoy dodging a swam of low-flying aircraft with all their pilots staring at the ground instead of toward you, then the Tulip Festival is perfect for you.

Airport Notes

Skagit Regional sits just outside the northeast edge of Whidbey's class C airspace. The lands around it are mostly flat, and there aren't any vertical obstacles to worry about.

Given the two active runways, listen carefully to AWOS and CTAF before committing to a runway pattern.

The main parking area and fuel dock (and restaurant) are off the 11/29 runway, to the northeast. The fuel dock is on the northwest end of that ramp, and the restaurant is toward the southeastern side.

Transportation

For local taxi options, you can try Skagit Transit at 360-757-4433. Uber does cover the area, but the level of coverage and availability can be sparse.

Food Options

Flyer's Restaurant & Brewery ✈

American (New), Breweries, Beer Gardens
0.0 miles or 0-minute walk
15426 Airport Way, Burlington, WA 98233
360-899-1025

Flyer's Restaurant & Brewery is an American style restaurant and brew house right on the airport. Their menu includes a variety of items: anything from breakfast, seafood, steaks, and tacos. They also have a wide variety of burgers and sandwiches. A lot of the sandwiches are named after different types of aircraft. They have six homemade beers, along with a seasonal variety, to enjoy your meal with. They accept reservations and credit cards, and are kid friendly, as well as open to large groups.[115]

Things to Do

Heritage Flight Museum

Museums
0.0 miles or 0-minute walk
15053 Crosswind Dr, Burlington, WA 98233
360-424-5151

Founded in 1996 by Apollo 8 astronaut Major General William Anders, the Heritage Flight Museum is a non-profit organization dedicated to the preservation and flying of historic military aircraft. Visitors are welcome to get an up-close look at the collection of memorabilia and artifacts, and a selection of flying World War II, Korean and Vietnam era aircraft.

The Heritage Flight Museum is on the field, about mid-point along the southeast edge of the 4/22 secondary runway. The museum is open Tuesday through Saturday from 9am to 3pm. Admission is $8 for adults and $5 for children over 5.

Flying displays of Museum and visiting aircraft are conducted on the 3rd Saturday of each month from April through October.

[115] At one point recently after they opened, the FATPNW (Flights Above The Pacific Northwest) aviation group hosted a fly-in to eat at the restaurant. The airport was utterly saturated with aircraft and pilots. The restaurant rapidly became standing-room only. And yet despite every table and chair being used, the restaurant brought out food at a steady clip without suffering any loss of quality. It was one of the most impressive displays of restaurant management I've ever seen.

OKH – A. J. Eisenberg Airport

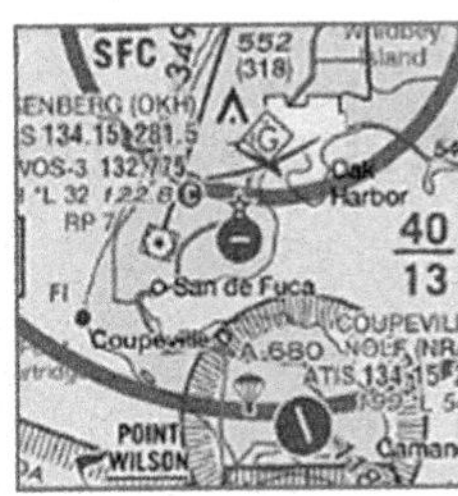

Location: 3 miles southwest of Oak Harbor
Coordinates: N48°15.09' / W122°40.42'
Altitude: 193 MSL
Fuel: 100LL (blue), Automotive Gasoline
Transient Storage: Tiedowns

About 3 miles outside of Oak Harbor is the little and easily overlooked A. J. Eisenberg Airport.[116] Oak Harbor itself is Whidbey Island's largest incorporated city, supporting over 22,000 people. It's the nearest city to the Naval Air Station Whidbey Island, so naturally it has a strong military influence.

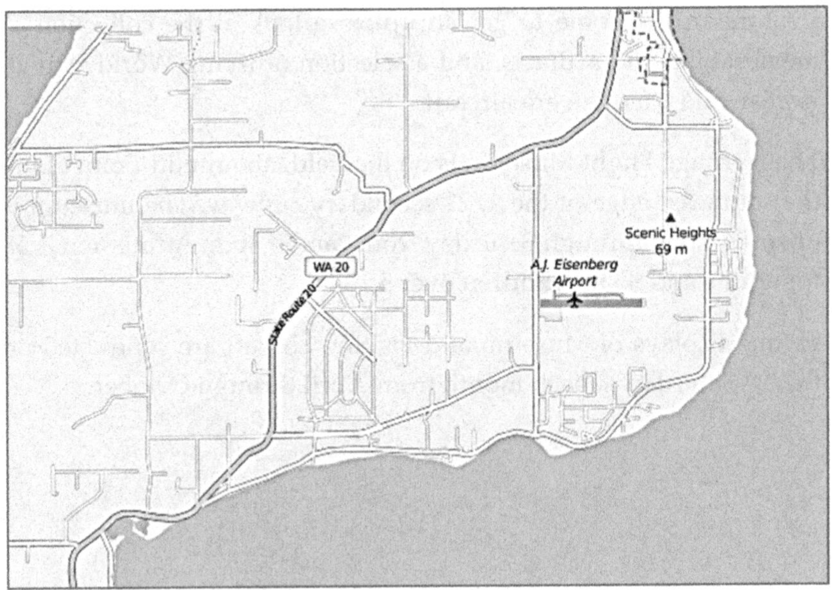

[116] This is to say, I overlooked it easily. I was flying with my family to meet up with my wife's cousin and his family, and Eisenberg was our intended destination. Despite talking to Whidbey, having a GPS moving map, and very clear conditions, I nearly overflew the field before I spotted it. I kept looking at the GPS moving map and saying, "It should be right here." Turns out, I was right.

Airport Notes

Eisenberg Airport runway is little more than a driveway, and its western end terminates at a 90-degree angle to Monroe Landing Road.[117] Traffic pattern is always to the south of the runway.

The runway slopes up to the east, but there's nothing but open farm land past the end toward the east for quite a ways, so you can come in pretty low without being overly concerned.

Note the rather non-trivial displaced threshold on 7 to keep you away from the road.

The airport's buildings, the pilot lounge, and transient parking are all at the western end of the runway.

Food Options

Whole "E" Cow BBQ Company

Barbeque
1.5 miles or 28-minute walk
1659 Scenic Heights Rd, Oak Harbor, WA 98277
360-914-0077

The Whole "E" Cow is a restaurant with a great name.[118] This place serves BBQ; their meat is home-smoked and everything is made by the people there. The food is made fresh and locally sourced. They serve meats from typical BBQ beef to Mexican style meat such as chicaron. They also serve many different types of breads to go along with your meal.

[117] Yes, I'm just making excuses.

[118] What I mean is, the name is something I would come up with for a business such as this, which means it's a great name that my wife and children thinks is groan-worthy.

Things to Do

Jet City Skydiving Center ✈

Skydiving
0.1 miles or 1-minute walk
1140 Monroe Landing Rd, Oak Harbor, WA 98277
206-497-3131

Jet City Skydiving Center is located on the field at Eisenberg. They are Whidbey Island's only skydiving center. They claim to have the "most scenic drop zone around."[119] Jet City is praised for being very accommodating for customers, having a welcoming atmosphere, and making sure customers feel safe while jumping. If someone has a question, the staff does what they can to answer them as quickly as possible. Overall, the company greatly cares about making jumping the best experience possible for the client.

Overnight Lodging

All the overnight lodging options presented here are not exactly close by the airport. They're a fairly long walk from the airport, in the range of 42 to 43 minutes. They're around Penn Cove in Coupeville. In all cases, call ahead to see if the place might be willing to pick you up from the airport.

[119] I know of about 7 other jump schools that might argue against that claim.

Cottage on the Cove

Hotels, Guest Houses
2.2 miles or 42-minute walk
6 NE Front St, Coupeville, WA 98239
360-678-0600

The Cottage on the Cove is a beautiful cottage with views of the water and literally just steps to a variety of local favorites including restaurants, coffee shops, and even grocery stores. The Cottage itself is large enough for a group or family and has two beds which are soft and comfortable. The owner, Reverend Barry, is a familiar face to the locals and is incredibly warm and friendly. The cottage's location combined with its charm make this a great place to stay in downtown Coupeville.

The Coupeville Inn

Hotels
2.2 miles or 43-minute walk
200 NW Coveland St, Coupeville, WA 98239
360-678-6668

The Coupeville Inn is located near the water, the Island County Historical Society, and downtown Coupeville. Some of the rooms have a beautiful water view while others have nice views of Coupeville itself. The rooms are spacious and clean, and some even include a balcony. All come with an included breakfast. You'll be within a short walk to many shops, restaurants, and even a park. The staff is friendly and welcoming and will be happy to give recommendations for what to do in the area.

Anchorage Inn

Hotels, Bed & Breakfast
2.3 miles or 43-minute walk
807 N Main St, Coupeville, WA 98239
360-678-5581

The Anchorage Inn is a nice Victorian style house in a small, old-time town with all the charm and class that one would expect when visiting. The Crow's Nest room, which is a suite by itself that spans the entire top floor, is a popular choice for many of the guests. The view of the sound from the upper rooms tends to be breathtakingly spectacular. The genuine hospitality enables guests to relax and feel comfortable. Guests are treated to fresh coffee and cookies around the clock, and the breakfasts are said to be delicious, unlike the typical continental breakfast of a generic motel. The Inn does offer wifi and cable in addition to the extensive DVD library. The charm and homey feel to the Inn will have guests wanting to return.

Coupe de Villa

Bed & Breakfast
2.3 miles or 43-minute walk
801 NW Tremont St, Coupeville, WA 98239
360-678-4686

Coupe de Villa, a bed and breakfast just minutes from the water in Coupeville with thoughtful hosts. Coupe de Villa is also a quick walk to downtown Coupeville and near a park so the kids can play or the adults can shop without needing to pack everyone into the car. The breakfast is especially well known to be quite tasty. The accommodations themselves received praise for being comfortable enough that guests to Coupe de Villa frequently stay again.

W10 – Whidbey Air Park Airport

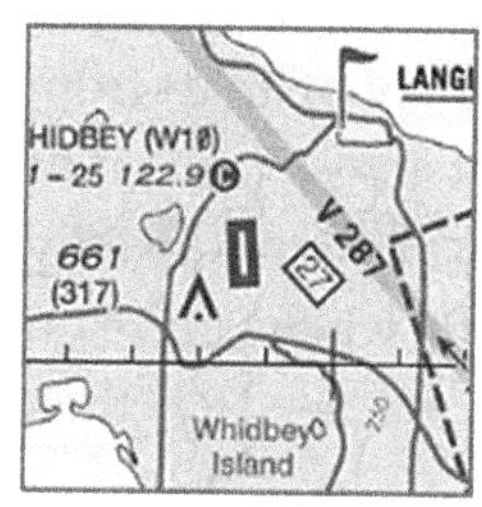

Location: 2 miles southwest of Langley
Coordinates: N48°1.05' / W122°26.26'
Altitude: 271 MSL
Fuel: None
Transient Storage: Tiedowns

The Whidbey Air Park is about 2 miles outside of Langley on Whidbey Island. Langley itself supports a population of a little over 1,000 people and overlooks the Saratoga Passage. Langley was founded in the 1800s by Jacob Anthes. It has a number of bed and breakfast options, and it's a lovely tourist attraction for this part of the island.

The Air Park itself is tucked out in the woods beyond the town. With tall trees on every side and narrow runway, it's a fun location to visit.

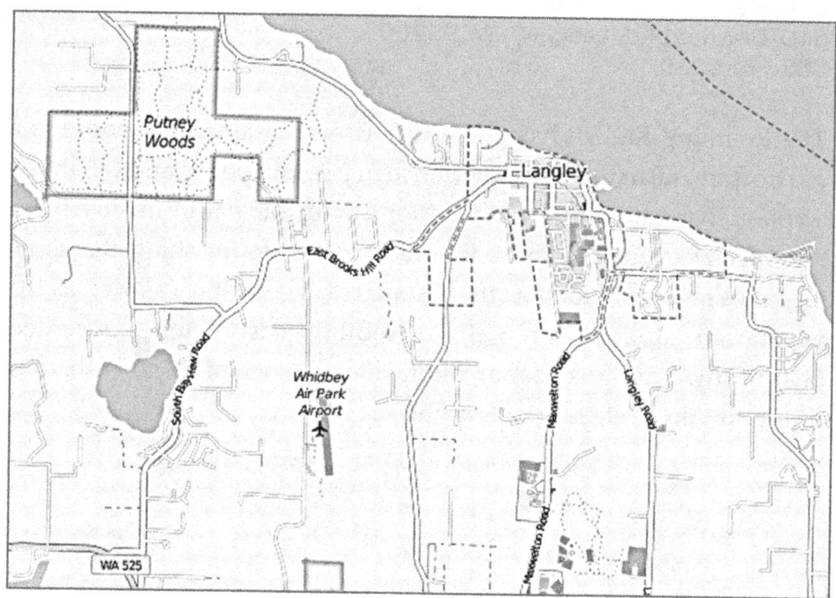

Airport Notes

As mentioned, there are trees everywhere, but other than those pesky obstacles, there's not much to be concerned about apart from the narrow runway. There's a road that cuts right across the end of 34, but it terminates at the hangars on the field and isn't heavily used. Regardless, keep an eye out for vehicle traffic when you're on final. The runway's 2470 feet long, so if you don't need all that, maybe imagine a displaced threshold on 34.

Parking is available on the north end of the field. Look for the hangars on the northwest corner, and park in front of the trees just to their south.

Food Options

Roaming Radish

Gastropubs, Venues & Event Spaces
0.5 miles or 10-minute walk
5417 Crawford Rd, Langley, WA 98260
360-331-5939

The Roaming Radish has a history of serving amazing food. It's a gastro-pub, farm to table experience in a re-purposed and rehabbed airplane hangar in the woods. Along with the eat-in facility there are special event accommodations that no doubt share the same elegance and great food as the restaurant. The entrees as well as the vegetarian options are all incredibly tasty and presented beautifully. You can order an old fashioned cocktail to go with your dinner if you're staying overnight.

Things to Do

Mukilteo Coffee Roasters

Local Flavor, Coffee & Tea
0.1 miles or 1-minute walk
3228 Lake Leo Way, Langley, WA 98260
360-321-5262

Mukilteo Coffee Roasters is quite popular and known for their grown, roasted, and packaged coffee. They also have a restaurant located right next door to the store called Our Café in the Woods which serves fresh food daily. The ingredients are supplied by local farmers every day to ensure freshness and great quality.

The Mukilteo Coffee Roasters has been slow-roasting their own coffee for over 30 years now, and they continue to share their passion with the rest of the community. There are many flavors of coffee that are available for purchase both online and in-store. The decor inside of the location is very unique and provides a comfortable atmosphere for everyone.

Overnight Lodging

Country Cottage of Langley

Hotels, Bed & Breakfast
1.9 miles or 36-minute walk
215 6th St, Langley, WA 98260
360-221-8709

Country Cottage of Langley is a bed and breakfast where guests can stay in one of six cottages on the property. Each of the cottages has a unique theme, but all have access to wifi and include a refrigerator, television, and a coffee maker. Breakfast is prepared each morning by the owners and can be served in either the dining room with other guests or delivered to the cottage for a private meal.

When not exploring Whidbey Island, guests can spend time relaxing or reading in the country garden on the grounds that is often visited by local wildlife.

The Inn at Langley

Hotels, Day Spas, Diners
2.1 miles or 39-minute walk
400 First St, Langley, WA 98260
360-221-3033

This cozy inn boasts 28 guestrooms, each with a view of the Saratoga Passage. They also include jetted tubs, private balconies, and fireplaces. Breakfast is served in the open chef's kitchen and guests are welcome to take a tray to enjoy in the comfort and privacy of their room. In the evening guests are invited to dine in the kitchen with Chef Matt Costello and watch as he prepares the freshest in season local foods. The Inn also offers a picnic basket for two packed complete with a bottle of wine and a blanket for an enjoyable experience. Beach access and sunsets help make this hotel experience relaxing.

Saratoga Inn

Hotels, Bed & Breakfast
2.1 miles or 40-minute walk
201 Cascade Ave, Langley, WA 98260
360-221-5801

This is a very quaint little bed-and-breakfast that will make for a nice stay. They do a really nice job of making their guests feel right at home during their stay. The rooms are nice, quiet, and comfortable so you can have a good trip. The scenery and the area is breathtaking, and it makes for a great vacation destination.

AWO – Arlington Municipal Airport

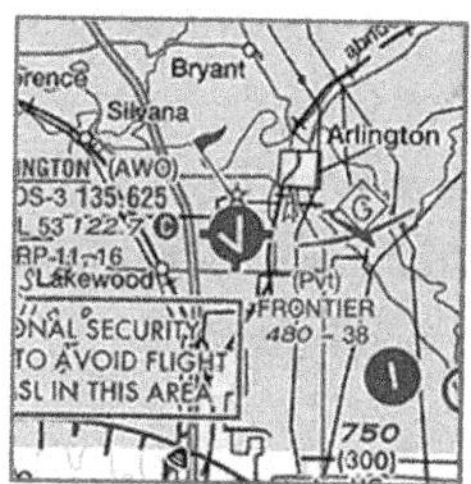

Location: 3 miles southwest of Arlington
Coordinates: N48°9.65' / W122°9.54'
Altitude: 141 MSL
Fuel: 100LL (blue), Jet-A
Transient Storage: Tiedowns

Arlington is a city in northern Snohomish County bordered by the city of Marysville to the south with a population of about 18,000. While founded later than other towns in the area, it grew at a faster pace.

The Arlington Airport sits just 3 miles outside of town. Construction was approved on February 23, 1934. The first airplane took off on June 13, 1934 and the airport was officially dedicated on July 4, 1935. The airport is host to several businesses making significant contributions to the aviation industry.

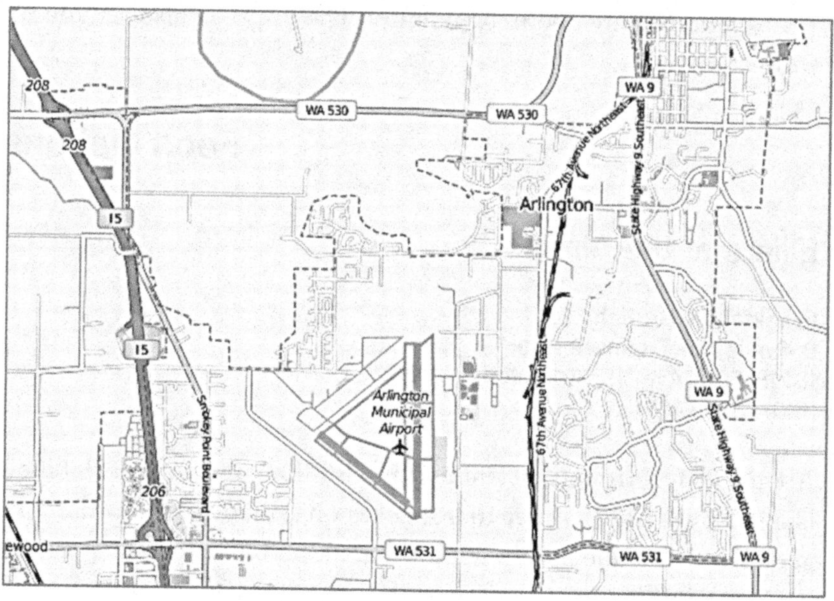

Airport Notes

Arlington makes for a great visit for a student pilot of his or her first cross-country solo. Its airspace is quite simple; class G at the surface covered by class E, then class A way up high. There's no tower and no other airspace considerations nearby. The pattern hosts friendly pilots. The runways and field are easy to see and navigate.

The two runways along with the ultralight strip form an obvious triangle easily visible from a long ways off. Traffic pattern is always to the outside of the triangle. 34/16 is the primary runway, but listen to AWOS and CTAF.

Transient parking is in a yellow box-like marked area about midfield on the east side of the field, west edge of the ramp near the taxiway, toward the north side of the ramp.

Transportation

A courtesy car is available. Contact Arlington Flight Services at 360-435-5700 to inquire about availability. The FBO can also set you up with a rental.

Food Options

Ellie's at the Airport ✈

Breakfast & Brunch
0.4 miles or 7-minute walk
18218 59th Ave NE, Arlington, WA 98223
360-435-4777

About 120 feet from transient parking is Ellie's at the Airport. Ellie's is a family-friendly diner that focuses on American food that'll be good for the whole family without breaking the bank. The portions are large and the food itself is fresh cooked as you order it.

These folks are typically very busy, so be prepared to wait a bit depending on load. The interior is clean and tastefully decorated.

Buzz Inn Steakhouse

American (Traditional), Steakhouses
0.7 miles or 14-minute walk
5200 172nd St NE, Arlington, WA 98223
360-658-1529

The Buzz Inn Steakhouse offers breakfast, lunch, and dinner with a full bar. There are a variety of meals to choose from that you can customize to your taste. They offer a seniors' menu and serve breakfast throughout the day. Buzz Inn Steakhouse is known for their steaks and offer a variety of wraps and sandwiches too. This is a no delivery and no reservations restaurant; however, you can order take-out. Attire is casual and there is an outdoor seating area for those who enjoy a good meal outside.

Things to Do

Airport Trail

Dog Parks
0.8 miles or 16-minute walk
43rdAve & 51st Ave at 172nd, Arlington, WA

The Airport Trail spans about 6 miles and takes about an hour or two depending on how fast of a walker you are. For those who want a bit shorter of a walk there are many places to stop and relax along the trail, each giving you differing wonderful views.

Best Western Plus

Hotels
1.1 miles or 21-minute walk
3721 172nd St, Arlington, WA 98223
360-363-4321

The Best Western[120] Plus of Arlington is a pet-friendly and affordable hotel located near Seattle Premium Outlets and the local casinos. There are many features available including good wifi, hot breakfast services, and a 24-hour front desk. There's a fitness center where guests can continue their daily workout; there is also a pool and a hot tub to relax in. There are 100 non-smoking rooms available and 5 rooms that are handicapped-accessible with many great features to help the physically challenged. Guests can also take advantage of the on-site convenience store for any last minute necessities.

Medallion Hotel

Caterers, Hotels
1.5 miles or 28-minute walk
16710 Smokey Point Blvd Ste 102, Arlington, WA 98223
360-657-0500

The Medallion Hotel is a recently renovated 97 room hotel. Standard rooms include a 42 inch flat screen television, microwave, refrigerator, wifi, and a complementary fresh breakfast. The property features a swimming pool, spa, restaurant, bar, convention center, and office space. The convention center has 9 available rooms which can accommodate between 10 and 250 guests each. The total size of the convention center is nearly 15,000

[120] Hey look! It's another Best Western.

square feet. The indoor pool also features a hot tub and chairs to relax on. Nearby attractions include a casino and outlet mall.

Hawthorn Inn & Suites

Hotels, Limos
1.5 miles or 29-minute walk
16710 Smokey Point Blvd, Arlington, WA 98223
360-657-0500

Hawthorn Inn & Suites located in Arlington, Washington offers free wifi and a hot breakfast with your stay. It's handicapped-accessible with an indoor pool for guests who like to enjoy a swim all year round. It's pet-friendly and has a bar and restaurant on-site for a bite to eat and a drink to help guest feel welcomed and relaxed while traveling. Flat screen TV's and DVD players are in the rooms and upgraded rooms offer whirlpool tubs, fire places, and balconies. Some suites will also have kitchenettes for extended-stay visitors who want all the comforts of home while on the road.

3W5 – Mears Field Airport

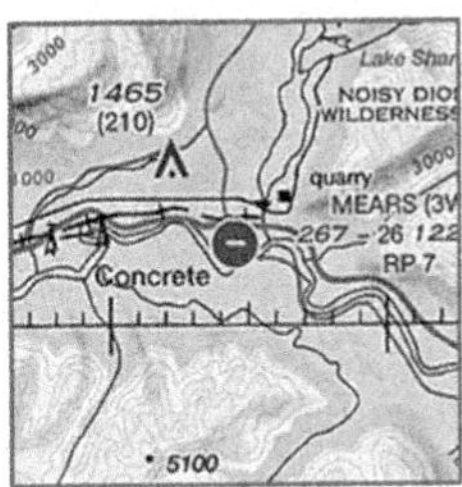

Location: 1 mile south of Concrete
Coordinates: N48°31.79' / W121°45.49'
Altitude: 267 MSL
Fuel: 100LL (blue)
Transient Storage: Tiedowns

Concrete is a little town of less than 800 people tucked up near where the Baker River merges with the Skagit River, a bit south of Lake Shannon. Back before 1909, it was actually two even tinier towns that merged after the Superior Portland Cement Company plant was built. It was in that merger the town was named Concrete.

The Concrete Airport, or Mears Field, sits slightly south of the town in the middle of an area of land formed by half arc in the Skagit River.

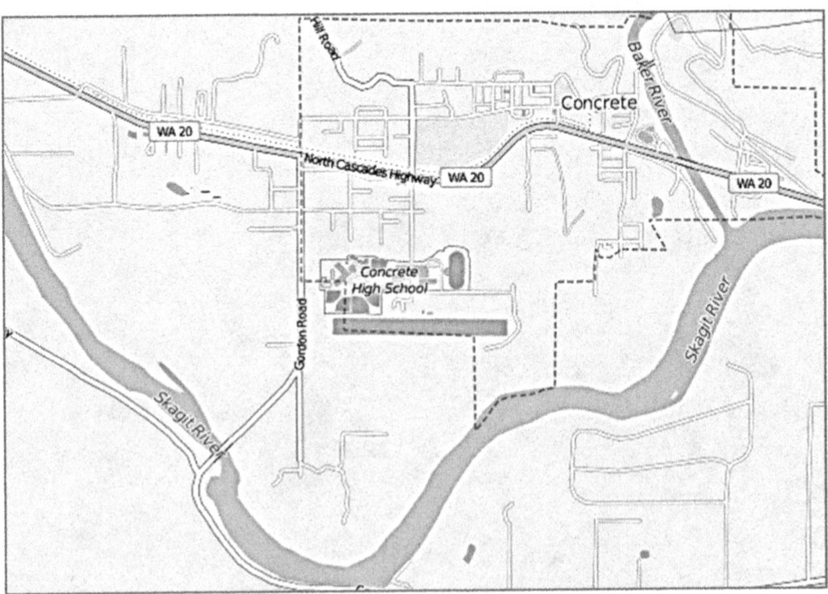

Airport Notes

This is an enjoyable airport to visit. As you get low, you'll be surrounded by mountains to the north and south, you'll likely overfly the river at least once or twice, and everywhere you look is natural beauty.

Traffic pattern is always to the south. Note with great care the tall trees at both ends of the runway. Despite its over 2600 feet of runway, it may be wise to consider using short-field technique.

Primary transient parking is midfield to the north on a very small paved ramp. If that area's full, you can park in the grass to the east end of the field, back from the runway. Don't park in front of someone's hangar or house that's right next to the runway, though.

Visit the pilot's lounge before you walk you way into town.

Food Options

Cascade Burgers

Burgers
0.4 miles or 7-minute walk
45292 State Rt 20, Concrete, WA 98237
360-853-7580

This place is known for old fashioned hamburgers and French fries. It's a great choice for folks who love to eat old fashioned food. Many people know this burger joint because their sauces are homemade and are put all over their burgers and French fries. They also have homemade dessert including pies. Their shakes are homemade and are made with outstanding ingredients such as a "secret" malt powder. While a lot of their food is fried, it's not dripping in grease.

5b's Bakery

Bakeries, Breakfast & Brunch, Sandwiches
0.7 miles or 12-minute walk
45597 Main St, Concrete, WA 98237
360-853-8700

If you're interested in gluten-free bakery goods, 5b's Bakery is for you.[121] The entire kitchen is gluten free, with offerings ranging from pot pies, calzones, quiche, "salads," sandwiches, to pastries. The decor is so inviting and incredibly well done. Whether you are looking for some great donuts, cookies, coffee, or a hearty meal you should be coming here and trying out this delicious food.

This is a locals' favorite spot for breakfast or an early brunch. But don't worry, they are open throughout the day.

Things to Do

North Cascades Vintage Aircraft Museum ✈

Museums
0.1 miles or 1-minute walk
7879 South Superior Ave, Ste 6, Concrete, WA 98237
360-770-4848

The small town of Concrete somewhat surprisingly has a great little museum dedicated to vintage aircraft. An ever-present tour guide will explain everything about the museum to you. Many of these aircraft are old and have seen a lot of flight hours.

The museum includes complete restoration facilities, and several active restorations are currently underway. The museum is dedicated to preserving and sharing the personal light aircraft that

[121] I'm not into gluten-free food. I enjoy gluten. I usually order my food with extra gluten on the side. Do you know that "gluten" is the German word for "yummy?" I do. Now you do too. And knowing is half the battle.

have trained and served generations of pilots, forming the backbone of general aviation for more than 80 years.

Overnight Lodging

Ovenell's Heritage Inn

Hotels, Bed & Breakfast
1.3 miles or 26-minute walk
46276 Concrete Sauk Valley Rd, Concrete, WA 98237
360-853-8494

If you need to stay overnight in Concrete, then you'll be glad you picked Ovenell's. The Inn is a comfortable place with nice size rooms and all of the amenities you would expect from a typical hotel. The staff is very friendly and can help you figure out your way around Concrete.

1S2 – Darrington Municipal Airport

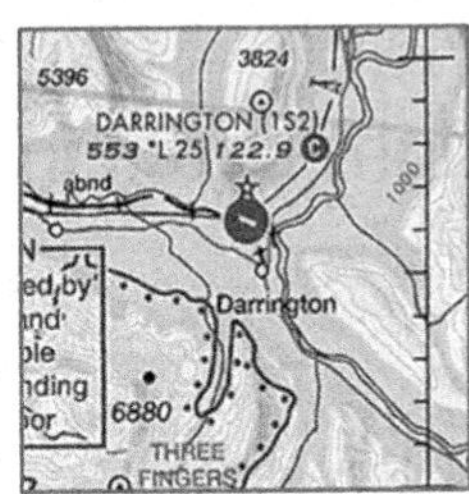

Location: 0 miles north of Darrington
Coordinates: N48°15.52' / W121°36.61'
Altitude: 553 MSL
Fuel: None
Transient Storage: Tiedowns

The town of Darrington sits on the southeast corner of what some pilots call the "Darrington Loop," with Concrete to its north. The town hosts a population of about 1,400.

At one point, the town was called "Starve Out" and later "The Portage," but it was renamed Barrington in 1895 following a community meeting. The U.S. Postal Department mistakenly changed the first letter to a "D," resulting in the current name.

The town is tucked into a valley between several small and mid-sized mountains.

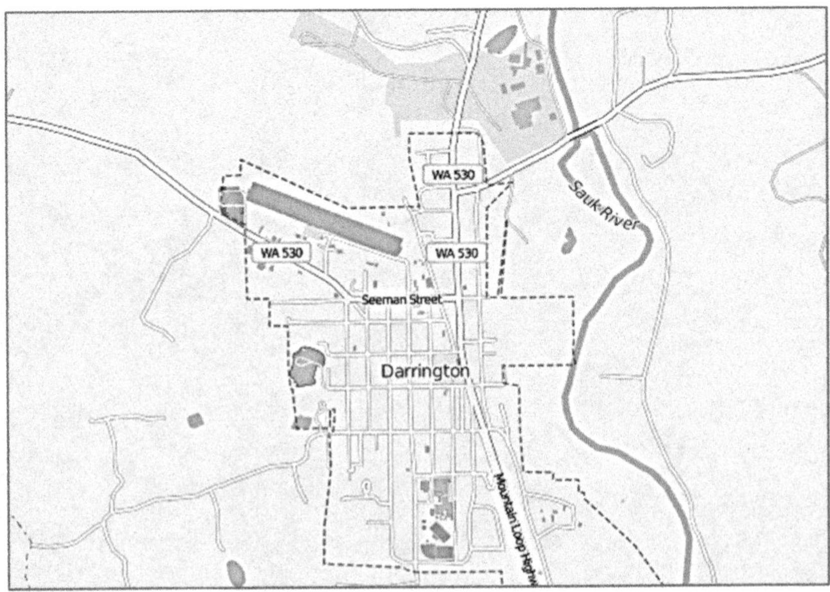

Airport Notes

As you drop into the valley and approach the airport, be ready for the wind to do some squirrelly things to your aircraft. The runway's right at the northern edge of town, between the two main roads that fork off north and west.

Note with caution the mountain to the east at over 2,000 feet MSL and less than 1nm away from the runway's eastern end. There's a small rise of terrain and trees to the north of the runway, but it's not much of a factor.

Transient parking is midfield to the south.

Food Options

Glacier Peak Café

Cafés
0.2 miles or 3-minute walk
1215 State Rte 530 NE, Darrington, WA 98241

Glacier Peak Café is just off the airport property and across 530 to the south. The café has a good variety on the menu and the food is quite tasty. The blue cheese burger is excellent as are the onion rings. For dessert, they serve real hard ice cream. The blackberry milkshake is also a delight. There also is a nice ambience here. You'll feel very comfortable as you sit and eat with your friends or loved ones.

Hawks Nest Bar & Grill

Sports Bars, American (Traditional)
0.2 miles or 3-minute walk
1215 State Rt 530 NE, Darrington, WA 98241
360-436-1500

The Hawks Nest is a nice bar and restaurant with a good atmosphere. It is a fun place to go with your pilot friends to hang out and maybe watch a game. It has a pretty wide menu and you will certainly be able to find some food that you like. There are many types of beer and other drinks available.[122] The staff takes pride in making sure that your night is an enjoyable one. They have a lot of TVs around so you will be sure to have a great view of the big game.

Bradley's Diner

Diners
0.2 miles or 3-minute walk
1215 Sr 530 Ne, Darrington, WA 98241
360-436-9345

Bradley's Diner offers the classic American diner experience for guests who are local to the mountain area or who are passing through. The diner is one of the few good sit-down restaurants in the town. Current hours are 6am to 8pm Sunday through Thursday and 6am to 9pm Friday and Saturday. The diner's menu includes omelets, biscuits and gravy, pancakes, pulled pork, homemade soups, and an Asian chicken "salad." They are also known for their locally made blackberry and apple pies.

[122] Available to your non-pilot passengers, to be precise.

Burger Barn

Burgers
0.4 miles or 8-minute walk
1020 Emens Ave N, Darrington, WA 98241
360-436-2070

Walk east along 530, then follow it as it turns north, and you'll quickly find the Burger Barn. If you're into fish and chips, you may want to order the fish burgers. They consist of crispy battered cod fillets, a generous pickle slices, and fresh, crispy lettuce.

The fries are delicious and served in extremely large portions. A medium is more than enough for 2 people.

Things to Do

Adventure Cascades

Rafting/Kayaking
0.4 miles or 8-minute walk
1080 Seeman St, Darrington, WA 98241
360-393-6815

The Adventure Cascades office is located on the bend in 530. You'll walk right past it from the airport on your way to the Burger Barn. They offer white water rafting adventures and other outdoor activities. The staff make the experience even better as they are beyond accommodating to their guests. They provide shoes and wetsuits.

The owner has been working this business for over 10 years. They usually have one person on the raft with the group and one other on a kayak staying close by in case someone falls. The guides are clear with their instructions, and they take their time making sure everyone is prepared.

Goat Lake Trail

Hiking
0.5 miles or 8-minute walk
Co-ordinates: 48.0537, -121.4113, Mt. Baker-Snoqualmie National Forest, Darrington, WA

The Goat Lake Trail is a 10.4-mile hiking trail offering opportunities for both day hikers and overnight camping. Hikers on the trail will traverse varied terrain, passing snow-capped mountains, forests, creeks, waterfalls, and the enormous blue-green lake which gives the trail its name. Goat Lake Trails features both uphill and downhill hiking at various elevations and offers opportunities for stream crossings. There are numerous spots along the trail that offer commanding views of the surrounding area, the highest point reaching 3,161 feet. At the lake itself, there are 15 camp sites and 2 open-air privies.

Mountain Loop Books and Coffee

Coffee & Tea, Music Venues
0.7 miles or 13-minute walk
1085 Darrington St, Darrington, WA 98241
360-630-7673

If you're into books and coffee,[123] you ought to make a point of stopping in at Mountain Loop Books and Coffee. The Zoka beans make great coffee drinks, and paired with handmade, not store bought, cakes and snacks, you really couldn't ask for more. Sipping coffee and snacking while on a personal layover can quickly turn into all-day adventure. Make sure you plan enough time to check out all the local art that adorns the walls in this shop.

[123] I know you're into books, because I know you're reading one right now. I'm psychic that way. Also, given that you're a pilot, you're also into coffee. If not, then I don't trust you. I don't trust any pilot who's not into coffee. I'm psychic that way.

Stagecoach Inn

Hotels
0.3 miles or 6-minute walk
1100 Seeman St, Darrington, WA 98241
360-436-1776

The Stagecoach Inn is nestled in the beautiful foothills of the Cascades. With scenic views and a rustic charm, this hotel provides a quiet sanctuary with convenient access to local outdoor recreational activities including fishing, rafting, rock climbing, and scenic hiking trails.

The hotel has two floors featuring kitchenette equipped rooms with wifi accessible to guests. The hotel grounds have picnic and grilling areas available as well with magnificent views of the nearby mountains.

Chapter 9

Methow and Western Okanogan

Some well-meaning folks suggest Washington is really two states, divided along the Cascade ridge. There's the wet side to the west and the dry side to the east. Unfortunately, this lumps the rich diversity of the east side all together. There are the flat dessert areas north and around the Tri-Cities, there's the Palouse region around Pullman, the western Rocky Mountain foothills near Spokane, and the fast Okanogan.

The Western Okanogan and Methow Valley regions sport a mixture of mountain slopes and drier foothills and climate relative to the western Cascades. Within the Okanogan region are numerous river valleys, some large and others small. Two of the largest are the Okanogan River valley and the Lake Roosevelt valley, both of which extend up into Canada.

The Methow River valley in particular is well-known for its natural beauty. The climate of the valley is diverse. In the south, the weather is notably dry, sometimes averaging only 10 inches of rain per year. Up north and west as you get into the Cascades properly the rainfall jumps up to 30 inches or more annually.

S35 – Okanogan Legion Airport

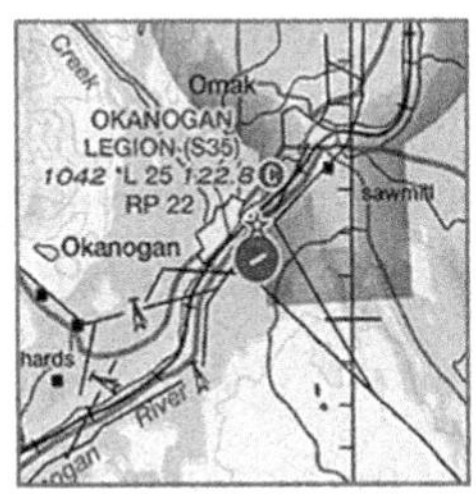

Location: 1 mile east of Okanogan
Coordinates: N48°21.72' / W119°34.05'
Altitude: 1042 MSL
Fuel: 100LL (blue)
Transient Storage: Tiedowns

The city of Okanogan sits along the Okanogan River in a narrowing of the valley south of the Omak area. Officially incorporated in 1907, the city currently supports about 2,500 people, the majority of whom live near the river.

This area is predominately agricultural, and the downtown has a charming mid-western feel to it. Walking into town from the airport, you'll cross over the Oak Street Bridge with the county court house several blocks in front of you to guide your way.

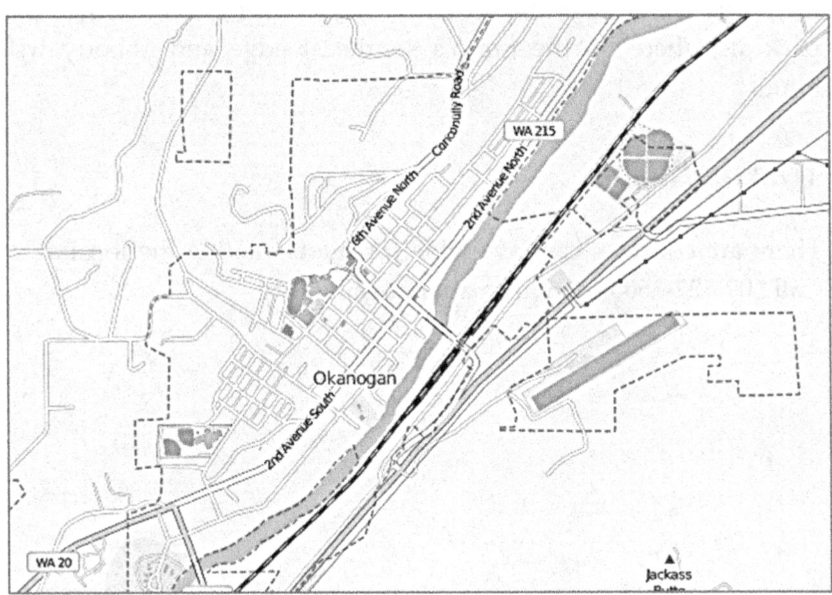

Airport Notes

Most of the town is on the northwest side of the river, and the airport is to the southeast side, up a bit on a small plateau or ridge. Traffic pattern is always to the northwest side of the field, toward the river, likely because of the rising terrain to the southeast of the field.

The wind usually blows up from downriver, but if in the rare cases it moves off to the northwest, watch for downdrafts over the runway. Likewise, if you get a healthy crosswind from the west, expect to float a bit longer than normal.

Both ends of the runway are clear of obstructions, but note the rising road just beyond the end of runway 4. If you're departing 22, you get a nice drop-off of land below you if you hang a slight right and head for the river.

There are 3 marked transient parking spots to the southwest end of the ramp. If those are filled, which they almost never are, you can park anywhere on the ramp's southeast edge and nobody will mind.

Transportation

There are courtesy cars available for pilots visiting the local area. Call 509-422-3600 to inquire about availability.

Things to Do

Okanogan National Forest

Public Services & Government, Parks
0.7 miles or 14-minute walk
1240 S. Second Ave, Omak, WA 98841
509-826-3275

Okanogan National Forest is a sprawling forest preserve, encompassing more than four million acres in total. North to south, the forest covers a distance of over 180 miles, which ensures that the forest is very diverse. Natural features of the forest range from alpine peaks of glacial rock to verdant valleys of ancient forest. Elevations throughout the forest vary from under 1,000 feet to over 9,000 feet.[124] There are countless recreational opportunities available to visitors of Okanogan National Forest, including hiking trails, campgrounds, horseback riding, mountain biking, fishing, hunting, climbing, skiing, snowmobiling and sightseeing. There are cabins available to rent that are connected to the forest by hundreds of miles of roads.

Overnight Lodging

Cariboo Inn

Hotels
0.7 miles or 14-minute walk
233 Queen St, Okanogan, WA 98840
509-422-6109

The Caraboo Inn, established in 1925, is independently owned and operated. Stepping into the lobby, the Inn resembles a hunting

[124] If you think it takes a long time to hike up to 9,000 feet, you should see how long it takes my airplane to climb that high…

lodge with two moose heads on the wall and one positioned above a welcoming fireplace.

The clean, newly remodeled rooms in this historic building offer guests free wifi and cable TV. Although the hotel offers the best of modern conveniences, the rooms are cozy. The antiques and traditional decor allows guests to travel back in time. Each bed has a welcoming, inviting, handmade quilt.

The food tastes like grandma's home cooking. Guests receive a free continental breakfast and are welcomed to dine for lunch and dinner at the on-site restaurant. The baked goods are amazingly delicious and lunch and dinner allow the guests to revel in the deliciousness and generous servings of comfort foods at their best.

Quality Inn

Hotels
1.3 miles or 24-minute walk
1 Apple Way, Okanogan, WA 98840
509-422-6431

This Quality Inn resembles many you might find elsewhere in the state. The wifi is reasonable, and access to the fitness center and laundry facilities are included with stay. Some of the rooms offered have sofa sleepers and/or mountain views. There's free breakfast with your room.

Rooms include a coffee maker, microwave, refrigerator, and hair dryer. The front desk is staffed 24 hours a day.

OMK – Omak Airport

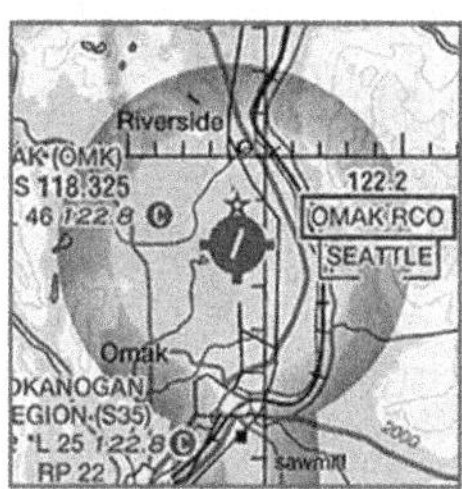

Location: 3 miles north of Omak
Coordinates: N48°27.87' / W119°31.08'
Altitude: 1304 MSL
Fuel: 100LL (blue)
Transient Storage: Tiedowns

North of the Okanogan Airport some 7 miles or so is the Omak Airport, located north of the town of Omak, set in an open flat valley some 4 or 5 miles wide.

The town itself supports about 5,000 residents. The land that is now Omak had been inhabited by various Native American tribes before the arrival of non-indigenous settlers in the early 19th century. The city began to develop after the completion of the Okanogan Irrigation Project affecting the Grand Coulee Dam and other nearby electric facilities.

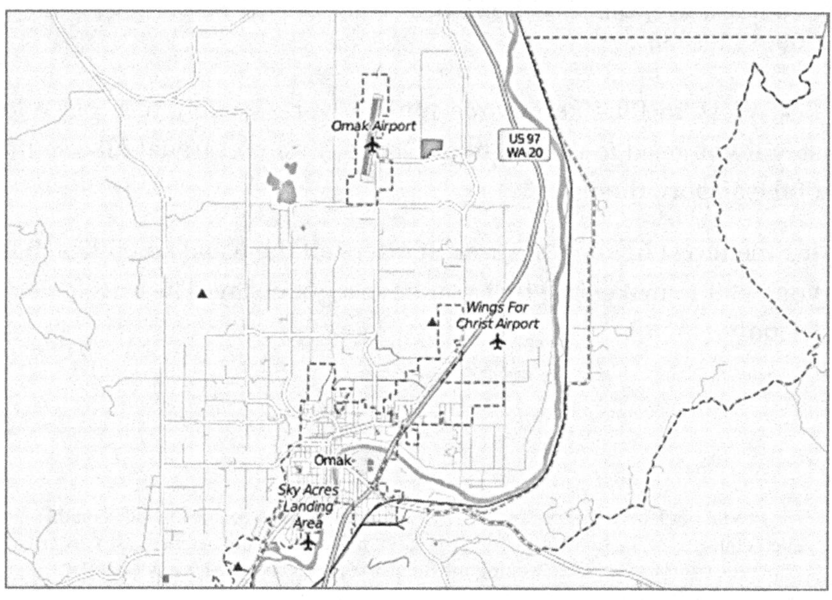

Airport Notes

The airport is easily visible at distance, north of town and west of the river. There aren't any obstacles on approach. There is, however, a really cool-looking 200 foot tall, 500 foot wide mini-mountain about 1.6nm north of the airport. It's worth a look.

Note after landing the extremely wide and tempting taxiway that's marked with large Xs. Don't use it.

Transient parking is on the smaller ramp to the south of the ramp that hosts the passenger and pilot lounge. Look for the fuel dock, which is on the eastern edge of the transient ramp.

Overnight Lodging

Best Western Plus Peppertree Inn

Hotels
3.1 miles or 59-minute walk
820 Koala Ave, Omak, WA 98841
509-422-2088

Best Western Plus Peppertree Inn[125] is a reasonably nice place to stay if you need to overnight in Omak. It's a non-trivial hike south of the airport, though.

It's the nicest hotel in the area. It offers all the usual amenities that you need to make sure that you have a good stay. The staff is very friendly.

125 Let's be frank here. Every Best Western is the same. They're like the McDonalds cheeseburgers of the hotel industry. This is not meant as a slam against Best Western. Quite the contrary. I enjoy checking into a Best Western because it's a good hotel with absolutely no surprises. I also enjoy eating McDonalds cheeseburgers.

W01 – Tonasket Municipal Airport

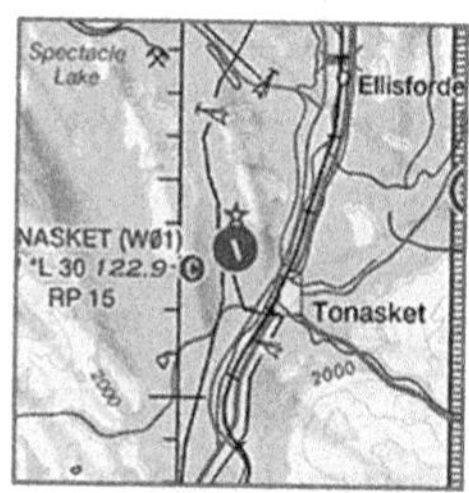

Location: 2 miles northwest of Tonasket
Coordinates: N48°43.49' / W119°27.94'
Altitude: 1311 MSL
Fuel: None
Transient Storage: Tiedowns

Continuing up north along the Okanogan River valley, you'll encounter the town of Tonasket. The town is small, supporting a population of just over 1,000. The city sits at about 900 MSL and is bordered on the north by Siwash Creek and the south by Bonaparte Creek.

Tonasket, which has been the site of a U.S. post office since 1901, was platted in 1910 and incorporated in 1927. It serves as a hub for agricultural and forestry industries in north central Okanogan County.

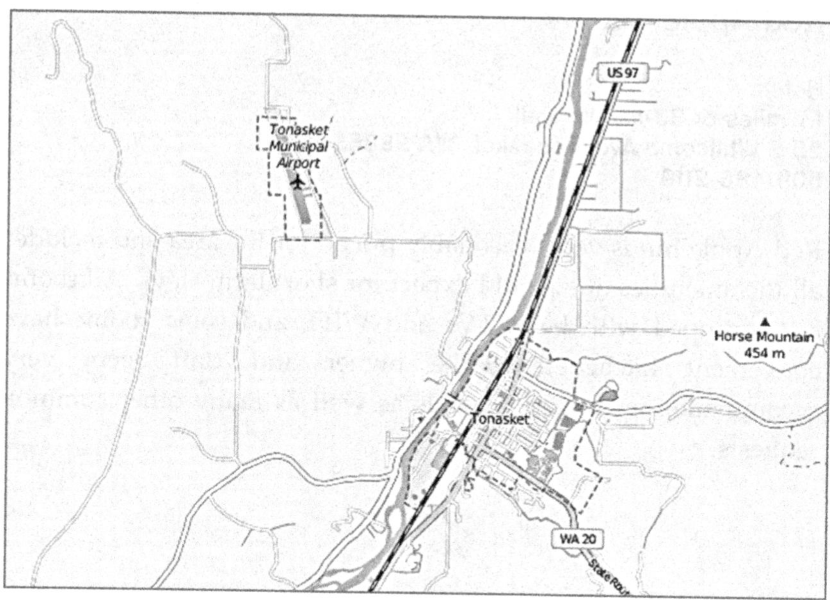

Airport Notes

The airport is easy to spot being that's basically in the middle of nowhere, northwest of town. Traffic pattern is always to the west of the field, away from the railroad tracks to the east.

As you're approaching, note the Whitestone Mountains to the north of the airport. They're not particularly tall, at about 2,400 MSL, but that's still about 1,100 feet over field elevation. These mountains are really a plateau that runs north-south west of the river, but from the ground, they look like mountains. If you're not on the clock, consider circumnavigating the formation. It's roughly 10 miles around. The best views are all along the south and up in the northwest corner.

Transient parking for 12 is well-marked midfield to the east.

Overnight Lodging

Red Apple Inn

Hotels
1.7 miles or 33-minute walk
20 S Whitcomb Ave, Tonasket, WA 98855
509-486-2119

Red Apple Inn is very reasonably priced for the area and includes all the amenities one would expect for short term stays. All rooms are equipped with large TVs and WIFI, and some rooms have convenient kitchenettes. The owner and staff seem very accommodating for late arrivals as well as many other common requests.

Junction Motel

Hotels
1.8 miles or 35-minute walk
23 W 6th St, Tonasket, WA 98855
509-486-4500

Junction Motel is a conveniently located motel with access to a wide variety of amenities and friendly staff. Amenities include in-room Keurig-brand coffee machine, mini-fridge, microwave, flat screen television, free wifi, and free coffee/hot cocoa. Pets are allowed, subject to a non-refundable deposit.

The motel is located at the junction of several highways and with convenient access to an adjacent convenience store and laundromat.

0S7 – Dorothy Scott Airport

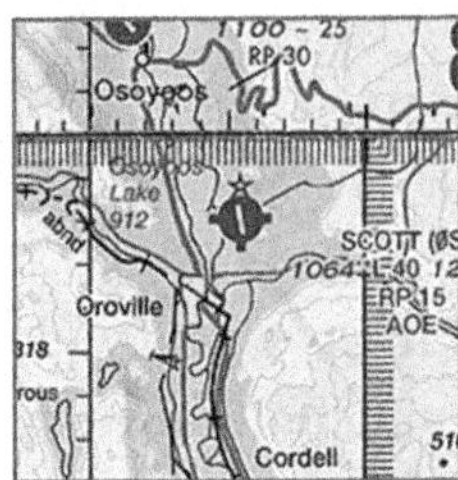

Location: 2 miles northeast of Oroville
Coordinates: N48°57.54' / W119°24.72'
Altitude: 1064 MSL
Fuel: 100LL (blue)
Transient Storage: Tiedowns

Follow the Okanogan River valley far enough north and you'll reach Osoyoos Lake and the Canadian border. Just to the east side of the south end of the lake is the Dorothy Scott Airport, a couple of miles northeast of Oroville.

Oroville supports about 1,700 people. Most of the economy of Oroville and the surrounding areas is based on agriculture. There are numerous orchards within the town limits and a few grape vineyards. During Oroville's heyday as a mining town, there were numerous saloons, restaurants, shops, and a drive in movie theater.

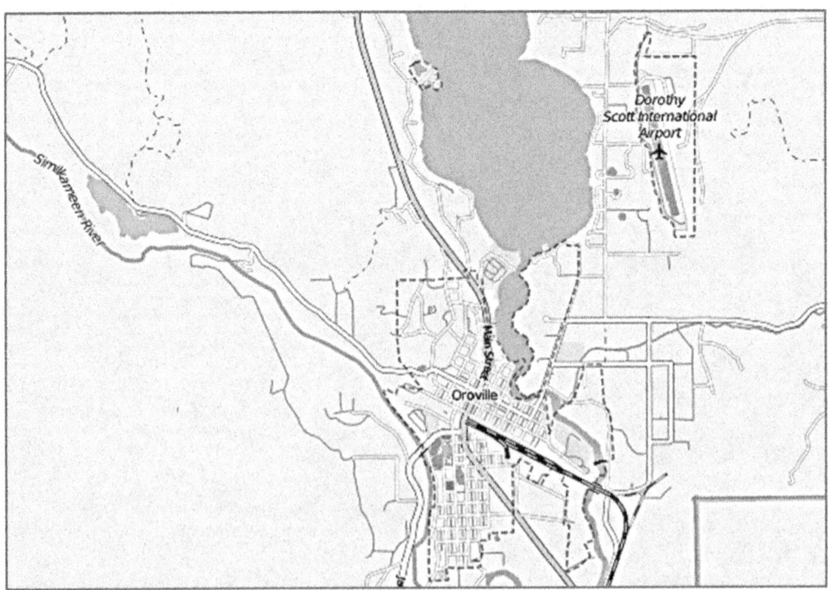

Airport Notes

Traffic pattern is always to the west of the field due to 2 very nifty-looking mountains of just a bit over 1,000 feet tall above the runway elevation and less than 1,800 feet east of the runway.

When the wind picks up, watch out for very strange and unexpected turbulence near the airport.

Transient parking is anywhere on the eastern side of the main ramp or to the west of the taxiway north of the ramp. If you park off the taxiway, ensure you're far enough back in the grass so as not to make someone taxiing worry about clipping the end of their wing.

Fuel dock is just south of the two very large helicopter landing zones midfield.

Overnight Lodging

Osoyoos Lake Veteran's Memorial Park

Campgrounds
1.3 miles or 24-minute walk
2207 Juniper, Oroville, WA 98844
509-476-3321

Osoyoos Lake Veteran's Memorial Park is a 47 acre park and campsite that straddles the 14 mile long lake. The park features plenty of green space and the lawns extend down to the shores of the lake. There is a 40 foot dock with two boat ramps and a daily permit is available for the launching of watercraft. Vehicle and trailer parking is included in the $5 cost of this permit.

Water sports are allowed and visitors who possess fishing licenses are allowed to use the lake for the fishing of certain species of fish including smallmouth bass, rainbow trout, and kokanee.

The park includes bathing facilities for swimmers. Ice skating and ice fishing are available in the winter when the lake is frozen.

Camaray Motel

Hotels
1.8 miles or 35-minute walk
1320 Main St, Oroville, WA 98844
509-476-3684

The Camaray Motel is a lovely place to say. The rates are quite reasonable, both their standard rates and especially their discounted weekly rates. Amenities and furniture are modern, clean, and comfortable. The place is clean with wonderful service.

The owners are really caring and provide a personal touch. For a small rural town, the decor was very nice and appeared to have been recently updated.

S52 – Methow Valley State Airport

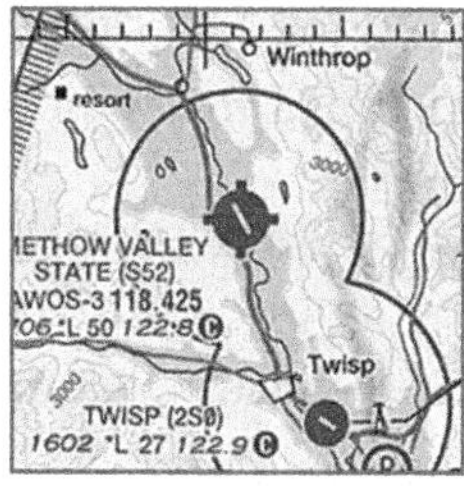

Location: 3 miles southeast of Winthrop
Coordinates: N48°25.50' / W120°8.75'
Altitude: 1706 MSL
Fuel: 100LL (blue), Jet-A
Transient Storage: Tiedowns

The Methow Valley has some sort of strange, almost magical draw to it, especially for aviators. Unlike the "wet" side of the state where seasons sort of bleed into each other, Winthrop experiences a winter that's really winter and a summer that's really summer.[126]

The population of the Winthrop area is around 2,000. Winthrop is known for the American Old West design of all the buildings in town, making it a tourist destination.

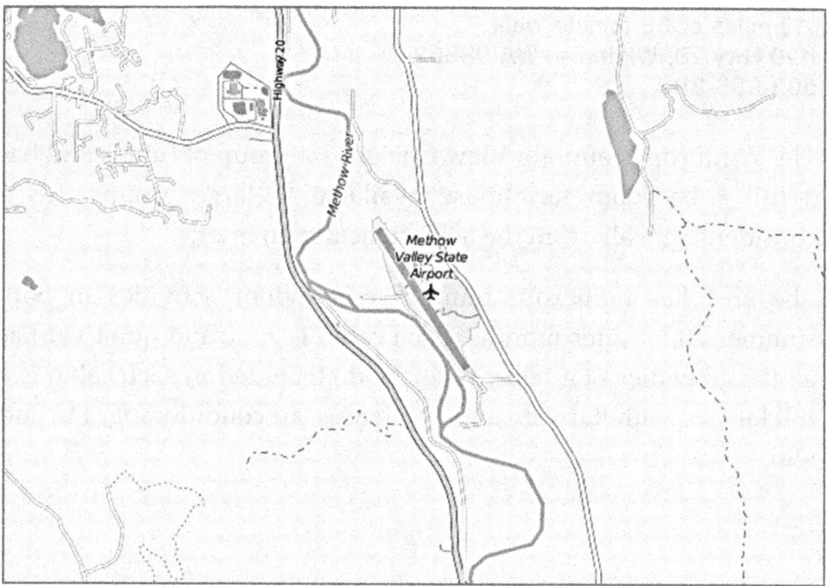

[126] Don't even get me started about autumn. Wow. Just, yeah. Wow.

Airport Notes

The airport is a 3 miles south of Winthrop, set just to the east of the river. The valley gets fairly narrow near the airport, so the winds can do some fun things at the surface. Exercise caution.

This airport is heavily used during fire season by smoke jumpers and other firefighting folks. During the fire season, keep an eye out for large aircraft operating on long final approaches.

There's fuel available about 100 yards north of the smoke jumper base.

Overnight Lodging

Winthrop Mountain View Chalets

Hotels
2.9 miles or 56-minute walk
1120 Hwy 20, Winthrop, WA 98862
509-996-3113

The Winthrop Mountain View Chalets is a group of cabins and has a full 6 bedroom farmhouse available to large groups. It's a considerable walk from the airport, nearly an hour.

The area has numerous outdoor and indoor activities in both summer and winter months. Each cabin is cozy and quiet yet has all the amenities of a fancy hotel room. Included in each cabin is a full kitchen with flatware and appliances, air conditioning, TV, and wifi.

2S0 – Twisp Municipal Airport

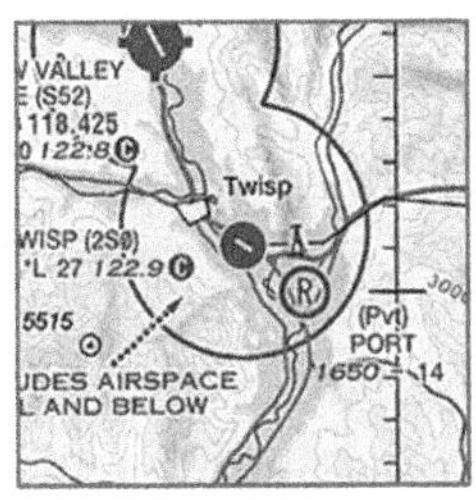

Location: 1 mile southeast of Twisp
Coordinates: N48°21.04' / W120°5.64'
Altitude: 1602 MSL
Fuel: None
Transient Storage: Tiedowns

Twisp is south of Winthrop and the Methow Valley airport a bit, still in the Methow Valley, on the Methow River at its confluence with the Twisp River. It's a small town of less than 1,000 people.

Twisp is called the "heart of the Methow Valley" by people who live in Twisp. Like their neighbors to the north, Twisp knows how to do a proper summer and winter. And even though the field elevation is only 1,600 MSL, watch for density altitude to creep up on you on hot summer days.

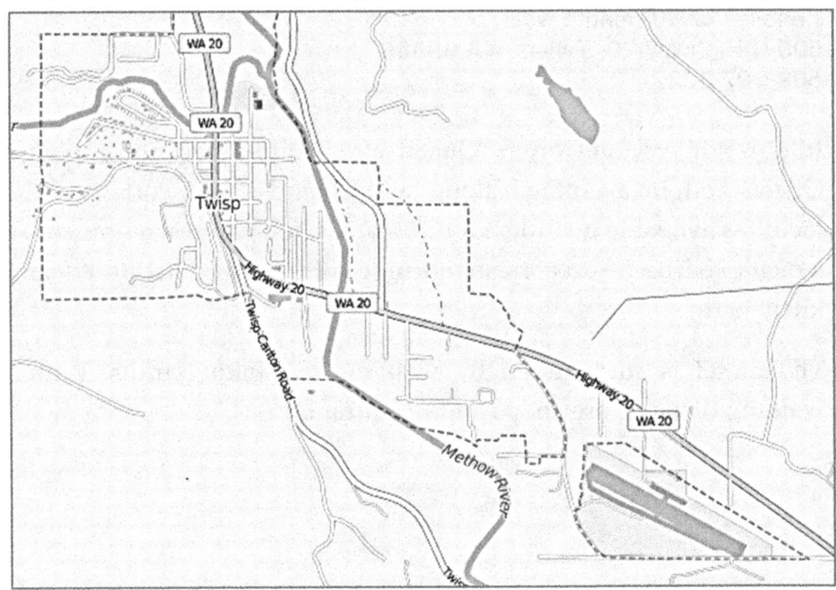

Airport Notes

The airport is southeast of town just to the southwest of highway 20. There are some rather non-trivial slopes out both sides of the runway, so watch out for curious and weird wind effects whenever there are crosswind conditions.

There are trees off the north end of the runway, but they're not directly in your way. There's a road directly to the south of the runway, hence the displaced threshold.

Transient parking is in the grass that's on the runway side of the taxiway that goes past the hangars.

Overnight Lodging

Idle-A-While Motel

Hotels
1.6 miles or 30-minute walk
505 N Highway 20, Twisp, WA 98856
509-997-3222

Idle-A-While Motel offers Queen and Double bedrooms plus a Queen bed in a cottage along with 2 and 3-bed cottages. The facilities available include hot tub, saunas, telephones, tennis court, a picnic/barbecue area, fresh morning coffee, wifi, satellite TV, and kitchenette.

The motel is surrounded by walking and biking trails. Within walking distance are shops and restaurants.

Methow Suites Bed & Breakfast

Bed & Breakfast
1.6 miles or 30-minute walk
Twisp, WA 98856
509-997-5970

Methow Suites has been a relaxing go-to spot in the Methow Valley since 2008. Owners and operators Sandy and Bill leave nothing to chance. Beautiful, quiet rooms with good WIFI and amazing homemade breakfasts and unlimited hot coffee are just a few of the reasons to fall in love with this spot.

There are numerous local attractions to be explored if you can pull yourself away the grounds of the B&B, which include a park with native plants and animals, and even a children's play area.

Methow Valley Inn

Hotels, Bed & Breakfast
1.6 miles or 30-minute walk
234 W 2nd Ave, Twisp, WA 98856
509-997-2253

This hotel will make you feel right at home. It's an old-fashioned, comfort-style inn in which you'll be served directly by the owners. This inn is available for groups of 4 up to 18. The rooms are well-sized, and the beds are very comfortable.

The Inn resides in a 100-year-old home. Their continental breakfast includes locally produced jams and compotes as well as a surprise dish of the day.

Twisp River Suites

Hotels
1.7 miles or 33-minute walk
140 W Twisp Ave, Twisp, WA 98856
509-997-0100

Just south of the Twisp River and near Division Street are the Twisp River Suites. A deck runs along the back of the building providing a wonderful place to enjoy a microbrew or a cup of Blue Star coffee. There are chairs down by the river if you prefer to be closer to the soothing gurgle of water.

The common area is warm and comfortable with a fireplace, leather furniture, and plenty of tables to enjoy a beverage, play cards, or eat a wonderful breakfast. Breakfast is a couple of egg casseroles, boiled eggs, fresh fruit, yogurt, fresh scones, cereals, bagels, bread pudding, and lots of accoutrements. They serve award-winning Blue Star Coffee.

W12 – Lost River Resort Airport

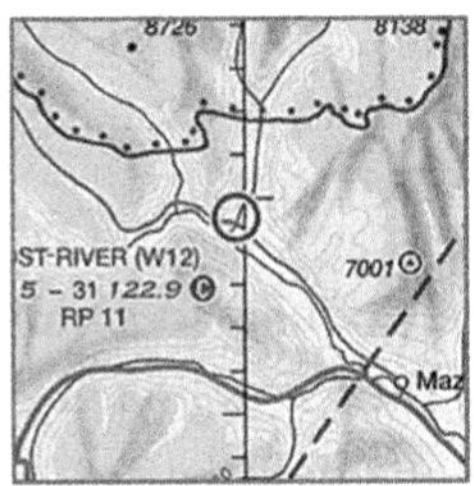

Location: 5 miles northwest of Mazama
Coordinates: N48°38.98' / W120°30.12'
Altitude: 2415 MSL
Fuel: None
Transient Storage: None

Tucked up securely into the Cascade Mountains northwest of the Methow Valley is the Lost River Resort Airport at Mazama. The area is heavily forested and enclosed by tall mountains on nearly every side.

Lost River flows down to the south, and there's a trench-like valley that it flows throw. The valley is sided by nearly vertical mountain walls that tower well over 2,000 feet over the valley floor. The valley is less than a mile wide.

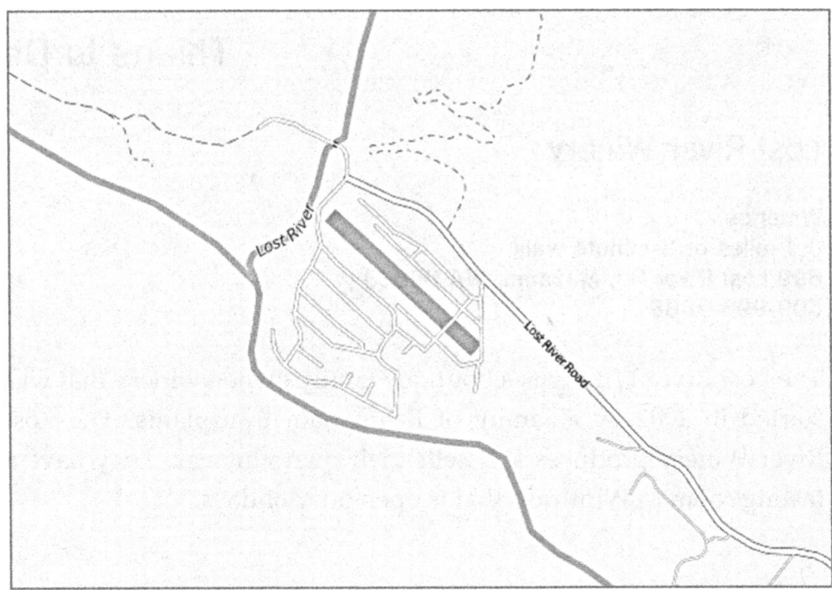

Airport Notes

As mentioned, this is a mountain valley with tight, tall walls. As you make your approach, hug the right side of the valley so you can comfortably make a 180 if conditions don't look favorable.

The airport is a grass strip just to the east of a merger of two small rivers. The northern end points right at a rather menacing mountain. Traffic pattern is always to the west of the field, over the river. The airport is closed in the winter, open from April through October.

The runway has roadways crossing it at various points. If you can, do a flyby to communicate your intentions to pedestrians and vehicles. Always be ready to abort your landing if necessary. There are vehicle access roads that run along both sides of the runway right up next to the grass field. Exercise extreme caution.

There's rarely any wind here, but regardless, be ready for anything.

Things to Do

Lost River Winery

Wineries
0.4 miles or 8-minute walk
699 Lost River Rd, Mazama, WA 98833
509-996-2888

The Lost River Winery is a boutique family owned winery that was started in 2002 by a family of Bellingham transplants. The Lost River Winery produces and sells their own vintages. They have a tasting room in Winthrop that is open on Mondays.

Monument Creek Trailhead

Hiking
0.4 miles or 8-minute walk
700 Lost River Rd, Mazama, WA 98833

The Monument Creek Trailhead provides access to the Monument Creek Trail #484 which accesses the Pasayten Wilderness. This trail is only maintained to where the bridge is washed out, at about 4 miles. The trail beyond Eureka Creek has not been maintained for over 25 years.

Overnight Lodging

Cedar Creek Cabin

Guest Houses
0.3 miles or 5-minute walk
24 Rainbow Road, Mazama, WA 98862
206-985-8472

Cedar Creek Cabin is located roughly 3 blocks southwest of the airport, a short walk from the runway. The cabin is fully outfitted and comfortable. The neighborhood is very quiet. The cabin is well ventilated, and together with the dry climate and evening breezes is comfortable even in hot weather. There is no air conditioning.

Lost River Resort

Hotels
0.3 miles or 6-minute walk
681 Lost River Rd, Mazama, WA 98833
509-996-2537

The Lost River Resort offers studio, family chalet, and other accommodations. A studio offers a fully equipped kitchen, rustic woodstove, queen beds, and double sofa sleepers.

Each studio sleeps up to 4 adults. The Chalet has a full kitchen, large wood burning stove, 2 bathrooms, and large open deck. The Chalet sleeps up to 8.

Chapter 10

Central Cascades

The Cascade Mountains extend from southern British Columbia through Washington and Oregon into Northern California, but their central core is right in the middle of Washington State. The highest peak in the range is Mount Rainier at 14,411 feet. The range is volcanic, and the most famous of the volcanic peaks is of course Mount St. Helens.

The Cascades can be a place of high ridges and peaks with deep and tight valleys. Winds can play strange games here, and frequently the mountains are visually obscured, especially on the western slopes but sometimes all the way through. Flying low from the east through the mountains has brought more than one pilot suddenly face-to-face with a wall of cloud. Even in perfect weather, it's doesn't take much to get disoriented and fly into a boxed canyon.

For those that carefully check the weather and opt to take the calculated risk, the area offers unparalleled majestic scenes at all altitudes. Peaks are rugged and elegant, and valleys are thick with trees, rivers, and lakes.

Tucked into various strategic locations in the area are a number of airports beckoning the adventurous pilot. And toward the eastern slopes are a number of other airports worth a visit that are considerably safer to fly around and through.

S88 – Skykomish State Airport

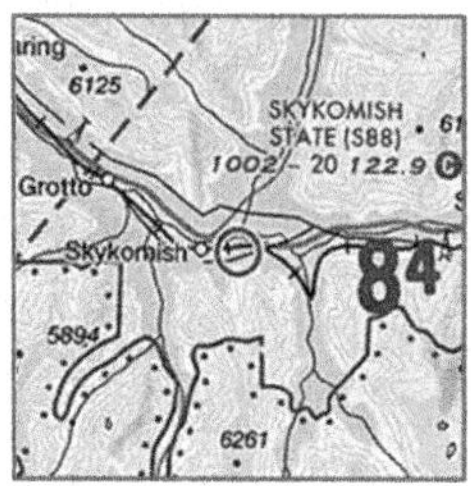

Location: 1 mile east of Skykomish
Coordinates: N47°42.66' / W121°20.34'
Altitude: 1002 MSL
Fuel: None
Transient Storage: Tiedowns

Skykomish is a very tiny town tucked up into the western side of a valley that carves into the heart of the Cascades along highway 2. It supports a population of about 200 people, but it was once home to several thousand in the 1920s.

Located in the Mount Baker-Snoqualmie National Forest, near Deception Falls on the Skykomish River, Skykomish was founded as a railroad town. Today, it's mainly a stopping point for recreational access to the surrounding mountains, including skiing at nearby Stevens Pass.

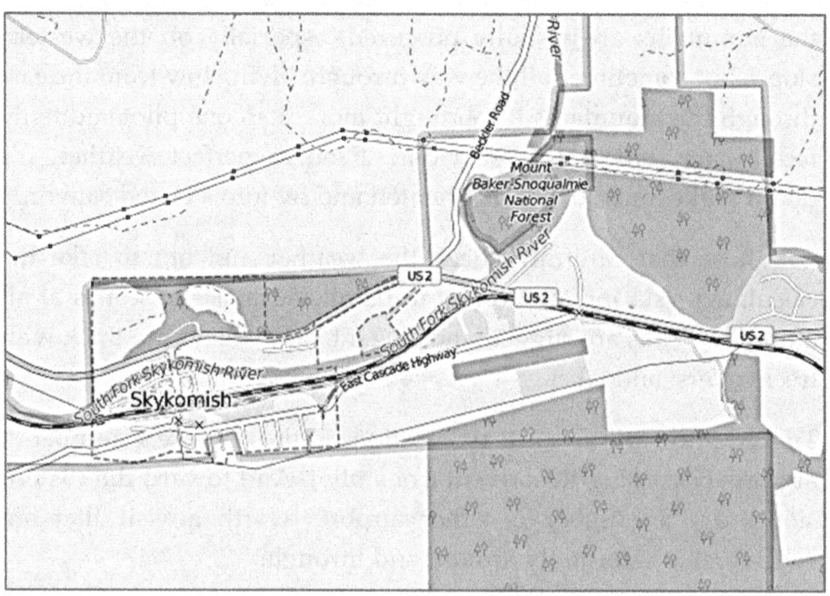

Airport Notes

The airport is just to the east of town. Both the airport and town are immediately south of the river, which is immediately south of highway 2. The valley is long and often acts as a wind tunnel, so expect winds to come out of the west. They tend to shift as you get closer to the runway. On an extended final at 2,000 feet AGL, you'll probably experience a right quartering headwind. At about 1,000 feet AGL, don't be surprised if the wind shifts to a left quartering headwind. Then as you flare, it'll probably be right down the runway.

There are trees off the eastern end of the runway. The runway itself is in reasonably good condition, but it's turf, so exercise the usual amounts of caution. The surface gets quite soft after a good rain. The runway is just over 2,000 feet long with terrain and trees just off to the left side as you depart to the west.[127] Before throttle-up, pick a safe abort point and don't push your risk envelope.

The runway is open only in the summer, from June through September. Watch out for pedestrians and vehicles on or near the runway.

Transient parking is on the north side slightly to the west of midfield. From there, you can easily walk out to the East Cascade Highway, then west into town.

[127] Although technically it's a left pattern both directions, I'd personally fly a right pattern if landing or departing to the east because of the nifty mountain to the airport's south. That said, winds are almost always from the west, so this is never really an issue.

Deception Falls

Hiking
0.8 miles or 15-minute walk
Rte 2, Skykomish, WA 98288

If you're looking for a cool place to go to enjoy natural beauty, then Deception Falls might be right. There are several good trails to walk and acres of thick forest all around. You could walk around here for hours and not see even a quarter of it.

To get to the falls, walk east along highway 2 until you reach Foss River road. Then follow that a bit until you hear the falls.

Great Northern and Cascade Railway

Trains
1.0 miles or 19-minute walk
101 N 5th St, Skykomish, WA 98288
360-282-6676

The Great Northern & Cascade Railway operates from May through October every year and is closed during the winter months. There are 2,700 feet of track, but it's currently expanding. The railway has one locomotive that has ten riding cars giving free rides to the public.

This is a non-profit organization that is always accepting donations to for upkeep and additions to the railway. It's fully funded by donations and ran by friendly volunteers. They offer discounted yearly memberships in various types but to ride the train is free.

Mysty Mountain Cabin

Vacation Rental Agents, Guest Houses
0.5 miles or 10-minute walk
73525 NE Stevens Pass Hwy, Skykomish, WA 98288
206-219-6427

Mysty Mountain Cabins are fully equipped vacation rentals. The cabins can be rented in any season and include pet friendly cabins, luxury cabins, and even honeymoon cabins. The rentals can accommodate large parties such as family reunions and company retreats. Each cabin is furnished and the kitchen is stocked with everything you might need except food. They team up with local attractions to offer great deals and discounts. Many of the cabins offer hot tubs, fireplaces, and wifi among numerous other amenities.

Cascadia Inn

Hotels, Diners
0.9 miles or 18-minute walk
210 Railroad Ave E, Skykomish, WA 98288
360-677-2030

The Cascadia Inn is a hotel and a café. The price ranges from $20 to $80 dollars. You can pay a lower price for a communal room with bunk beds and a shared bath, or you can pay a higher price for a private room with a private bath and TV. Breakfast and an open bar are available. The hotel lounge has games and wifi. The café on the other side serves appetizers, lunch, and dinner. The hotel also offers a do-it-yourself tour which allows you to learn the history of the city.

27W – Lake Wenatchee State Airport

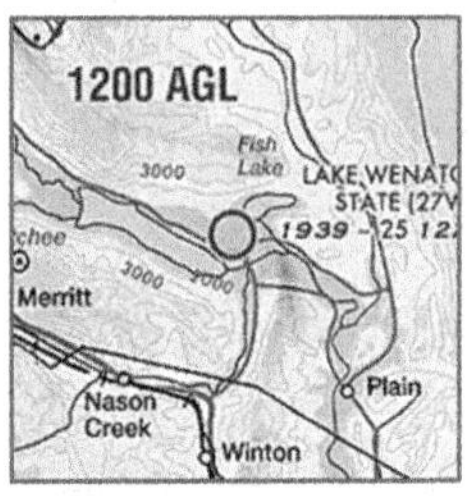

Location: 14 miles northwest of Leavenworth
Coordinates: N47°49.16' / W120°43.19'
Altitude: 1939 MSL
Fuel: None
Transient Storage: Tiedowns

Lake Wenatchee is a glacier and snowmelt-fed lake located in the Wenatchee National Forest on the eastern slopes of the Cascades. Lake Wenatchee covers nearly 2,500 acres with a depth of 244 feet. It's the source of the Wenatchee River.

Lake Wenatchee State Park is a publicly owned recreation area at the eastern end of the lake. The park is nearly 500 acres split into two parts: the north shore park and the south shore park. These two sections are separated by the Wenatchee River. On the southern shore is a beach about 800 feet long and 180 feet wide.

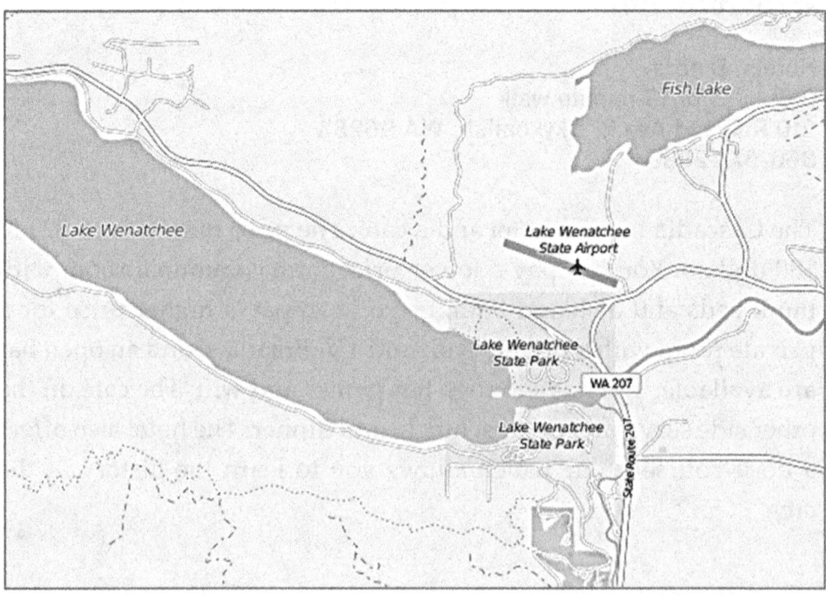

Airport Notes

First of all, if you're lucky enough to own a seaplane, just land on the lake. At over 24,000 feet in length, you'll have no problems. Note that the lake surface elevation is a bit under 2,000 MSL, so on hot summer days the density altitude may factor in, but you'll have a lot of lake to give things a try.

For everybody else, the airport is on the northeast corner of the lake, sandwiched between Lake Wenatchee and Fish Lake. Despite its mountain proximity, the land around the airport is relatively flat without too much to worry about in terms of tall obstructions.

The airport's only open from June through the end of September. There are access roads along all sides of the runway, so keep an eye out for pedestrians and others in and around the runway.

Park on the eastern end in the open area north of the building.

Food Options

Headwaters Pub

Dive Bars, Restaurants
0.8 miles or 15-minute walk
21328 State Route 207, Leavenworth, WA 98826
509-763-3501

Headwaters Pub is a casual restaurant with a full bar. There's free wifi, TV, and an outdoor patio where smoking is permitted. It's good for eat in or take out with the busiest nights being Friday, Saturday, and Sunday.

This establishment is not recommended for kids as it can get somewhat "lively" at times. There is a juke box and karaoke for dancing, plenty of parking for cars or bikes, and lots of room for groups of almost any size. No reservations are needed or taken, and all major credit cards are accepted. The food is excellent and the owners are happy and willing to make your visit a memorable one.

Things to Do

Icicle Outfitters & Guides

Parks, Hiking, Horseback Riding
1.0 miles or 18-minute walk
14800 State Park Rd, Leavenworth, WA 98826
509-763-3647

Icicle Outfitters & Guides is a company that offers customers guided horseback riding trail tours and riding instruction for youth. The trail tours offer scenic views of the wilderness. Tours range from a couple of hours to multi-day tours and are guided by experienced guides who provide entertainment during the trip with stories and jokes. During the winter months, horse-drawn sleigh rides are available. The sleigh rides end with coffee, tea, cocoa, and warm apple cider to warm travelers up. Customers also have the option of booking private tours instead of taking the normal large group tours.

Lake Wenatchee State Park

Parks
1.1 miles or 21-minute walk
Lake Wenatchee State Park, Leavenworth, WA 98826

Lake Wenatchee State Park covers almost 500 acres and is dedicated to camping, boating, and other activities. During the summer, it's open from 6:30am to dusk. The park is divided into the south park which has been developed for park activities and the north section which is mostly wilderness. There is winter camping available in designated areas from November 15 through April 1. There are two kitchen shelters along with 54 uncovered picnic tables. Bathroom facilities are available. It contains miles of hiking, biking, and horse trails. Many water activities are available such as boating, swimming, and water skiing. During the winter you can cross country ski, ice climb, or sled. For camping enthusiasts, there are tent sites along with sites with electricity and water available. The park also has two ADA campsites. During the summer months, a Junior Ranger program is available along with various evening programs.

Overnight Lodging

Cove Resort

Hotels
1.4 miles or 27-minute walk
Fish Lk, Leavenworth, WA 98826
509-763-3130

Cove Resort is a campground located on Fish Lake. There is a camp store on the grounds which sells food and bait and tackle for fishing on the lake. 14, 16, and 20 foot boats are available for rental to use for fishing. Some fish found in the lake are rainbow trout and yellow perch, and fishing season is all year round. Rates for a campground start at $20 per night for an unpowered site and $28 per night for a powered site, and there is also one cabin available for rent at $85 per night.

Kahler Glen Golf & Ski Resort

Golf, Ski Resorts
1.7 miles or 33-minute walk
20700 Clubhouse Dr, Leavenworth, WA 98826
509-763-4025

The Kahler Glen Golf and Ski Resort is a beautiful, peaceful retreat. Those who enjoy the calm and serenity of rolling and hills and lakes surrounded by wooded land will love this peaceful picturesque setting. The resort itself is luxurious and spacious but is completely surrounded by nature. Guests can play round of golf in the afternoons to unwind or simply take a walk around the grounds and enjoy a picnic along the hillside. This resort is the perfect getaway to enjoy the mountain views and the water on Lake Wenatchee all year round.

Pine River Ranch Bed & Breakfast

Hotels, Bed & Breakfast, Venues & Event Spaces
2.9 miles or 56-minute walk
19668 State Rt 207, Leavenworth, WA 98826
509-763-3959

If you're looking for a good romantic getaway, this place might be right. Pine River Ranch Bed and Breakfast is south of the airport a fair walk, but call ahead and ask for a pick-up from the airport.

Pine River Ranch is renowned for its romantic getaways, complete with propane rock fireplaces in every room, jetted tubs, hand-peeled arbor log beds, breakfasts delivered to your room every morning, and the seclusion of twenty-three acres. During the winter it's a gorgeous getaway with snow on the ground, snowshoes to borrow, and miles of places to walk through fresh powder.

8S2 – Cashmere-Dryden Airport

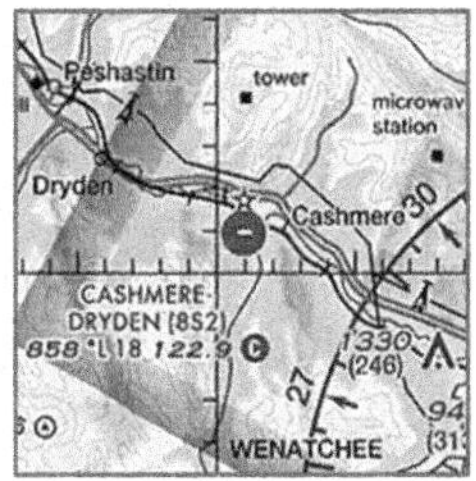

Location: 2 miles southwest of Cashmere
Coordinates: N47°30.88' / W120°29.08'
Altitude: 858 MSL
Fuel: None
Transient Storage: Tiedowns

Cashmere is a city in Chelan County that supports a population of something north of 3,000 people. The Cashmere area has a rich history of tree fruit production, starting with the first pioneers. With the construction of the Peshastin irrigation ditch in the 1890s, ranches and sagebrush gave away to lush orchards climbing up the walls of the valley.

Cashmere is the closest open airport to Leavenworth,[128] some 10 or more miles to the northwest.

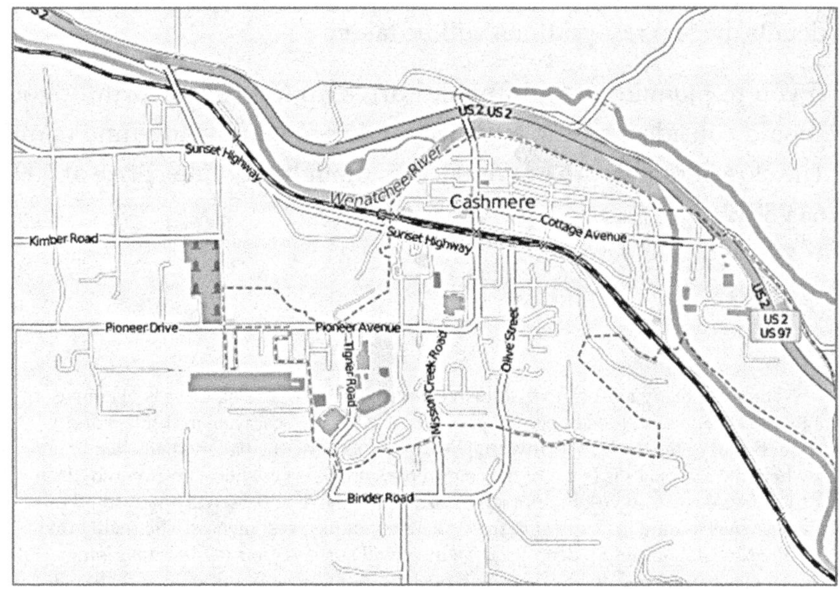

[128] In Leavenworth, you can eat chocolate-covered, deep-fried Twinkies. No joke.

Airport Notes

The airport is fairly easy to spot, being southwest of town right about at the part where residential homes give way to farms. The airport property is strangely both tight and open, depending on what you're talking about. North of the runway is a wide and open area of grass, but to the south are densely packed hangars just to the south of the taxiway.

Transient parking is limited with only 2 spots tightly packed into the southeastern corner of the airport property. If these are taken, you can elect to park in the grass area to the north of the field. If you do so, park pointed either west or east so that when you depart your prop wash won't blow quite so badly into the residential properties along the northern perimeter.

Transportation

There is a courtesy car available. Call 509-782-3321 to inquire about details, but no reservations will be taken.

If you're planning a flight in and drive up to Leavenworth,[129] you should consider renting a car if you'll be spending any time there. The closest rentals are in Wenatchee, though. Try Enterprise at 509-663-8812.

[129] There are many reasons to visit Leavenworth. Primary among these is of course the spectacular and life-changing opportunity to eat the best wienerschnitzel and sauerkraut in the Pacific Northwest. During Octoberfest, the bakery that's just under where the Starbucks is (west of the central park area) serves chocolate-covered, deep-fried Twinkies. And yes, I'm not joking. They are real. I've personally consumed this awesomeness, and I can attest to the epic nature of its awesomeness. The reality that is the chocolate-covered, deep-fried Twinkie will surpass your wildest imaginings. As you consume one, the heavens will open, flights of angels will sing, and all will seem right with the world. You might think I'm exaggerating. Eat one and try to prove me wrong. I dare you. I triple dog dare you.

Taqueria El Chavo

Mexican
0.6 miles or 11-minute walk
5647 Sunset Hwy, Cashmere, WA 98815
509-782-3590

Taqueria El Chavo is a Mexican restaurant known for authentic, affordable favorites and a robust menu of choices for those who enjoy variety when dining out. The presentation and atmosphere of the restaurant are quite modest, which contribute to its reputation as a local secret among "those in the know" Mexican food aficionados.

Mondays are a great day for the uninitiated to give Taqueria El Chavo a test drive: tacos are only $1. Other menu favorites include green mole enchiladas, ceviche tostadas, grilled burritos, and chile rellenos. The beverage menu features Mexican beers as well as a variety of fresh fruit juices and sodas.

Country Boy's BBQ

Barbeque
0.9 miles or 18-minute walk
400 Aplets Way, Cashmere, WA 98815
509-782-7427

Barbecue tastes great all year round but it's even better in the summer. If you are looking for a new barbecue place try Country Boy's BBQ. They know how to do barbecue the right way. Whether you were looking for brisket, pulled pork, baked beans, or any type of BBQ, they know how to do it. Meat is tender and juicy. The flavor is smoky, deep, and complex. Even the side dishes are excellent.

The staff is super nice and friendly. They'll come around to make sure everything is okay and do beverage refills. A sweet and enthusiastic bunch.

Club Crow

Restaurants
0.9 miles or 16-minute walk
108 1/2 Cottage Ave, Cashmere, WA 98815
509-782-3001

Club Crow[130] is a casual dining restaurant with a full bar. There are different activities to participate in such as billiards and live music. The restaurant has a smoker for their meat, which can be paired with a beer or your favorite soft drink.

The prices are affordable which makes this a location a popular spot for larger groups of friends. Since there is a full bar, it's not necessarily an appropriate location for children.

Blue Flame Asian Bistro

Chinese, Japanese, Thai
0.9 miles or 16-minute walk
102 Aplets Way, Cashmere, WA 98815
509-782-0298

The Blue Flame Asian Bistro is a combination Chinese, Japanese, Thai restaurant that's fairly classy yet not expensive. They offer sushi, Pad Thai, sesame chicken, and the usual Thai and Chinese dishes you'd expect to see. They also do a lot of fusion dishes like

[130] The term "eating crow" is an American colloquial idiom meaning humiliation by admitting wrongness or having been proven wrong after taking a strong position. The theory is that the meat from a crow bird is presumably foul-tasting in the same way that being proven wrong might be emotionally hard to swallow. Eating crow is of a family of idioms having to do with eating and being proven incorrect, such as to "eat dirt" and to "eat your hat" or shoe, all probably originating from "to eat one's words," which first appeared in print in 1571 in one of John Calvin's tracts, on Psalm 62: "God eateth not his words when he hath once spoken."

the "Blue Flame Spicy Chicken," which is essentially General Tso's chicken fused with spicy orange chicken.

The staff are friendly and attentive, and the food is prepared at lightning speed.

Hitching Post Tavern

Restaurants
1.0 miles or 18-minute walk
5720 Vale Rd, Cashmere, WA 98815
509-782-3250

The Hitching Post Tavern is a full service bar that includes a full menu. There are bar menu favorites and interesting entrees, all made to order. They have a large menu and are known locally for having a great burger selection. You can sit at the bar, have a seat at a table, or even get your meal to go.

The moderately priced food menu and drink specials are very satisfying and the friendly atmosphere will make you an instant regular when you're in town. It's a place you will want to return to often and try something new each time.

Things to Do

Brian's Bulldog Pizza & Bowling

Pizza, Bowling
0.9 miles or 17-minute walk
107 Cottage Ave, Cashmere, WA 98815
509-782-1505

Brian's Bulldog Pizza & Bowling is a family entertainment center that features a variety of activities. The main attraction is a four lane bowling alley. There is also a large gaming area with skee ball, air hockey, pinball machines, a basketball machine, and a large arcade with modern gaming cabinets.

The restaurant primarily serves pizza with 12 different specialty pizzas and a pizza buffet. Other food options include a "salad" bar with 50 items, calzones, chicken wings, and iced cream.

Reservations are accepted and special packages can be purchased which include bowling and pizza.

Action Rafting Company

Rafting/Kayaking
1.0 miles or 18-minute walk
105 E Pleasant St, Cashmere, WA 98815
509-782-1191

The Action Rafting Company offers a range of river activities. Their highly trained and qualified guides have years of expertise and can offer a wide selection of experiences from a relaxing float down the river to adrenaline-filled whitewater rafting.

Small group sizes keep the experience personal, and the guides are knowledgeable about the local area. Action Rafting Company or ARC supplies all essential equipment, including wet-suits, life jackets, and (optionally) lunch, ensuring you the utmost safety and comfort.

Cashmere's Village Inn Motel

Hotels
1.0 miles or 19-minute walk
229 Cottage Ave, Cashmere, WA 98815
509-782-3522

Cashmere's Village Inn is a family-owned hotel. The hotel itself is a little outdated. But despite its dusty appearance, the place is very well kept. The staff is friendly and accommodating. This is a good hotel if you're looking for the essentials. There's an ice maker, the rooms have balconies, and the hotel is close to town.

ESW – Easton State Airport

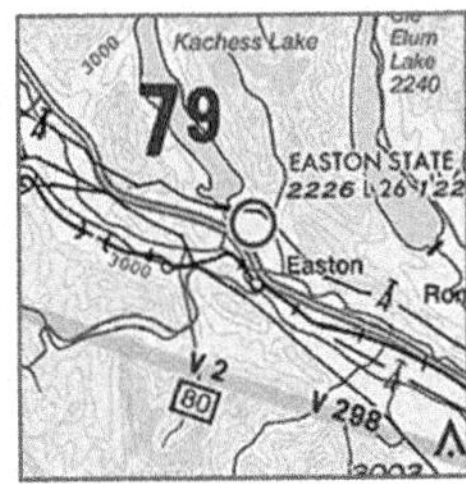

Location: 2 miles north of Easton
Coordinates: N47°15.25' / W121°11.13'
Altitude: 2226 MSL
Fuel: None
Transient Storage: Tiedowns

Easton is a small town spread along I-90 west of Cle Elem. It supports a population of about 500 people. The region experiences dry and warm but usually not too hot summers, with no average monthly temperatures above 72°F.[131]

It's home to Lake Easton and the associated state park, the Iron Horse State Park, and miles of hike-able wilderness. To its north is the enormous Kachess Lake.

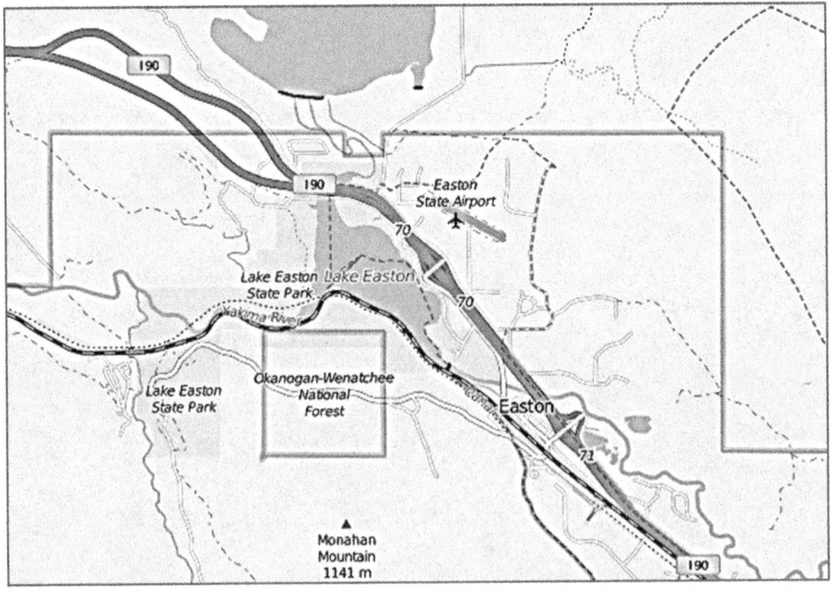

[131] That said, there are some days in July and August where it can get over 90°F. The air can get quite thin. You can almost feel it. Watch out for density altitude.

Airport Notes

Being just east of the Snoqualmie summit, Easton is usually about the dissipation point of whatever cloud layers are hugging up the western slopes. Don't let clear skies over Easton fool you into thinking the pass is passable.

It was constructed in the 1930s by the federal government as an emergency field for DC-3s crossing the Cascades through Snoqualmie Pass. It was acquired by the state in 1958 to preserve it for future use.

Field elevation is 2,226 feet, and density altitude problems can be encountered in the summer. Trees surround the airport and there are trees in both approaches close in. Deer, elk, and motorcyclists also enjoy the airport. The surface is somewhat rough, and will be soft when wet. An overflight is recommended to check field conditions and obstructions. The airport is generally open from June through September.

Best place to park is probably on the south side about a quarter of the distance from the eastern edge.

Food Options

Mountain High Hamburgers

Burgers
0.5 miles or 9-minute walk
2941 W Sparks Rd, Easton, WA 98925
509-656-3037

Mountain high burgers is just south of the airport right on Sparks Road. It's a wonderful place to have a fun, friendly meal. The multiple variety of shakes and tasteful flavors are appealing. The place is upbeat and family friendly; kids welcomed. Food is made promptly.

They sometimes offer venison and elk hamburgers, depending on the season.[132]

Backwoods Café

Barbeque, Coffee & Tea
0.4 miles or 8-minute walk
2480 E Sparks Rd, Easton, WA 98925
509-656-0124

Backwoods Café is a Barbeque Joint located south and slightly east of the airport just past Silver Creek. They're open 4 days a week, closed Monday, Tuesday, and Wednesday. They offer barbeque or hamburger meals and feature beer and wine to drink along with other beverages. The décor is rustic, decorated much like a cabin, and they feature many sides good for barbeque such as beans and coleslaw. Backwoods Café does not accept reservations, but they do accept credit cards, and are friendly to both children and large groups.

[132] Here's the thing about venison and elk burgers: They can be very yummy if done just right. But you have to do it just right. It's easy to get it wrong and end up with a mostly tasteless brick of dry meat. Cow is far easier to prepare well. That said, a lot of these mountain-based restaurants that serve venison and elk know what they're doing. But of course, a lot depends on who's on shift as cook that day. Fortunately, for most of these mountain burger joints, the wait staff are friendly and quite willing to let you in on who's on shift and whether you should order a venison, elk, or cow burger.

Back Woods BBQ Café

Coffee & Tea, Breakfast & Brunch
0.6 miles or 12-minute walk
2480 E Sparks Rd, Easton, WA 98925
509-656-0124

Back Woods BBQ Café specializes in great ribs. With a very diverse menu for a BBQ restaurant, you really are going to want to keep coming back to sample everything they offer. They even offer free wifi.

Things to Do

Lake Easton State Park

Parks
0.7 miles or 12-minute walk
150 Lake Easton State PA, Easton, WA 98925
509-656-2586

Lake Easton State Park is a camping park located around Lake Easton and upriver along and around the Yakima River. It's 516 acres long with about 24,000 feet of freshwater access.

The park's design and location allow it to host festive activities all year long. These include hiking in the summer and cross country in the winter. The park is also known to be good for kids and easy to explore. As the campsites are close together but laid out in a way that doesn't feel clustered or small.

Waterspring Inn

Hotels
1.0 miles or 19-minute walk
4193 E Sparks Rd, Easton, WA 98925
509-674-8156

Waterspring Inn is located east of the airport up Sparks Road as it heads toward its terminus up the side of a mountain. It's is a two-story log home. This is a very nice place to stay and has a serene and peaceful feel to it. They have immediate access to miles of off road recreational trails for hiking, biking, fishing, hunting, ATVs, cross country skiing, snowmobiling, and more.

The Inn offers charming rooms with a queen size bed and a private bath for couples looking for a quiet retreat. To complete the Bed and Breakfast experience, they offer a variety of breakfast menus that may include made-to-order omelets, Belgian waffles with fresh fruit, and whipped cream or sausage gravy and biscuits.

The owners of the hotel are on site and are very helpful for all of their guests. Kent and Cathy, the owners, are some of the nicest and warmest people you'll ever meet. You will not find a more attentive, welcoming, and friendly couple.[133]

133 Full disclosure: I know these guys personally. Kent and I are pastors and leaders in the Pacific Northwest Church of God movement. My wife and I have spent a few weekends with Kent and Cathy at various church events and functions. They've been married over 40 years, and they've lived in Easton since the early 1980s. You will not find a friendlier, more welcoming and accommodating pair. If you find yourself in Easton, I highly recommend you book your stay with them.

Silver Ridge Ranch

Hotels, Bed & Breakfast
0.6 miles or 11-minute walk
182 Silver Ridge Ranch R, Easton, WA 98925
509-656-0275

Silver Ridge Ranch is a Bed & Breakfast located in a scenic mountain environment. Family owned and operated, facilities include a dining room where a full family style breakfast is served.

Seven guest rooms comfortably accommodate up to 27 people and include various amenities such as big screen television and DVD player. Bathrooms are both shared and private depending on the room, and beds range from twin size to king size. A large common room features a fire place, ping pong table, pool table, and views of the surrounding area.

Adjacent campground features 45 RV sites with electricity and water provided. Private horse corrals have horses available to rent and the property features several miles of horse trails. Depending on the time of year, snowmobile rentals are available.

S93 – Cle Elum Municipal Airport

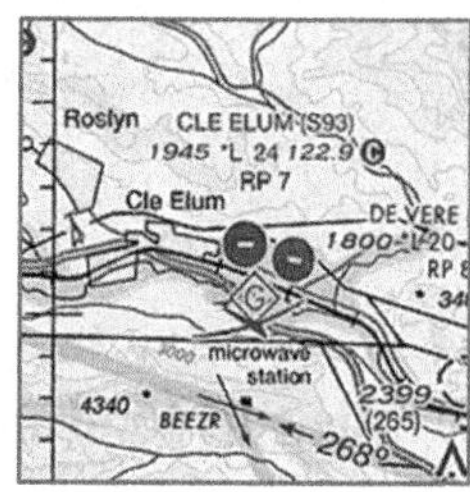

Location: 1 mile east of Cle Elum
Coordinates: N47°11.65' / W120°53.04'
Altitude: 1944 MSL
Fuel: None
Transient Storage: Tiedowns

Cle Elum is a city supporting a population of about 2,000. Incorporated in 1902, the city was predominately a coal mining and lumber town.[134] The name Cle Elum, which means "swift water" in the language of the Kittitas Indians, was given to a river, a town, and also a beautiful tranquil lake created by the construction of the Cle Elum Dam.

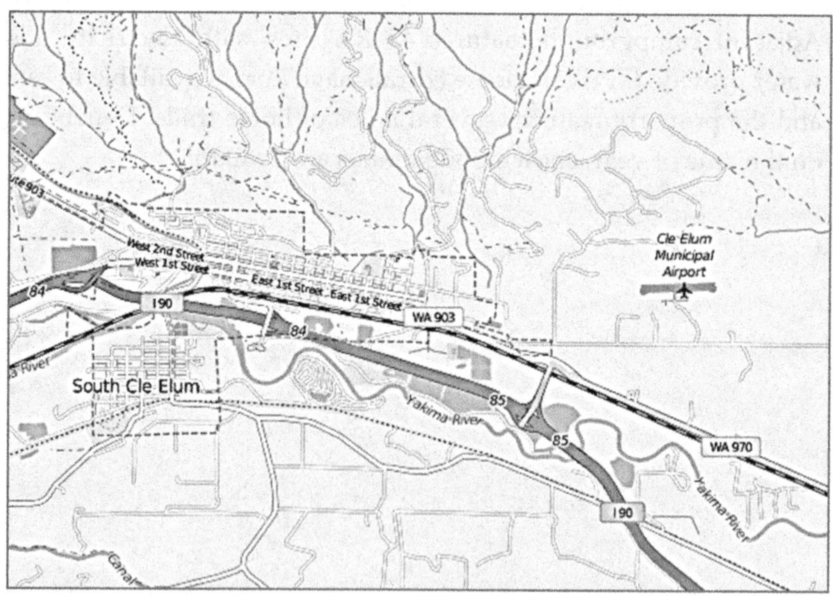

[134] Founded in 1902, tragedy followed in 1908 with two train car loads full of blasting powder exploded, killing at least 9 people including a family with children. In 1918, a huge fire wiped out over 70 acres of the city. 30 businesses and 205 homes were destroyed, leaving 1,800 homeless. The town was also the birthplace of astronaut Dick Scobee, the commander of the Space Shuttle Challenger on its final mission.

Airport Notes

Cle Elum Municipal Airport is located one mile east of the City of Cle Elum on a bench and is surrounded by forested mountains to the immediate north and across the valley to the south. Traffic pattern is always to the south so as to avoid the rising terrain to the north.

Directly to the east of the field is a cow pasture, so if you're landing 25 or departing 7, you get to buzz some cows.[135]

The runway and taxiway segments are in good condition, but there's no paved ramp, just grass. But it's fairly well maintained. Transient parking is in the grass area in front of the hangar buildings.

Food Options

Gunnars Bistro

Burgers, Sandwiches, Desserts
0.5 miles or 9-minute walk
811 Hwy 970 Suite 6, Cle Elum, WA 98922
509-674-6774

From the airport, walk south then east on Airport Road, and you'll find yourself at Gunnars Bistro. This bistro has a friendly atmosphere and offers games of chess and checkers. They are reasonably priced offering soups, several "salad" choices, wraps, sandwiches, and grilled sandwiches. There is a separate menu for the café offering a variety of coffee selections and desserts like a banana split or berry crepes. Bistro offers free wifi and TV with indoor and outdoor seating available.

[135] In my experience, the cows don't seem to notice. Out of a herd of maybe 20 head, not a single one looked up or even noticeably paused from their grazing.

ELN – Bowers Field Airport

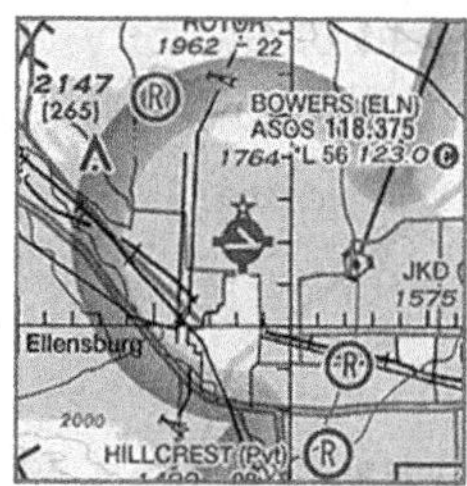

Location: 2 miles north of Ellensburg
Coordinates: N47°1.98' / W120°31.84'
Altitude: 1763 MSL
Fuel: 100LL (blue), Jet-A
Transient Storage: Tiedowns

Ellensburg is a city supporting a population of just a bit below 20,000 people. The surrounding Kittitas Valley is internationally known for the timothy hay that it produces. There are several local hay brokering and processing operations that ship to Pacific Rim countries. Downtown Ellensburg has many historic buildings, many of which were constructed in the late 19th century.

Historically, Ellensburg at one time tried to bid to be the Washington State capital, but it lost to Olympia. Ellensburg is home to Central Washington University.

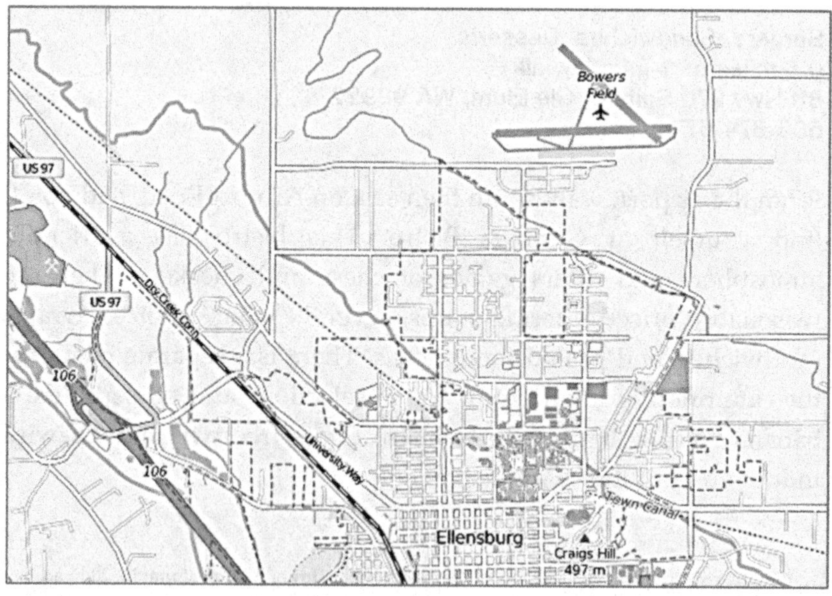

Airport Notes

The airfield was established in 1943 as Ellensburg Army Airfield and manned by the 302nd Base Headquarters and Air Base Squadron. The airport is named after Ensign Keith Bowers, the first man from Kittitas County killed in World War II.

The wind can really pick up here, but it's usually steady and predictable. If you get it straight down the runway, it can make your takeoffs happen in inches, which is fun.

There's a lot of transient parking on a nice looking ramp to the east of the FBO and fuel island.

Transportation

The FBO has a courtesy car available for use. Contact 509-962-7523 to inquire about availability.

Overnight Lodging

Guesthouse Ellensburg

Hotels, Bed & Breakfast
2.5 miles or 49-minute walk
606 N Main St, Ellensburg, WA 98926
509-962-3706

Guesthouse Ellensburgh is a cozy little hideway. Instead of staying at a hotel, why not stay in a charming, restored Victorian house all to yourself? Each room is decorated with English antiques and features a giant, comfy, four post bed with its own private bathroom. There is also free wifi, flat screen television, and complimentary juice, coffee, and tea.

21W – Ranger Creek Airport

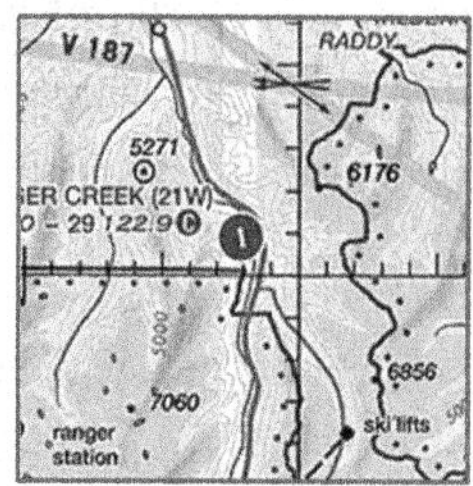

Location: 10 miles southeast of Greenwater
Coordinates: N47°0.79' / W121°32.02'
Altitude: 2650 MSL
Fuel: None
Transient Storage: None

Ranger Creek airport is located just outside the northeast corner of Mount Rainier National Park. It's a favorite of many pilots due in part to its challenging arrival and departure through the Cascades, but also due to the extensive hiking and camping opportunities right off the runway.

The airport is only open from June through September, but during that time, a number of pilots make the trek. The airport is well maintained due in no small part to the volunteers who each spring fly and drive in to conduct spring maintenance.

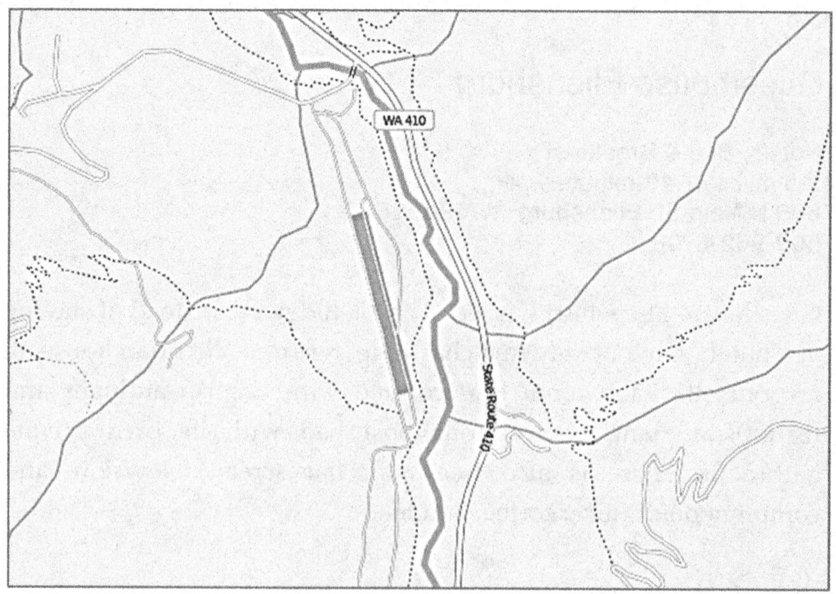

Airport Notes

There are several different opinions about approaches and departures at Ranger Creek. Typically, a strategic approach is from the north through a wide channel in the mountains following highway 410 from Greenwater and Enumclaw. As you're making your approach or departure along this path, stay to the right and observe VFR altitudes when possible.

Tactically, there are two major opinions: Some pilots recommend landing always to the south and departing always to the north because around the runway itself the sides of the valley get a little tight.

The other opinion is that it's perfectly safe to make a landing on on 33 or departure on 15 so long as you respect the tight space. Flying a left pattern for 15 landing does put you pretty close to a mountain on base, but not too close. Downwind for 33 will put you close to a mountain to your right, but again, not too close, so long as you flight tight patterns.

Departing 15, I wouldn't make an immediate left turn to crosswind but would slip a bit to the right and extend my upwind a bit because there's more space to the south of the field.

Best parking spots are midfield to the west side.

Things to Do

Ranger Creek Trailhead

Hiking
0.2 miles or 4-minute walk

From the airport, walk north then slightly east and across the bridge to highway 410. Then cross the road to find the Ranger Creek

Trailhead. This trail snakes through and around the mountain that's just to the north of the runway. Near the top of the mountain is a lovely little log cabin useful for resting up before you continue onward.

Suntop Trailhead

Hiking
0.2 miles or 4-minute walk

At the southern end of the runway, cross west over access road and you'll encounter the Suntop Trailhead. This trail initially climbs over the mountain that's just to the west of the airport, but then it continues for many miles up and down through valleys and other ridges to the west and northwest of the airport.

Overnight Lodging

Buck Creek Campground ✈

Camping
0.1 miles of 1-minute walk

The Buck Creek Campground is located toward the north end of the runway, off to the east side. There are numerous campsites dispersed around the area. They're fairly primitive without picnic tables, but they are quite spacious.

The campsites serve as an excellent rendezvous spot for large groups. Due to the fact that there's no camping fee or any on-site camp hosts, the campground tends to draw a younger and sometimes rowdier crowd.

Alta Crystal Resort at Mt. Rainier

Ski Resorts
0.6 miles or 10-minute walk
68317 SR 410, Greenwater, WA 98022
360-663-2500

The Alta Crystal Resort is along highway 410 just south of the field a bit. It's not a far walk from the airport as the crow flies, although you will have to brave the tight shoulder of 410.

Once there, the walk will be considered worth it. This is a wonderful place to take a vacation with some of the best natural surroundings in the country. They offer log cabin style rooms that are immaculate and relaxing.

Every aspect of your stay will be excellent. The staff are friendly and helpful. The resort offers a heated pool and hot tub. The pool glows a beautiful blue color in the evenings and looks incredibly inviting. The staff puts on complimentary evening events like a movie night with free snacks and a bonfire with s'mores.

Chapter 11

Grand Coulee Area

The greater Grand Coulee Area, really the central Columbia Basin northeast of Ellensburg, is home to a number of interesting airports worthy of a visit; however, most of these have no restaurants, things to do, or overnight accommodations worthy of your time within walking distance of the airport. Some notable airports in this category include Ephrata (EPH), home of an annual air race and where part of the movie *Always* was filmed. Lake Chelan (S10) is an extraordinarily interesting airport to fly into because of the topography around it. Moses Lake (MWH) is a gigantic airport, and there's also a courtesy car available, but not enough of note within walking distance. As such, these airports and others aren't included herein, but you may want to consider visiting them anyway.[136]

The area around this region is dry, typically quite flat for mile and miles, but then spiked with unexpected geological features that in their own way are quite stunning. Southwest of Quincy about 6nm are cliffs looming over the Columbia and strangely beautiful formation of finger lakes. The Odessa area is eerily tranquil in it's stark emptiness. And the Grand Coulee area is saturated with epic picture taking opportunities.[137]

[136] There are PBYs at both EPH and MWH. Even if you're just stopping for fuel, those can be nice attractions right on the ramp.

[137] I don't mean just pictures of the dam, which is certainly impressive, but there's so much more. Banks Lake, Steamboat Rock, Northrup Canyon…

3W7 – Grand Coulee Dam Airport

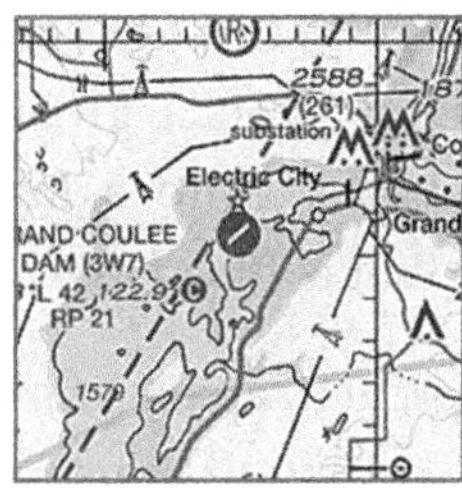

Location: 2 miles southwest of Electric City
Coordinates: N47°55.32' / W119°4.98'
Altitude: 1588 MSL
Fuel: None
Transient Storage: Tiedowns

The Grand Coulee Dam and Bank Lake area is about as visually stunning a location as you'll find in Washington State. It's almost like a miniature Grand Canyon experience. The Grand Coulee is an ancient river bed with an amazing geological history.

The area surrounding the Grand Coulee is shrub-steppe habitat, with an average annual rainfall of less than 12 inches. And cut deep into this are features like the Columbia, Banks Lake, and Northrup Canyon, which provide patches of deep green and sharp topography useful for pictures to share on social media.

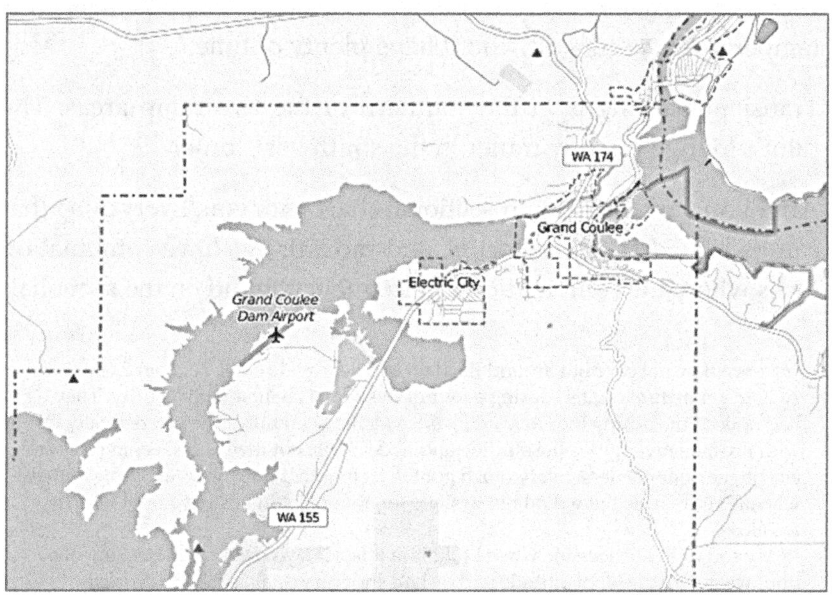

Airport Notes

The Grand Coulee airport is southwest of the dam, Grand Coulee city, and Electric City. It's extremely easy to spot from a great distance. Look to the northeastern end of Banks Lake, to a fat peninsula sticking out into it. Right on the end of that is the airport.

There's not too much to worry about on your approach, apart from ensuring your focus on your approach instead of getting distracted with all the picture-taking opportunities. You can fly over the dam and circle it, but do so with a rather significant vertical clearance. The general rule is that you can't fly lower than 1,000 feet over a dam. Unlike the other dams in Washington State, who take their security seriously, Grand Coulee Dam takes its security very, *very* seriously.[138]

Traffic patterns is always to northwest of the field, over the water.

When departing, if you're departing to 21, you'll see a big mountain that looks like it's sitting right at the end of the runway. It's not.[139] As long as density altitude doesn't force you to wait for temperatures to cool off, you'll have plenty of time.

Transient parking is in the southern of the two ramp areas. The pilot's lounge is a tiny trailer in the southwest corner.

After you park, bring your sectional chart with you. Everything that can be locked at the airport is, and most things have combination locks where the combination is a frequency found on the sectional.

[138] I once flew not over but around the dam in a very wide circle at about 2,000 feet AGL to get pictures. Later, during a tour of the dam, I chatted with security. They had noticed me during the circle and were watching carefully. They were totally OK with my maneuver given the altitude and wide circle, but they were keeping a close eye on me none-the-less. I very much got the feeling that these guys are professionals who are reasonable but would not hesitate for a moment in busting a pilot who flew too close.

[139] My son didn't believe me when I told him this. He was pretty well freaking out until we got a little bit of altitude and he had enough visual context to properly gauge the distance.

Transportation

A courtesy car is made available by the local Chamber of Commerce. You can call 509-633-1319 for information, but no reservations are accepted. You can get the keys by unlocking a box using "super secret" frequencies from your sectional. Leave your name and number on the board so if other pilots fly in and need the car, they can call you.

Remember to keep your sectional chart with you at all times. Otherwise, you won't get far even in the courtesy car.

Overnight Lodging

Osborn Bay Campground

Campgrounds
1.1 miles or 20-minute walk
51052 Hwy 155, Electric City, WA 99123

The Osborn Bay Campground is a great place to stay for your next camping trip. Don't worry about reservations as they aren't necessary. Also, they cater to the late traveler, and late arrivals are OK. Once you arrive, paying is quick and easy at the self-serve pay station.

The campground includes all the normal amenities such as fire pits and cozy campsites, plus additional benefits like bathroom facilities. Top the night off with scenic views of the surrounding areas, watching for deer sightings, and gazing at the stars in the sky at your cozy site.

Sunbanks Lake Resort

Resorts, Hotels
1.3 miles or 25-minute walk
57662 Hwy 155 N, Electric City, WA 99133
509-633-3786

Sunbanks Lake Resort offers multiple variations of accommodations to fit most needs including villas, cabins, cottages, and sites for tents and RVs. Their seasons are busy so booking in advance is a good idea.

Since 1992, the resort has been attracting families with the beautiful landscape and full range of services and entertainment. There is full service dining experience in the restaurant and lounge, an espresso café for the early birds, and even a general store on location for items of convenience you may need to purchase during your stay.

43D – Odessa Municipal Airport

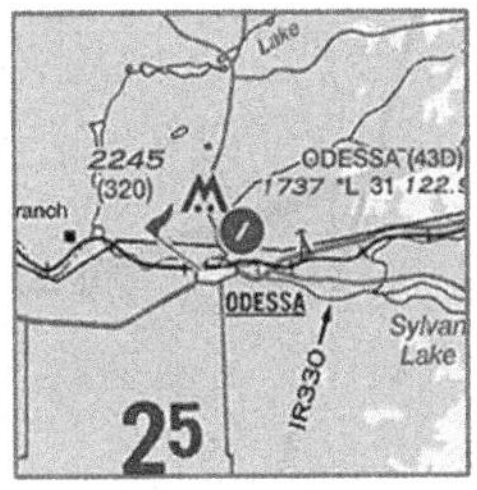

Location: 1 mile north of Odessa
Coordinates: N47°20.85' / W118°40.64'
Altitude: 1737 MSL
Fuel: None
Transient Storage: Hangars, Tiedowns

Odessa is a small town of less than 1,000 in Lincoln County. Officially incorporated in 1902, Odessa was first settled in 1886. The Great Northern Railway built its line through the valley in 1892. The railroad siding was named Odessa Siding by railroad surveyors after the Ukrainian city Odessa, then in southern Russia, because of the German-speaking Russian wheat farmers in the area.

Each year the town hosts the Odessa Deutschesfest, which occurs on the 3rd weekend in September. Several thousand guests travel from distant places to experience the German festival.[140] German music plays its way into your ears, sausage and strudel tease your appetite, and the locals claim that the fun, excitement, and friendliness "capture your heart."[141]

[140] I haven't attended the festival yet, but it seems really awesome. You can't go wrong with German food.

[141] I'm not sure I want my heart captured like that. Seems like that's just a poetic way of saying heartburn. Of course, if the heartburn comes from eating German sausage and strudel, then I suppose it's worth it.

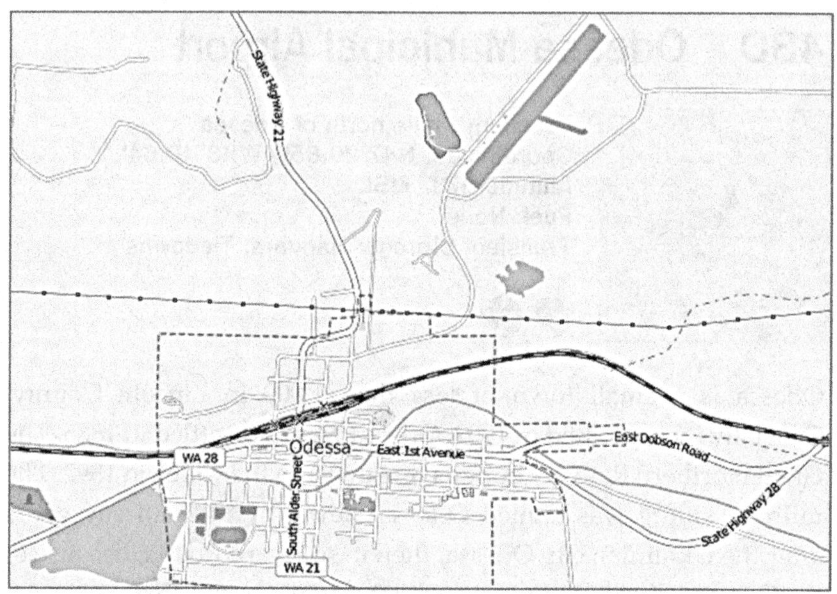

Airport Notes

The airport is just north of town. It's easily visible because it's well outside the city limits and surrounded by mostly nothing.

Transient parking is about midfield, north of the hangars and what not.

Food Options

Chiefs Bar & Grill

American (Traditional), Breakfast & Brunch, Burgers
1.2 miles or 22-minute walk
17 E 1st Ave, Odessa, WA 99159
509-982-2999

The Chiefs Bar & Grill is traditional American restaurant. The price range is low. They are open every day with different hours. Sunday and Monday it's open from 8am to 2pm. From Tuesday through Thursday and Saturday their hours are from 8am to 8pm. On Friday they stay open until 9pm.

The attire is casual. They also have a full bar. The restaurant has a catering service. They don't accept reservations. Most customers are pleased with their experience.

Odessa Drive-In

Restaurants
1.2 miles or 22-minute walk
206 W 1st Ave, Odessa, WA 99159
509-982-0111

The Odessa Drive-In is a really neat 50s style diner that offers a variety of traditional American fare. They are best known for their old-fashioned hamburgers, fries, and milkshakes. This is a great place to take the kids, but it's also a great place to meet-up with friends. The restaurant is decorated with 50s style signs and decorations, and they have really cool old-style red and white chairs and formica tables.

Das Kraut Haus

Restaurants, Meat Shops
1.2 miles or 22-minute walk
11 W 1st, Odessa, WA 99159
509-982-2701

Das Kraut Haus is a German restaurant and meat shop in one location. The restaurant features reasonably priced traditional German fare including items like German sausage and kartoffel. Patrons can come in for dinner and a Hofbrau (German beer), or they can order take-out. The staff is very friendly, and the restaurant is especially popular during the Deutches Fest in the fall.

La Callage Inn, Odessa Motel

Hotels
1.0 miles or 19-minute walk
609 E 1st Ave, Odessa, WA 99159
509-982-2412

The La Callage Inn was previously known as the Odessa Motel. Its rooms are quiet and clean. Each room includes heat, air conditioning, a flat screen TV, a refrigerator, and a microwave. Many of the rooms are decorated in different styles. Wifi is provided.

80T – Quincy Municipal Airport

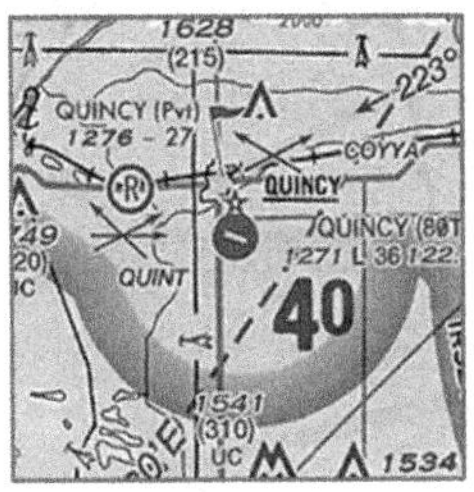

Location: 2 miles southeast of Quincy
Coordinates: N47°12.70' / W119°50.39'
Altitude: 1271 MSL
Fuel: None
Transient Storage: Tiedowns

Quincy is a city in Grant County, which is home to some 7,000 people. During the spring, the whole of the greater Quincy area shifts toward green with all the farming activity. Quincy has long had an agricultural economy, which was enhanced by irrigation made possible with the Grand Coulee Dam. Major crops include potatoes, wheat, and grass. Orchards and vineyards are also appearing in Quincy. Although George is the closest town to the Gorge Amphitheatre, Quincy is the closest town that offers services such as motels and a full grocery store.

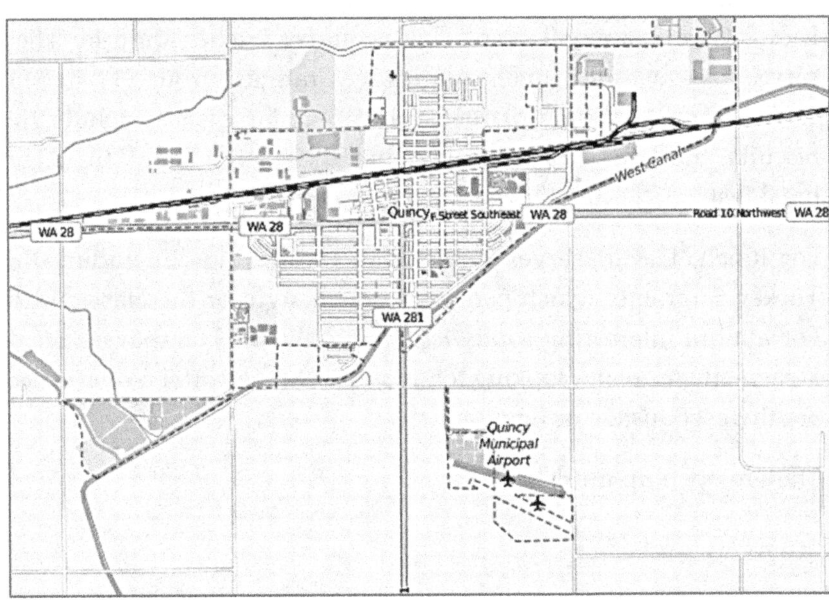

Airport Notes

The airport is somewhat tricky to spot as it's southeast of the town a bit and blends very well into the farms around it. There are also some nearby irrigation channels that look from altitude a lot like airport runways. Basically, look at the center of town, find the big canal to its south, then count down two square farm grid spaces, and you'll see the runway's western end.

Transient parking is easy to spot at the southern end of the field.

Food Options

L & R Café

Cafés
1.3 miles or 24-minute walk
1114 Central Ave, Quincy, WA 98848
509-787-2210

L & R Café is a small home-style, country kitchen dine in. They serve breakfast and lunch, with prices ranging from $11 to $13. They offer wifi. Some of their more popular dishes include the biscuits and gravy or pancakes, but they serve more than just breakfast.

For lunch, L & R serves sandwiches of all kinds, including the Turkey Supreme, which comes on sourdough, or the classic BLT. For a more interesting sandwich, they offer the Hamburger Steak Hoagie. If you're not looking for a sandwich, they offer a dish called Southwest Sausage of Eggs.

They're open up until 1pm.

Time Out

Pizza
1.5 miles or 29-minute walk
610 F St SE, Quincy, WA 98848
509-797-8888

Time Out is a restaurant specializing in pizza; however, it also offers sandwiches, burgers, and "salads." It's a casual restaurant that serves lunch, dinner, and dessert. It does offer delivery, takeout, and inside dining. There is a limited bar that serves beer and wine. It's child-friendly. The price for a pizza can range from $12 to $26 for the more elaborate pies, and they can also be made to order.

Central Market

Fast Food, Mexican
1.5 miles or 29-minute walk
726 Central Ave S, Quincy, WA 98848
509-787-5100

The Central Market is a gourmet Mexican-style restaurant. The folks here serve authentic tacos, homemade salsas, and fresh carne asada. Many people come to see the different types of fruits and wide variety of meats. The Market caters to large groups. People come from all over the area to try the steak and shrimp burrito. Others say that their fresh produce is what brings them in.

Quincy Inn and Suites

Hotels
1.8 miles or 34-minute walk
500 F St SW, Quincy, WA 98848
509-787-1919

It may not look amazing from the outside, but once you step in you will be very happily surprised. The service at the Quincy Inn and Suites is great, and the rooms have all you need from a hotel. For the price, this is a good place to stay and in a good location. Breakfast in the morning is a nice touch.

Crescent Hotel

Hotels
2.0 miles or 37-minute walk
710 10th Ave SW, Quincy, WA 98848
509-797-7001

The Crescent Hotel is a newly constructed facility with many amenities for both the business and leisure traveler. Each room in the hotel is a suite, and every room is equipped with a microwave, refrigerator, and coffee maker. Some rooms are available with fully equipped kitchens to accommodate a longer stay. A free breakfast is included in the breakfast room. Wifi is available, and fax service is available at the reception desk.

Chapter 12
Spokane and Eastern Okanogan

Within the greater Spokane area and Eastern Okanogan, you'll find a variety of topographies including rolling low hills covered in farm lands, tight urban areas in Spokane itself, and the seemingly endless sea of low mountains of the Okanogan.

The climate usually trends widely with large seasonal temperature differences. Summers are hot and winters are cold. As a result, fall is an actual season here.[142] There are grasslands that rise up into low mountains covered with various evergreen trees. River valleys carve long and wide gaps between the ranges.

It's a bit difficult for the layman to note where the Okanogans end and the western slopes of the Rockies begin, since they more or less link up together.[143] As such, as you're flying around the eastern Okanogans, you can often feel connected to the vastness of the Rocky Mountains in their run from northern British Columbia through Idaho, Montana, Wyoming, Colorado, and New Mexico. Be vigilant in your obsessive observance of weather conditions.

142 This is unlike most of the rest of the State. West of the Cascades, there are only two seasons: "wet" and "dry," the latter of which is sometimes known as "somewhat less wet." In the south-central and southeast, there are three seasons: winter, "plants can grow now," and "Plants? What plants?" In the greater Spokane area and Eastern Okanogan, they're rather progressive with four seasons.

143 I tend to think of the Rocky Mountains starting from the west around about at Priest Lake and Lake Pend Oreille, roughly.

R49 – Ferry County Airport

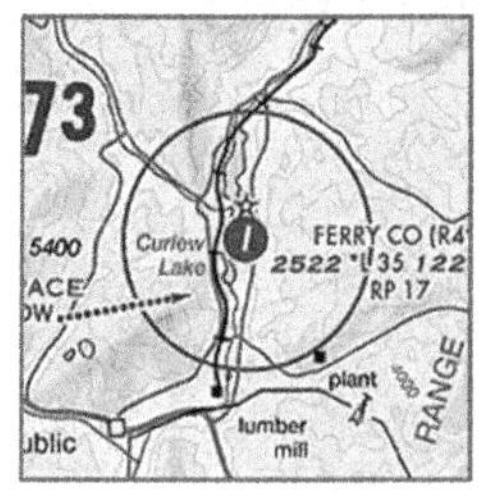

Location: 6 miles northeast of Republic
Coordinates: N48°43.09' / W118°39.39'
Altitude: 2522 MSL
Fuel: None
Transient Storage: Tiedowns

Curlew Lake is a 921-acre lake located in the glacier-carved Curlew Valley northeast of Republic. The lake hosts a number of native and introduced fish including trout, bass, and squawfish. Many recreationists enjoy the lake for its fishing, swimming, and waterskiing options.

Near the southern end of the lake and immediately to the west of the airport is the Curlew Lake State Park. Park activities include camping, hiking, cycling, and wildlife viewing. The park's 123 acres is not far from a public access paleontology site at Stonerose.

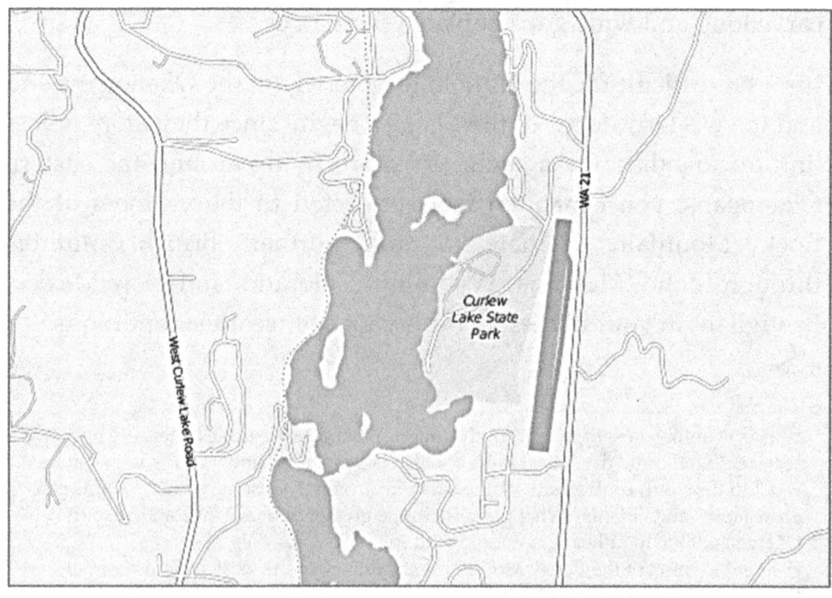

Airport Notes

The airport runway is in good condition and sits up from the State Park on a mini-plateau. The ground drops down suddenly toward the water about 200 feet to the west of the runway. To the northeast are tall hills that come up quickly. As a result, traffic pattern is always to the west.

If you're attempting a 17 landing at night, stay above glide slope to avoid the rising terrain off the north end of the airport property.

Transient parking is on dirt ramp at the south-end. Park opposite the hangars, and favor the northern side of the ramp if possible.

Overnight Lodging

Curlew Lake State Park

State Parks, Recreation Locations
0.3 miles or 6-minute walk
62 State Park Rd
Republic, WA 99166
509-775-3592

Although located immediately to the west of the airport, you'll have to walk north along highway 21 until you're just past the north end of the airport property before you can head toward the beach.

The State Park itself is down the slope from the airport right on the water. It feels almost hidden from the real world. The camp hosts are extremely nice. There's ice and ice cream sold at the campground, clean bathrooms with coin operated showers, and lots of sites that are next to the lake or at least with views of the lake.

Black Beach Resort

Hotels, Convenience Stores
0.9 miles or 18-minute walk
80 Blacks Beach Rd, Republic, WA 99166
509-775-3989

The Black Beach Resort is on the west side of the lake, so the walk around may get annoying. Call ahead to see if they can pick you up from the airport.

The resort is an ideal place to visit if you're looking for a nice relaxing get away with some access to water activities. The customer service is superb. You have the option of bringing your own RV,[144] setting up a tent, or renting from a variety of cabins that are available.

Tiffany's Resort

Hotels, Convenience Stores
2.5 miles or 48-minute walk
58 Tiffany Rd, Republic, WA 99166
509-775-3152

Tiffany's Resort is also on the west side of the lake, further north than Black Beach.

This resort is an inexpensive camp ground and RV park. The resort focuses on outdoor activities and as such offers access to a host of outdoor recreation, including but not limited to: fishing and boating, volleyball, basketball, and even horseshoes on the beach. Guests also enjoy easy access to the area's hiking, horseback riding and biking trails. The resort's amenities include wifi, a small convenience store and a coin laundry. The resort provides bike parking and a concrete boat launch.

[144] Or if you fly a large enough airplane, you can pretend your airplane is an RV. That said, I doubt you'd want to drive your airplane the 0.9 miles to the resort.

63S – Colville Municipal Airport

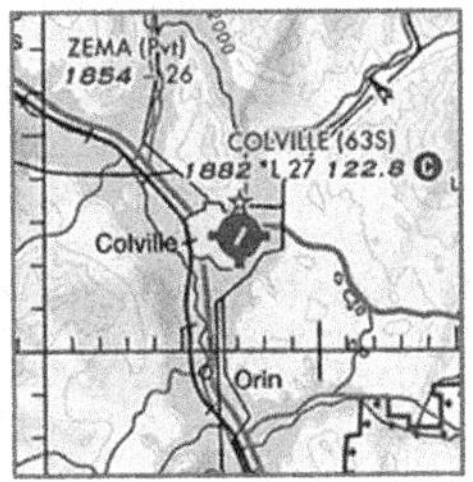

Location: 1 mile east of Colville
Coordinates: N48°32.63' / W117°53.03'
Altitude: 1882 MSL
Fuel: 100LL (blue)
Transient Storage: Tiedowns

Colville is a city of about 5,000 located east of Lake Roosevelt in a valley that extends north from Spokane. Colville itself, being about three-quarters of the way from Spokane to the Canadian border, is well-entrenched in the foothills of the Okanogans, but in an open valley with short rolling hills with a mixture of forests and farming.

This climate region is typified by large seasonal temperature differences. Average summer temperatures are in the 80s with spikes into the 100s. Winter sees low 40s with drops well below 0.

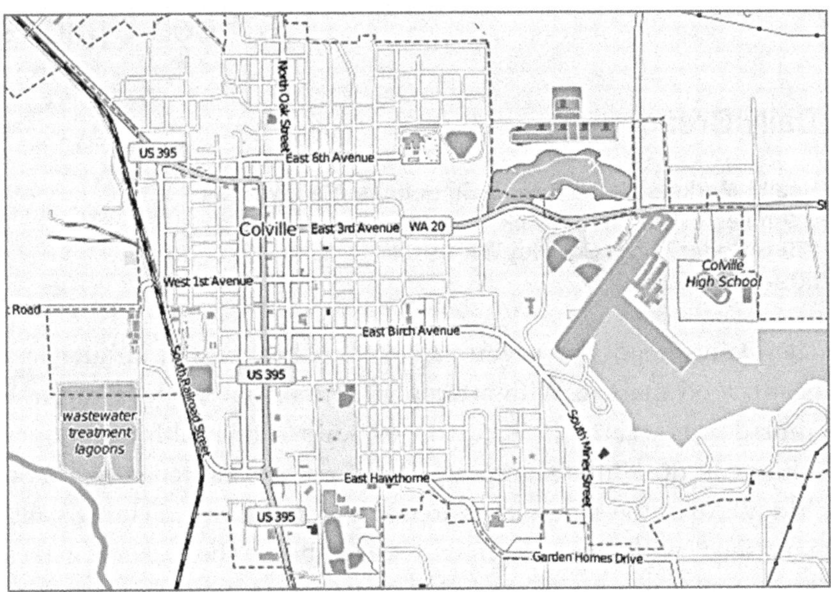

Airport Notes

The airport is located along the eastern edge of town. Highway 20 runs right past the northern end of the runway. Note the displaced threshold as a result.

The runway is in fair condition with some bumps. The temperature swings for the area between summer and winter make it more difficult to maintain than more temperate locations.

Transient parking is on the main ramp to the southeast side of the airport. Park opposite of the hangars to the southwest of the fuel dock.

Transportation

There are 2 courtesy cars available. Call 509-675-1041 to inquire about availability.

Food Options

Daily Bread

Health Markets, Juice Bars & Smoothies, Sandwiches
0.9 miles or 18-minute walk
139 E Cedar Loop, Colville, WA 99114
509-684-3627

The Daily Bread is a vegan café with a bakery and an attached health food market. With afternoon hours from Monday through Thursday, you can enjoy sandwiches, soups, and healthy smoothies while you do a little shopping. The store has shortened hours on Friday. All of the sandwiches are served on homemade breads and garnished with fresh fruit and vegetables. The bakery makes cookies, cinnamon rolls, and pizzas along with their assortment of breads. All items are vegan and incredibly satisfying.

Selkirk Motel

Hotels & Travel
1.0 miles or 19-minute walk
369 S Main St, Colville, WA 99114

The Selkirk Motel is a very affordable motel owned by a friendly couple. It can be pretty busy during the week and slightly less busy at weekends. Even when it's busy with many other guests, noise does not travel between rooms, making it surprisingly quiet. Some rooms are newer than others, and the owners have put some effort into renovating since they took over. Rooms have clean kitchenettes attached, and pet owners will be pleased to hear that animals are welcome.

Benny's Colville Inn

Hotels, Guest Houses, Sports Clubs
1.1 miles or 21-minute walk
915 South Main Street, Colville, WA 99114
509-684-2517

Benny's Colville Inn offers a central location to many amenities within walking distance. A continental breakfast is provided, and the staff are friendly and helpful. Some of the rooms have been updated while others have not. Every room is clean and comfortable. There is also the availability of reserving a deluxe room that provides a TV, microwave, and refrigerator. The hotel also offers guests an indoor pool.

S23 – Ione Municipal Airport

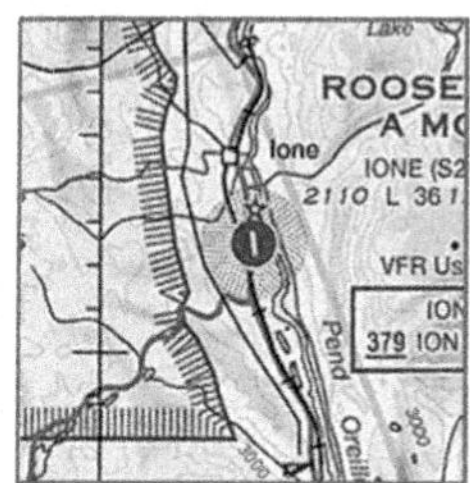

Location: 2 miles south of Ione
Coordinates: N48°42.51' / W117°24.79'
Altitude: 2109 MSL
Fuel: None
Transient Storage: Tiedowns

Ione is a tiny town of only a few hundred[145] that sits along the Pend Oreille River as it flows northward from its lake source into Canada.

Ione was first settled in 1894 and incorporated in 1910. Since then, it has grown only slightly, mostly being the center for local commerce supporting the farms and ranches near its location along the river.

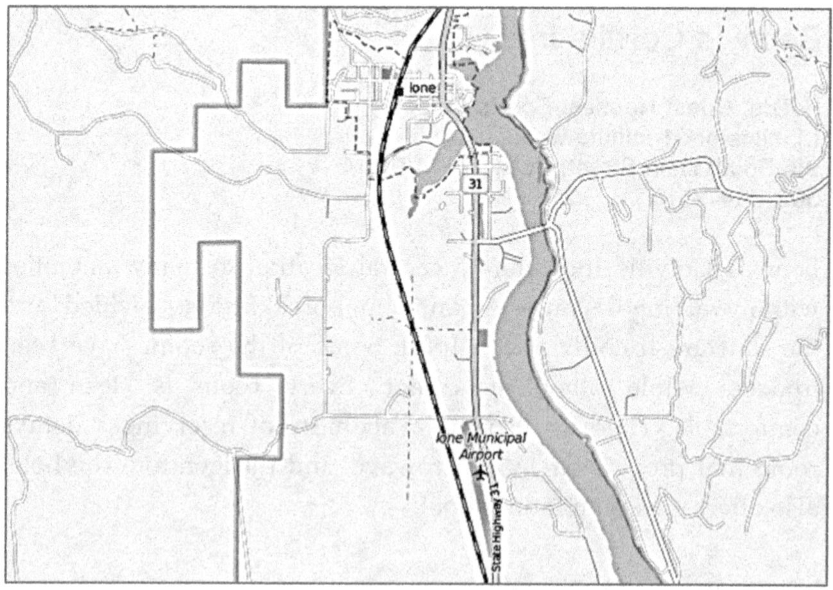

145 There are several conflicting estimates, but I saw in one report that as of 2014, the population had dropped to under 300, a reduction of more than 35% since 2000.

Airport Notes

The airport is about 2 miles to the south of town, but it seems a greater distance because of the small size of Ione itself. The runway is just to the west of the main highway.

There's a rather significant displaced threshold to the south end to avoid vehicles on the highway, but the road is sunken compared to the runway, so it's really not an issue.

The runway is in good condition, but there's no taxiway along the runway. That fact wouldn't be a big deal except that on the southern end the turn-around area is tight. It's not wide, and the perimeter fence rides up close to the east side. Turn sharply and with caution.

Parking and what not is on the north end. Park to the east side of the north end, past the hold-short markers. There's a grass area at the very northern end. If that's filled, park off the second paved hangar taxiway in the grass along its northern side.

Overnight Lodging

Riverview Inn

Hotels
1.9 miles or 36-minute walk
122 Riverside Ave, Ione, WA 99139
509-442-2990

The Riverview Inn is north of the airport along 31 just before you would cross the causeway into Ione proper. The inn has a dock and large patio area that look out over the expansive river and into the mountains. Wifi is available.

1S9 – Sand Canyon Airport

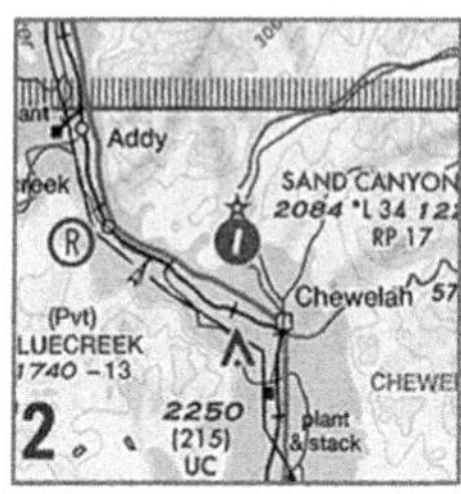

Location: 2 miles north of Chewelah
Coordinates: N48°18.84' / W117°44.60'
Altitude: 2084 MSL
Fuel: None
Transient Storage: Tiedowns

Chewelah in Stevens County, hosts a growing population of over 2,600 south of Colville along highway 395. The name of the town comes from a Kalispel word meaning watersnake or gartersnake.

Much like Colville, the climate is humid continental, typified by large seasonal temperature differences. The wide valley is home to numerous farms that stretch out from either edge, with highway 395 running mostly through the middle. The town of Chewelah itself is the only dense development in about 8 miles, situated just as highway 395 turns northwest from due north.

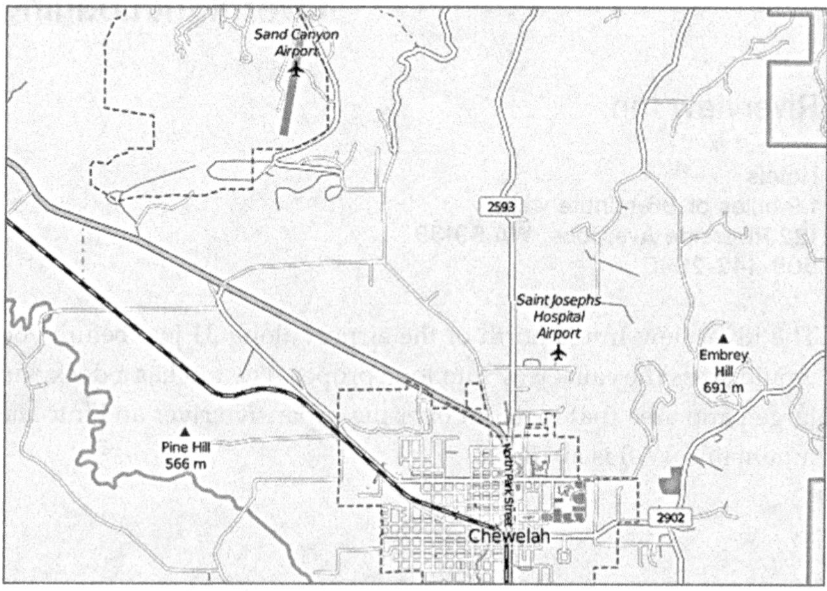

Airport Notes

The airport is northwest of town by about 2 miles. It's perched on a small plateau that rises from the valley floor a bit over 200 feet below. A residential golf course sits just to the west of the field. There are nice looking hills to the southwest and northeast. Traffic pattern is always to the west of the field.

Overnight Lodging

Nordlig Motel

Hotels
2.4 miles or 47-minute walk
101 W Grant Ave, Chewelah, WA 99109
509-935-6704

The Nordling Motel is a cheap yet great motel built in an historic home. It's clean and comfortable. It's also within walking distance to a grocery store. The staff is eager to please. Continental breakfast is included. The food is homemade, and the beds feature extra pillows. They are pet-friendly and offer wifi.

49 Degrees North Mountain Resort

Ski Resorts
2.9 miles or 56-minute walk
Chewelah, WA 99109
509-935-6649

The 49 Degrees North Mountain Resort is the perfect place for someone who loves cold winters skiing down mountain sides. Whether you have a passion for skiing or this is your first time ever trying it out, the staff is very knowledgeable and will be able to answer every question you have.

GEG – Spokane International Airport

Location: 5 miles southwest of Spokane
Coordinates: N47°37.14' / W117°32.11'
Altitude: 2385 MSL
Fuel: 100 (green), 100LL (blue), Jet-A
Transient Storage: Hangars, Tiedowns

This region of the State is not all small towns and quiet airports. Spokane, being the second largest city in Washington, is home to a population of well over 200,000 just within its city limits, let alone including the surrounding communities.

The first humans to live in the area, the Spokane people, arrived about 10,000 years ago. Their name comes from the Salishan word meaning "children of the sun." The modern city features Riverfront and Manito parks, the Smithsonian-affiliated Northwest Museum of Arts and Culture, and the Davenport Hotel.

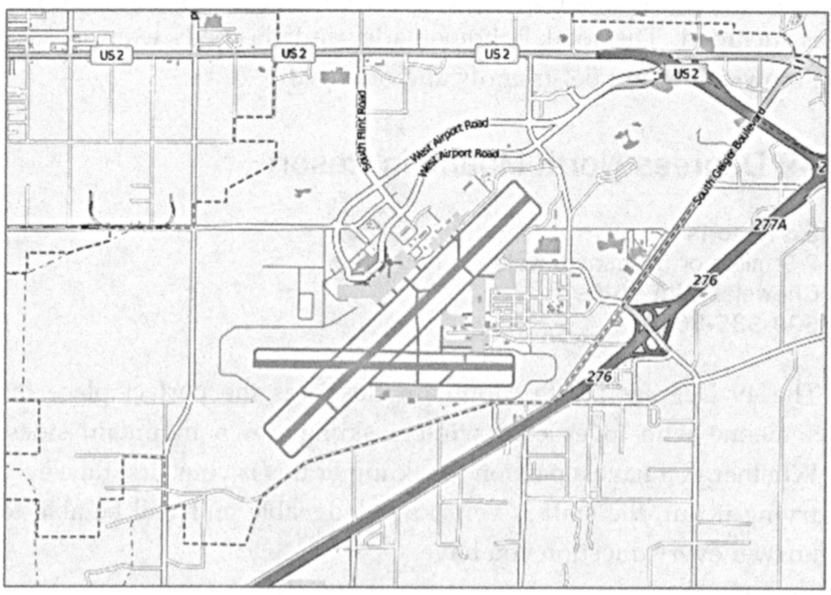

Airport Notes

Spokane International, while not sporting the traffic congestion like SeaTac, is still the only class C airspace in Washington State us non-military mortals can legally land at. That said, it's not a particularly scary experience at GEG. If you're flying VFR, just call up sufficiently ahead of time for airspace clearance and to inform the controllers of your intentions.

GEG is to the west of Spokane just north of interstate 90 as it heads northeast into Spokane. It's tremendously easy to spot from several lightyears away. Note with great care Fairchild Air Force Base about 4nm to the west of GEG. Don't land at Fairchild.[146]

Traffic pattern is, technically, to the northwest of the big runway and south of the small runway. Expect the controllers to give you explicit approach instructions if you're flying under VFR.

Parking is available on the northeast corner of the "south pilot ramp," which is near the Customs office, east side of the field between the two runways. Call the FBO ahead of time to ensure there's a spot open for you and to coordinate if necessary. The airport can get busy, so plan ahead.

Transportation

Uber has reasonable coverage for the area; however, car wait times can get long relative to what you might expect in the Seattle area. If you want to try Anywhere Transportation at 509-389-9155.

The FBO can always set you up with a taxi they prefer or a rental car for longer stays. Depending on your needs, you can also call for a shuttle from nearby hotels.

[146] Otherwise, big guys with guns.

All the food and overnight lodging options are far enough away (and typically on other side of the field) that having a vehicle is a better option than trying to walk the distances.

Food Options

Remington's Restaurant & Lounge

American (New), Lounges
0.7 miles or 13-minute walk
Ramada Inn, 8909 W Airport Dr, Spokane, WA 99224
509-838-5211

Remington's Restaurant and Lounge, located in the Ramada Inn on the northwest side of the airport, has a relaxed and comfortable atmosphere with televisions and wifi for all its patrons. You can choose to eat in the restaurant or in their outdoor seating area when it's nice outside. They have a full bar that features many local wines and great happy hour specials, which makes this restaurant a great place to meet with friends after work. Remington's is open Monday through Friday from 6am to 10pm and on Saturday and Sunday from 6am to 11pm.

Rusty Moose Bar and Grill

American (Traditional), Gluten-Free
1.1 miles or 20-minute walk
9105 W State Rd 2, Spokane, WA 99224
509-747-5579

Follow South Flint Road from the airport terminal area (or more likely, drive around the airport from the FBO until you reach the entrance to South Flint Road from the north), and you'll find The Rusty Moose.

This place has a relaxed atmosphere, is clean, simultaneously elegant and rustic, and sports a great menu of traditional American food. The service is fantastic.

Overnight Lodging

Best Western Plus Peppertree Airport Inn

Hotels
1.3 miles or 25-minute walk
3711 S Geiger Blvd, Spokane, WA 99224
509-624-4655

The Best Western Plus Peppertree Airport Inn[147] offers spacious, clean, and comfortable rooms. The wifi is reasonable throughout the hotel. The flat-screen TVs in every room come with premium channels (including HBO). Also featured is a full size indoor swimming pool, an indoor gym and exercise area, and a guest laundry room that are all open 24/7. Continental breakfast is offered every morning. Pets are welcome to stay for free. Shuttle service is available to and from the airport as well as to nearby restaurants and the Quest casino.

Hilton Garden Inn Spokane Airport

Hotels
1.6 miles or 31-minute walk
9015 W Hwy 2, Spokane, WA 99224
509-244-5866

The Hilton offers good wifi, comfy beds, an indoor pool, and a hot tub. The lobby and exercise rooms are quite beautiful. Their staff is very friendly and cares about you like family. The Garden Grill downstairs is delicious.

[147] Yes, another Best Western.

Northern Quest Resort & Casino

Casinos, Hotels, Venues & Event Spaces
3.0 miles or 59-minute walk
100 N Hayford Rd, Airway Heights, WA 99001
509-242-7000

Northern Quest Resort & Casino is a suitable hotel for a family or couples. Upon passing the entrance, there are valets that greet and help guests. The casino is filled mostly with slot machines and some table games. It contains a non-smoking area and a smoking area. There are foods and beverages available for purchase while gambling. Nearby the casino is a spa, gym, and the luxurious hotel with large and comfortable rooms. The bathrooms are modern and fit with multiple shower heads.

SFF – Felts Field Airport

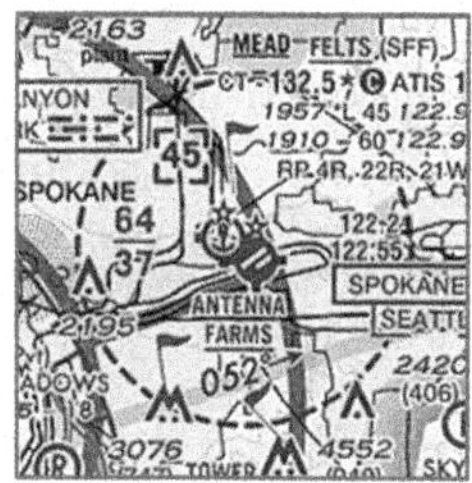

Location: 4 miles northeast of Spokane
Coordinates: N47°40.98' / W117°19.35'
Altitude: 1956 MSL
Fuel: 100LL (blue), Jet A-1+
Transient Storage: Tiedowns

East of the central part of Spokane, wedge between the Spokane River and the railroad tracks, is an airport out of history. Felts Field feels like a special place, and it's. It was once the only major airport for Spokane, offering commercial service.

Aviation activities began in 1913. In September 1927, the airport was renamed Felts Field after James Buell Felts, a Washington Air National Guard aviator killed in a crash that May. After World War II, commercial air traffic moved to Geiger Field, later renamed as Spokane International Airport.

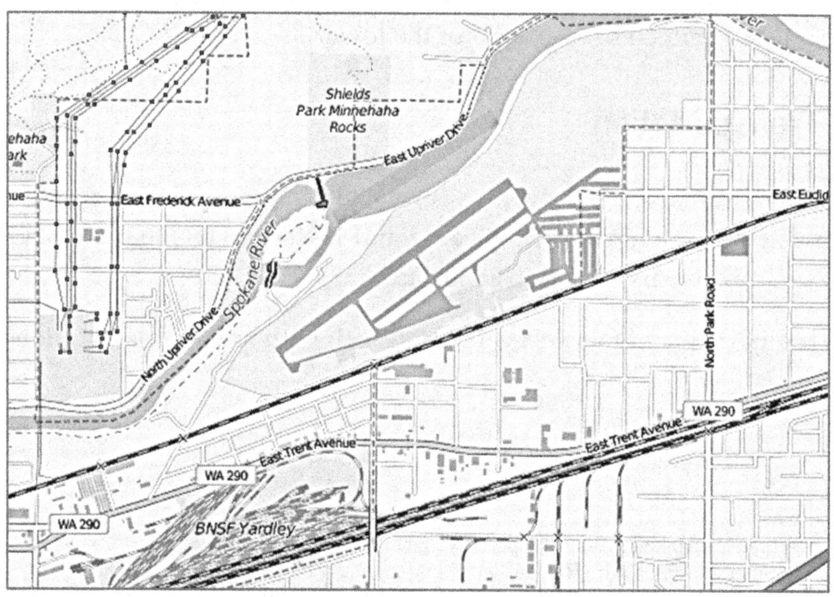

Airport Notes

Felts sits underneath the eastern edge of GEG's class C airspace. As such, it's usually a good idea to call Spokane Approach if you're arriving anywhere from the western side of things. They can route you around commercial traffic and get you safely lined up for Felts without your having to do aerial contortions.

Note the rising terrain to the east. It's really of no major concern since the rise isn't significant; however, after departure with high DA, you might be getting a closer look at the housing on the ridge than what you might like. If departing on the longer runway, the tower will sometimes give you an optional right base call so you can follow the valley a bit longer while you climb.[148]

Transient parking is available directly in front of the tower (opposite side of the taxiway nearest to the tower) and in a smaller transient ramp to the west. Ground control is very friendly and can progressive you to the right spot.

The fuel island is to the west of the restaurant in the old terminal building, which itself is west of the tower.

Transportation

Uber has reasonable coverage here. Wait times are a bit longer than what you might expect in Seattle, but better at Felts than at GEG. You can also try City Cab at 509-455-3333.

The FBO has rental cars available as well with great deals for pilots.

[148] I fly an airplane that's not especially known for its great climbing ability. On a hot summer afternoon with full fuel, 4 passengers, and a 100 pounds of luggage, permission to turn to right base from 4L sounds wonderful.

Skyway Café ✈

Cafés
0.1 miles or 1-minute walk
6105 E Rutter Ave, Spokane, WA 99212
509-534-5986

Walking into the terminal at Felts, you might feel transported back in time to the golden age of aviation. Just to the right after you enter from the ramp resides the Skyway Café. The café is appropriately named as the interior design theme is all airplanes.

The café opens early and serves breakfast and lunch 7 days a week. The menu is extensive and the portions are large. The restaurant is large with plenty of seating. It's a casual seat-yourself experience. The staff is friendly and service is fast. The restaurant has a great dessert menu of homemade pies, cakes, and even cinnamon buns that can cross over from a breakfast treat to a mid-day snack. The prices are reasonable, and the wifi is good.[149]

Smacky's On Broadway

Sandwiches
1.3 miles or 25-minute walk
6415 E Broadway Ave, Spokane Valley, WA 99212
509-535-4230

Smacky's On Broadway is known for their deliciously unique sandwiches. They offer 45 different sandwiches, French dips, wraps, and Paninis. Some of their most popular items are the

[149] Skyway has become for me a favorite stopping point for lunch on trips into northern Idaho. I really enjoy the friendly controllers (approach, tower, and ground). And there's something pretty cool about flying into Felts. Charles Lindberg flew in to Felts once, as he did several other airports in the Pacific Northwest; but for some reason, at Felts, you can almost imagine it happening.

Gourmet Roast Beef Sandwich, the Avo-albacore Melt, Tycoon Hawaiian Dip, and the Grilled Club Panini. All of their sandwiches are served with pretzels and a pickle.

The restaurant is open during the workweek from Monday through Friday, 10:30am until 3pm. They are closed Saturday and Sunday. You don't have to worry about parking because they have street parking available plus a private lot.

Mike's Burger Royal

Burgers
0.5 miles or 9-minute walk
6115 E Trent Ave, Spokane Valley, WA 99212
509-534-3113

Mike's Burger Royal is a fairly priced drive-in restaurant featuring all-American favorites such as burgers, pizza, and calzones. The Stromboli is a favorite for many patrons. The staff is friendly and helpful. Think American nostalgia. There is an extensive menu featuring classic favorites as well as lessor seen fare such as sweet potato fries and a huckleberry milkshake. This family-friendly spot has a drive-thru and take-out. All of the food is delivered with great service.

Sri Prasert Thai Bar & Grill

Thai
1.3 miles or 25-minute walk
5908 E Broadway Ave, Spokane Valley, WA 99212
509-534-3040

Sri Prasert Thai Bar & Grill features a full scale bar along with fantastic and unique interpretation of Thai food. The spices and seasonings are wonderful. The Pad Thai is a great option. The staff, like the food, can be fiery. Another bonus is that food can be ordered very late.

Food aside, this is a true dive bar setting. There is karaoke along with very strong drinks. A designated driver is a good idea. However, those looking for good Thai food and good drinks won't be let down.

Broadway Diner

American (Traditional), Burgers, Diners
1.4 miles or 26-minute walk
6606 E Broadway, Spokane, WA 99212
509-534-7445

The Broadway Diner has been serving the area since 1963 with the family motto of: "We go the extra mile." The restaurant is clean, the prices are low, and the staff is friendly. There is everything from ham and steak and eggs to strawberry banana pancakes for breakfast. The dinner options are just as varied and tasty such as the chicken fried steak, pot roast sandwich, and biscuits and gravy. Many just pop in for a slice of pie and coffee despite the menu being so large and creative.

Zip's Drive In

Restaurants
0.5 miles or 9-minute walk
5901 E Trent Ave, Spokane Valley, WA 99212
509-534-5899

Zip's Dive In is a family oriented restaurant with a variety of menu options to satisfy everyone in the family. The sell burgers, fish, and chicken in various styles. The chain has been serving good food fast since 1953. Along with their sandwich options they serve ice cream and milkshakes in a very relaxed and clean environment. You can dine in or get your food to go. The menu contains old favorites and a few new creations that change out every so often for even newer tasty creations.

My Place Bar and Grill

Bars, American (New)
0.6 miles or 12-minute walk
6520 E Trent Ave, Spokane Valley, WA 99212
509-413-1387

My Place Bar and Grill, as its name suggests, is an American style bar that offers a selection of dining possibilities as well. A recent visitor thought highly of one of the particular types of hamburger on the menu as well as her associates experience with the "build your own" option. My Place Bar and Grill also offers what they call "red beer," draft beer served with a type of tomato juice. The restaurant offers three different types of fries: the standard seasoned variety, another type seasoned with parmesan and garlic, and "tiger fries," a combination of sweet and regular potatoes.

Things to Do

Fenwyr Cellars

Wineries
1.2 miles or 23-minute walk
928 N Lake Rd, Spokane, WA 99212
509-362-8903

Fenwyr Cellars is a mead production facility. They make mead, a type of honey wine. They currently produce 2 sweet and 2 dry meads. The sweet meads are their signature Sweet Mead and the Huckleberry Sweet. Their two dry meads are the Lhug Sereg (Dragon's Blood) which is spicy and warm and the Huckleberry Dry which is light and flavorful. The business was established in 2012 by a Master Mead Maker and three other partners including his wife. Their mead has earned two awards at the Spokane Interstate Fair in 2012 and 2013.

Knipprath Cellars

Wineries
0.4 miles or 8-minute walk
5634 E Commerce Ave, Spokane, WA 99212
509-534-5121

This is a small, family owned winery specializing in various port wines. It's located in a rebuilt old schoolhouse with a beautifully refinished tasting room. It's open Wednesday through Saturday from 12pm to 5pm. This winery has award winning Pinot Noir and is one of the first producers of port in the region. Several different varieties of their famous port wines include chocolate and coffee flavors. Customers can buy a bottle or a glass of wine or port and wander the beautiful grounds at their leisure.

Shields Park/Minnehaha

Hiking, Climbing, Mountain Biking
0.3 miles or 6-minute walk
5701-5721 East Upriver Dr, Spokane, WA 99217

John C. Shields Park (Minnehaha) is an outdoor recreational park for outdoor enthusiasts. The 29-acre park is best known for its massive outcrop of granite with a vertical height of over 300 feet that offers rock climbers a variety of 20-foot to 80-foot routes. The park also offers plenty of winding trails for both beginners and experienced hikers and bikers. Once marred by graffiti, the park is part of a large-scale beautification project sponsored by the Spokane Mountaineers.

Rodeway Inn & Suites

Hotels
1.3 miles or 25-minute walk
6309 East Brdway, Spokane, WA 99212
509-535-7185

This hotel is one of the many hotels offered by Choice Hotels. Rodeway's beds are comfortable, and the hotel offers good wifi, ample parking, and continental breakfast. There's an outdoor heated pool available during the summer. There are also computers with internet service available for guest use.

68S – Davenport Airport

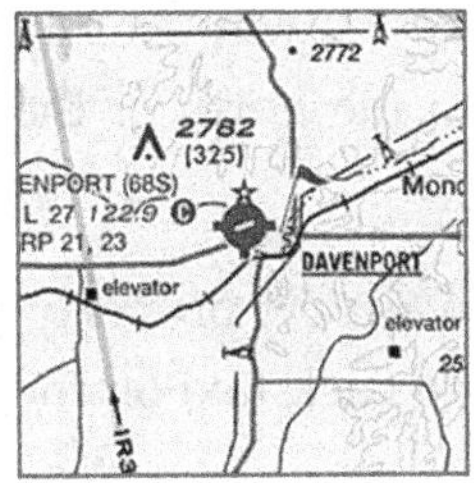

Location: 1 mile west of Davenport
Coordinates: N47°39.21' / W118°10.13'
Altitude: 2421 MSL
Fuel: 100LL (blue)
Transient Storage: Tiedowns

Directly west of Spokane and Fairchild Air Force Base along highway 2 sits the town of Davenport. Supporting a population of about 1,800 people, the town is surrounded by miles of open farm lands.

Davenport was first settled in 1880 and has always been predominately an agricultural economy. It's centrally located in the northern wheat belt of the Columbia Basin.

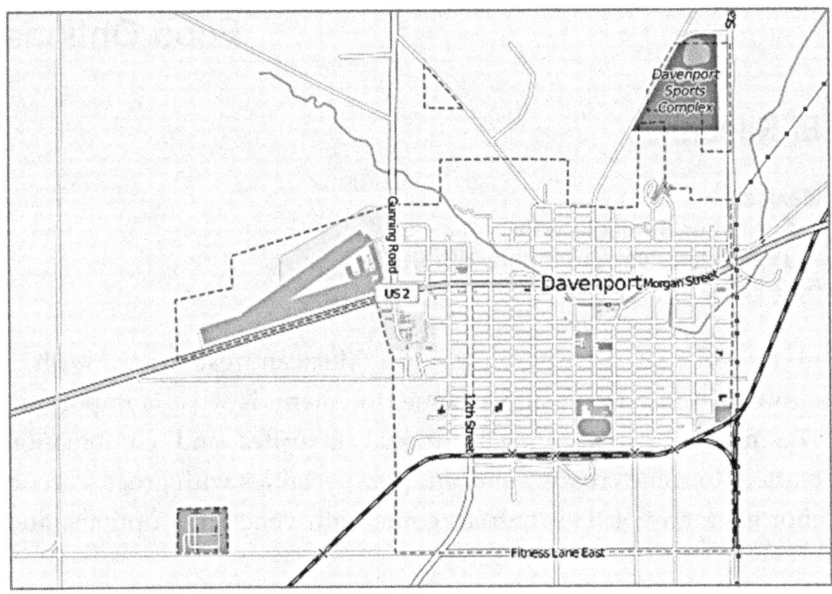

Airport Notes

The airport is just west of the edge of town. The runway closely parallels Highway 2. Traffic pattern is always to the north of the runway.

There is a taxiway along the northern side of the airport property, but depending on your tires, you may just want to back-taxi on the runway.[150]

Transient parking is along the eastern edge of the airport property, north of the runway 23 threshold.

Transportation

A courtesy car is available. Contact 509-725-4352 to check on availability or if you have any questions.

Food Options

El Ranchito

Mexican
0.4 miles or 8-minute walk
1325 Morgan Ave, Davenport, WA 99122
509-725-2030

El Ranchito is a very busy little Mexican restaurant. With a minimalist interior design scheme, the menu is what is important. The menu ranges from traditional favorites and combination platters to some creative and unique specialties with great seafood choices. Many of their entrees come with vegetarian options, and

[150] I have emotionally sensitive tires. I need to keep them off gravel. They prefer pavement, grass, and water. I think it has something to do with trauma suffered in their youth, when someone kicked them.

the variety ensures that everyone, even children, find something that they enjoy.

Some of the local favorites include the guacamole and chips, the house made sangria and the picadillo. Fair prices, friendly staff, and top notch Mexican cuisine keep this restaurant busy all year round.

Overnight Lodging

The Davenport Motel

Hotels
0.5 miles or 9-minute walk
1205 Morgan St, Davenport, WA 99122
509-725-7071

The Davenport Motel is on highway 2 just in to town from the airport, on the corner of 12th street. The service here is good. The rooms are clean and comfortable. The motel is pet-friendly.

Black Bear Motel

Hotels
1.3 miles or 24-minute walk
30 Logan, Davenport, WA 99122
509-725-7700

This motel has many rooms that are all themed around different types of populations and cultures ranging from gunslinger to pioneers. Black Bear is designed for comfort and is somewhat small compared to most hotel chains. Their rooms consist of clean beds, bathrooms with showers, comfy beds, and flat screen TVs.

Chapter 13

Yakima and Tri-Cities

Just about in the center of the state latitudinally and a bit on the south-side longitudinally resides and abides the Yakima River Valley. Its watershed stretches northwestward past Ellensburg and Cle Elum, but its focal point is the city of Yakima, where nearby the Naches River and Ahtanum Creek merge into the Yakima. Flowing south, the Yakima passes by a series of towns and communities in the valley including Wapato, Toppenish, Sunnyside, Prosser, and Grandview. It finally ends at the Tri-Cities where it merges with the Columbia. The Yakima River ends up being the longest river that's entirely contained within Washington State.

The Yakima River provides irrigation for the dry but fertile land in the valley, and irrigated agriculture is the economic base. Agricultural land totals 1,000 square miles, including irrigated pastures, orchards, grapes, hops, and field crops. A significant portion of Washington apples and cherries are grown in the valley, as well as about 75% of the United States' hops.

Where the Yakima merges with the Columbia are the three neighboring cities of Richland, Kennewick, and Pasco. The cities are actually located at the confluence of both the Yakima and Snake rivers with the Columbia. The Tri-Cities are in a semi-arid climate, receiving an average of less than 7 inches of rain annually.

YKM – Yakima Airport, McAllister Field

Location: 3 miles south of Yakima
Coordinates: N46°34.09' / W120°32.64'
Altitude: 1098 MSL
Fuel: 100LL (blue), Jet-A
Transient Storage: Tiedowns

Yakima is the state's eleventh largest city by population with a direct population of 92,000 residents, but if you include the surrounding area with communities like West Valley[151] and Terrace Heights to the east, the number jumps to almost 250,000. The Valley is an extremely productive agricultural area. Crops include apple, wine, and hops.

Yakima has a semi-arid climate with a Mediterranean precipitation pattern. Summers can get extremely hot and spike density altitude.

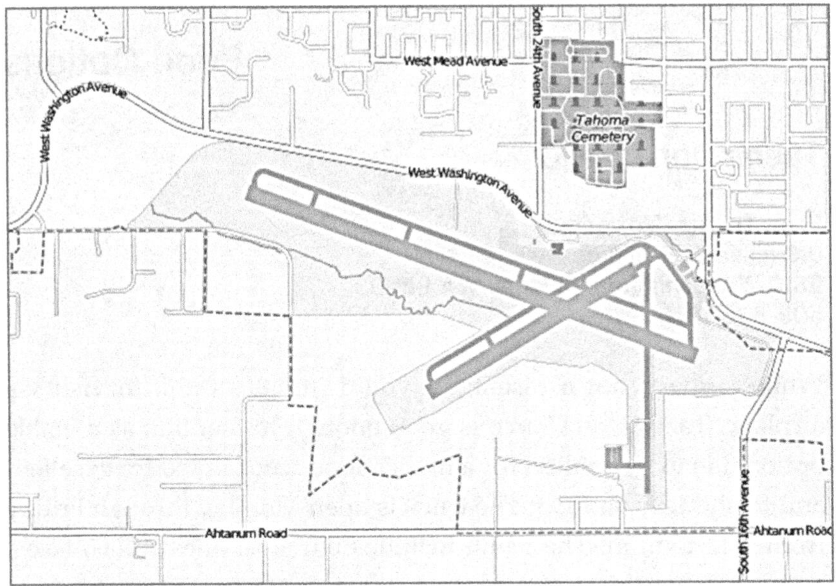

[151] West Valley is the western part of the Yakima Valley.

Airport Notes

The Yakima Valley itself is bordered by shallow mountains on its north and south. Once you cross these, there are no major vertical obstacles on your approach. The airport is located just on the southern edge of the dense residential neighborhoods of Yakima, west of the river.

The tower is professional and friendly.

Review the airport diagram with attention to detail prior to arrival. The FBO is west of the main terminal building, just east of taxiway A4.

Transportation

McCormick Air has a courtesy car available. Give them a call at 509-248-1680 to inquire about availability. They can also set you up with a rental for longer stays.

Food Options

Tacos Don Chayo

Food Trucks, Mexican
0.3 miles or 6-minute walk
2810 W Washington, Yakima, WA 98903
509-833-1814

While perhaps not a restaurant you'd initially think to visit via airplane, Tacos Don Chayo is good enough to mention as a viable option due to its quality. It's a mobile food truck noted for excellent and fresh Mexican food. The truck is open Monday through Friday from 9am to 5pm. The menu includes burritos, quesadillas, tacos, and tortas with a choice of chicken, beef, pork, tongue, and shredded pork. The salsas are fresh and the green is spicy and hot.

The prices are very reasonable with friendly service and a very clean environment.

Flying Pig BBQ

Barbeque, Coffee & Tea
0.3 miles or 6-minute walk
7 N Front St, Yakima, WA 98901
509-759-7350

The Flyin' Pig[152] is a newly-renovated BBQ joint and is a lunch and dinner favorite with locals and visiting pilots. They serve hand-smoked BBQ fare including ribs, pulled pork, kielbasa, brisket, and chicken along with sides of cole slaw and baked beans. They serve sandwiches as well as platters. The Flyin' Pig serves D&M Coffees and is set up to make a full array of espresso drinks as well as energy mixer iced drinks.

Kyoto Japanese Steakhouse

Japanese
0.3 miles or 5-minute walk
2405 Washington Ave, Ste 150, Yakima, WA 98903
509-571-1919

At Kyoto Japanese Steakhouse, as you would expect from any Japanese steakhouse, they cook the food right in front of you. Reservations are required, so call ahead. Kyoto offers many well-known Japanese style dishes including scallops, tempera, hibachi chicken, and of course steak. The steaks are coated with a homemade sauce which adds to the flavor.

[152] Did you know that pigs have been flying since the early days of aviation? And no, I'm not talking about overweight pilots. I mean the ham and bacon sort of pigs.

If sitting in front of a grill with a crazy Japanese cook while he builds flaming volcanoes out of onions isn't your thing,[153] Kyoto offers seating away from the grilling area.

MOD Pizza

Pizza, Fast Food
1.2 miles or 22-minute walk
2550 W Nob Hill Blvd, Ste 100, Yakima, WA 98902
509-759-7364

MOD Pizza is a pizza restaurant where you can design your own pizzas, take recommendations from the crew, or copy the classics. Their pizza is made fresh to order and only takes about 5 minutes from order to ready. They have several different sizes to cater to your appetite. They also have milk shakes and other sweet treats. The prices are in line with the amount of food you receive and the pizzas are set at a standard price regardless of the number of toppings.

Taj Palace

Indian
1.2 miles or 22-minute walk
2710 W Nob Hill Blvd, Yakima, WA 98902
509-494-1001

The Taj Palace is a small Indian restaurant with a menu that features traditional fare. Diners can choose from both vegetarian and meat appetizers and entrees. At lunch time, the Taj Palace offers a buffet option as well as a traditional ala carte menu. The restaurant serves offers family style dining options. The Taj Palace is open seven days a week, from 11am to 9pm for lunch and dinner.

[153] It's a flaming volcano made out of onions! Come on, people! That's cool, but not in the temperature sort of way.

Kabob House

Mediterranean, Greek
1.1 miles or 21-minute walk
2706 W Nob Hill Blvd, Ste 103, Yakima, WA 98902
509-469-0504

If you're a fan of Greek or Mediterranean food,[154] then the Kabob House might just be the perfect place. No matter what part of the world you're from, the staff treats you well makes you feel at home. The setting is perfect, the building is clean and spacious, and the food perfect. From common recipes to more edgy ones, there's something on the menu that's sure to grab your attention.

Things to Do

Kissel Park

Parks
0.7 miles or 13-minute walk
1525 S 32nd Ave, Yakima, WA 98902

Kissell Park is conveniently located in a quiet area of town and it is a great place for kids to play. This park features basketball courts, tennis courts, a playground, and a walking path. The playground includes swings, a slide, monkey bars, and many other things for kids to play on. The walking path runs around the perimeter of the park so parents can keep an eye on their children playing while they get in some exercise. This is one of the cleanest parks in the area.

[154] And if you're not a fan of Greek food, then I feel very sorry for you. You're missing out.

Rosedell Bed & Breakfast

Bed & Breakfast
2.1 miles or 40-minute walk
1811 W Yakima Ave, Yakima, WA 98902
509-961-2964

The Rosedell Bed & Breakfast is set in a home built in 1905 and restored with all the modern amenities, yet it keeps its original charm. Each room has good wifi, a mini fridge, and cable TV. Unlike most other bed and breakfasts, breakfast is served to each room at their desired time.

The house has a large front porch to lounge on, and some rooms have their own private porches. Each room has its own unique theme but still flows with the theme of the home. The hostess is very knowledgeable of the surrounding areas and attractions nearby, and the home itself is not far from the downtown area.

A Touch of Europe Bed & Breakfast

Hotels, Bed & Breakfast, Restaurants
2.4 miles or 45-minute walk
220 N 16th Ave, Yakima, WA 98902
509-454-9775

If you're a fan of the typical Mom-and-Pop bed and breakfast, then you will love A Touch of Europe Bed and Breakfast. From the gorgeous scenery to the comfortable beds, there's something here for everyone to enjoy.

M94 – Desert Aire Airport

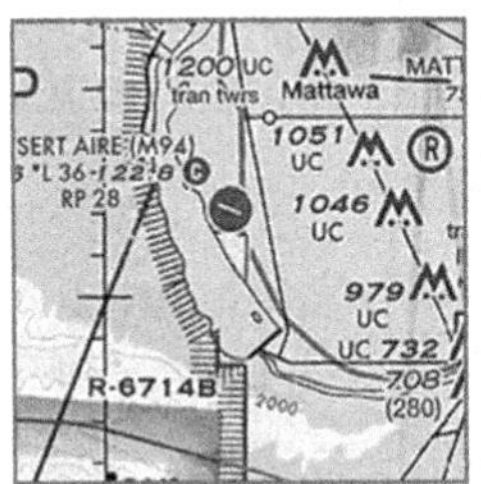

Location: 3 miles southwest of Mattawa
Coordinates: N46°41.24' / W119°55.18'
Altitude: 586 MSL
Fuel: None
Transient Storage: Tiedowns

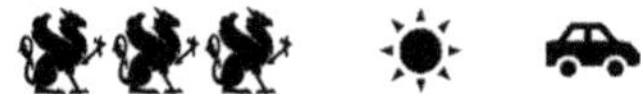

Desert Aire is a community on the shores of the Columbia River just a bit upstream of the Priest Rapids Dam. Its home to a population of about 1,200.

In the early 1970s, a group of investors bought 3,200 acres of land along the Columbia and developed the community of some 1600 homes centered on a golf course and marina. The area is sometimes referred to as "The Palm Springs of Washington,"[155] a moniker also proclaimed by a billboard at the entrance to the community.

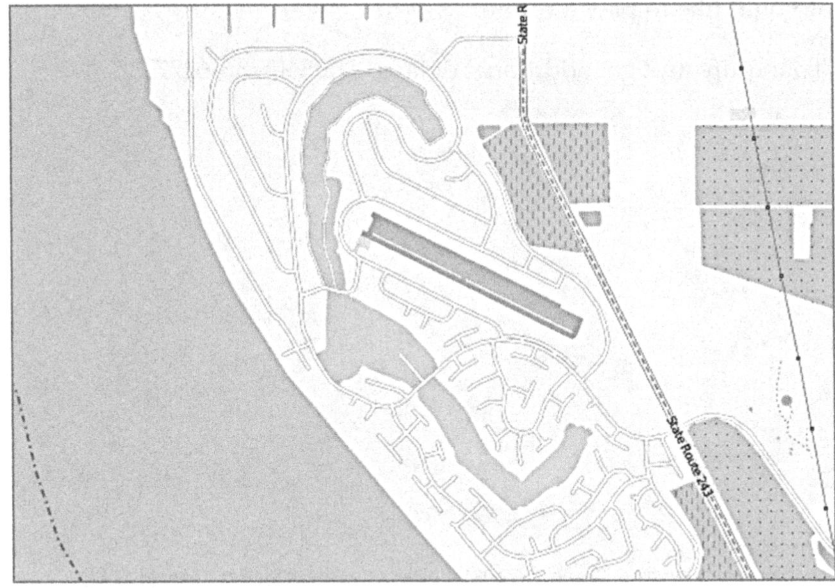

[155] I've heard Yakima called the same thing. I've also seen a billboard claiming such.

Airport Notes

The most important note, of course, is avoid overflying all lands west of the river.[156] Very dangerous. Therein reside military folks with big guns, binoculars, and the FAA on speed-dial.

The airport itself is easily visible, right in the middle of the community, with the greens of the golf course bracketing the runway like a giant letter C. Traffic pattern is always to the north of the runway.

Transient parking is on the far west end of the runway.

Transportation

There's technically no courtesy car here; however, the airport manager has stated he'll happily drive anyone anywhere as needed. The golf course, although within walking distance, will also be happy to pick you up in a golf cart and transport you to the course if you'd like to play a round.

To inquire and get additional details, call 360-436-6277.

[156] Approaching from the northwest, I typically use the bridge at Vantage as a checkpoint, staying to its north and then east, then follow the east side of the river south to the airport.

Food Options

Tumbleweeds Bar & Grill

Bars, American (Traditional)
0.8 miles or 14-minute walk
124 Frontier Way W, Mattawa, WA 99349
509-932-3100

Tumbleweeds Bar & Grill, which opened in 2013, is owned by a couple who are pursuing their dream of owning their own restaurant. It is a full-service restaurant that serves breakfast, lunch, and dinner. Some of the top breakfast selections are the chicken fried steak and biscuits and gravy. For lunch, try a Tumbleweed burger. The dinner menu includes rib-eyes, chicken breast, and prawns. The owners are friendly and will go out of their way to ensure that you have a warm meal and excellent experience.

Things to Do

Desert Aire Golf Course

Golf
0.5 miles or 9-minute walk
504 Clubhouse Way W, Mattawa, WA 99349
509-932-4439

If you're a golf lover as well as pilot, a visit to Desert Aire ought to include a round at the Desert Aire Golf Course. Course information is available on its website where you can book tee times, view greens fees, shop its online store, and access a printable PDF of its tournament schedule. The first nine of its eighteen holes opened in 1972, and the back nine followed in 1993. The course has recently been redesigned. The source is challenging, as are its penalties for the overly aggressive. Food, beverages, a pro shop, and lessons are all available.

Overnight Lodging

Priest Rapids Recreation Area Campground

Campgrounds
0.6 miles or 10-minute walk
302-A Desert Aire Dr N, Mattawa, WA 99349
509-754-0500

Priest Rapids is a small community campground. It has a boat launch located along the water. There's also a beach area set apart from the launch. There are no showers, but the campgrounds does have pit toilets and one water tap. There is a natural swimming area for adults and children. The nights are quiet, and fellow inhabitants are friendly and tend to keep to themselves.

RLD – Richland Airport

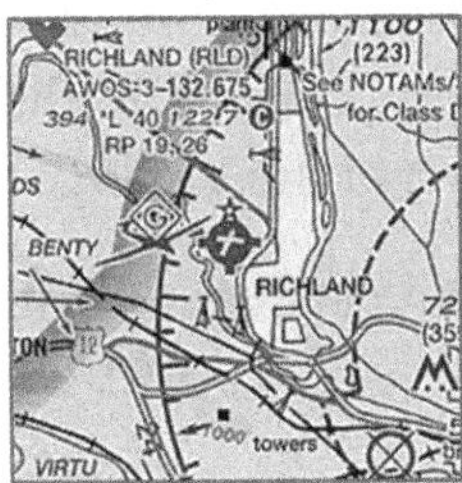

Location: 2 miles northwest of Richland
Coordinates: N46°18.34' / W119°18.25'
Altitude: 394 MSL
Fuel: 100LL (blue), Jet-A
Transient Storage: Tiedowns

Richland is a city in Benton County in the southeastern part of Washington, just north of where the Yakima River merges with the Columbia. The city supports a population of just around 50,000. However, given its inclusion as a member of the Tri-Cities area, it's really one part of a much larger city.

Richland was a small farm town until the US Army purchased some 640 square miles of land during World War II and evicted the then 300 residents. Some say those wounds have not yet fully healed.[157]

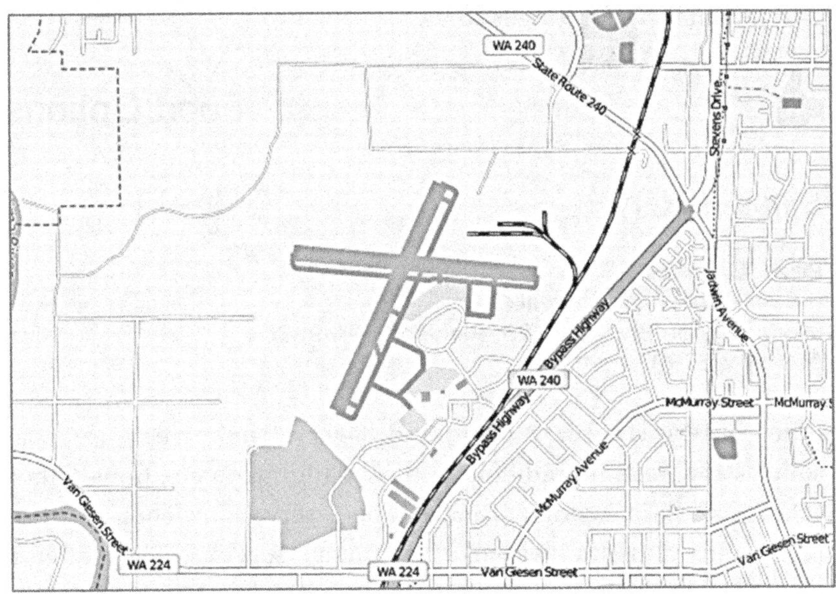

[157] The history of West Richland avoiding incorporation into Richland is fascinating.

Airport Notes

The main part of Richland sits between the Yakima and Columbia rivers and runs more or less north-south. The airport is off to the west of this, toward the northern end, but still east of the Yakima.

Due in part to the flat terrain of the area, winds can get rather, well, windy here. Traffic pattern is always to the north or west of the active runway.

There are two main ramps. The first is immediately southeast of the nexus of the two runways. The second, larger ramp is off to the south, set back from the runway behind a few 4 sets of hangars. This is where you can pick up fuel.

Transportation

Sundance Aviation provides a courtesy car. Give them a call at 509-946-2515 to inquire about availability. The FBO can also set you up with a rental car for longer stays.

Food Options

Ethos Bakery

Pizza, Bakeries
0.9 miles or 17-minute walk
2000 Logston Blvd, Ste 125, Richland, WA 99354
509-942-8799

Ethos Bakery is a pizza bistro and bakery. The owners use local sources for fresh ingredients in their daily made creations. Ethos caters to walk-in customers and accepts reservations. They are open for groups and families alike for dinner services. They offer a variety of baked goods and ice creams as well as many types of pizza. Everything is made in an open kitchen that allows customers to watch their food being made from start to finish.

Shrub Steppe Smokehouse Brewery

Breweries
0.9 miles or 17-minute walk
2000 Logston Blvd, Ste 122, Richland, WA 99354
509-375-9092

Shrub Steppe Smokehouse and Brewery is open seven days a week for lunch and dinner. They serve a full menu of assorted meats including brisket, sausages, wings, and pulled pork as well as various sides. The meats are coated in their signature dry rub then slowly smoked for 12 hours over hickory, mesquite, and alder woods. Sandwiches served on a toasted roll. Their weekday Happy Hour specials consist of several ½ sandwich and side selections and $1 off pints and wine. They have 7 of their own beers on tap which change seasonally as well as 6 rotating guest taps. They offer dine-in or take out and growler fills.

Things to Do

Buckskin Golf Club

Golf
0.7 miles or 13-minute walk
1790 Bronco Lane, Richland, WA 99354
509-942-0888

Buckskin Golf Club has great training courses as well as knowledgeable staff members. This 9-hole golf course is kid-friendly, so it's a positive environment for the younger golf enthusiasts. This location has been open since 1998 and is most commonly used as a beginner or training course due to the smaller golfing area. The green is thick and plush, which can make it a tad more challenging; however, it's great for practicing and preparing for more difficult course play. Golf carts are available for added convenience.

Columbia Basin Racquet Club

Gyms, Trainers
0.7 miles or 13-minute walk
1776 Terminal Dr, Richland, WA 99354
509-943-8416

Columbia Basin Racquet Club is open 7 days a week. They have a wide variety of programming, group classes, and private lessons with professional equipment. They have a clean pool inside and another one outside and well-kept tennis courts. They have reasonable membership fees and provide private family changing areas. There is a cafeteria and a daycare facility making it very convenient for the entire family. Services include massage therapy, physical therapy, karate classes, and even offer birthday party accommodations. The children's programs include a nursery room, tot room and even a rock climbing wall. There are diverse classes and events every single day.

White Bluffs Brewing Company

Breweries, Pubs
0.9 miles or 18-minute walk
2034 Logston Blvd, Richland, WA 99354
509-578-4558

The White Bluffs brewery is an independent micro brewer of craft beers. The property that the brewery sits on features a great view of the Yakima River, Benton City, and the Horse Heaven Hills, which you can explore beer in hand. The tasting room also features wine. Leading up to the tasting room from the outside is a stunning long wooden vine-covered archway.

Homewood Suites Richland

Hotels
2.3 miles or 43-minute walk
1060 George Washington Way, Richland, WA 99352
509-374-1550

The Homewood Suites is considered by some to be one of the best places to stay in the whole region. The rooms are spacious, cleaned, and comfortable; the staff is wonderful. They will go above and beyond just to make sure you feel at home. On top of the great customer service and delicious food there is a beautiful view that's breathtaking.

Red Lion Hotel Richland Hanford House

Hotels
2.5 miles or 47-minute walk
802 George Washington Way, Richland, WA 99352
509-946-7611

This is a spot widely selected for combining business with pleasure. Situated idyllically on a river bank, guests can go on long walks on the nearby park or on paved walking trails. The rooms are well decked with their signature mattress and pillows. This 3-star lodge has proven its versatility in providing for event planning and tools for business conferences and social gatherings alike. Guests typically take off on fishing or jet skiing expeditions. This hotel has good wifi, and it offers a shuttle to and from the airport.

Paragon Suites

Hotels, Apartments
2.7 miles or 52-minute walk
2550 Duportail St Apt K262, Richland, WA 99352
509-943-0500

Paragon Suites housing is designed for those looking for an extended stay. The property has many of the features found in a hotel yet has the space and privacy of an apartment. Each suite is fully furnished including flat screen TVs, internet, and fully applianced kitchens. On-site staff are available to assist with specific requests such as cribs or a recliner. Housekeeping service is provided to keep your suite tidy and make your stay enjoyable. Multiple size apartments are available. Paragon Suites will hold special appeal for those on a temporary assignment away from home or as a base of operations if looking to relocate.

PSC – Tri-Cities Airport

Location: 2 miles northwest of Pasco
Coordinates: N46°15.88' / W119°7.14'
Altitude: 410 MSL
Fuel: 100LL (blue), Jet A-1
Transient Storage: Hangars, Tiedowns

Pasco is another of three cities that make up the Tri-Cities region. It directly supports a population of about 60,000. Combined with the other cities and communities of the area, the total population jumps to 280,000.

On October 16, 1805, the Lewis and Clark Expedition camped in the Pasco area at a site now commemorated by Sacajawea State Park. In the 1880s, the Northern Pacific Railway was built near the Columbia River, bringing many settlers to the area. Pasco was officially incorporated in 1891.

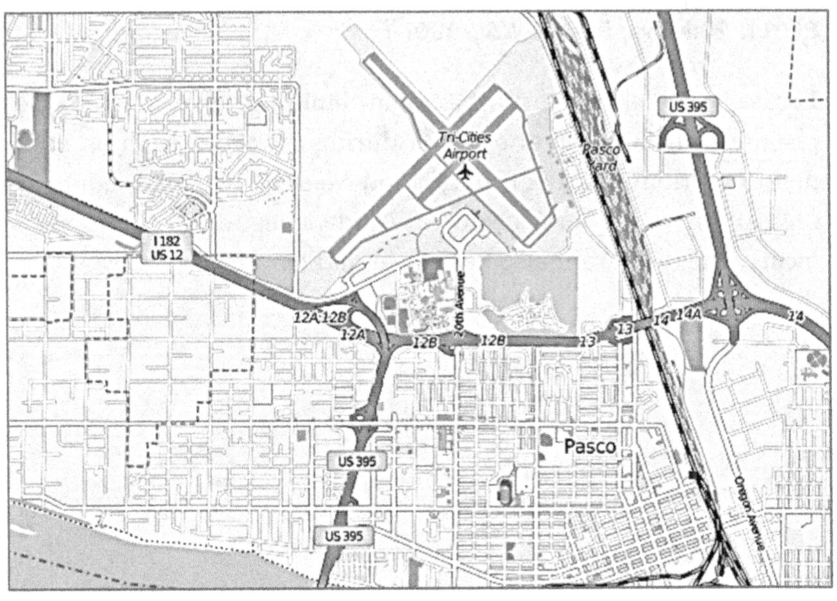

Airport Notes

Wind conditions can get extreme here when a Chinook wind gets blowing in just the right way. Use caution.

The tower is friendly but can get busy, so plan your approach and taxi ahead of time. Transient parking and the FBOs are all on the eastern side of the airport.

Transportation

A courtesy car is available from Bergstrom Aircraft. Give them a call at 509-547-6271 to inquire about availability.

Food Options

3 Eyed Fish ✈

American (New)
0.5 miles or 10-minute walk
3601 N 20th Ave, Pasco, WA 99301

Located inside the airport's main building, the 3 Eyed Fish restaurant hosts different events during the week such as music night on Fridays and Saturdays, and Meet the Maker Wednesday nights. This place serves cold-cut sandwiches with your choice of meats. The restaurant also has a beer and bar area.

Grizzly Bar

Dance Clubs
1.0 miles or 20-minute walk
2525 N 20th Ave, Pasco, WA 99301
509-547-0701

The Grizzly Bear is a hotel bar which doubles as a good music venue. The bar staff are very helpful and friendly, and they serve a good selection of beers and cocktails. Drinks are well priced, and there is also a happy hour. Bar food is served. If pool is your game, there are tables situated in the bar. Monday Night Football is shown on Mondays when in season. Friday night is Salsa night, which is very popular and makes for a good atmosphere.

Things to Do

Roasters Coffee

Coffee & Tea
1.0 miles or 20-minute walk
2525 N 20th Ave, Pasco, WA 99301
509-547-2481

Roasters Coffee is an inexpensive coffee shop open from 5:30am to 7pm on weekdays and 7am to 5pm on weekends. Roasters' is passionate about supporting their local community and customers. The baristas are friendly, attentive, and can cater to many unique drink orders, including the use of almond soy and hemp milks and irregular syrup flavors. The coffee shop also sells cookies and other baked products. They also offer their own signature drinks like the Red Bull Twist, Iced Snickers, and White Rocket.

Best Western Plus Pasco Inn & Suites

Hotels
0.8 miles or 15-minute walk
2811 N 20th Ave, Pasco, WA 99301
509-543-7722

This Best Western includes a free breakfast with all the traditional options plus an excellent omelet station.[158] The facility has a sauna, pool hot tub, and a gym. The rooms are clean and stocked with linen; they contain a small refrigerator and good wifi coverage. The staff is friendly, and they can accommodate late arrivals as well as group reservations. The hotel is clean and affordable and with all the amendments you would expect.

[158] It's a Best Western, folks. They all have this stuff. Everything is the same. And yet, because of my dedication to the craft of writing, I have written up a unique review for the place. That's how dedicated I am. But it's at the cost of my sanity, because there's only so many Best Western reviews you can write before you go crazy. Hopefully this is the last for this book.

1S5 – Sunnyside Municipal Airport

Location: 2 miles east of Sunnyside
Coordinates: N46°19.62' / W119°58.22'
Altitude: 767 MSL
Fuel: 100LL (blue)
Transient Storage: Tiedowns

Sunnyside is a city along the Yakima River between Yakima and the Tri-Cities that supports a population of about 16,000. It's predominately an agricultural community. Originally founded in 1902, it started with barely over the minimum 300 people required by law to incorporate. The population boost was stimulated by the immigration of a religious community from South Dakota. Later, in the 1930s, refugees from the Dust Bowl also moved to Sunnyside.

Noted NASA astronaut Bonnie Dubar is a graduate from Sunnyside High School.

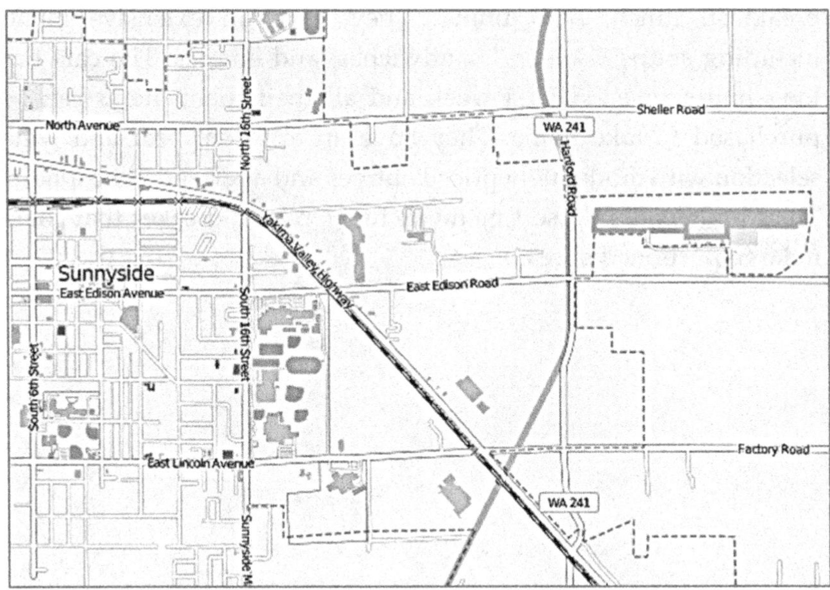

Airport Notes

The small airport can be a bit tricky to spot. It's east of town, separated from the density of Sunnyside proper by a maybe half a mile or more. The airport property is entirely surrounded by farms.

There's plenty of transient parking in the middle of the property toward the south, and an even greater amount of parking along the ramp to the east.

Food Options

Green Olive Café

Coffee & Tea, Italian, Breakfast & Brunch
1.4 miles or 26-minute walk
2926 Covey Ln, Sunnyside, WA 98944
509-837-9009

The Green Olive Café can accommodate small and large parties for breakfast, lunch, and dinner. They have an extensive menu including soups, "salads," sandwiches, and entrees. The café has long hours seven days a week and all their menu items can be purchased to take home. They have an excellent beer and wine selection with moderately priced entrees and a relaxed atmosphere. Their homemade dessert menu includes pies and cakes that come in large portioned slices.

Panda Garden

American (New), Szechuan
1.3 miles or 24-minute walk
3210 Picard Pl, Sunnyside, WA 98944
509-839-0018

Panda Garden is a restaurant serving Szechuan style Chinese food. It is open seven days a week. Reservations can be made by calling their number listed. They have a private room that can host company parties or family get togethers. The restaurant is clean and comfortable and the prices are reasonable. Typical Chinese food can be found here including: chicken chow mein, pork egg foo young, hot and sour soup, orange beef, and walnut prawns. Vegetarian and seafood options are available.

Overnight Lodging

Quality Inn

Hotels
1.3 miles or 25-minute walk
3209 Picard Place, Sunnyside, WA 98944
509-837-5781

Quality Inn Sunnyside offers free continental breakfast served to visitors every morning with selections ranging from cold cereal to hot waffles. During their stay, visitors can work out with the hotel's exercise equipment or enjoy the hotel's pool. Rooms are kept clean and are well maintained by the friendly attentive staff. Rooms are furnished with personal refrigerators, microwaves, and flat screen TVs. Reasonable wifi is available to guests.

Best Western Plus Grapevine Inn

Hotels
1.5 miles or 28-minute walk
1849 Quail Ln, Sunnyside, WA 98944
509-839-6070

Best Western[159] Plus Grapevine Inn has a friendly staff and clean, spacious rooms. The bed are comfortable and include extra pillows. Each room has a mini fridge and large business desk. There are pet-friendly rooms, and wifi is provided at no extra charge. Roll-away beds are available for $10 per night. Guests have access to a fitness room, pool, and hot tub. A continental breakfast is provided each morning. The inn provides a lovely view, great customer service, and many complimentary amenities for a moderate price.

[159] Oy. YABW. (Yet Another Best Western). I'm starting to lose my mind writing these reviews. Have you ever considered how difficult it would be to write a review of every McDonalds in Washington State? Yet, I persist, because I'm just that dedicated.

S40 – Prosser Airport

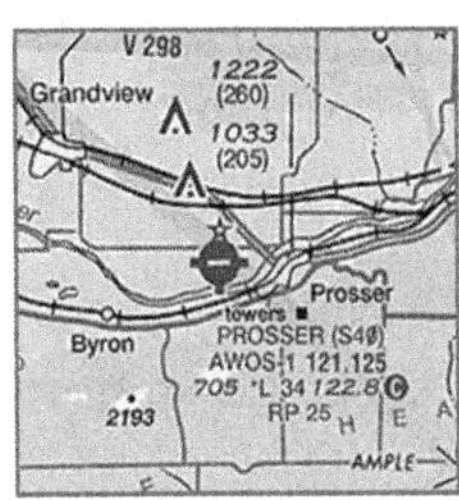

Location: 1 mile northwest of Prosser
Coordinates: N46°12.80' / W119°47.73'
Altitude: 705 MSL
Fuel: 100LL (blue)
Transient Storage: Hangars

Prosser sits along the southern edge of the Yakima Valley, snug up against the edge of the Horse Heaven Hills with the Yakima River rolling over its northern side. The town supports a population of nearly 6,000 residents.

The climate here is semi-arid with summer temperatures averaging in the 70s with spikes up into the 90s. Winters can get cold with average lows dropping into the 20s. Prosser's location on a major river and with highway access has encouraged a growing wine business and associated tourist industry.

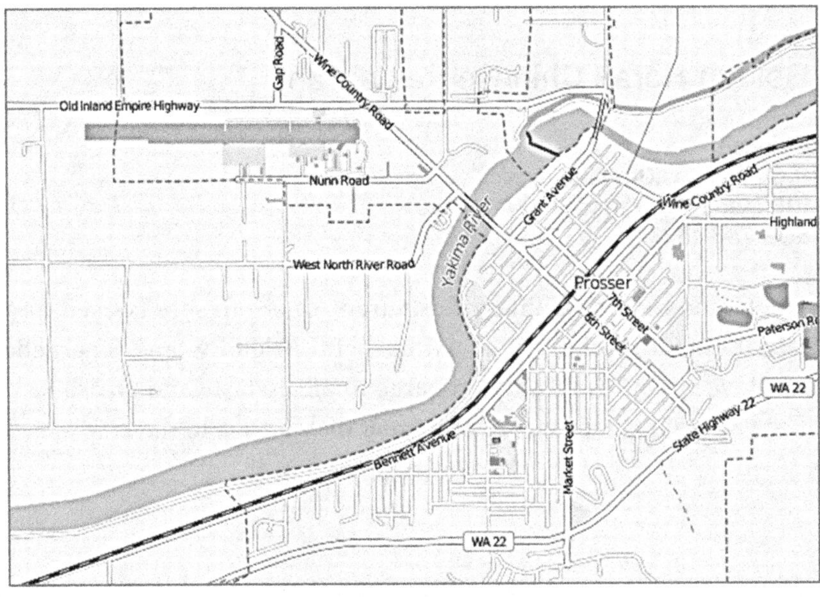

Airport Notes

The airport is fairly easy to spot. Just look for the "bulb" shape the Yakima River makes as it passes through Prosser. From there, the airport is just to the northwest at less than a mile.

Traffic pattern is always to the north of the field. Note the rather significant displaced threshold on 26, intended to keep you up from Wine Country Road.

There are two ramp parking options. The larger of the two is the main ramp in the middle of the field. The smaller ramp to the east is preferred since that's where you'll find the fuel.

Transportation

There is a courtesy car available. Contact 509-786-2053 to inquire about availability.

Food Options

Golden Horse Chinese Restaurant

Chinese
0.6 miles or 10-minute walk
108 Merlot Dr, Prosser, WA 99350
509-786-1578

The Golden Horse Chinese Restaurant offers freshly cooked and rapidly-made dishes. It's staffed with friendly and energetic employees. Dishes that are prepared in oil are tasty and grease-less. The variety of soups make for a great dish on a cold day.

The Roza Grill

American (Traditional), Cafés, Diners
0.6 miles or 10-minute walk
413 Wine Country Rd, Prosser, WA 99350
208-781-6315

The Roza Grill serves traditional American diner cuisine. It's noted locally for having a cozy and welcoming atmosphere. The Roza Grill serves a variety of food, including classic breakfast dishes such as pancakes and traditional favorites like biscuits and gravy. There's both indoor and outside seating.

El Rancho Alegre

Mexican
0.6 miles or 11-minute walk
364 Chardonnay Ave, Ste 3, Prosser, WA 99350
509-786-3558

El Rancho Alegre is a locally owned Mexican restaurant. It has low to mid-priced dishes. The decoration is colonial Mexican-style. It's open for business every day. They also take reservations and have a private dining room for special occasions. It has a full bar and an outdoor sitting area. Televisions are placed around the restaurant.

Things to Do

Canyon's Edge Winery

Wineries
0.5 miles or 9-minute walk
10 Merlot Dr Ste D, Prosser, WA 99350
509-786-3032

Canyon's Edge Winery is run by a father and son team. The grapes for their wine come from the Aldercreek Vineyard in Horse Heaven

Hills. Their tasting room opened in 2007 with the experience and passion of wine maker John P. Haw. Featured daily in their tasting room are their Sage Brush Red table wine, their merlot and syrah, and Jeremiah's Chocolate Port. Their tasting menu is exceptionally diverse and all encompassing. The owners and operators have extensive knowledge and offer excellent recommendations.

Yakima River Winery

Wineries
0.8 miles or 14-minute walk
143302 W North River Rd, Prosser, WA 99350
509-786-2805

The Yakima River Winery is a small, off the beaten track winery owned and ran by a couple who have been making wine for over 35 years. They make 4 wines and 2 stouts. The tasting room is in the back of their house, complete with a taxidermy collection. Tasting is free of charge. The owners are both friendly and knowledgeable.

Overnight Lodging

Barn Motor Inn

Hotels
0.4 miles or 8-minute walk
490 Wine Country Rd, Prosser, WA 99350
509-786-2121

The Barn Motor Inn is a comfortable and economic place to stay. The staff is quite friendly. It's a very quiet hotel, so you can come here for a vacation and relax in peace. It isn't particularly fancy, but it is clean. There's a pool for guests. New owners Rob and Jayne bought the inn in 2013 and have been making steady improvements ever since.

Best Western Plus

Hotels
0.7 miles or 13-minute walk
259 Merlot Dr, Prosser, WA 99350
509-786-7977

The Best Western[160] is a hotel that features a large swimming pool, hot breakfast served each morning, and friendly staff. Rooms feature a very spacious design as well as flat screen TVs, microwaves, and refrigerators. Every room is kept very clean and is well maintained. Pets are welcome.

Seven Gables Pensione

Bed & Breakfast
0.8 miles or 16-minute walk
257 Wamba Rd, Prosser, WA 99350
206-499-2200

Seven Gables Pensione is a bed and breakfast inn set in a renovated house. Rooms are very well maintained by the owners. The owners themselves are very friendly. Each room features its own shower and bath and is stocked with bath products. Two cats roam the grounds and are friendly to patrons. The breakfast served is old fashioned and home cooked. The inn itself is unique, and there's a bit of mystery to the house. The owners promise to delight would be patrons with the history of their inn.

[160] OK, please make it stop. No more Best Western reviews. Please.

Chapter 14

Pullman and Walla Walla

The far southeast of the state offers a diverse and stunning landscape. In the northwest of the southeast area lies Ritzville and Pru Field, essentially a Moses Lake sort of topography with flat farm lands as far as the eye can see. Along the southern edge of the state resides Walla Walla, a town so nice, they named it twice. Walla Walla's area too is surrounded by farm land, but it has a bit more vertical range. Even more interesting is that it's snuggled up near the western edge of a blub of the Rocky Mountains that sticks out westward. This, to some extent, increases precipitation over the area as compared to the Tri-Cities just to its northwest. Then finally along the far eastern edge of the state stands proudly the city of Pullman, home of Washington State University.

Pullman sits in the heart of the Palouse region, which technically includes Walla Walla as well and extends into northern Oregon, western Idaho, and even up into a small section of the Okanogans. The Palouse regions is a major agricultural area, primarily producing wheat and legumes. Peculiar and picturesque loess hills characterize the Palouse Prairie. The hills are underlain by wind-blown sediments of the Palouse Loess. In late spring and early summer, the vast region turns into rolling low hills covered in almost perfect green as far as the eye can see. By fall, this effect turns to gold.

33S – Pru Field Airport

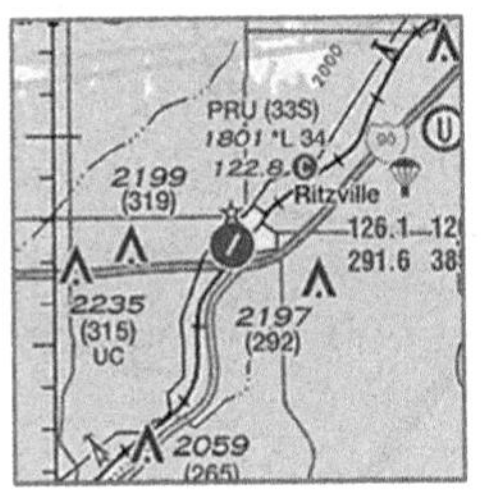

Location: 1 mile west of Ritzville
Coordinates: N47°7.41' / W118°23.36'
Altitude: 1801 MSL
Fuel: None
Transient Storage: Tiedowns

Up in the northwest corner of this, the southeast corner of Washington resides the city of Ritzville. It supports a population of about 1,700 people. It was first settled in 1880 a quickly grew as a result of settlers arriving via the train, which passed through town.

Ritzville experiences a semi-arid climate. Annual precipitation averages just under 12 inches. Average temperatures in January are around 30°F and climb in July to about 70°F.

The primary industry in the area is farming, of course.

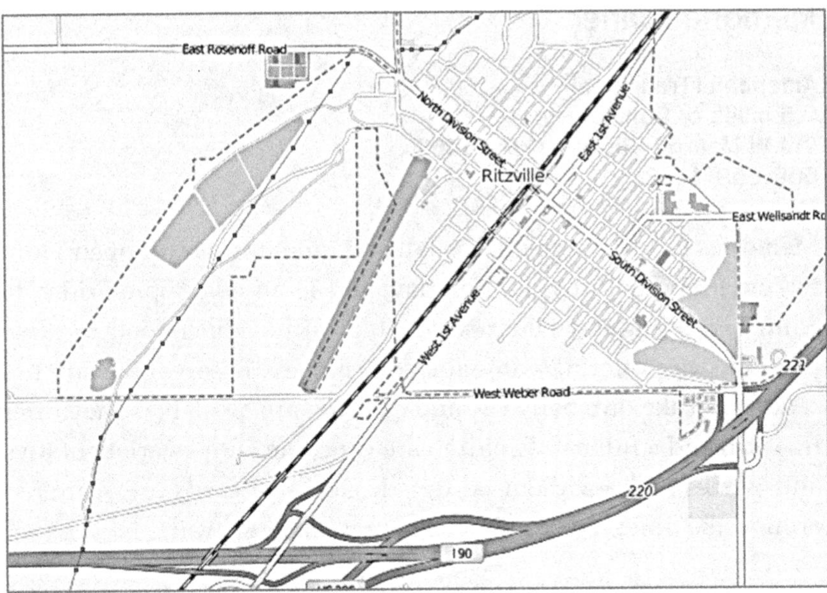

Airport Notes

The town and airport are easily visible from a long way off. The runway itself sits between two small rises in the land, the larger of which is to the west. They aren't anything to be concerned about from an obstacle perspective, but they can cause some interesting wind effects close to the runway if the winds aren't particularly strong.

Note the rather significant displaced threshold on 19 to keep aircraft up from the residential neighborhood just off the north. If you're departing on runway 1, consider an early crosswind turn to avoid overflying.

Transient parking is on the ramp at the northern end of the field, east side. The airport doesn't have a fence around its perimeter.

Food Options

Memories Diner

American (Traditional)
0.5 miles or 9-minute walk
214 W Main St, Ritzville, WA 99169
509-659-4652

Memories Diner is a small, casual, and quiet restaurant open 11am to 7pm Monday through Thursday, and 11 am to 8:30pm Friday to Saturday. Memories Diner serves typical hot diner food in large portion sizes, offering value for your money. Reservations are not required. Take out, delivery, and catering are available. They offer free wifi and a full bar. Children are welcome with a variety of toys and games to keep them occupied. Decks of cards are scattered around the diner for patrons to enjoy while they wait.

Soup It Up

Soup, American (Traditional), Sandwiches
0.5 miles or 9-minute walk
116 W Main Ave, Ritzville, WA 99169
509-659-0503

Soup It Up is a traditional American style restaurant that specializes in house-made soup and sandwiches. It's in the lower end of the price range at less than $10 per person. The restaurant is owned by a couple who focuses on healthy, quick meal options. They're open five days a week for lunch: Monday through Thursday from 10am to 2pm and Fridays from 9am to 3pm. Soup It Up doesn't offer delivery service, but they do offer carry out. For dining in the restaurant, reservations are available.

Jake's Café

American (Traditional)
0.5 miles or 9-minute walk
1604 W 1ST Ave, Ritzville, WA 99169
509-659-1961

Jake's Café is a great place to get traditional American fare. The restaurant is a classic old-fashioned truck stop diner with great food. The restaurant serves breakfast, lunch, and dinner. Some of the most popular menu items are the chicken fried steak and eggs, cheeseburger deluxe, patty melt, cube steak sandwich, grilled German sausage, pork chops, beef stew, and deep fried chicken strips. And of course, like the sign on the road says, Jake's is known for their steaks. The portions are great and the atmosphere is laid-back and relaxed. This is a great place to bring kids and large groups. There is something for everyone on the menu.

Top Hat Motel

Hotels
0.6 miles or 12-minute walk
210 E 1st Ave, Ritzville, WA 99169
509-659-1100

Top Hat Motel is an affordable mom-and-pop roadside motel. It has a friendly and accommodating staff. The rooms are quaint but clean and are equipped with refrigerator, flat screen TV, microwave, and air conditioning. The motel is located near a railroad, and guests can easily walk through the historic downtown to shop, sight-see, or visit local attractions such as the railroad museum or the nearby waterpark. It has a garden at the front where guests can have a picnic and barbecue or just plain relax. However, being that it's near the railroad tracks, some guests may be put off by the sound of passing trains.

Best Western Plus Bronco Inn

Hotels
1.1 miles or 21-minute walk
105 Galbreath Way, Ritzville, WA 99169
509-659-5000

The Best Western[161] Plus Bronco Inn is a low to mid-priced inn. It's open every day, all hours. It serves complimentary breakfast to all guests. The check-in is at 3pm and check-out is at noon. The bedrooms have free wifi and TV with access to several popular channels. The inn also has an indoor swimming pool, gym, and a variety of other amenities for guests to enjoy. It is also pet friendly.

[161] Oh no. It's another Best Western review. I can't keep writing these. I'm going insane now. Seriously. Sent help. Tell the first responders I'll be the guy holding a keyboard and slowly rocking back in forth.

PUW – Pullman Regional Airport

Location: 3 miles northeast of Pullman/Moscow
Coordinates: N46°44.63' / W117°6.57'
Altitude: 2554 MSL
Fuel: 100LL (blue), Jet-A
Transient Storage: Tiedowns

Pullman is the largest city in Whitman County with a population of well over 30,000. Pullman is noted as a vastly fertile agricultural area known for its many miles of rolling hills and the production of wheat and legumes. It is best known as the home to Washington State University and the international headquarters of Schweitzer Engineering Laboratories.

The Palouse climate is classified as humid continental with four distinct seasons. It's typified by warm, dry summers followed by cold, snowy winters with short transitional seasons in between.

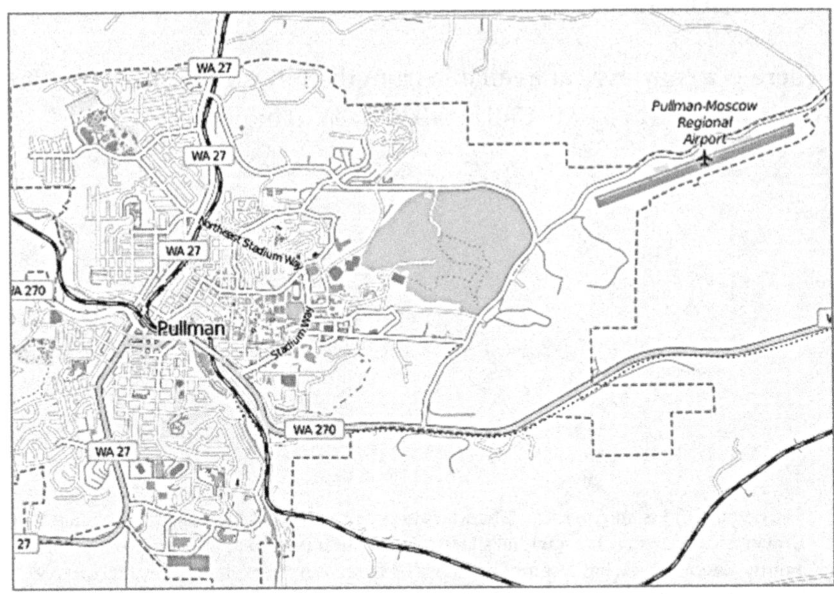

Airport Notes

Pullman is a dense-looking city that immediately cuts away to the open farmlands of the Palouse. As such, it's extremely easy to spot from a great distance. The airport is off to the east and is separated from the city by a golf course.

The runway is lengthy, and there are no serious obstructions or issues with it. For those pilots used to the "wet" side of the state with its airports a few hundred feet above sea level, think through weight and density altitude considerations at this 2,555 MSL airport on hot summer afternoons.

Transient parking is to the east of the FBO midfield. There are two long stretches of ramp parking. Any spot in those two rows should be fine.

When you stop in at the FBO, be sure to buy some Cougar Gold.[162] The FBO sells the 30-ounce tin cans of the stuff.

Transportation

There is a courtesy car available from the FBO. Inter-State Aviation has a car for $15 a day. Call 509-332-6596 to inquire.

[162] Cougar Gold is an American Cheddar cheese produced at the Washington State University Creamery. It's a white, sharp cheddar that is aged at least one year. It has a nutty flavor somewhat resembling Swiss or Gouda. Approximately 250,000 cans of Cougar Cheese are produced annually, with around 80% being Cougar Gold.

Wawawai Canyon Winery

Wineries
1.2 miles or 22-minute walk
5602 State Route 270, Pullman, WA 99163
509-338-4916

The Wawawai Canyon Winery is a small winery using traditional methods of production and fermentation to create their wines. Since 1994 this family owned and operated winery has produced wines such as Cabernet Franc, Syrah, and Sauvingon Blanc.

The tasting room at the winery is open from noon untill 6pm Thursday through Saturday and also by appointment. The tastings are free, the pours are generous, and you will probably bump into the wine maker himself: Ben Moffett. Wines are available for purchase at the tasting room and on the winery's website.

ALW – Walla Walla Regional Airport

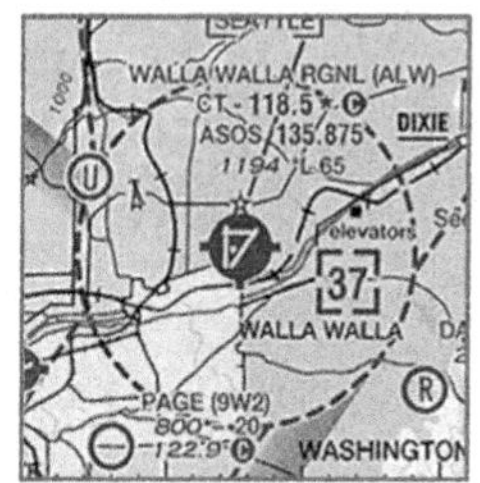

Location: 3 miles northeast of Walla Walla
Coordinates: N46°5.71' / W118°17.16'
Altitude: 1194 MSL
Fuel: 100LL (blue), Jet-A
Transient Storage: Tiedowns

Walla Walla, the town so nice, they named it twice,[163] is the largest city in its county with a population of over 32,000. But that number is a bit misleading. Walla Walla is surrounded by two suburgs: the town of College Place and unincorporated East Walla Walla. These two together bring the total population up to nearly 50,000.

Walla Walla Valley includes rolling Palouse hills that give way to the Blue Mountains east of town. Various creeks meander through town before combining to become the Walla Walla River.

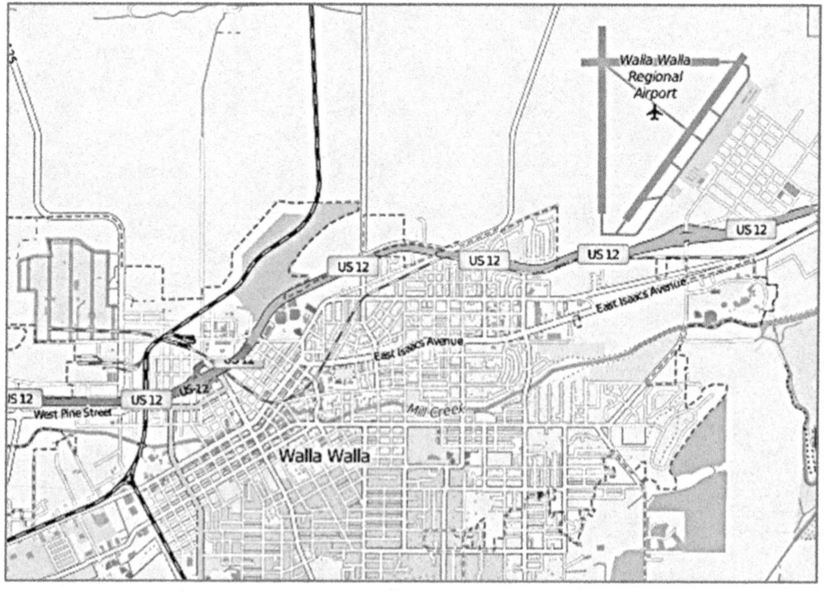

[163] A joke so unfunny, I told it twice.

Airport Notes

The airport is tucked up to the northeast corner of town, just beyond where the density of the residential neighborhoods give way to the open farm lands.

It's a fairly typical-looking class D with professional and friendly controllers. Transient parking is on the ramp to the north of the main terminal building.

Food Options

Hidden Valley Bakery

Bakeries, Specialty Food, Gluten-Free
0.5 miles or 10-minute walk
45 Terminal Loop Rd, Walla Walla, WA 99362
509-386-3460

Hidden Valley Bakery specializes in gluten-free baked goods. It opens just in time for breakfast at 6am then closes at 6pm Monday through Friday. It closes early at 4pm Saturday and is closed on Sunday. This is a casual, family-friendly bakery that accepts orders over the phone for pick-up and offers a delivery service. Pricing is estimated to be under $10. The give customers quite a menu to look through with items such as gluten-free bacon quiche and cups of coffee.

Mr Ed's

American (Traditional), Breakfast & Brunch, Burgers
1.3 miles or 24-minute walk
2555 E Isaacs Ave, Walla Walla, WA 99362
509-525-8440

Mr Ed's is a family friendly restaurant that offers moderately priced, traditional American cuisine including breakfast, brunch and burgers. Mr. Ed's doesn't offer delivery or take reservations, but they do have carry-out available. The restaurant serves beer and wine. It's open seven days a week from 6am to 8pm.

Things to Do

Cavu Cellars

Wineries
0.6 miles or 12-minute walk
175 E Aeronca Ave, Walla Walla, WA 99362
509-540-6352

Cavu Cellars is a great local winery. Tours are available throughout the week and they have a very nice event space available for weddings, family get-togethers, and corporate events. The winery's tasting room is very unique. It used to be a World War II air hangar. The place is decorated with all kinds of memorabilia, including photos of the planes the owner once flew when he was a pilot in Vietnam. A tour of the winery would make for a great romantic night out.

Elegante Cellars

Wineries
0.7 miles or 13-minute walk
839 C St, Walla Walla, WA 99362
509-525-9129

Elegante Cellars is a winery run by Doug Simmons who is a retired chemistry teacher. The award winning wines are created in small batches and are very high quality. There are wine tastings and wines available for purchase. The wine list is extensive and the tours are personal and incredibly informative. The staff is passionate and knowledgeable and can usually ship your purchases the same day. The winery is open 7 days a week for tastings, tours, and purchases. Established in 2005, these wines are only sold through their tasting room.

Tempus Cellars

Wineries
0.7 miles or 14-minute walk
1110 C St, Walla Walla, WA 99362
509-270-0298

Tempus Cellars is a family-owned boutique winery featuring hand-crafted, signature Walla Walla Valley wine. They feature a variety of selections from Rieslings to Rosé, Syrah, and Cabernet Sauvignon. Tempus Cellars supports local vineyards, and their wine is made using locally sourced grapes and fruits. The tasting room at Tempus Cellars is friendly and intimate. The owner and brewmaster is frequently in house and is well known to impart his love of wine and brewing to curious customers, answering any questions and making recommendations.

Figgins Wine Studio

Wineries
1.1 miles or 20-minute walk
2900 Melrose Street, Walla Walla, WA 99362
509-522-7808

Figgins Wine Studio is guaranteed to bring you a wonderful experience. The service is delightful and the wine is amazing. For a family owned wine studio, The Friggins produce some of the world's greatest wines. No hassle reservations at all and with much convenience through the website. The wines are extraordinary. The first, an Oregon Pinot Noir from Toil, a sub-label, is a beautiful light purple and smells of strawberry, cranberry, mushroom and rose petal. Very delicate on the palate and drank like a cool climate Burgundy.

Ensemble Cellars

Wineries
0.5 miles or 10-minute walk
145 E Curtis Ave, Walla Walla, WA 99362
509-525-0231

Ensemble Cellars is a winery which offers quality wines. The customer can try a variety of wines that will not be found in regular stores. This winery is not in a crowded area but rather offers an experience that is more intimate and personal. Ensemble Cellars wines are typically in the more expensive category. This out-of-the-way experience is unique. The winery is run by the Nelsons who have expertise in wines pleasing to the palette. They enjoy sharing their knowledge along with providing a unique experience in wine tasting.

Revelry Vintners

Wineries
0.7 miles or 13-minute walk
720 C St, Walla Walla, WA 99362
509-540-5761

Revelry Vintners is a moderately priced winery with an intimate setting for their tasting room. It is a family friendly location with handicapped-accessibility for customers of all kinds. You can visit their website as well for online shopping and delivery for the customers who are not able to make it into the physical store. There is also a tab that is specified for any events that may be happening for customers with interest. You can also join their Wine Club for member exclusives.

Patrick M. Paul Vineyards

Wineries
0.5 miles or 8-minute walk
124 W Boeing Ave, Ste 3, Walla Walla, WA 99362
509-526-0676

Patrick M Paul Vineyards is one of the few original great wineries across Washington. Patrick Paul has got some history with the town and because of that customers continue to pour in day after day, week after week. Regardless of your Wine preferences or tastes there's wine here for everybody. The amount of different choices of wine is incredible and will make people come back to try new flavors and the rest of the menu.

Patit Creek Cellars

Wine Tasting Room
0.5 miles or 9-minute walk
325 A St, Walla Walla, WA 99362
509-522-4684

Patit Creek Cellars are open 6 days a week, Tuesdays through Sundays specializing in Cabernet Sauvignon and Merlot but equally known for their German style Riesling. More than just wine tastings they offer live music and artisan cheese. You can buy their wine and their cheese at tasting events all year long. They have a reasonably priced wine club with four different levels of membership to choose from. Wine club membership includes exclusive per-shipments quarterly and automatic discounts on wine purchases. It's free to join.

Buty Winery

Wineries
0.9 miles or 16-minute walk
535 E Cessna Ave, Walla Walla, WA 99362
509-527-0901

Buty Winery creates and sells Buty and Beast wines. There are tastings available in their small tasting room Monday through Saturday, 11am to 4pm. The wine tasting fee that is paid up front can be refunded upon the purchase of a bottle of their wine. Their wines may be purchased at the tasting room or through their website on the internet. The tasting room is small and very busy especially around new wine release weekends so calling ahead to make sure they have what you are looking for in stock might be necessary if you plan to purchase something specific.

Walla Walla Super 8 Motel

Hotels
1.3 miles or 25-minute walk
2315 Eastgate Street N, Walla Walla, WA 99362
800-536-9326

Walla Walla Super 8 Motel is a motel with recently remodeled rooms. Rooms are kept clean and the hotel is well maintained. The staff is friendly. Each room is furnished with a microwave, refrigerator, hair dryer, flat screen television, coffee maker, and free wifi. A swimming pool and jacuzzi are available to all guests, as is a washing machine and dryer. A variety of vending machines can be found at this location. Pets are welcome at this location.

Colonial Motel

Hotels
1.3 miles or 25-minute walk
2279 E Isaacs Ave, Walla Walla, WA 99362
509-529-1220

The Colonial Motel is a privately owned budget motel. The rooms in this quaint old-fashioned hotel are relatively small but clean, and they come with all the modern amenities you might need. Each room has a flat-screen television, fridge, microwave, and coffee maker. The motel accepts credit cards and it offers free wifi to all of its guests. Located between the airport and downtown areas, this hotel is conveniently near many shops and attractions you can easily walk to. Guests can also enjoy the BBQ grill on the grounds along with the garden.

S95 – Martin Field Airport

Location: 1 mile west of College Place
Coordinates: N46°2.82' / W118°25.03'
Altitude: 746 MSL
Fuel: 100LL (blue), Automotive Gasoline
Transient Storage: Tiedowns

College Place is a suburb of Walla Walla, a town so nice, they named it twice.[164] College Place supports a population of about 9,000 and is the home of Walla Walla University, a Seventh-day Adventist operated Liberal Arts University.

Because of the primary Adventist population, most downtown College Place businesses close on Saturday, reopening in most cases on Sunday.

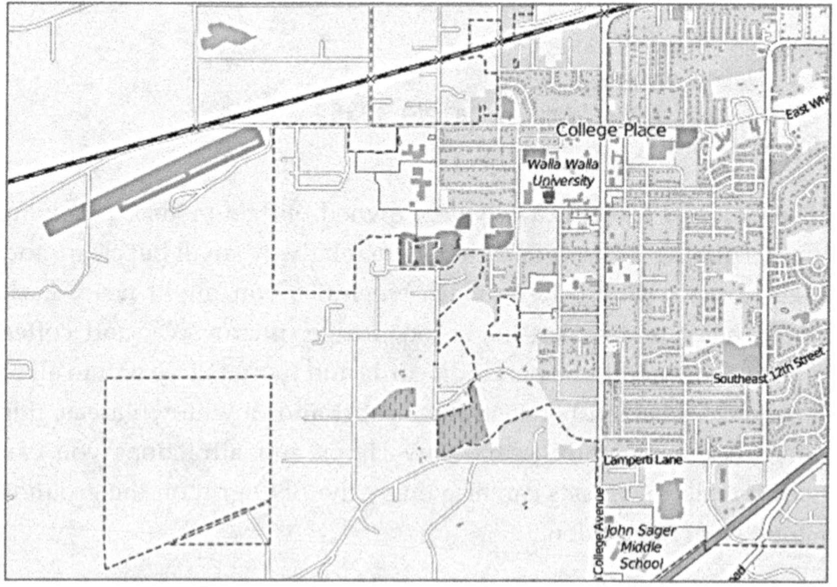

[164] I can't help myself. I know it's not a particularly funny joke, but I can't not retell it over and over. It's a sickness. Send help.

Airport Notes

Martin Field is west of the main body of the town. It was an air training base during World War II, but is now a private airfield open to the public.

A few things to note about this airport: There's a road immediately off the end of runway 23. There isn't a displaced threshold marked, so it may be wise to fly in with a fairly steep angle of descent or image a displaced threshold.

A little over 700 feet from the end of runway 5, a private driveway cuts over the runway.[165] Watch for vehicles.

Transient parking is on the main ramp mostly near the north end along the edge of the ramp that faces the runway, essentially right across from the fuel island.

Food Options

Cugini Import Italian Market

Grocery, Italian
1.1 miles or 21-minute walk
960 Wallula Ave, Walla Walla, WA 99362
509-526-0809

The Cugini Import Italian Market is a full service Italian café inside of a full service Italian Deli. When weather permits, there's outside seating adding to the already authentic atmosphere of the café and market. The café serves lunch but may also accommodate an early dinner crowd.

Both the café and market are closed Sundays and Mondays. Prices are moderate for genuine imported Italian cuisine, and the

[165] Yes, you read that correctly. It's simultaneously cool and scary.

restaurant is known equally for the charcuterie and their cannoli. The friendly staff treat all the shoppers and diners like family and create a memorable dining experience.

Things to Do

Skylite Cellars

Beer, Wine & Spirits, Wineries
1.5 miles or 28-minute walk
25 Campbell Rd, Walla Walla, WA 99362
509-529-8000

Skylite Cellars is open daily for wine tastings and purchases. You may join their Copper Top Wine club in person at the winery or online via their website. Membership includes quarterly shipments of premium wines, tasting fees waved, and complimentary access to many Skylite events. The winery is dog friendly and the staff is knowledgeable and friendly.

There are numerous wines to taste and purchase and the atmosphere is cozy yet inspiring. All the wines are moderately priced considering the quality and the experience of the location. The wines available for tastings vary from week to week your current options can be found on their website or call in and the eager staff can tell you what they are serving this week in the tasting rooms.

A Room with a View

Bed & Breakfast
1.7 miles or 33-minute walk
28 Roland Ct, Walla Walla, WA 99362
509-529-1194

A Room with a View is a bed and breakfast located on a hilltop acre. Here you can relax in casual elegance, watch the world drift by, and marvel in the glorious view of the Walla Walla Valley with the manicured fields below, the winding tree-line of the Walla Walla River, and an ever changing light on the foothills of the Blue Mountains.

In the morning, the staff serves breakfast for you at a table with the whole family. Each room is themed around a different era or place. The rooms all have windows from which you can see for miles.

Chapter 15

Departure

There's an amazing world out there to explore. As pilots, we get to explore more of it and from a very special point of view. The greatest regrets come from what we don't do. There's nothing quite so depressing as an unused airplane.

If the idea of yet another $100 hamburger doesn't excite you anymore, try a spur-of-the-moment overnight visit to some random airport in Washington State. Find a B&B, walk the town, soak in the experience, and enjoy. Even just a day trip somewhere is often more than worth the expense and effort.

Each year, just after I get my wings back from annual, I set for myself flight goals. They're usually in the form of fly such-and-such hours and visit so-and-so number of airports new to me. I've hung a few sectionals together on a wall in my office, and each time I visit a new airport, I put a pin in the chart.

For some of us, competition spurs. So consider a friendly competition with pilots from your home airport. Who can see the most number of new airports this year? Who can fly the most hours non-commercially? Find a few pilots and challenge each other to find errors and missing information in this book. Fly to airports I didn't list and prove to me I should've included them. Contact me at g@shfr.us with your findings.

Buy this book for new pilots and for pilots visiting from out-of-state. If you're a CFI, give this book as a gift to your students as congratulations on passing their checkride.

GiggleFest

Each summer, our family of 4 loads up way too much luggage and sets off on a flying adventure. Each morning, after I've been appropriately obsessive about understanding the weather, we open up a sectional, look at airports an hour or two away, and pick a destination. We stay in hotels and B&Bs, we eat out a lot, and we experience the special features of each town we find ourselves in.

The first year we did this, we found ourselves one morning on our way westward to from Kalispell to Coeur d'Alene. The sky was an unbroken blue, the air as smooth as glass. We were fairly high up, crossing over the Rockies on our way back to Idaho. And we heard giggling. Our two children in the back were making faces at each other, giggling unceasingly for over an hour. And so the trip was forever called GiggleFest.

Each year since, we've flown a new edition of GiggleFest. It has given our children an unparalleled opportunity to see things from a new and special point of view. The time we've spent together as a family is invaluable.

Schrödinger

We fly in a Lake Buccaneer. We're N8003H on the radio, and we sport a Star Wars Rebellion emblem on our tail.[166] I was once reading a fine book about Lake aircraft in which the author wrote that, "the Lake has a power-off glide-slope of a dead cat." Given that it's difficult to tell our power setting without looking inside the

[166] Yes, I'm a nerd and geek. Proudly.

cockpit at the throttle and thus collapsing the superposition, we call our airplane Schrödinger.

If you happen to see us around an airport, stop over and say hello. We mostly hang out on the wet side of Washington, but we get out to Spokane, Pullman, and beyond on a semi-regular basis.

Why

We don't fly because it's particularly cheap or perfectly safe. We invest wisely and calculate assumed risks. The payoffs are the experiences our earth-bound brothers and sisters will never receive nor fully understand. To them, our hearts yearning always skyward is foolishness. I am blessed to be such a fool. To the Creator of the atmosphere we all breathe and in which a few of us fly, I am grateful.

Appendix A

Best Places for Stuff

Many ask me where to go for the best stuff. I'll quickly list out my opinions[167] on a few topics:

Best Fish and Chips

1. Madrona Bar & Grill (ORS)
2. Airport Diner (PWT)
3. Cask and Schooner (FHR)

Best Other Dishes

- Pie: Spruce Goose (0S9)
- Patty Melt: Skyway Café (SFF)
- Wild Boar: Bruno's Family Restaurant & Bar (2W3)

Best B&Bs

- Westport Bayside B&B (14S)
- Waterspring Inn (ESW)

[167] My opinions are well-researched facts. I wrote a book on the subject, turns out. You're free to disagree, but you'd be wrong.

Best Coffee

This is a highly debatable topic and one which really should be debated regularly and with great interest and care due to the significance of the subject matter. Avgas makes airplanes go. Coffee makes pilots go.[168] Without coffee, aviation wouldn't be where it is today.[169]

There are many locations in Washington State from which a pilot can acquire good coffee.[170] However, stipulating where the best place is within walking distance of an airport is challenging for many reasons, not the least of which is the heavy weight of responsibility in making such a pronouncement.

With this in mind, the best coffee within walking distance of an airport is:

- Mukilteo Coffee Roasters (W10)

As a final thought, there's actually a place you can get to from a Washington State airport that has even better coffee, but technically it's in Idaho. Fly to Pullman (PUW), ask the FBO for the courtesy car, and drive east into Idaho.

The Filling Station

Café, Bakery
19.1 miles or 28-minute drive
504 S Main St, Troy, ID 83871
208-835-2300

[168] Both "go" in terms of movement and "go" in terms of visits to restrooms.
[169] It is by coffee alone I set my mind in motion. It is by the juice of the bean that thoughts acquire speed, the teeth acquire stains, the stains become a warning. It is by coffee alone I set my mind in motion.
[170] There are even more places where a pilot can acquire bad coffee.

CPSIA information can be obtained
at www.ICGtesting.com
Printed in the USA
FSOW04n0103160816
23745FS